WHEN LIFE AND CHOICE COLLIDE

WORDS IN CONFLICT SERIES

It would be difficult to dispute the fact that rhetoric is one of the dominant instruments of change in human affairs and that social movements convey their ideologies largely through the dynamics of persuasive discourse. But while the importance of rhetoric in transforming society may be quite obvious, what is not so obvious is how that rhetoric actually takes shape.

The Words in Conflict Series attempts to make more evident the scope and efficacy of rhetoric in promoting important social values. The focus of the series will be on contemporary issues in biomedical ethics, including especially —but not limited to—abortion and euthanasia. And because the study of rhetoric is much broader than any single academic discipline, each volume will provide a variety of insights from a number of specialties.

It is a governing principle of the series that controversial issues in bioethics belong exclusively to no privileged academic elite but to society as a whole and to every thinking person. There are no special academic qualifications for any essayist herein, beyond the depth and breadth of understanding he or she may provide. Accordingly, each essay is selected for its ability to increase the reader's rhetorical awareness.

WORDS IN CONFLICT SERIES

WHEN LIFE AND CHOICE COLLIDE

Essays on Rhetoric and Abortion

Vol. 1

TO SET THE DAWN FREE

Edited by
David Mall

With an Introduction by
Nat Hentoff

KAIROS BOOKS, INC. LIBERTYVILLE, ILLINOIS

Permission has been granted to reprint the following materials:

*Diagram, p. 119, "Hierachical Structure Map for
Hypothetical Airline Study," Journal of Advertising Research,
Copyright © 1984 by the Advertising Research Foundation.
Visuals, pp. 131-35, Secretariat for Pro-Life Activities,
United States Catholic Conference.*

*Published by Kairos Books, Inc.
P.O. Box 708
Libertyville, Illinois 60048*

*Printed in the United States of America
1 3 5 7 9 10 8 6 4 2*

*Library of Congress Cataloging in Publication Data
and colophon are located on the
final printed page of this book.*

BOOK DESIGN BY CAROL TORNATORE

Contents

To
Ginny and Ken
this book and all its progeny
in grateful appreciation

*It was once said
that the moral test of government is how
that government treats those who are in the
dawn of life, the children; and those who are in the
twilight of life, the elderly; and those who are in the
shadows of life—the sick, the needy, and the
handicapped.*

Hubert H. Humphrey

*When God sends the dawn,
he sends it for all.*

Miguel de Cervantes

Preface

Early in the film version of *Gone with the Wind*, Rhett Butler, that paragon of gallantry and cynicism, admonishes a group of Southerners gathered for a party at the Wilkes' plantation of Twelve Oaks. In a display of flint-edged realism, he asserts, "I think it's hard winning a war with words, gentlemen."

Now, if Rhett's observation were true for slavery and the American Civil War, it is doubly true for what has been termed America's "New Civil War"—the prolonged and bitter controversy over induced human abortion. Fortunately, however, for all those who arc witnessing this more recent struggle, the contenders do not marshall armaments, only arguments. And the battleground is neither North nor South but the human mind and heart in conflict with each other.

The abortion controversy has indeed become an undeclared or, at least, an unacknowledged civil war. In fact, so clearly has this been the case that it would be relatively easy to defend the claim that no conflict in U.S. history has relied on the subtlety of language as a lethal weapon quite so much as has abortion. It seems appropriate then that the abortion struggle be labeled a "War of Words."

Yet even in the face of an escalating verbal warfare, for too many Americans the abortion debate has become clouded and confused. But while the public support for abortion has ebbed and flowed over the years, the editor believes that now the average citizen seems more willing to be confronted by the truth. And because the abortion debate often shows how human reason can be mesmerized by distorted perceptions and held hostage by raw human emotion, any objective analysis of that debate must ultimately devolve into a rigorous test of critical thinking. Accordingly, what this in turn suggests is that ridding the abortion debate of its most striking deficiencies in logic should begin with a rehabilitation of language. It is largely toward this end that the ensuing essays are directed.

The editor thinks it appropriate to warn the reader at the outset that this is a partisan book—a book designed to upset an individual's moral equilibrium. Those, in fact, who are unalterably convinced that the abortion freedom should always and everywhere remain an unassailable part of the American social fabric need read no further. But, on the other hand, those who may possess only the faintest glimmer of doubt about the ultimate success of the abortion experiment in America will likely find these pages to be stimulating, enlightening, and intellectually challenging.

The essays to follow support the thesis that in the abortion debate truth itself is a partisan, that in its struggle with falsehood truth will inevitably enjoy an unshakable alliance with social justice. The editor believes that truth's preferred habitation is the mind of the unconvinced where it can cast doubt, counter misconceptions, and confound intellectual pretense. And because truth's natural inclination is to associate mainly with what is magnanimous and noble in human nature, the editor enthusiastically endorses Schopenhauer's observation that "the truth works far and lives long" and the resulting dictum that we should therefore "speak the truth." The essayists writing herein have kept faith with Schopenhauer.

The book's theme is maintained through five integrated parts. Part One, "Barriers to Communication," considers the problem of movement justification and describes how an elitist culture can depict a social movement as marginal and irrelevant. Part Two, "Language and Public Opinion," suggests how a movement can adjust its message to assure maximum clarity and impact.

Part Three, "Lessons from History," analyzes the dominant historical analogies imbedded in the public mind and sometimes misused. Part Four, "Insights from Rhetoric and Philosophy," deals
with hidden symbolisms that can help explain human motivation
but which are often lost to awareness or underutilized. And, finally, Part Five, "Strategies for Persuasion," explores the best available
means by which rhetoric can alter or reinforce the status quo.
Thus does each part of the anthology contribute to a better understanding of how movement messages are communicated.

The scholars contributing to this volume—from both the United States and Canada—have brought their work out of the ivory
tower to make it available to society as a whole. This is not scholarship to feather academic nests. The essays contained herein represent a scholarship that mingles with the real world of everyday
human concern. And if the best scholarship is created from the
living clay of controversy, it is natural that there will be a crossing
of intellectual boundaries and at times even a de-emphasis of traditional academic disciplines such as law, medicine, and ethics.
This book emphasizes the social sciences and the humanities.

The writers were selected for their ability to enlarge the public's understanding of the hotly contested issue of abortion. Each
is a committed scholar driven by a desire to identify and explain
the truth. They approach their subjects with insights gained from
rich and diverse backgrounds. The reader will also find that some
of the essays are dispassionately self-critical. And although the
essayists may not agree on the exact steps to be taken to solve the
abortion problem, they are nonetheless united in their deference
to sound and responsible scholarship. Each essay can be considered an indicator of a social movement's maturity and of a realistic
approach to achieving its goals.

This book will be the first in a projected series of books dealing with the complex bioethical issues of the day, including abortion, infanticide, and euthanasia. The common thread that binds
the essays together will be the illumination each gives to the
process of transmitting important social values. Underlying this and
all future volumes are certain assumptions of which the following
two are foundational: first, that truth is intrinsically stronger than
falsehood and, second, that America is not a nation of bystanders.
Both assumptions relate to each other in subtle and compelling
ways and bolster the editor's confidence in the efficacy of

rhetoric. The first assumption arises from the structure of logic and the second from the character of the American people.

To begin with, in a free and pluralistic society the truths of social movements are proclaimed and defended primarily through the power of persuasion. Even such a long-standing defender of abortion as Laurence Tribe of Harvard University recognizes that the final arbiter is neither executive, legislative, or judicial but the force of public opinion. Of course, in such an environment no one makes or certifies the rules of rhetorical engagement. The arguers must rely on an unwritten code of civility. But when the debate occurs in a democracy like the United States, the arguers are forced to rely on channels of communication that are undistorted and ideologically uncontrolled. Yet to say that these conditions have been satisfied in the abortion debate in America thus far is to believe in a great fiction. On the contrary, it would be much closer to reality and the truth to assert that abortion in America has been aided and abetted, sustained and expanded largely by sympathetic print and broadcast media that have been carefully cultivated by those who know how to manipulate them.

Any impartial critic of the abortion controversy can easily substantiate the claim of media bias. Olasky's detailed history (1988) of how American journalism has dealt with abortion for over a century and a half draws attention to some serious ethical irregularities. His longitudinal indictment was updated recently by Shaw's exposé in the *Los Angeles Times* (1990). Shaw trenchantly explained how those who oppose abortion have had difficulty reaching their audiences with messages that are accurately reported.

Giving a pro-life message often means running a media gauntlet that leaves the message seriously denatured. The Hartford study (1981) and the more recent Rothman-Lichter reports (1983 and 1991) provide telling insights concerning how media elites have successfully attempted to restrict and shape abortion information to satisfy their own highly secularized world view. Put bluntly, the media in America have consistently placed the right-to-life movement in an unfavorable light; they have attempted to belittle and weaken it by discrediting its leaders and by making it seem an enemy of poor people and the emerging aspirations of women and minorities. In the face of such media hostility, it is much easier to appreciate McLuhan's claim that "the media are engaged in a Luciferian conspiracy against the truth."

When all is said and concluded about media bias, however, one thing is certain. What is logically and ethically correct about abortion will be decided in favor of justice and love only if rhetoric is left free to assist the process of public decision making. Thomas Jefferson perhaps said it best when he wrote: "We are not afraid to follow truth wherever it may lead, nor to tolerate any error so long as reason is left free to combat it." In authoring the Declaration of Independence, he also, in turn, supplied the trade name for the right-to-life movement and spoke for all those contributing to this anthology who believe in the proposition that any idea no matter how distasteful must be given a chance to be disproven. Stripped to its essentials what this means is an unflinching belief that truth is not only stronger than falsehood but that it cannot be bested in an unhindered encounter.

But in the largest view, if those who oppose abortion do not prevail, it will not be solely because of the media strengths of those who support it. On the contrary, victory for those who favor abortion will arise only from the hardened hearts of the indifferent. In the editor's opinion the major problem of movement rhetoric is to overcome public apathy and to drive home the regrettable truth that not to be involved is ultimately to favor what is proposed and thus to encourage it. To be indifferent to an evil is not only to allow it to continue but to let it expand and flourish. Yet given enough time and a level playing field, Americans have always seemed able to marshall sufficient resources to subdue any troublesome opponent. Part of this book's success, then, might well be its ability to adapt to the American genius by helping to subdue indifference while encouraging a renewed personal commitment.

For one of the great social issues of the twentieth century, there has hardly been a fair encounter between the competing points of view or, in the words of Justice Scalia in his *Casey* opinion, "the satisfaction of a fair hearing and an honest fight." Had there been such an encounter, however, the debate could have concluded long ago. But with a hostile journalism arrayed against it, there can be little wonder that the right-to-life movement has not yet prevailed. And what is probably just as amazing is that even with its media advantages, the pro-abortion philosophy has not solidified its hold on the public mind. So the battle continues and a constructive outcome still remains in doubt.

What is the prognosis for an acceptable outcome to America's "New Civil War" or the "War of Words" over abortion? To such a key question there is as yet no clear and unqualified answer. The editor's greatest wish is that what the reader encounters in the pages of this book may become part of an answer. At least that is the most sanguine note with which he feels compelled to conclude his preface.

And lest we be intimidated by Hentoff's conception of the "barbarian" as depicted in his introduction, let us hope that once the abortion controversy has been resolved in America, the American people will have the courage, foresight, and good sense to debate future issues in the public forum without a media favoritism that can lead to unhappy and socially debilitating results. And, finally, let us also hope that once we have debated an issue thoroughly, we as a nation have the ability and determination to change direction if and when the facts so warrant.

The editor wishes to acknowledge the generosity of those who helped in producing this book. Particularly, he wishes to thank Kenneth Kaplin and Virginia Reuter whose unstinting support kept the project alive and on schedule. He also wishes to thank the contributors for their excellent suggestions for improvement and for their uncommon patience in awaiting the final result. To the many who provided assistance, the editor extends his deepest appreciation.

Introduction

Nat Hentoff

There Is More to Abortion than Abortion

I met Derek Humphry, the Hemlock Society's guiding spirit of darkness, at a conference on euthanasia. I was eager to find out if a report I had heard concerning a speech of his in Chicago was accurate.

He had said, I was told, that during his first years as an advocate of euthanasia in the United States, he did not receive a very warm reception. But then, suddenly, "all the doors opened!"

The turning point was *Roe v. Wade*. Once the Constitution of the United States legitimized the killing of developing human beings, then death became a welcome visitor in certain parts of American society. And euthanasia became far more acceptable a prospect than ever before.

"Is this true?" I asked Derek Humphry. "Did the doors open for you once abortion became legal"?

"Yes, of course," he said.

What remained to be done was to secure "the right to die," which—as University of Michigan law professor Yale Kamisar notes—is actually "the right to kill." Again, the bond between abortion and euthanasia was clear. For, as Dr. Ron Paul has pointed out, "Abortion means to kill a fetus, and to speak of abortion *rights* is equivalent to *killing* rights."

1

Once the barriers to killing start coming down, it becomes easier and easier to designate who can and should be killed. To begin with, over a million and a half developing human beings are aborted each year. After all, it is said, they are not "persons." Since they're nonpersons, they can be exterminated at will.

Once this rationale for convenience killing becomes rooted in the consciousness of many Americans, the ending of other lives not worthy of living becomes "justified" by the example of the "legitimacy" of abortion. Baby Does—"severely handicapped" infants whose parents did not want to bear the emotional and financial cost of rearing them—were allowed to starve to death. This had happened before *Roe v. Wade*, but now the cutting off of those lives was to be considered a matter of "late abortions."

As for Derek Humphry—so grateful at the advent of *Roe v. Wade*—he and his organization continue to flourish. They are trying in various states, and will eventually succeed, in having a law passed that will allow physicians to directly kill their patients. It's called "aid-in-dying," and the statutes are titled "Death with Dignity" acts.

There is much more to abortion than abortion. It has numbed, as if with Novocain, a respect for life in American society. Or, put another way, *Roe v. Wade* has established a consistent ethic of death.

Even worse, if worse is possible, is that the abortion mindset—that unwanted life can and should be disposed of—has now been extended to attempts to create a "perfect" child. And if genetic screening in the womb indicates an imperfection, then it is simple and "natural" to abort him or her.

A grimly historic milestone in this return of eugenics—by way of abortion-on-demand—occurred in the Maryland legislature in February 1991. It could not be more clear that if it had not been for *Roe v. Wade*, the following American version of the "perfection" of the race would not have happened.

The Nazis gave eugenics a bad name. But there are still many people in this country who would like to purify the stock. Some are racists—the kind that delighted at the coming of *Roe v. Wade*. As a commentator on WCBS Radio in New York said when that state legalized abortion—two years before the Supreme Court did nationally—"Abortion is one sensible method of dealing with such problems as overpopulation, illegitimacy, and possible birth defects. It is one way of fighting the rising welfare rolls and the increasing number of child abuse cases."

Others who look forward to the age of eugenics are concerned with costs. It is expensive, they say, to care for certain people born with certain genetic defects, and since their "quality of life" is going to be so meager anyway, why not give the taxpayers a break and kill defectives in the womb.

Then there are those people, and they are legion, who are not concerned with any of these questions, but just want a perfect baby.

For all of these advocates of making abortion even more commonplace than it is now, the Maryland state legislature has provided a solution—and a precedent that, I expect, will be followed by other state legislatures unless there is concerted resistance from those who fear the kind of society this is becoming: a land where death is increasingly the preferred option over life.

The Maryland legislature passed a bill intended to ensure by state law the freewheeling abortion rights guaranteed by *Roe v. Wade* if the Supreme Court overturned that decision.

Included in the final bill—and ignored by the press—was a section declaring that a fetus may be aborted "at any time during the woman's pregnancy" if THE FETUS IS AFFECTED BY GENETIC DEFECT OR SERIOUS DEFORMITY OR ABNORMALITY." (The capital letters are in the original statute.)

So much for the fiction that viability may save a fetus. Also, with regard to "deformity or abnormality," there is a qualifier in the Maryland law. Those conditions have to be "serious," whatever that means.

But there is no qualifier to "genetic defect." As Robert Destro—a law professor at Catholic University in Washington who specializes in these matters—told me: "If myopia is discovered, you could, by the language of this section, abort a nearsighted fetus in the seventh month or later." It's not likely to happen at first, but once killing of any kind is legal, it becomes easier, with time, for the harvest of death to increase. And once anything is legal, most people believe that it is moral.

In the years to come, there will be pressure on more and more states for laws that will protect the right to kill developing human beings—no matter what the Supreme Court does. Included in many of these laws will be a genetic rationale for killing.

Women have been doing this all along since *Roe v. Wade*, but making it explicitly lawful to end the lives of those with genetic defects (no matter how slight) will make it easier for women to decide on this course. Moreover, having eugenics as part of a state's system of law will eventually lead—as abortion inevitably did—to more killing of the imperfect *after* birth.

As for greater future increase in killing before birth, it should be remembered that in time nearly all genes will be mapped, making the Perfect Race possible.

Meanwhile, for years—and the practice has been increasing—developing human beings have been prevented from being born because they were of the wrong gender. In debates I've had with pro-abortion leaders, this has been vehemently denied. Yet long articles in newspapers like *The New York Times* have documented this killing by sex. And, although pro-abortion advocates claim to be feminists, more female fetuses are killed this way than male.

Here again, the legalization of—indeed, the constitutional imprimatur on—abortion has created such coarseness of sensitivity that developing human beings in the United States are extinguished only because they are of an undesirable gender.

The Maryland statute that advocates eugenics also permits abortion because of gender. To permit this is to encourage it.

On the other hand, the pro-life movement is broadening considerably. The stereotype of a pro-lifer that the killing-rights forces cherish and try to disseminate is that of a male Catholic past the age of sixty who looks very much like Jesse Helms and is a staunch advocate of capital punishment while greatly preferring to spend tax money on arms than on prenatal care and services for poor women once they give birth.

Actually, those with respect for life, all life, are rather exhilaratingly diverse. There are Feminists for Life of America and JustLife who are working toward a society in which women will have the support, financial and emotional, that will make it unnecessary to even think of abortion.

And there are more and more of us libertarians and egalitarians who agree with Mary Meehan who wrote in *The Progressive*:

> Some of us who went through the anti-war struggles of the
> 1960s and early 1970s are now active in the right-to-life
> movement. We do not enjoy opposing our old friends on

the abortion issue, but we feel that we have no choice. We are moved by what pro-life feminists called the "consistency thing"—the belief that respect for human life demands opposition to abortion, capital punishment, euthanasia, and war. We don't think we have either the luxury or the right to choose some types of killing and say that they are all right, while others are not. A human life is a human life; and if equality means anything, it means that society may not value some human lives over others.

Meehan cites Graciela Olivarez, a civil rights and anti-poverty activist: "The poor cry out for justice and equality and we respond with legalized abortion. . . . I believe that in a society that permits the life of even one individual (born or unborn) to be dependent on whether that life is 'wanted' or not, all its citizens stand in danger. . . . We do not have equal opportunities. Abortion is a cruel way out."

Mary Meehan said something else, and I focus on it whenever I speak on abortion at colleges and universities to liberal students. I am often asked by them how come I, on the Left—and an atheist as well—am pro-life. I tell them what Mary Meehan says:

> . . . [I]t is out of character for the Left to neglect the weak and helpless. The traditional mark of the Left has been its protection of the underdog, the weak, and the poor. The unborn child is the most helpless form of humanity, even more in need of protection than the poor tenant farmer or the mental patient or the boat people on the high seas. The basic instinct of the Left is to aid those who cannot aid themselves—and that instinct is absolutely sound. It is what keeps the human proposition going.

That depends, of course, on how you define "human."

The ethos of death that has become the underside of the American Way—euthanasia, the hastening of capital punishment by the Supreme Court, the welcoming of eugenics, the killing by abortion of over a million and half lives each year—is in danger of greatly diminishing the American instinct to "aid those who cannot aid themselves."

My reason for opposing abortion—in addition to a desire to stop the mass killing—is that it is anesthetizing the society.

Dr. Leo Alexander served as an expert at the Nuremberg trials, particularly with regard to the attitudes and backgrounds of the German physicians who took part in the German programs of death.

In the July 14, 1949 issue of the *New England Journal of Medicine*, Dr. Alexander explained: "The beginnings at first were merely a subtle shift in emphasis in the basic attitude of the physicians. It started with the acceptance . . . that there is such a thing as life not worthy to be lived."

A book that profoundly influenced the German medical profession to choose death was *Permitting the Destruction of Unworthy Life*, published in Germany in 1920. Its co-author, Karl Binding, professor of law and philosophy, wrote: "It will take time, but society must come to accept that merely individual existence is meaningless when compared to the interest of the whole. . . . Once upon a time, barbarians eliminated all unfit lives; now we preserve unfit lives. As society progresses in a spiral, we will again come to see the higher morality of destroying the unfit."

The barbarians have returned. From abortion, they have moved on. And on. They can be stopped only by the life force— by those of us who have not been mesmerized by them.

PART ONE

Barriers to Communication

CASSIDY   Crucial to an understanding of how Americans debate public issues is an appreciation of the complex and sometimes contradictory beliefs which they hold about authority and legitimacy. The abortion question brings out these patterns with unusual clarity. Among the legitimating principles and sources of personal authority appealed to are "democracy," the claim to speak for "the public interest," professional and upper class status, the claim that one represents "the poor and disadvantaged," the appeal to libertarian principles, "equality," "the sanctity of life," and "the family." In general, supporters of abortion have been more successful than its opponents in appealing to and manipulating these claims to authority and legitimacy. Pro-lifers must understand and come to terms with the structures of authority in America. Two approaches are possible: one sees America as in need of fundamental change and challenges existing structures of power and authority; the other sees it as fundamentally sound and in need only of reform within the existing framework. The example of the abolitionists suggests that both perspectives are useful and can profitably coexist.

POTTS   In 1983, *Newsweek* magazine published an article indicating that only a very narrow category of abortions is permitted in the last three months of pregnancy. Thus began a series of events that resulted in a case being decided against *Newsweek* by The National News Council. *Newsweek* not only could not reliably describe a ten-year-old Supreme Court decision that meant abortions are readily permitted throughout all nine months of pregnancy, but, of concern to The National News Council, *Newsweek* refused to correct the error in a way that readers would understand.

These events led to an investigation of how *Newsweek*, during a four and one-half year period starting with January of 1980, covered the matter of when during pregnancy and for what reasons abortion is permitted. *Newsweek* covered the matter six times, got it wrong five times out of six, and was inconsistent even about what it got wrong those five times. *Newsweek* coverage was as if *Newsweek* not only had not read *Roe v. Wade* but had not even read *Newsweek*.

The events leading up to The National News Council decision, the decision itself, and the inconsistent and unreliable *Newsweek* coverage during this time are reported and analyzed in this essay.

Abortion and the Rhetoric of Legitimacy

Keith Cassidy

A mericans cherish an image of their society as open, free, democratic—a society in which every person is at liberty to speak on public affairs and in which characteristics such as class (when that concept is even conceded to be meaningful in America) are irrelevant to the exercise of this democratic right.

It would be a mistake to dismiss this image as wholly false, but it is equally clear that America, like all societies, has certain fundamental understandings about the sources and nature of authority and about basic legitimating principles, and that these are intimately linked to ideas about who has the right to speak, how they are to speak, and, more crucially, whether they have a right to be heard. In fact, of course, the right to speak is not seriously questioned: In America, the *formal* barriers to participation in public discussion are few, and anyone with a soap box has the right to harangue passers-by. What is problematic is *effective* participation in public policy debates, for while eccentrics may harangue, no one listens or grants them access to the real forum of debate, namely the mass media. Effective participation demands that one be seen as a legitimate participant, playing the game by unwritten but widely understood rules. Central then to the analysis of how America goes about debating and deciding on public policy is an understanding of its concepts of authority and legitimacy.

To even begin the discussion of these subjects is to open an intellectual Pandora's box: The philosophical and social science literature on these topics is vast and controversial, and it is hard to find agreement on the definition of basic words.[1] For purposes of this paper two concepts are central. The first is *authority,* understood here as a quality to be distinguished from raw power on the one hand and persuasion on the other; people with authority are presumed to have a right to help shape public policy, by virtue of some attribute which they possess.[2] Such attributes might be social class, education, etc. Over time the American understanding of the social and personal bases of authority has varied considerably; only now are historians reconstructing those changes.[3]

The second concept, obviously linked with the first, is that of *legitimating principles.* Even someone with little actual authority may claim a right to influence public policy by professing to speak on behalf of principles widely regarded as legitimate and significant. The exact nature of these principles has of course changed dramatically over time: In the seventeenth century an appeal to the principle of racial equality would have impressed few, while in the late twentieth century suspicion that someone does not accept it acts to disqualify the legitimacy of their utterances on a variety of issues. It is impossible to produce a complete list of such legitimating principles, but they would certainly include democracy, individual freedom, gender equality, compassion, religious freedom, etc. It is apparent, of course, that these principles are not of equal strength, nor are they necessarily consistent with one another. It is also clear that what constitutes a crucial principle for one segment of society— say religion, or the family—is either less important or wholly irrelevant for another.[4]

What this points to is that America is too large and variegated for there to be a single "public": What constitutes the limits of discourse in a liberal arts college in Massachusetts is not the same as in a Baptist church in rural Mississippi. Nonetheless, to be influential on the national stage it is necessary to receive the recognition of certain institutions which are informally recognized as having the right to legitimize participation. These institutions include powerful communications media, prestigious universities, big corporations, large labor organizations, professional bodies, and national religious denominational organizations.

Many policy debates occur between those who wield similar titles to authority. Thus when economists differ, however bitterly, it is often understood that as long as they both have the appropriate piece of paper—a Ph.D. degree from a high status university— they have a right to be heard and to have their ideas considered. More commonly, groups with various claims to legitimacy find themselves in conflict. In such circumstances there is a strong temptation to try to win the debate not by refuting arguments but by suggesting that your opponent has no right to be heard. Thus when environmental activists are locked in public disputes with businessmen it is easy to suggest that the business viewpoint need not be considered seriously because it represents the opinion of a "selfish" group that ignores "the public interest," that it is, in short, a "special interest" group whose views *ipso facto* lack legitimacy. What is being appealed to here is the sense that contravention of the legitimizing principles of the society rules out one's effective participation in public debate. The group under attack may reply not only by denying that it contravenes a legitimate principle, but also by invoking legitimating principles of its own—in the case of business it might appeal, for example, to the widespread respect for property rights.

Groups such as the Ku Klux Klan, which are widely perceived to have violated basic legitimating norms, are simply not part of public debate. The Klan may have attention paid to it, but only as a menace, not as a voice in the public forum. The case of the Klan illustrates a crucial point: The boundaries of legitimate discourse are constantly shifting. In 1924, the Klan was a real power in many states, and the Democratic Party refused to denounce it by name in its election platform. Within a few years, however, membership was a disgrace which one attempted to conceal. The changing fortunes of the Communist Party illustrate the same point.

Studying the language used by groups seeking public policy input permits us to see what strategy they are using to lay claim to a recognized place in the public arena. They may stress their claims to authority, making clear, for example, their connections with an authoritative institution. Thus, they may emphasize that a prominent member is a law professor at a prestigious university.

They may also stress their attachment to legitimating principles—
the ways in which the group's program advances racial equality or
individual freedom, for instance. Normally groups will do both
and will also suggest that their opponents speak less authoritative-
ly and are linked to attacks on widely revered principles. Hence a
group may suggest that its members are doctors, lawyers, and university professors selflessly working to advance racial justice and
that its opponents are ill-educated members of the lower class
who are racial bigots. If this is done skillfully enough, it will
never be necessary to actually defend the group's policy—on busing, for example, or anything else—for it will have delegitimated
the opposition at the same time that it has established its own credentials. Close attention to the language used lets us see the legitimating and delegitimating strategy at work.

It should be noted that when speaking of a "strategy" of
legitimation it is not meant that the process is fully conscious. It
is precisely because Americans have so internalized their society's
unwritten rules that they can apply them almost by instinct and
know how a particular audience will respond to certain cues.

At this point reference must be made to something alluded to
earlier: the complex and ambiguous character of authority and legitimacy in America. It is not possible here to trace the shifting
sources of authority in America, but the point must be made that
over time new and successful claims to authority have been made:
In the late nineteenth century, for example, professionalism became
a source of authority.[5] Older sources of authority may undergo a relative or absolute decline, but they never fully disappear. Thus high
social class, so important in colonial America, still produces some
authority for its possessors. Age, wealth, sex, religion—all act in different ways to produce authority. Since it is almost impossible to
produce a clear and coherent list, in relative order of importance,
of the sources of authority, and of the principles recognized as crucial by society, the situation may accordingly appear hopelessly
complex. In fact, however, it is one that everyone who has grown
up in America understands intuitively, although foreigners are
sometimes baffled by the curious rituals and conventions to which
it gives rise. Put bluntly, under its open, simple, and democratic
exterior, America is a nation in which all do not share equally in
authority and in which the sources of authority are tangled and
opaque. The way in which citizens react to issues makes clear that

they understand these ambiguities and inequalities. Indeed it is often those most quick to take a stand on democratic principle who are most adept at manipulating the symbols of authority.

James Davison Hunter has argued that the abortion debate is part of a much larger "Culture War" in American society. In his analysis of this "war" he discusses the rhetorical strategies which the combatants employ. Each makes a "positive" appeal "By grounding the 'rightness' or legitimacy of their claims in logic, science, humanitarian concerns, or an appeal to tradition or God." They also wage "negative" campaigns, "the deliberate, systematic effort to discredit the opposition," through "a strategy of public ridicule, derision, and insult."[6]

The abortion debate is particularly fascinating because while it can be seen quite plausibly as part of the "war" Hunter describes, it cuts across numerous other lines of fracture in America and brings out more fully than most conflicts the complexities of the American cultural situation. It illustrates vividly the ways in which groups attempt to gain rhetorical advantage over each other by their use of the language of legitimation and delegitimation. It may be suggested that while the abortion debate in other countries would tend to reflect, in general terms, the same themes, the rhetoric of legitimacy in America would have special characteristics, reflecting the country's distinctive traditions with respect to authority and legitimating principles.[7]

An important source of authority in America is democracy: the claim to be representing "the public." In fact, neither pro-choice nor pro-life forces may claim majority public support for their positions; as Judith Blake and others have pointed out, there are profound ambiguities in the public's attitude.[8] Notwithstanding this fact, pro-choice forces early staked out a claim to the authority of democratic support by their ingenious use of public opinion polls. Examples are legion, but take *Ms.* magazine's claim in April 1973, that "Politicians quaked before the shrill outcries of the vocal, Right-to-Life groups and ignored the fact that a 1972 Gallup Poll showed 64 percent of the general population and 56 percent of the Catholic population to be in favor of a woman's right to choose." That a later Gallup poll showed a different result was of no consequence: The rhetorical point had been made, that pro-choice views had the authority of democracy behind them.[9]

Allied to the claim of democratic legitimacy is the larger and vaguer claim to be speaking for "the public interest," rather than that of any narrow or limited "special interest group." As Joseph Sobran pointed out some years ago, the pro-choice tactic of labelling pro-life views as "Catholic" is effective not principally because of the anti-Catholic bias it enlists (although that is not negligible), but because it *places* opposition to abortion, *localizes* it: "It suggests that opposition to abortion can be dismissed, explained away, accounted for as a state of mind confined to people of a peculiar background (it hardly matters what that background is) whose arguments can be safely ignored."[10]

More convoluted is the maneuvering to claim the authority conferred by professional status and by upper and upper-middle class social status. Both are, of course, valuable sources of prestige and legitimacy, but their use is not without its perils. Too enthusiastic an employment of them leaves one open to the charge of "elitism." In the complicated world of American authority patterns, the *absence* of high social status can be in itself a source of authority, if a claim can be made to "victim status" and if one can assert a right to speak as one of the poor, the dispossessed, and the oppressed. The pro-choice handling of this difficulty has been nothing short of brilliant.

From the first, full use was made of the professional status of pro-choicers. In his revealing book *Abortion II: Making the Revolution,* Lawrence Lader discusses the strategy employed by pro-choicers in Colorado in 1967: "An important part of the strategy was to avoid public furor, and draw support from medical, religious, and legal leaders. . . ." He quotes Richard Lamm, then leader of the pro-choice forces, as saying that "It was our opinion that one letter from a doctor or minister supporting the bill, particularly if the legislators knew the person writing, was worth twenty adverse letters."[11] Lader is quite clear about the elite character of the strategy: He notes the flood of pro-life petitions, letters, and pickets and says, "Realizing they could not match this deluge numerically, Lamm and Steel concentrated on sending the Governor letters from supporting medical and clerical committees."[12]

The pro-choice movement drew not only upon the authority conferred by professional and, by inference, class position, it also benefitted from the financial support of wealthy foundations, such as the Rockefeller Foundation. The obvious danger was a charge of elitism; the response was to claim to speak on behalf of poor and black women. Now, in fact, women, the poor, and non-whites were less likely to support abortion than males, the wealthy, and whites; but the claim to represent their interests was insistently and, at least for public relations purposes, successfully made. Thus pro-choicers could claim the legitimacy which accrued to both high and low class positions. Where did this leave pro-lifers? They were portrayed as members of the lower-middle class, as Archie Bunkers, as part of the class in America which is granted the least right to speak on public affairs.

This can not be done crudely or overtly, but the impression has to be conveyed by suggestion and indirection. Occasionally, however, the matter is dealt with more clearly. Connie Paige's *The Right to Lifers* is a useful illustration of this tactic. In describing the Edelin case she sets it in the context of a "hundred-year-old history of antagonism between the Protestant Yankee settlers and the immigrant Irish." She portrays the Irish as having risen to political power, but as now on the defensive with challenges coming from blacks and Hispanics. To shore up their "ethnic pride," some of the Irish attack busing, while "others chose abortion as their target."[13] What seems to be suggested are sullen and resentful middle- and lower-middle-class Irish Catholics facing a Harvard educated elite of white, British-stock Protestants on the one hand and the black and Hispanic poor on the other. The inference is clear: The opinions of pro-lifers need not be considered seriously, for they lack the social and moral authority of their opponents. It might be noted that to achieve this effective rhetorical gambit certain facts had to be downplayed, namely that there was no reason to believe that Boston's black and Hispanic residents were any more accepting of abortion than its Irish population, and that indeed the Catholic Archbishop, Humberto Medeiros, was himself an immigrant from Portugal who had developed close ties with the Hispanic community.

A more common strategy is to portray pro-lifers as unrepresentative of any class or major group, as marginal, irrelevant and isolated from major centres of legitimacy and authority. This impression is conveyed in a variety of ways. Thus one *Ms.* magazine contributor, in an article entitled "I Was a Spy at a Right-to-Life Convention," presented it as a freak show, exhibiting "paranoia and in-group catch phrases."[14] A letter to the editor in a subsequent issue touched on a difficult point: While she agreed that pro-lifers "do indeed sound like crazy fanatics at times," she had to admit that "they can sound quite reasonable when presenting their views to the general public."[15] The message is clear: Right-to-life arguments may sound reasonable, but need not be taken seriously because we know that pro-lifers are actually eccentrics. The logic of this may be weak, but as rhetoric it is effective.

It is this desire—conscious or not—to show the marginality of right-to-life support, and conversely the cultural centrality of pro-choice, which led Garrett Hardin to include as an appendix to his book, *Mandatory Motherhood: The Real Meaning of "Right to Life,"* a list of organizations supporting ready access to abortion.[16]

Again the same approach is revealed in Gloria Steinem's comment, made as an aside in an article, that the remarks she quotes by pro-lifers are "bizarre and exceptional," and that right-to-lifers, who "don't trust the major media," "have created their own media world of right-wing newsletters, pamphlets and books distributed through churches and local organizations." In the same article she refers to the *Handbook on Abortion* as "obscurely published."[17]

The point of all this seems clear enough: to delegitimate the pro-life position by suggesting that it is culturally and psychologically marginal and to thus bring into play the powerful currents of conformism in American society. As Alexis de Tocqueville suggested a century and a half ago: "In America the majority raises formidable barriers around the liberty of opinion; within these barriers an author may write what he pleases, but woe to him if he goes beyond them."[18] It is precisely to suggest that those who contemplate pro-life advocacy risk exclusion from the circle of legitimate discourse that such remarks are made.

A different approach, an early sample of which is found in Deirdre English's analysis of the right-to-life movement in the radical magazine *Mother Jones,* is to profess a certain sympathy for the movement, or rather for the women in it. In the eyes of Deirdre English, the movement "is not merely for motherhood and the family but also openly—and virtually across the board—in favor of male domination." She argues that men in the movement "stand to gain a measure of male control over women," but the women "are fighting a battle for their own sexual submission." Why is this, since these women are "neither stupid nor incompetent"?

The answer lies in the fact that contraception and abortion have radically altered the nature of motherhood. Once the birth of a child became a choice, the old rules of male-female relations changed. "Women of all classes and religions" welcomed the new freedom. However, English asserts, the economy did not change as quickly, and a woman without a man is still severely disadvantaged. Especially in bad economic times, this sort of pressure leads some women into "the anti-feminist backlash." "In short, the anti-feminist woman is, like all other women, grappling with the weight of her oppression." Her response, however, is "defensive: reactionary in the sense of reacting to change with the desire to return to the supposedly simple solutions of the past."[19]

No proof was offered for this hypothesis, which has been taken up and embellished by others. The point, of course, was not to provide a disinterested scientific analysis of the origins and motivation of the right-to-life movement, but to provide an explanation which could recognize, but then dismiss as spurious, the movement's claims to speak on behalf of moral principles. Female pro-lifers could now be seen as victims of male oppression, rather than as simply villains (male pro-lifers, of course, continued to be clearly villainous). The advantages were obvious: An apparent sympathy could mask a patronizing and dismissive contempt for those who lacked the clear vision and strong will of the true feminist. More importantly it was possible to deal in a rhetorically effective fashion with one of the most salient facts about the movement: its heavily female character. It was now possible to dismiss on feminist grounds a largely female movement.

Another strategy is illustrated in the *Ms.* magazine coverage of the 1978 International Women's Year meeting in Houston. Pro-lifers are invariably referred to in these articles as "right wing" or, more commonly, as "ultra right." Since pro-lifers are not all right wing, and indeed the correlation is weak, the author, Lindsy Van Gelder, had to deal with the fact that on some crucial issues pro-lifers did not vote with right wing delegates.[20] Rather than face the implications of this, which would undercut her rhetorical point, she resorted to the claim that the "ultraright machinery" had "unoiled, squeaky joints."[21] The assertion that right-to-life is "right wing" has proven to be too valuable to discard, even in the face of evidence to the contrary.

The reader may at this point ask why it is rhetorically useful to label right-to-life as "right wing." After all, do not a large number of Americans see themselves as being "right of center"? In fact a poll taken in the mid-1980s showed 36% of the population so describing themselves, with only 18% saying they were "left of center." However, nearly half the population—46%—say they are "middle of the road."[22] It is this preference by so many for a non-polarized, nonideological politics which is being appealed to by the use of the label "right-wing" for pro-lifers, who are thereby pictured as being outside the safe, central consensus of American politics. Pro-lifers have, of course, sometimes tried the reverse strategy, that of hanging the "left-wing" label on pro-choicers. This has not been successful, in part because of the skill of pro-choicers in associating their cause with "establishment" figures. Also, since the career of Senator Joseph McCarthy, the "left-wing" label has tended to create more suspicion about the person doing the labelling than the ones labelled. A similar problem does not exist for those who brand opponents as "right-wing."

It may be suggested that there is another purpose served by hanging the "right-wing" tag on pro-lifers. It serves to make their cause unpalatable to those on the Left, some of whom are only weakly committed to abortion, and to keep them from defecting to a right-to-life position. It is impossible to understand why *Ms.* magazine, for example, spends so much time excoriating right-to-life unless it is aware that, though they are preaching to the converted, some are only weakly converted. Right-to-life must be made to appear illegitimate to potential supporters on the Left. To actually grapple with right-to-life arguments would be counter-productive: It is far easier to inhibit people from ever examining those arguments.[23]

It might be asked if pro-abortionists are not painting themselves into a corner by their attack on right-to-life as "right wing." In fact, and this is a stroke of rhetorical genius, pro-abortionists avoid an exclusive association with the Left by simultaneously employing, as legitimating principles, slogans and themes fully compatible with a right wing perspective.

The invocation of "a woman's right to control her own body" touches a responsive chord for those on the Right who subscribe to doctrines of possessive individualism. By basing much of the defense of abortion on grounds which are essentially libertarian and individualistic, pro-choicers have been able to tap the deep currents of anti-authoritarianism and individual freedom in American society. As one observer has noted, the characteristic form of radicalism in America is anarchism, not collectivism.[24] Indeed the very term "pro-choice" mirrors the ideology.

A characteristic expression of this appeal is found in Lawrence Lader's remark that "We [early pro-choice leaders] were determined to prove that radicalism hadn't been washed out of the American dream. It was a test of individualism against church and bureaucracy."[25]

A striking example of how extraordinarily flexible pro-choicers could be in their appeals to authority is provided by Lawrence Lader, in the very book from which this ringing evocation of the individualistic tradition was taken. A few pages away a very different source of legitimacy is tapped: the managerial-professional-bureaucratic tradition which has been so significant since the late nineteenth century. Citing the threat of a "population explosion," Lader advocated compulsion in population control, declaring that "some form of compulsion . . . is not only healthy, but imperative."[26] As part of this program of coercion he urged that the minimum age of marriage be raised to 23 and the state levy "economic penalties against couples who bear three or more children."[27]

This ready acceptance of the power of the state to regulate family affairs appears strange from a "pro-choice" advocate who appeals to the American tradition of individualism. In fact it mirrors the profound ambivalence with which Americans approach questions of authority: The upper-middle classes to whom Lader addressed himself retain a respect for older values, even as they are integrated into the professional-bureaucratic value system with its acceptance of "social engineering." A successful rhetoric of legitimacy will touch all bases, with both author and reader likely unaware of the contradictions: They have so thoroughly internalized them that it would require a major effort of self-discovery for their existence to be perceived.

Not all pro-choicers, of course, would endorse Lader's naked coercion. It is true, however, that the frequently expressed linkage of abortion and the "population crisis" belies the notion that abortion is sought as a simple expression of personal freedom. The failure of most pro-choicers to condemn coercive Chinese birth control programs—including compulsory abortion—makes the same point.[28]

Right-to-life advocates, of course, lose on both sides of these appeals: They are condemned for interfering with the "privacy" of individuals and, at the same time, for failing to see the need for an attack on the "population problem" which would subordinate the rights of individuals to the power of the state.

The same rhetorical genius can be seen in the pro-choice argument that right-to-lifers are males who wish to block the liberation of women. The principle appealed to here is that of equality, one of the great sources of legitimacy in American life. Its use in this fashion preempts the rhetorical field and diverts serious attention from the fact that most right-to-life activists are women; that men are consistently more in favor of abortion than women; and that such targets of feminist wrath as Hugh Hefner's Playboy Foundation have been major financial supporters of the pro-choice movement.

The danger of too successfully portraying right-to-lifers as a small, marginal, ill-educated, irrelevant group of "loonies" is to invite the question how such a group could command the influence it does. This leads to a further problem: If too successful in persuading readers that right-to-lifers are weak, then pro-choice advocates may find it difficult to arouse their followers from apathy and lead them into battle.

The rhetorical solutions to these difficulties are interesting. Pro-lifers were portrayed as "well-financed," "well-organized," and supported by the Roman Catholic hierarchy (but not by other Catholics). These attributes plus their "fanaticism" and willingness to show "gory pictures" account for their influence. It was important that while pro-choicers despised their opponents and allowed to them no claim to authority or legitimacy, they were never to underestimate the danger these people represented.

The amount of time and energy spent attacking the motives and personalities of pro-lifers is not fully explicable unless it is recognized that it is an essential element in a rhetorical strategy aimed at preserving a claim to legitimacy. For pro-choicers the problem is this: Pro-lifers have appropriated the American tradition of equality ("a person is a person no matter how small") and the general Western concept of the sacredness of life. Portraying them as lower-class, right wing, culturally marginal Roman

Catholics will help to delegitimate them, but will not be enough if they can continue to claim to speak out on behalf of principles widely regarded as legitimating. Two answers to the pro-life claim are possible: The first is to argue that these principles point to pro-choice conclusions; the second, and more rhetorically powerful approach, is to suggest that pro-lifers do not *really* espouse these principles. Thus, it is claimed, pro-lifers are "inconsistent": They should oppose capital punishment and war, but, it is maintained, they do not. They are "callous," "only care about life before birth, not after," and are "violent."[29]

That pro-choicers sense that their opponents have not wholly lost a claim to speak as the legitimate voice of these principles is attested to not only by these continued assaults (you do not, after all, continue to fire at a dead enemy), but also by explicit admissions. Thus Rosalind Petchesky, in her *Abortion and Woman's Choice: The State, Sexuality and Reproductive Freedom,* concedes that abortion's "legitimacy has been shaken," and that "escalation of the 'right-to-life' propaganda campaign . . . has apparently influenced how people feel and talk about abortion."[30]

At this point we should turn to an examination of that "right-to-life propaganda campaign." When we turn from pro-choice rhetoric to that of the pro-life movement we are forcibly struck by the degree to which it is a reaction. Very early in the abortion debate pro-choicers were able to largely define the rhetorical ground and set the terms of the argument. Thus pro-lifers were thrown on the defensive, and felt compelled to demonstrate, among other things, their compassion and concern; the diverse religious backgrounds of their members; the acceptance of women's rights, etc. Their pro-choice opponents were under no such obligation; having made the charges they could sit back and watch their opponents try to defend themselves from diverse and sometimes contrary accusations (thus right-to-lifers were simultaneously reproached for being single issue fanatics and the bearers of a whole range of right-wing programs). The task was obviously hopeless.

Pro-lifers did, of course, try to mount their own campaigns for recognition as authoritative speakers. Where medical doctors could be found who would work actively for the cause their prestige was used. More generally, the authority of science was employed, and arguments based on medical evidence about prenatal development became a stock in trade of the movement.

A serious problem they encountered was that the class/educational background of most right-to-life members tended to confer less personal authority than that of pro-choicers, who were on average better educated and wealthier. Sensing this, right-to-lifers defiantly made a virtue of their positions and presented their movement as a "grass-roots" phenomenon, which by implication possessed greater democratic legitimacy than that of their opponents.

In general terms, however, pro-lifers recognized their best chance for success lay not with claims to personal authority but with appeals to legitimating principles.

They had an enormous advantage in that the pro-choice victory had not come through the democratic process, but by a Supreme Court decision. It was easy to argue that this was an imposed victory, that it lacked the legitimacy of one obtained through the legislatures. As Karen Mulhauser of the National Abortion Rights Action League put it, referring to the 1973 decision, "the country wasn't with us at that point. Had we made more gains through the legislature and referendum processes, and taken a little longer at it, the public would have moved with us."[31]

As indicated earlier, the two chief principles appealed to were that of equality and the sanctity of life. Two historical parallels were frequently used to dramatize these: slavery and the Holocaust. The parallels between slavery and abortion, and right-to-life and the abolitionists were made early and often. In this way right-to-life was able to place itself in the mainstream of American history and to portray itself as being the true heir of the liberal tradition.[32]

The parallel with the Holocaust served to delegitimate the opposition, by linking it with one of the greatest crimes of human history. That it was effective was demonstrated by the fury of the pro-choice response.[33]

These themes all appeared early and simply received greater elaboration over time. One innovation which did have considerable power was the linkage of abortion with attacks on the family. Placing the opposition to abortion in the context of a "pro-family" policy and drawing on the legitimating power of the family threw the pro-choice movement on the defensive and showed the power of a more aggressive and less reactive approach to the debate.

How successful has the right-to-life movement been? Even though it has often been on the defensive, and has suffered from its opposition's overwhelming power in the mass media, it has not been without effect. For one thing the public opinion polls demonstrate that the shift to a pro-choice position, so marked in the 1960's, slowed substantially with the emergence of a broad-based right-to-life movement.[34] More intriguing is the testimony, from pro-choicers themselves, that "right-to-life," "sanctity of life" appeals have tremendous potential support. Thus Barbara Grizzuti Harrison, in a *Ms.* magazine review of Linda Bird Francke's *The Ambivalence of Abortion,* found "an irony that feminists now find themselves locked in battle with people who describe themselves as 'pro-life'," and warned that "the consequence of not discussing the moral ambiguities of abortion is that we allow pro-lifers to catch the moral ball and run with it."[35]

Even clearer are the remarks, some quoted earlier, by Rosalind Petchesky, writing from a Marxist and feminist perspective: "Recently, a rash of disclaimers and apologies by liberals, leftists and even some feminists in the popular media, confessing 'ambivalence' about abortion, reveal the extent to which 'right-to-life ideology' has penetrated the dominant culture and fostered guilt, even without a change in the law."[36]

What this points to is that if right-to-life appeals have not succeeded in fully persuading many, they have served to prevent the full acceptance of the pro-choice position. That they have done so, despite the formidable rhetorical skills and advantages possessed by pro-choicers in asserting their own authority and the legitimacy of their cause, is extraordinary. It is clear that a pro-life rhetoric which went on the offensive and questioned the legitimacy and consistency of the pro-choice position on a variety of fronts would have a substantial impact.

What form might such attack take? They could focus, for example, on the inconsistencies between the libertarian rhetoric of abortion advocates and their frequent willingness to employ the coercive power of the state for social control projects. Similarly, pro-lifers who are charged with inconsistency because some support capital punishment might more aggressively turn the tables and demand to know how their opponents can denounce war and yet kill the unborn. Those who denounce human rights violations at home and abroad could be queried about their views on the rights of the unborn. A more aggressive, less reactive, strategy would likely prove to have more impact. Yet in the long run it would not prove sufficient.[37]

Ultimately, pro-life must recognize and come to terms with the structures of authority in American society. Put simply the problem is this: While relatively successful in appealing to legitimizing principles, the movement has largely failed to speak with the authority which arises from social status, educational background, or institutional support. Indeed, the only authoritative national organizations to fully endorse pro-life have been the Catholic Church and some of the Protestant denominations. In fact, so complete is the alienation of the nation's most authoritative classes and institutions from pro-life that the leaders of those institutions sense that a general triumph of pro-life principles could result in a serious challenge to their claims to moral authority and leadership. Should pro-life principles win general and recognized acceptance, the very groups which have claimed to act as the keepers of the nation's conscience might stand condemned as false prophets. The fury with which pro-lifers are attacked is not fully explicable unless it is recognized that what is at stake is not only abortion, but the moral authority of some of the most powerful groups in America. That they should be challenged by those very people—lower middle class, personally religious, less well educated—whom they most despise seems to them an incredible affront. In a very real sense the pro-life movement, precisely because many in it perceive it as a populist, grass-roots challenge to major portions of the American establishment, is, ironically enough, a radical force in American society, for it raises questions about the authority of major American institutions. Thus the abortion issue has certainly been a major factor in making clear the political character of the Supreme Court, depriving it of some of its aura of being "above politics." Not only did the original *Roe v. Wade* decision contribute to this, but subsequent battles over presidential nominations to the Court have added to the process. A significant portion of the pro-life movement has always felt attracted to this approach, in which a prophetic minority calls society to the bar for judgement.

The alternative has also always been a part of the movement. Rather than seeing itself as a revolutionary force, profoundly at odds with corrupt and illegitimate institutions, it can see itself as a reform movement, attempting to turn around institutions which, though fundamentally sound and legitimate, have gone astray. This approach points not to confrontation but to a sustained effort to penetrate and turn around those dominant institutions—universities, the media, the professions—which are pro-choice bulwarks. It brings to mind the call by German radicals in the 1960's for a "long march through the institutions." While the pro-life movement has always had elements which opted for this view of its role, it has not, in general terms, seen major institutions as the subjects of long-term and systematic courtship. Thus, for example, pro-life work on campuses has been limited. Certainly due recognition must be given to those groups which work in that field, but as a general rule the university, one of the central authority generating institutions in society, has been tacitly conceded to pro-choice forces by most in the movement.

In short, it appears that pro-life can be, as one option, a revolutionary force, appealing to the great principles of equality and the sanctity of life to delegitimate those powerful institutions which promote a pro-choice viewpoint. In this case the movement's very alienation from these dominant institutions becomes a source of pride and comfort, as it sees itself in the prophetic role of an outcast group representing the "real" America. Conversely, it can see itself as a reform movement, in which case its rhetoric is likely to be less confrontational, and it will use a logic of incremental demands to gradually drive pro-choice to a defensive and marginal position.

It might be profitable at this point to look again at a historical group with whom the pro-lifers are fond of comparing themselves: the abolitionists. Both tendencies, just cited, flourished in the anti-slavery movement which contained those who, like Garrison, regarded the whole political system as intrinsically corrupt (Garrison once burned a copy of the Constitution, calling it "a covenant with death and an agreement with hell") and who refused even to vote.[38] It also contained those who saw slavery as a blemish on an otherwise sound nation and who felt they could work within the system. The parallels are not exact, but in similar fashion the pro-lifers must come to terms with the structure of authority and legitimacy in American society and decide on their response to it.

It may well transpire that, like abolitionism, the movement has room—and need—for both analyses.

As one historian has noted, "Abolitionist quarrels were not between competing ideologies: They took place within a parameter of assumptions." He has also argued that the "institutional disarray [of the movement] did no harm. Rather than discouraging abolitionists, the very diversity after 1840 probably encouraged the maximum number of people to enlist in the cause." He further claims that the divisions were not rigid, and that over the years partisans of each tendency showed signs of movement toward the opposing viewpoint.[39]

The implications of this for the pro-life movement seem clear enough. While pro-lifers should be aware that members of their movement have chosen different strategies, they should also recognize that the differences are not immune to dialogue, change, and accommodation, and that by opting for a variety of strategies pro-lifers are following a well established pattern in American politics. Such a recognition might make them more tolerant of their fellows who have decided on a different route.

Notes

1. Particularly useful is Richard T. DeGeorge, *The Nature and Limits of Authority*, Lawrence, Kansas: University Press of Kansas, 1985. See also R. Blaine Harris, ed., *Authority: A Philosophical Analysis*, Tuscaloosa, AL: University of Alabama Press, 1976, which has a useful bibliography by Richard T. DeGeorge. Also useful are Richard E. Flathman, *The Practice of Political Authority: Authority and the Authoritative*, Chicago: University of Chicago Press, 1980; April Carter, *Authority and Democracy*, London: Routledge and Kegan Paul, 1979; E. D. Watt, *Authority*, London: Croom Helm, 1982; Harry Eckstein and Ted Robert Gurr, *Patterns of Authority: A Structural Basis for Political Inquiry*, New York, John Wiley and Sons, 1975; Leonard Krieger "The Idea of Authority in the West" *American Historical Review*, Vol. 82, No. 2 (April 1977), pp. 249-70.

2. This approach is based on that of Robert L. Peabody. "Authority" *International Encyclopedia of the Social Sciences*, Vol. 1, pp. 473-77.

3. There is no adequate review of the relevant literature. Some of the titles which suggest themselves however are Laurence Veysey, ed., *Law and Resistance: American Attitudes toward Authority*, New York: Harper and Row, 1970; David Potter "The Quest for the National Character" in John Higham, ed., *The Reconstruction of American History*, New York: Harper and Row, 1962, pp. 197-220; Michael Kammen, *People of Paradox: An Inquiry Concerning the Origins of American Civilization*, New York: Alfred Knopf, 1973, especially Chapter 2, "The Quest for Legitimacy in Colonial America," pp. 31-56, T. H. Breen, *The Character of the Good Ruler: Puritan Political Ideas in New England, 1630-1730*, New Haven and London: Yale University Press, 1970; Thomas S. Haskell, *The Emergence of Professional Social Science: The American Social Science Association and the Nineteenth Century Crisis of Authority*, Urbana: University of Illinois Press, 1977. John P. Diggins and Mark E. Kahn, eds., *The Problem of Authority in America*, Philadelphia: Temple University Press, 1981; William Graebner, *The Engineering of Consent: Democracy and Authority in Twentieth-Century America*, Madison: University of Wisconsin Press, 1987. A related theme, inspired by the work of Antonio Gramsci, which has attracted considerable attention is that of "hegemony." In *The Rise and Fall of the American Left*, New York: W.W. Norton, 1992, p. 415, footnote 1, John Patrick Diggins notes that "The scholarship on Gramsci is an endless growth industry. . . ." In addition to the works cited by Diggins in this note, see also T. J.

Jackson Lears, "The Concept of Cultural Hegemony: Problems and Possibilities," *American Historical Review,* Vol. 90, No. 3 (June 1985), pp. 567–93.

4. This area has not been adequately studied. For a good introduction to the subject of changing American values, see Thomas C. Cochran, *Challenges to American Values: Society, Business and Religion,* New York: Oxford University Press, 1985. See also Robert Bellah *et al., Habits of the Heart: Individualism and Commitment on American Life,* Berkeley: University of California Press, 1985.

5. See Haskell, *The Emergence of Professional Social Science,* also, Robert Wiebe, *The Search for Order, 1877-1920,* New York: Hill and Wang, 1967; Thomas Haskell, ed., *The Authority of Experts: Studies in History and Theory,* Bloomington, Indiana: Indiana University Press, 1984; Burton J. Bledstein, *The Culture of Professionalism,* New York: W.W. Norton and Co., 1976. See also Don K. Price, *America's Unwritten Constitution: Science, Religion and Political Responsibility,* Cambridge: Harvard University Press, 1983.

6. James Davison Hunter, *Culture Wars: The Struggle to Define America,* New York: Basic Books, 1991, p. 136. This book appeared after this essay was prepared and provides a very useful context for its argument.

7. Two studies, which like Hunter's appeared after this essay was prepared, are of direct relevance and contain some very useful insights. They are Celeste Michelle Condit, *Decoding Abortion Rhetoric: Communicating Social Change,* Urbana and Chicago: University of Illinois Press, 1990 and Marsha L. Vanderford, "Vilification and Social Movements: A Case Study of Pro-Life and Pro-Choice Rhetoric," *Quarterly Journal of Speech,* Vol. 75 (1989) pp. 166–182. A helpful account of press treatment of the abortion issue is Marvin Olasky, *The Press and Abortion, 1838-1988,* Hillsdale, NJ: Lawrence Erlbaum Associates, 1988.

8. Judith Blake, "Negativism, Equivocation and Wobbly Assent: Public 'Support' for the Pro-Choice Platform on Abortion," *Demography,* Vol. 18, No. 3 (August 1981), pp. 309–20.

9. The deficiencies of the 1972 poll as a guide to abortion attitudes are explicitly addressed by Peter Skerry on p. 72 of his article "The Class Conflict over Abortion," *The Public Interest,* 52 (Summer 1978), pp. 69–84.

10. M. J. Sobran, "The Abortion Sect," *The Human Life Review,* Vol. 1, No. 4 (Fall 1972), p. 104.

11. Lawrence Lader, *Abortion II: Making the Revolution,* Boston: Beacon Press, 1973, p. 63. (All citations are from the clothbound edition.)

12. *Ibid.* p. 65.

13. Connie Paige, *The Right-to-Lifers: Who They Are, How They Operate, Where They Get Their Money,* New York: Summit Books, 1983, pp. 13–14.

14. Louise Farr, "I Was a Spy at a Right-to-Life Convention," *Ms.,* February 1976, p. 77.

15.   *Ms.*, June 1976, p. 9.

16.   Garrett Hardin, *Mandatory Motherhood: The Real Meaning of "Right-to-Life."*

17.   Gloria Steinem, "Feminist Notes: The Nazi Connection," *Ms.*, October 1980, pp. 88, 89.

18.   Alexis de Tocqueville, *Democracy in America,* Vol. 1, New York: Vintage Books, 1945, p. 274.

19.   Deirdre English, "The War against Choice: Inside the Anti-abortion Movement," *Mother Jones,* February/March 1981, pp. 16–32.

20.   The factors which act as the most powerful predictors of abortion attitudes are education and degree of religious commitment. Political ideology is only weakly correlated with them, a fact observed in a number of studies. Thus Donald Granberg declared in "Abortion Attitudes, 1965–1980: Trends and Determinants," *Family Planning Perspectives,* Vol. 12, No. 5 (September/October 1980), pp. 250–61 that "political ideology is only weakly correlated with approval of abortion." Similarly Ross K. Baker *et al.* in "Matters of Life and Death: Social, Political and Religious Correlates of Attitudes on Abortion," *American Politics Quarterly,* Vol. 9, No. 1 (January 1981), pp. 89–102, declared "in an analysis not reported here, we found no relationship between the abortion scale and questions which tapped attitudes on the government's role as a guarantor of employment and its role in aiding minorities" (emphasis in original). In a recent review of survey data relating to abortion attitudes, James Davison Hunter, in "What Americans Really Think about Abortion," *First Things,* No. 24, (June/July, 1992) pp. 13–21, declared that ". . . individuals who identified themselves as being 'pro-life' were, with but a few exceptions, as 'liberal' as, and in most cases even more 'liberal' than, the so-called socially progressive abortion rights group" (p. 20).

21.   Lindsay Van Gelder, "Behind the Scenes at Houston: Four Days That Changed the World," *Ms.*, March 1978, p. 90.

22.   *The Gallup Report,* Report No. 230 (November 1984), p. 23. A later poll, and the most recent reported by Gallup on this topic, showed 20 percent describing themselves as "liberal," 28 percent as "conservative," and 45 percent as "moderate." *The Gallup Report,* June 1986, No. 249, p. 19. The different wording may account for the change in percentages.

23.   Something of the ambivalence of many on the Left to abortion can be glimpsed by the reactions to Mary Meehan's article "Abortion: The Left Has Betrayed the Sanctity of Life" in *The Progressive,* Vol. 44, No. 9 (September 1980), pp. 33–34. Letters in subsequent issues both excoriated the editors for even running the piece and agreed with Meehan's views. Again, the Deirdre English article referred to supra footnote 19 drew a mixed reaction, even in a journal as left-wing as *Mother Jones.* As one writer put it, "I know I am not the only person of left-leaning philosophy who has found the abortion issue a difficult one. Many progressives oppose abortion on the same grounds they oppose nuclear weapons and the exploitation of Third World countries." (*Mother Jones,* May 1981, p. 2).

In an interview with the author held on October 28, 1982, Julie Loesch, founder of Pro-Lifers For Survival, declared that "there is a deep potential split on the Left over this issue. [There are] many closet pro-lifers on the Left who have been intimidated into silence by hysterical feminists."

24.   David De Leon, *The American as Anarchist,* Baltimore: The Johns Hopkins University Press, 1978. The libertarian basis of the claim of "a woman's right to control her own body" and its clash with a left wing emphasis on the power of society has attracted the unfavorable attention of Elizabeth Fox-Genovese in *Feminism without Illusions: A Critique of Individualism,* Chapel Hill and London: University of North Carolina Press, 1991. She notes ". . . many feminists continue to found some of their most important claims—above all, the right to 'reproductive freedom' and abortion—firmly in individual right, even as they ground others . . . in a repudiation of individualism. . . . Either they do not perceive the contradiction, or worse, they cynically assume that others will not perceive it." (p. 57)

25.   Lader, *Abortion II,* p. 225.

26.   *Ibid.* p. 218.

27.   *Ibid.* p. 222.

28.   For a discussion of this, see Joseph Sobran, "'Choice': The Hidden Agenda," *Human Life Review,* Vol. 10, No. 4 (Fall 1984), pp. 5–14. For a pro-choice work which protests compulsory abortion, see Betsy Hartman, *Reproductive Rights and Wrongs: The Global Politics of Population Control and Contraceptive Choice,* New York: Harper and Row, 1987.

29.   Some of these themes are treated in Vanderford's "Vilification and Social Movements." Attacks on some of these stereotypes can be found in James R. Kelly, "Beyond the Stereotypes," *Commonweal,* November 20, 1981, pp. 654–59; see also Kelly's "Turning Liberals into Fascists: A Case Study of the Distortion of the Right-to-Life Movement," *Fidelity,* July/August, 1987, Vol. 6, No. 8, pp. 17–22. Discussion of some of these stereotypes by a pro-lifer can be found in Dave Andrusko, "Zealots, Zanies, and Assorted Kooks: How the Major Media Interprets the Pro-Life Movement" in Dave Andrusko, ed., *To Rescue the Future,* Toronto and Harrison, NY: Life Cycle Books, 1983, pp. 183–200. For a discussion of media bias in the discussion of the abortion issue by a journalist who is not a member of the pro-life movement, see David Shaw, *Los Angeles Times,* July 1–4, 1990.

30.   Rosalind Pollack Petchesky, *Abortion and Woman's Choice: The State, Sexuality and Reproductive Freedom,* New York: Longman Inc., 1984, p. 242, 365.

31.   Quoted in Roger M. Williams, "The Power of Fetal Politics," *Saturday Review,* June 9, 1979, p. 12.

32.   See, for example, J.C. Willke, *Abortion and Slavery: History Repeats,* Cincinnati: Hayes Publishing, 1984 and William Brennan, *The Abortion Holocaust: Today's Final Solution,* St. Louis: Landmark Press, 1983. A full and scholarly discussion of both parallels is found in James Burtchaell, *Rachel Weeping and Other Essays on Abortion,* Kansas City: Andrews and McMeel, 1982.

33.   See, for example, Gloria Steinem, "If Hitler Were Alive, Whose Side Would He Be On?" in *Outrageous Acts and Everyday Rebellions,* New York: Holt, Rinehart and Winston, 1983, pp. 305-26.

34.   Judith Blake in "The Supreme Court's Abortion Decisions and Public Opinion in the United States," *Population and Development Review,* 1977, pp. 45-62, declared "Although negative views have declined and positive ones increased over time, it seems clear that the largest changes took place in the late 1960's. Both the Gallup and the NORC surveys evinced relatively little change beginning in 1973." *The Gallup Report,* Report Nos. 244-45 (January/February 1986), pp. 17-18, found that 45 percent opposed and 45 percent supported the Supreme Court's 1973 abortion ruling. Until 1989 the tendency was for some variation to occur, with no stable increase in support of the ruling over the years. After the 1989 *Webster* decision, the percentage of those supporting the 1973 *Roe v. Wade* decision rose, as did the percentage of those who believed that abortion should be legal "under any circumstance." Nonetheless, a majority of the population continued to support restrictions on abortion. See *The Gallup Poll Monthly,* January 1992, No. 316, pp. 5-7. Given the enormous media support for unlimited access to abortion, the fact that the percentage of those who believed that abortion should be legal "under any circumstance" only rose from 21 to 31 from 1975 to 1992 represents substantial evidence of the impact of the pro-life movement.

35.   Barbara Grizzuti Harrison, "On Reclaiming the Moral Perspective," *Ms. Magazine,* June 1978, p. 40.

36.   Petchesky, *Abortion and Woman's Choice,* p. 341. Some of those reservations about abortion are abundantly on display in Elizabeth Fox-Genovese's *Feminism without Illusions.*

37.   One author who has given serious thought to the problems of pro-life political strategy is James R. Kelly. See "Abortion: What Americans Really Think and the Catholic Challenge," *America,* Vol. 165, No. 13 (November 2, 1991), pp. 310-16, which has a very useful discussion of public perception of the abortion issue and of the right-to-life movement. See also Mark Cunningham, "The Abortion War," *National Review,* Vol. 44, No. 21 (November 2, 1992), p. 42.

38.   Merton L. Dillon, *The Abolitionists: The Growth of a Dissenting Minority,* New York: W.W. Norton, 1979, pp. 133-134, and James Stewart Brewer, *Holy Warriors: The Abolitionists and American Slavery,* New York: Hill and Wang, 1976, pp. 98-99.

39.   Ronald G. Walters, *The Antislavery Appeal: American Abolitionism after 1830,* New York: W.W. Norton and Company, 1984, pp. 18, 5, 17.

The Fourth Estate on the Third Trimester:

Legal Analysis of This and Other Fiction in *Newsweek* Magazine

John J. Potts*

You shall know the truth, and the truth shall make you free.[1]

Public understanding of the United States Supreme Court depends almost exclusively on the news media. . . .[2]

Introduction

T he purpose of this essay is to evaluate coverage by *Newsweek* magazine of certain aspects of the abortion controversy. The essay will explain the trimester system under *Roe v. Wade*[3] with regard to the timing involved and to the standards employed. It will analyze the accuracy of *Newsweek*'s own standard for reporting. Finally, the essay will explore how *Newsweek*'s coverage has affected the legal process.

---

* I am indebted to my colleagues in academia, Professor Richard T. Stith, of Valparaiso University School of Law and Professor Alex Y. Seita, of Albany Law School, Union University, for commenting on a draft of this essay. I am also indebted to my research assistants, Mr. Robert Brown, Mr. Tallum I. Nguti, Mrs. Linda D. Potter, and Mr. Richard J. Rupcich for their invaluable assistance in connection with this essay, which was completed in the spring of 1985.

33

Scope

Inaccurate reporting on the abortion controversy in the national print media is apparently widespread.[4] Demonstrating this, however, is not the purpose of this essay. Present space allows analysis of no more than a few limited aspects of the controversy,[5] and then only in a single national publication and only for part of the time since *Roe v. Wade* was handed down by the Supreme Court of the United States on January 22, 1973. This essay will focus on coverage of the abortion controversy by *Newsweek* magazine from the beginning of 1980 through the middle of 1984. This period is late enough for the magazine to have had sufficient time to absorb the court cases involved and long enough to justify reaching conclusions concerning the magazine's coverage. Because *Roe v. Wade* and its sister case *Doe v. Bolton*[6] were nearly eight years old when this time period began, *Newsweek*'s coverage of the conclusions reached in these cases should have been accurate. Erroneous statements concerning the trimester system cannot be dismissed with the excuse that they concern a late-breaking development.

The trimester system established by the *Roe-Doe* axis constitutes the focal point of this essay.[7] What the cases in fact say will be used as a standard against which *Newsweek*'s reporting on the cases will be tested. The results of that comparison will then be tested against *Newsweek*'s own standard for reporting.

Stith and Potts v. *Newsweek*

In June 1983, *Newsweek* magazine published an article on abortion that included a description of the trimester system.[8] This report quickly became the subject of a dispute, and in August 1983 it became the subject of proceedings before The National News Council.[9]

The trimester system has two relevant features. It tells *when* certain standards apply as well as *what* those standards are. Attention must first be given to these aspects of the trimester system in order to appraise the accuracy of *Newsweek*'s reporting.

Legal Background for Proceedings

Certain conclusions of the Supreme Court in *Roe v. Wade* and *Doe v. Bolton* are clear. It is clear, for instance, that states may impose no restrictions at all on abortions performed by doctors with the consent of the mother in the first trimester,[10] the first three months of pregnancy. It is clear that no restrictions relating to the reason for the abortion may be imposed in the second trimester,[11] the middle three months of pregnancy. Under *Roe v. Wade* and *Doe v. Bolton*, for the first six months of pregnancy an unborn child is subject to abortion for any reason "or for no reason at all."[12]

Only in the last trimester, the final three months of pregnancy, may restrictions be imposed on the basis of the reason for which the woman wishes an abortion.[13] A line is drawn by the term "life or health" of the mother.[14] *Roe* held that a state may not prevent a woman from having an abortion "when it is necessary to preserve [her] life or health."[15] If her life or health are at issue, then a state may not prevent the abortion. If her life or health are not at issue, then the abortion may be proscribed.[16]

This distinction does not mean that a state is *obligated* to proscribe third-trimester abortions when there is no life or health reason for the abortion. Rather, a state is *permitted* to prohibit such abortions. Under *Roe v. Wade* and *Doe v. Bolton* there is no constitutional objection to a state allowing abortion for any reason or for no reason at any time during pregnancy.

In the *Roe* decision, the Supreme Court describes the trimester system *twice,* no doubt in order to be as clear as possible. After one description, in the words of the Court "To summarize and to repeat,"[17] the Court gives another description. Neither description allows state interference with an abortion decision on the basis of the reason for the abortion prior to viability, which the Court said "is usually placed at about seven months (28 weeks) but may occur earlier, even at 24 weeks."[18] Both descriptions make clear that states may not proscribe post-viability abortions undertaken to preserve "the life or health of the mother."[19]

Appraising the restrictiveness permitted a statute in the last trimester therefore requires an understanding of the Supreme Court definition of the phrase "life or health." The Court provided the definition the same day it handed down *Roe v. Wade*, in *Roe*'s sister case *Doe v. Bolton*. Referring to *Doe, Roe* says, "That opinion and this one, of course, are to be read together."[20]

In the words of the Court in *Doe,* the word "health" is interpreted to include consideration of "all factors—physical, emotional, psychological, familial, and the woman's age—relevant to the well-being of the patient."[21] In other words, the meaning is so broad that it is fair to say that even in the last trimester abortions are permitted, in effect, on demand.

Factual Background of Proceedings

Trimester System Explained to Newsweek. In early June 1983, a spokesman for Americans United for Life Legal Defense Fund, a public interest law firm based in Chicago, was interviewed by a *Newsweek* reporter for a story concerning developments then taking place. In that conversation, the spokesman "painstakingly describe[d] the extreme nature of the opinions" in *Roe* and *Doe*,[22] making particular reference to the availability of abortion in the third trimester for reason of maternal health and explaining the meaning of the word "health" as used in the abortion context.

What Newsweek Said. In reporting on the last trimester, *Newsweek* magazine on June 27, 1983, wrote that in *Roe v. Wade* the Supreme Court "held that states . . . in the final months, *except where a mother's life was at stake*, . . . could prohibit abortions entirely to protect the unborn child"[23] (emphasis added). *Newsweek*'s statement stands in striking contrast to the conclusions of the *Roe-Doe* axis. The statement is not just misleading. The error is not a judgmental difference. Neither is it merely arguably wrong. It is absolutely and categorically false.

As previously stated, abortions are permitted in the last trimester not only when a mother's life is at risk but also when her health is threatened. *Newsweek*'s words when discussing the third trimester include no reference whatsoever to the health exception, an omission made particularly important by the extreme breadth of the health standard. *Newsweek*'s error would make the reader incorrectly think that only the grave situation of a threat to the mother's life could be used to authorize such abortions. This constitutes an egregious error on an important matter.

Error Reported to Newsweek. The error was promptly brought to *Newsweek*'s attention on June 23, 1983. I did so personally as reflected in the following excerpts from my letter:

[The above-quoted statement] is absolutely and categorically false. A reading of *Roe v. Wade* and its companion case
Doe v. Bolton, makes clear that under *Roe* abortion must
be permitted in the last trimester for reasons that in no
way threaten the mother's life.

. . . .

It is difficult for an informed national debate to take place
when the media so misinforms the public. You really
should read court decisions more carefully before reporting on them, especially when you've had over 10 years to
read one of them[24] (emphasis in original).

My colleague, Professor Richard T. Stith, also called the error
to *Newsweek*'s attention.[25] We wrote to them separately on June
23, 1983. Nothing.

Follow-up Letter. On July 18, 1983, we followed up by joint-
ly writing a letter to *Newsweek*. In that letter, we informed
Newsweek that we were considering filing a formal complaint
concerning the distortion. We indicated we had no interest in
seeing our own letters in print, nor in exposing or otherwise
harassing *Newsweek*, but rather in seeing that the public was "not
given absolutely false information on this important issue," in
short, in "having the truth reported."

If our initial letters, mine telling *Newsweek* that its reporting
was "absolutely and categorically *false*" and Stith's stating that
"*Newsweek* continues to misinform its readers," did not get
Newsweek's attention, we certainly thought that our very strong
follow-up letter concerning the potential filing of a complaint
deserved some response. Still nothing.

Filing of Complaint. More than a month later, two months
after initially writing to *Newsweek*, we brought the matter to the
attention of The National News Council by letter dated August 24,
1983. We simultaneously sent a copy of this letter to *Newsweek*.

***Newsweek*'s First Letter.** *Newsweek* finally responded for the
first time by letter dated September 9, 1983. In it, *Newsweek*
apologized "that an unusually heavy volume of mail delayed [its]
response and necessitated [our] having to write twice." The letter
also stated, in part:

The fact is that *Newsweek* has consistently covered the controversial issue of abortion in an evenhanded and responsible fashion. It is *never* our purpose to mislead our readers, and every article is carefully researched and double checked. Of course typographical and machine errors are a constant peril in our business and you were quite correct in pointing out that *Roe v. Wade* affirms the right of women to third-trimester abortions for reasons of maternal life or *health*. The sentence in question was inadvertently truncated while proceeding through the editorial process; unfortunately the omission was not detected until after our story had gone to press. Although we were unable to print your comments in our Letters column, your letters were brought to the attention of the appropriate members of the *Newsweek* staff[26] (emphasis in original).

This letter is interesting in a number of respects. First, even though the error was acknowledged privately to us, clearly *Newsweek* did not think that the error warranted a public correction by way of publishing one of our letters or otherwise. Second, although *Newsweek*'s letter was dated sixteen days after we sent *Newsweek* a copy of our letter to The National News Council, it did not reflect an awareness of that letter. Third, part of the quoted language from the *Newsweek* letter is important because it sets forth a journalistic standard to which *Newsweek* holds itself: "every article is carefully researched and double checked."

Newsweek's Second Letter. *Newsweek* responded again by letter of September 14, 1983, indicating that it had "just received a copy of [our] letter to The National News Council, which seem[ed] to have crossed [*Newsweek*'s] letter to [us] in the mail." This letter was dated twenty-one days after our August 24 letter to The National News Council and suggested that our August 24 letter was not known to the author of the September 9 letter from *Newsweek* to us.

Publication of Letter. In the October 17, 1983, issue *Newsweek* did publish Stith's brief letter in truncated form.[27] If the letter had been published in July, I would have been pleased and would not have written this essay. By October, however, there were several things wrong with *Newsweek*'s handling of this matter, some of which I would not have thought about in July. For one thing, the delay was very long. For another, publication of a letter alone is an ineffective way of correcting a major error in an article.

Newsweek had placed the abortion article under a two-column headline—"The Court Stands by Abortion"—and had given it prominence by making it the only article in the "JUSTICE" section.[28] The article's title had been under a two-column-wide, 3 5/16-inch-high photograph of a woman lying on a table at an abortion-providing location with a man who might reasonably be taken to be an abortionist standing by. A member of the general public having the slightest interest in the subject would probably have noticed this article upon an even casual perusal of the magazine. By contrast, Stith's letter[29] appeared as one of 16 letters in the Letters column and shared its page with two advertisements which consumed two-thirds of the page, the left and middle columns. His letter shared the leftover column with four other letters.

In addition, although *Newsweek* privately admitted its error, it did not do so publicly. Two or three words following the Stith letter indicating agreement would have sufficed.

Moreover, while The National News Council had no enforcement powers but only the power to issue press releases, *Newsweek*'s publication of the Stith letter does not seem to have been voluntary. *Newsweek* seems to have responded to pressure from The National News Council proceedings rather than to have demonstrated its own desire to set the record straight.

The Decision

The findings of The National News Council are set forth in its decision in the matter of *Richard Stith & John J. Potts against Newsweek*.[30] The decision reports that in response to the two June 23 letters and the July 18 letter sent to *Newsweek*, "*Newsweek* replied to Stith and Potts, with a copy to the News Council, on September 9, acknowledging that its report had been wrong."[31]

Among other things, the Council's decision also says:

> Council staff asked *Newsweek* whether the magazine plans to publish a correction. The magazine replied that Stith's letter was to be published after all in the October 17 issue. The letter, slightly edited, was published without an editor's note acknowledging that the magazine's report had been wrong.[32]

This language, in the context of *Newsweek*'s statement in its September 9 letter that it was "unable to print [our] comments in [its] Letters column," certainly makes it appear that Stith's letter was ultimately published because of the involvement of The National News Council. The decision also points out that the Stith letter was published without an editor's note acknowledging that *Newsweek* had been wrong.

Concerning the matter of what constitutes a correction, the decision goes on to say: "Council staff asked *Newsweek* if the magazine believed the publication of the letter without an editor's note did indeed set the record straight."

William Broyles, Jr., Editor in Chief of *Newsweek*, said yes. He wrote: "If a letter corrects a matter of fact and we accept the correction, the letter runs without reply; it is assumed to speak for itself. If there is a dispute over a matter of fact, we print a reply stating our position."[33] This position is interesting. A letter correcting a matter of fact amounts to "a dispute over a matter of fact." But *Newsweek* seems to think that its saying "X" and a letter saying "not X" ceases to be a dispute of fact if *Newsweek* decides, wholly *sub silentio* as far as the reading public can discern, that *Newsweek*'s original fact was not a fact. This would require that the reading public itself discern that the failure of *Newsweek* to state that there is a continuing controversy is to be taken to mean that the facially apparent controversy no longer exists. This expectation is unrealistic since reading the article and the letter together, or even just the letter by itself, clearly reveals that there is a controversy. In other words, a dispute is not a dispute unless it is disputed twice.

This matter of "whether the publication of a letter challenging reported facts"[34] is sufficient correction "when the letter is not accompanied by an editor's note saying whether the letter is right or wrong"[35] was the most important issue to The National News Council. It reported that *Newsweek*, *Time,* and *U.S. News and World Report* all follow the same practice in this matter, that letters challenging facts are published "only when the magazine believes its facts were wrong and the letter writer is right."[36] It also reported that *Newsweek*, *Time,* and *U.S. News and World Report* all "believe that their readers understand that the publication of a fact-challenging letter amounts to a correction."[37] "Editor's notes," The National News Council's decision states, "are more likely to be used in the rare case of a 'real blooper,' as one editor expressed it, or as another said, to appease an important news source."[38]

The decision goes on to state:

> In contrast with news magazine practice, newspapers increasingly publish fact corrections in correction columns that appear regularly in the same place in the newspaper. Newspapers increasingly devote their letter columns to expressions of opinion instead of challenges of fact. On the rare occasion when a newspaper finds it warranted for one reason or another to publish a letter containing a fact challenge with which the newspaper does not agree, editors frequently append a note saying the paper stands by its report.[39]

Understandably, all of this would confuse the reading public. A reader commonly realizes that he sometimes sees letters disagreeing with the print media, that sometimes there is an editor's note admitting error or standing by a report, but that normally neither appears. For a reader to understand the significance which *Newsweek* attached to publication of Stith's letter, the reader would mentally have to divide letters to the editor into expressions of opinion versus corrections of fact (while realizing that the rules concerning corrections in a correction column or by way of an editor's note appended to a letter differ between magazines and newspapers) and understand that a magazine will sometimes follow the newspaper rules if there has been a "real blooper" or to "appease an important news source." In short, for the reader to be able to understand what *Newsweek* meant by publication of Stith's letter he would have to be a reader of minds.

By the time of The National News Council decision, the initial error was really no longer an issue since *Newsweek* had admitted the error—privately. The Council found "that the corrective action[40] [of publishing Stith's letter] was not prompt."[41] The Council also indicated that it did not believe "that readers understand that if the magazine publishes a letter challenging its facts, the publication amounts to an admission that the facts were wrong."[42] On these bases the Council found warranted "the complaint that the correction was inadequate." The Council's final words were:

> The Council encourages news organizations to publish edi-
> tor's notes in order to set the record completely straight,
> or to devise some other method clearly to inform readers
> that the publication of letters challenging facts is an admis-
> sion that the facts were wrong.[43]

Highlights of the decision were carried on the Associated Press
wire.[44]   This action was the only sanction within the Council's
power; it could issue a press release.

It is a tragic footnote that on March 22, 1984, the AP wire
carried the information that The National News Council "voted to
end operations at the end of this month."[45] The report said, in
part, that "the main reason for closing after 11 years was not
money but lack of press support."[46] In its 11 years of existence
the Council "investigated 242 complaints and said 82 were warranted."[47] This was one of them.

Trimester System Coverage

Generally

Newsweek claimed, you will recall, that it had "consistently
covered"[48] this matter in a "responsible fashion,"[49] that "every
article is carefully researched and double checked,"[50] that the
error in this case occurred only because "typographical and
machine errors are a constant peril in [its] business,"[51] and that in
this case the "sentence in question was inadvertently truncated
while proceeding through the editorial process."[52] One would
think that this was an isolated example of such a mistake and that
Newsweek's presentation of the trimester system should normally
be correct. In the articles under analysis here, however, the
trimester system is reported six times.[53] In them, Newsweek misreported the trimester system by making either misleading or categorically false statements five out of six times.

George Will, in an authored column appearing in Newsweek,
accurately described the trimester system.[54] This column constitutes the only occasion when Newsweek correctly stated the
trimester system. In its regular articles, as distinguished from
columns, Newsweek misreported the trimester system every time.
Mr. Will's erudition stands out strikingly in a swamp of ignorance.

Newsweek's trimester fantasies will shortly be described in
detail, but two aspects of the Will column, other than his report-

ing of the trimester system itself, deserve comment. For one thing, in chronological order, Will's is the second of the six presentations of the trimester system. So the correct information concerning the trimester system was not unavailable to *Newsweek* employees. They needed only to read their own columnist. For another thing, the occasion for Will's rendering of the trimester system was that a different magazine, *The New Republic,* misreported the trimester system. Will was reporting on that fact and correcting that magazine. This might additionally have sensitized *Newsweek* to the presence of misreporting of the trimester system in the media.

Specific Reporting of Exceptions

First Instance. The first article to be considered appeared in *Newsweek*'s issue dated January 28, 1980. In this article, *Newsweek* reports:

> In 1973, the U.S. Supreme Court decided that any woman has the right to an abortion during the first trimester of her pregnancy. Four years later, the Court refused to go further and held that states do not have to pay for poor women's *elective* abortions[55] (emphasis in original).

The first sentence quoted is factually accurate as to when abortions are permitted. Its misleading quality lies in the fact that it states only one-third of the truth. It mentions the permissibility of abortions in neither the middle trimester (for any or no reason), nor the last trimester (for reasons of maternal life or "health"). It would leave the reader with the mistaken impression that the Supreme Court did not decide that a woman is permitted to obtain an abortion after the first trimester.

In this case the problem is heightened by the language in the second sentence quoted, which reads "Four years later, the Court refused to go further. . . ." Clearly, on a careful reading of the full quote given above, this latter language may be read to refer to a refusal to go beyond declaration of a "right" and to hold that state funding is also required,[56] rather than referring to going beyond the first trimester in time. Nevertheless, the juxtaposition could heighten a reader's misunderstanding, particularly since the conjunction "and" in the middle of the second sentence quoted above allows a person to conclude that the sentence says two things, that four years later the Court: (1) "refused to go further," and (2) "held that states do not have to pay for poor women's *elective* abortions." Realizing that it is possible to break the sentence apart mentally in this way, it would not be difficult to see the reader reading in the words "in time" after the words "refused to go further."

The juxtaposition of the two sentences, given their phraseology, is particularly unfortunate, rendering as it does the analysis of the distortion of the trimester system rather complicated in this case. The juxtaposition of these two sentences, however, does seem to be the kind of unavoidable confusion one expects in everyday use of the language, including in the print-news media.

Without diminishing the extent to which the juxtaposition heightens the possibility for confusion about the trimester system and renders the total effect egregiously wrong, it is in the first quoted sentence standing by itself that the principal error was made. That sentence is misleading with or without the second sentence. And if the first sentence were not inherently misleading concerning the trimester system, then the second sentence, written as is, would not have created confusion on this point. The insensitivity to the facts reflected in the second sentence follows from the dangerously misleading quality of the first sentence.

Even *The New York Times* has admitted the danger in a reference to the trimester system which is incomplete in describing the time when abortion is permitted. On July 26, 1982, it wrote to Mr. Douglas Johnson, Legislative Director of the National Right to Life Committee: "As you indicate, the phrase 'in the first three months of pregnancy' might be incorrectly interpreted to mean that abortions in the last six months of pregnancy remain illegal."

Second Instance. The second article—that authored by George Will and mentioned above—reports:

> Some defenders of the Supreme Court's 1973 abortion decision may have been so busy applauding it that they have not read it. *The New Republic* recently praised the decision as "fair," explaining it this way: "Abortions are freely available in the first trimester, subject to medical determination in the second trimester, and banned in the third, when the fetus is viable." But the Court actually

decreed that there can be no serious impediment to even third-trimester abortions. It said that even in the third trimester states cannot prevent any abortion deemed necessary to protect a mother's health from harm, and that harm can include "distress."

There is, effectively, abortion-on-demand at every point.[57]

Will's article appears in *Newsweek*'s issue dated June 22, 1981. It is a fair and accurate presentation of the trimester system. Will's description lacks full elaboration, but he so captures an accurate sense of the system as a whole that he cannot be faulted. Space considerations are an important and legitimate constraint in a news magazine. Within this stricture, Mr. Will demonstrates how simply and briefly the trimester system can be presented when he writes that we have, "effectively, abortion-on-demand at every point" during pregnancy.

Third Instance. *Newsweek*'s third article, of January 11, 1982, occurred nearly seven months after the Will column. *Newsweek* employees had had adequate time to absorb Will's message, or to forget it. They did the latter. What *Newsweek* reported was: "The Supreme Court attempted to address the issue in 1973, when it held that the law gives full protection to the lives of fetuses only from the time they are capable of living outside the womb, which the court fixed between 24 and 28 weeks."[58] This time *Newsweek* is not being merely misleading. The statement actively denies the availability of abortion in the last trimester which results under the Supreme Court's life or health exceptions. We do not give "full protection to the lives of fetuses" until birth, if then. Furthermore, this is precisely one of the mistakes made by *The New Republic* when it wrote that abortions are "banned in the third" trimester "when the fetus is viable," which Mr. Will attacked in *Newsweek* itself.

Also, this description of the trimester system is inconsistent with *Newsweek*'s first attempt considered here. On January 28, 1980, *Newsweek* left readers thinking that second-trimester abortions are not permitted at all but here told them that "full protection [for] the lives of fetuses" is not then applicable, with both reports based explicitly on what the Supreme Court wrote in 1973.

Fourth Instance. The fourth article considered here appeared on January 31, 1983—more than a year after the third. By this time *Roe v. Wade* and *Doe v. Bolton* were ten years old. This time *Newsweek*'s description was different yet again. It was as follows:

> Another form of restriction being reviewed by the court is requirements that some abortions be performed in hospitals rather than clinics. In *Roe v. Wade*, the court gave a universal green light to all abortions in the first trimester of pregnancy, but held that states and localities could regulate second-trimester abortions in the interest of protecting the mother's health. Twenty-one states now require hospitalization for second-trimester abortions—but many physicians believe that precaution is no longer necessary. Since 1973, abortion techniques have advanced to the point that dilation and evacuation—a relatively simple procedure— can be performed safely well into the second trimester, and experts say there is no reason that it cannot be performed in clinics.[59]

As with *Newsweek*'s first effort, the reader would be led by negative inference to conclude that abortion is not permitted after the time period specified, here the second trimester. As such, the description is misleading.

This description is also inconsistent with *Newsweek*'s first presentation of the trimester system, even though the nature of the error is the same. On January 28, 1980, *Newsweek* left readers thinking that second-trimester abortions are not permitted while here it allows that they are permitted, with both reports again based explicitly on what the Supreme Court wrote years earlier. Of course, for a reader to understand that *Newsweek*'s language in this fourth instance means that abortions are allowed in the second trimester, the reader would have to realize that to "regulate" does not mean to prevent. It is likely that some readers would not understand.

The problem is that there are two health standards—one in the second trimester that does *not* involve inquiry into the reason for which the abortion is sought and therefore does *not* require a health reason for an abortion, and one in the third trimester that does require a health reason for an abortion.[60] The second-trimester health standard bears on performing the abortion under such circumstances as will minimize health risks to the mother. She is permitted to have the abortion as long as it is done safely for her.

One does not speak of the requirement for other procedures to be performed in hospitals as meaning there is a "form of restriction" involving "requirements" under which states may "regulate" the availability of those procedures. Why speak of a requirement that abortions be performed in hospitals, or in clinics for that matter, that way—especially when a medical reason is necessary for the other procedures and not for abortion? And why do so in a sentence which addresses the time during pregnancy when abortion is allowed?

The important aspect of the degree of restrictiveness of regulation of abortions relates to the *reason* why the abortion is sought. The important point is that no reason is required, in effect, for the full nine months of pregnancy. This is permissive availability, not restrictive availability.

In a sense, this presentation might be read as at least being consistent with *Newsweek*'s erroneous third presentation. A negative inference here that abortion is not allowed in the third trimester does accord very roughly with the earlier statement that "the law gives full protection to the lives of fetuses"[61] when they are "capable of living outside the womb."[62]

Fifth Instance. The next example, *Newsweek*'s fifth presentation on June 27, 1983, is the one discussed above in connection with proceedings before The National News Council. It was a case in which a statement by *Newsweek* omitted the health exception from discussion of the third trimester and was absolutely and categorically false.

But there are more things wrong with *Newsweek*'s presentation of the trimester system in this instance than the single most important and glaring distortion which was the subject of The National News Council proceedings. A larger excerpt from *Newsweek*'s presentation, which includes the language previously quoted, is as follows:

Ten years ago, in the court's seminal abortion ruling (*Roe v. Wade*), the justices found that a woman's constitutional right of privacy included opting for an abortion. But like other fundamental rights, abortion was not an absolute; states could restrict abortions in order to protect their "compelling interests" in public health. The court held that states had virtually no legitimate interest during the first trimester of a pregnancy, but could regulate abortions to protect a mother's health during the second trimester— and in the final months, except where a mother's life was at stake, they could prohibit abortions entirely to protect the unborn child.[63]

One additional problem in this presentation relates to use of the term "public health" in a general sentence and the word "health" specifically in connection with regulation of abortion during the second trimester. The problem here is similar to the problem with use of the word "health" in the fourth instance, above, of misleading reporting related to the use of the health standard. Elsewhere in the article, examples of second-trimester abortion regulation are given, but they are less closely associated with the misleading language than in the fourth instance. They are therefore even less likely in this instance adequately to soften the impact of any placement of health regulation language in the second trimester. The presence of the word "health" as a standard relating to regulation of abortions in the second trimester heightens the impact of its exclusion from the presentation's description of permitted abortions in the third trimester. Not only is health not listed as an exception in the third trimester, but its use in connection with the second trimester would leave the reader with the impression that consideration had been given to whatever relevance the health standard had, even if the reader already knew that a health standard was relevant sometime. The reader would think there was some meaningful regulation of abortions in the second trimester and that no health standard was relevant in the third trimester.

If the reader already had some idea that a health standard was somehow relevant, he would think he had just read what its relevance was. If an acquaintance told him that an abortion could be had in the third trimester for nonlife-threatening health-related reasons, then he might wonder who was right, his acquaintance or *Newsweek*, if the only problem were that the health standard had been left out in connection with the third trimester. Of course he would probably think his acquaintance wrong and *Newsweek* right, such being the power of the national media. But given the presence of some discussion of regulation during the second trimester for reasons of health, he would be confident that his acquaintance was wrong. With such reporting, public debate deteriorates.

Many persons, including persons in the media, are simply out of touch with reality in their understanding of the lack of restrictions on abortion in this country. They think there is some meaningful restriction on when and why a woman may seek to have an abortion. There is not.

It can be difficult to get someone to believe what the situation really is in the second trimester, and, especially, in the third trimester. The surprisingly extreme positions of *Roe* and *Doe* are undoubtedly part of the difficulty. The persistence with which the media distorts the matter is unquestionably also an important part of the problem.

As in the fourth instance, the phraseology here could lead the average reader to think the mother must have a health reason for an abortion in the second trimester, although in fact, as has been seen, there is no requirement for a reason, and the regulation has only to do with conducting the abortion in such a way that there is some protection for the mother's health. And, it must be remembered, successful attempts to regulate second-trimester abortions in ways designed to maximize protection for the mother's health are virtually nil.[64] Even the requirement that the abortion be performed in a hospital has been struck down.[65] A requirement that a doctor perform the abortion and that he do it in a "licensed clinic" is not a significantly meaningful restriction in the context of the abortion debate. To insinuate discussion of regulation of abortions to protect the mother's health during the second trimester into a discussion of the degree of liberality of the present abortion situation is misleading.

Sixth Instance. The error in the immediately preceding passage was promptly pointed out to *Newsweek* by two different people in separate letters. Because *Newsweek*'s practice is to put as the date of an issue the last day on which it will be available on newsstands, the two correcting letters were mailed before the date on the magazine and may have arrived while that issue was still on sale.

This did not prevent *Newsweek* from making precisely the same mistake, but in a way that was even worse, just three weeks later in the issue of July 18, 1983. In it *Newsweek* wrote: "[Justice] O'Connor pointed out the fatal flaw that may be lurking in the Court's abortion-law rationale that states may forbid abortions once the fetus is viable."[66] Unlike the fifth instance, in which *Newsweek* reported that states could prohibit abortions in the last trimester unless the "mother's life was at stake,"[67] which omits the radically broad "health" exception, this sixth description not only omits the health exception but does not even list the "life" exception. It leaves the reader believing that, without exception, "states may forbid abortions once the fetus is viable." This is obviously not the situation, and the mistake is not O'Connor's.

Newsweek not only repeated the same mistake it made three weeks earlier by leaving out the health exception, and did so after the error was pointed out, but even left out the life exception and thereby described the trimester system inconsistently with the way *Newsweek* itself described it only three weeks earlier. Perhaps the right person had not read my letter or Professor Stith's letter. Perhaps the internal distribution system of this news organization takes more than a couple of weeks to circulate information. Our letters might have gone to someone responsible for handling letters from readers and the letters could have simply sat for a while before being analyzed and before reaction was made to them.

But doesn't *Newsweek* at least read *Newsweek*? *Newsweek* is not only consistently inconsistent with itself, but here it utterly contradicted itself on an important matter in a space of three weeks. And the report was absolutely wrong both times.

Newsweek has wandered so far into wonderland that it would be useful at this point to remember a few things. First, the *Roe-Doe* axis was over ten years old at this point. Second, George Will explained it to them accurately in their own magazine over two years earlier. Third, as *Newsweek* told us in its September 9, 1983, letter, "*Newsweek* has consistently covered the controversial issue of abortion" in a "responsible fashion," "every article is carefully researched and double checked," but "typographical and machine errors are a constant peril in [its] business." And the mistake in the June 27, 1983, issue, the fifth instance, occurred because "The sentence in question was inadvertently truncated while proceeding through the editorial process; unfortunately, the omission was not detected until after our story had gone to press."[68] This leaves one with the impression that *Newsweek* itself caught the error quickly but not quite in time, which would mean that *Newsweek* should have known about the health exception in the July 18 issue. Of course, *Newsweek* did not truncate the life exception in the June 27 issue, and yet if one believes *Newsweek* is adhering to the responsible, carefully-researched-and-double-checked standard of truth which it claims, then it would appear that both the life and health exceptions were "inadvertently truncated" in the July 18 issue.

Maybe typographical and machine errors being a constant peril in *Newsweek*'s business and the possibility of inadvertent truncation lurking behind every corner of every page might explain why *Newsweek* got the trimester system wrong five out of six times. Maybe war can be misspelled "p-e-a-c-e." Maybe.

Now the word "inadvertent" means "1: not turning the mind to a matter: inattentive" or "2: unintentional,"[69] and the word "truncate" means "1: to shorten by or as if by cutting off: lop."[70] Applied just to these last two instances it seems exceptional that both could be explained by inadvertent truncation (although of course it must be remembered that *Newsweek*'s explicitly made inadvertent-truncation explanation applied on its face only to the first of these last two instances). It seems even less likely that inadvertent truncation could explain the third presentation wherein *Newsweek* said ". . . the law gives full protection to the lives of fetuses only from the time they are capable of living outside the womb. . . ."[71] It is difficult to see what could have been truncated. Conceivably, of course, accurate exceptions, life or health, could have been truncated, but adding properly understood life-or-health exceptions to that presentation of the trimester system would completely gut any meaning from the expression "full protection." The word "truncation" just does not seem to apply. And in the third instance, in addition, the words "full protection" would have to have been inadvertently added.

The word "inadvertent," of course, might apply in all the misleading situations. *Newsweek* does not seem adequately to have turned its mind to this matter. But it is very clear, taking five out of the six presentations together, that a standard of "consistently" and in a "responsible fashion" covering this matter and having "every article" "carefully researched and double checked" does *not* apply. Careless disregard for the truth may come closer. Hopefully any disregard for the truth, if it is present, occurred on the part of *Newsweek* sources rather than on the part of *Newsweek* itself. But it is extremely difficult to see how *Newsweek* could get the matter wrong five out of six times if the articles were "carefully researched and double checked." All *Newsweek* had to check was the *Roe* decision itself to see the applicability of the life or health exceptions in the third trimester. In *Roe* the trimester rules are both stated and repeated.

I sincerely want to believe that disregard for the truth by anyone is not the explanation. Other possibilities do suggest themselves. One of the articles, the column, has a named author. Four of the articles have a by-line. One of the articles has neither. Proceeding on the basis of names which are so given, there are a total of eight names associated with these six articles. The number of names associated with an article varies from none to three. Of these eight names, only two appear more than once; both of them appear twice. The two names which appear twice are together on the same article only once.

The rate at which *Newsweek* seems to have different people cover the same subject would certainly seem a possible contribution to confusion over this matter on the part of any particular *Newsweek* reporter, although that would not obviate the reporter's responsibility to report accurately. And it would not explain away responsibility on the part of whoever was responsible for editing these articles.[72] For whatever reason, *Newsweek*'s coverage of the trimester system is not even consistent, much less accurate.

Conclusion

This essay has presented the extreme breadth of the health standard. It has documented that *Newsweek* typically omits mention of this broad health standard in the third trimester from its presentations of the trimester system. It has shown that *Newsweek* has reported a health restriction in the second trimester, but has failed to mention that the health standard which nominally restricts the reasons for having an abortion applies in the third trimester.

In all six of these instances, the health standard, as an explanation for the reason a child is being aborted, was discussed fairly only once. The one breath of fresh air came in the column by George Will. *Newsweek* must be credited with publishing George Will's column, but *Newsweek* must be faulted for never properly placing in time or describing the health standard in a regular type of article.

When the trimester system came up during the four and one-half year period under consideration, *Newsweek* got it wrong five out of six times. That is an 83% error rate. And when the trimester system came up other than in an authored column, the error rate was 100%. There is therefore no reason for the reading public to trust *Newsweek* magazine's coverage of this subject and every reason to distrust it. *Newsweek* has repeatedly failed properly to inform its readers concerning the timing dimensions of the trimester system—what standard applies when. *Newsweek* has repeatedly failed to inform its readers of abortion in the third trimester under the "health" exception, and to explain the breadth of that exception. *Newsweek* has failed abysmally to measure up to the standard of reporting to which it claims to subscribe—carefully researching and double-checking every article.

Legal Process

At the abstract level, the rightness or wrongness of the competing positions in the abortion controversy is not determined by who convinces whom in the debate. It is not subject to vote. At the practical level the victors may be considered those whose values are institutionalized and are given effect by the power of government. Values are necessarily adhered to, one side's or the other's, no matter how the present controversy is resolved.

Also at the practical level, the principal battleground may well be the public mind. If the public overwhelmingly favors the present situation, then the situation can probably be counted on to continue. If the public overwhelmingly disapproves of the present situation, change will probably follow. The resolution of the matter in the public mind will not make the resolution right or wrong, but it can affect the result.

What cases say about abortion is of course important to which abortions occur. Taking a snapshot of the state of affairs at any given moment, what the Supreme Court says is of more importance than what the national print media say. But what the media say may well be more important, in the same context, than what almost anyone else says.

The national print media have the power to lead the thinking of a nation. *Newsweek* seems to have used this power to induce acceptance of the *post-Roe status quo.* But that very leadership is holding back the maturation process of the nation's thinking about abortion, largely because the radically altered *status quo* created by the Supreme Court generally is not being accurately reported to the nation.

As the pro-life movement has sought to change the Constitution, the role of *Newsweek* and other media institutions has been less than helpful in promoting informed debate. With changing the Constitution not being a matter concerning which courts have much say, the role of the national print media becomes paramount. If the American people think abortions are restricted more than they really are, and if they think some real health reason is required in the third and even in the second trimester, then they will not as readily consider an amendment restricting or reversing *Roe v. Wade.*

There is a real sense in which we are talking about politics. But we are talking about the politics of what is said to be the "law"[73] on an issue of fundamental legal rights and of how the result will or will not change—in short, the politics of civil rights. We are talking about the process by which legislators, federal and state, are chosen by voters, and how they in turn might vote regarding statutory changes pertaining to abortion, or regarding changes in federal or state constitutions. We are talking about the process by which legislators decide how to vote on a call for a constitutional convention, because we are talking about the process by which voters decide which legislators they want. We are talking about the process by which presidents are elected and therefore Supreme Court justices are appointed. This process is politics, but in this case it is also the substance, fiber and fabric of legal process.

In the abortion controversy, at the very least the print media should not take sides favoring abortion. They particularly should not do so in such a way that the public is left largely uninformed, or worse, misinformed about the issue.

This essay has discussed a pattern of distortion in *Newsweek* magazine which misleads the public about when and why a woman is permitted to have an abortion. *Newsweek*'s reporting fails to disclose the present radical availability of abortion. Every *Newsweek* distortion favored the same side in the controversy. Even if unintentionally, *Newsweek* has *de facto* taken sides and by falsehoods and distortions has actively contributed to perpetuation of the *status quo*. *Newsweek*'s columnist George Will is its only saving grace.

It is the responsibility of the press in a free society to enlighten the citizenry on important matters. *Newsweek*, as part of "the press," has taken up this issue. Rather than enlightening the public, however, *Newsweek* has obfuscated the matter. Once *Newsweek* magazine chose to cover this issue, it assumed the duty to do so responsibly. *Newsweek* has failed in its responsibilities.

Notes

1.   John 8:32.

2.   Everette E. Dennis, "Another Look at Press Coverage of the Supreme Court," *Villanova Law Review,* Vol. 20, No. 4 (March 1975), p. 765.

3.   410 U.S. 113 (1973).

4.   "News organizations frequently err, even ten years after [*Roe v. Wade*], when they try to state simply what the court said." Decision on Complaint of Richard Stith and John J. Potts against *Newsweek,* No. 54–83, at 3, August 24, 1983, The National News Council. August 24, 1983 is the date the complaint was mailed, which the Council considered to be the date it was filed. It is not the date of the decision, which itself bears no date other than the date the complaint was filed. See note 9, *infra.* Further discussion concerning this decision is contained below.

5.   All are related to the trimester system.

6.   410 U.S. 179 (1973).

7.   Obviously, not every article containing the word "abortion" is included in this analysis. Nor is there included every article that is relevant to abortion but which does not focus on abortion, such as articles on fetology. The articles covered herein deal explicitly with the subject of abortion. Those dealing with the subject sufficiently to be classified under the word "abort," or various forms of that word, in a computer search in the DIALOG Information Retrieval Service, Magazine Index (File No. 47) are included. The search in this system is based on words in titles or in "descriptors." There are 18 such articles (not counting one dealing with abortion in wild horses and another dealing with an aborted economic recovery). A much broader computer search reveals an additional 43 articles in *Newsweek* during this time period which are arguably relevant to the subject of abortion, but which are not sufficiently focused on abortion to be classified under the word "abortion." Of these 43 articles, only articles dealing with the trimester system, the focus of this essay, are included. There was one such article. A total of 19 articles were therefore considered in the primary universe for detailed analysis for this essay. Articles which referred to abortion having been "legalized," but neither indicating when during pregnancy an abortion could be obtained nor making reference to the trimester system, were not considered to be within the scope of this essay; a statement that the Supreme Court authorized abortion is as consistent

with the thought "for the first trimester" as it is with the thought "for the full nine months of pregnancy." See note 26, *infra.* Only the six articles analyzed herein qualified for inclusion in this essay under these criteria.

8. By-line Aric Press with Diane Camper in Washington, "The Court Stands by Abortion," *Newsweek,* June 27, 1983, p. 62, col. 2.

9. An independent media watchdog group. See note 45, *infra,* and associated text.

10. *Roe, supra* note 5.

11. *Id.*

12. *Id.* and *Doe v. Bolton,* 410 U.S. 179, at 221 (1973) (White, J. and Rehnquist, J., dissenting from both decisions). A longer excerpt from this dissent, which was written by Justice White, explaining this aspect of the majority opinion reads as follows:

> At the heart of the controversy in these cases are those recurring pregnancies that pose no danger whatsoever to the life or health of the mother but are, nevertheless, unwanted for any one or more of a variety of reasons—convenience, family planning, economics, dislike of children, the embarrassment of illegitimacy, etc. The common claim before us is that for any one of such reasons, or for no reason at all, and without asserting or claiming any threat to life or health, any woman is entitled to an abortion at her request if she is able to find a medical advisor willing to undertake the procedure.

> The Court for the most part sustains this position: During the period prior to the time the fetus becomes viable, the Constitution of the United States values the convenience, whim, or caprice of the pregnant woman more than the life or potential life of the fetus; the Constitution, therefore, guarantees the right to an abortion as against any state law or policy seeking to protect the fetus from an abortion not prompted by more compelling reasons of the mother.

> With all due respect, I dissent. I find nothing in the language or history of the Constitution to support the Court's judgments. The Court simply fashions and announces a new constitutional right for pregnant women and, with scarcely any reason or authority for its action, invests that right with sufficient substance to override most existing state abortion statutes. The upshot is that the people and the legislatures of the 50 States are constitutionally disentitled to weigh the relative importance of the continued existence and development of the fetus, on the one hand, against a spectrum of possible impacts on the mother, on the other hand.

> . . . .

> The Court apparently values the convenience of the pregnant woman more than the continued existence and development of the life or potential life that she carries.

Id. at 221–22.

13.   *Roe, supra* note 5 at 164.

14.   *Id.* at 163–64.

15.   *Id.*

16.   *Id.*

17.   *Id.* at 164.

18.   *Id.* at 160.

19.   *Id.* at 164–65. The conceptual tie in *Roe* between the concepts involved in the "life or health" exceptions and the point in time when a statute may require that the exceptions be met in order to have an abortion is viability. As stated in the text, *Roe* said viability "is usually placed at about seven months (28) weeks but may occur earlier, even at 24 weeks" as an expression of *when* *Roe* thought the health standard could be applied in 1973. In *Planned Parenthood of Central Missouri v. Danforth,* 428 U.S. 52 (1976), the Supreme Court upheld a definition of viability as the capability of the fetus to live outside the mother's womb, albeit with artificial aid. The point during pregnancy when viability is reached should have changed since 1973 and should continue to change. Nevertheless, research revealed no court decision moving the applicability of the health standard earlier in time into the second trimester. This essay therefore discusses the breakdowns of pregnancy in time as trimesters. The use of the trimester system as a conceptual framework in this essay therefore is not inconsistent with *Roe.* This cannot be unfair to *Newsweek,* which expresses the period of late pregnancy differently at different times, because *Newsweek* generally makes clear that it is reporting 1973 developments.

20.   *Id.* at 165.

21.   *Doe, supra* note 6 at 192.

22.   Letter from Mr. Steven Baer, Director of Education, Americans United for Life AUL Legal Defense Fund to Friends of AUL, dated July 1, 1983.

23.   Press, *supra* note 8.

24.   My letter to *Newsweek* dated June 23, 1983. The letter refers to "one" case, *Roe v. Wade*, as having been available for reading for over ten years, because the *Newsweek* article on which I was commenting discussed *Roe v. Wade* by name and a number of 1983 cases which the article did not name. But *Newsweek* did not in its article discuss *Doe v. Bolton.* It is, of course, true, besides, that a reading of *Roe v. Wade* cannot be completed without completing a reading of *Doe v. Bolton.* The cases conceptually, and in what cases the justices decide to discuss by name, simply blend into one another. See text associated with note 20, *supra.*

25.   See note 27, *infra,* for text of Stith letter.

26.   Letter from *Newsweek* to Richard Stith and John J. Potts dated September 9, 1983. The language of positivism ("right" in this quote and words like "law" in other quotes) was left in the quotes to keep them accurate. Positivism in this context means that the "law" is whatever authority posits or says the "law" is. When fundamental human rights are violated, when natural law is vio-

lated this way, when crimes against humanity are thus authorized, one can see that positivism and its language must be rejected. That is what many people thought was decided at Nuremberg.

27.　　*Newsweek,* October 17, 1983, p. 12, col. 3. The full text of the Stith letter, with *Newsweek* truncations prior to publication shown in brackets and *Newsweek*'s additions shown in double parentheticals, is as follows:

> [Astonishingly,] *Newsweek* [continues to] misinform((ed)) its readers about the 10-year-old *Roe v. Wade* abortion decision ((JUSTICE, June 27)). You [write] ((wrote)) [(June 27, 1983, p. 63)] that the [*Roe*] court held that "in the final months, except where a mother's life was at stake, they [(the States)] could prohibit abortions [entirely to protect the unborn child]." [*Newsweek* omitted start of new paragraph here.] In fact, not only a mother's life but also her health constitutionally outweighs the fetus' life right up to birth. [And the fetus never merits the word "child" because, according to *Roe,* it remains only a "potential" life throughout pregnancy.] If *Roe* ((*v. Wade*)) were as you state((d)), the opposition to it would surely be far less.

28.　　See Press, *supra* note 8.

29.　　*Supra* note 27.

30.　　Decision on Complaint of Richard Stith and John J. Potts against *Newsweek, supra* note 4. See note 44, *infra.*

31.　　*Id.* at 1. The statement in the quoted language that *Newsweek* replied to Stith and Potts ("with a copy to The News Council, on September 9") might make one wonder how this could be since *Newsweek*'s September 14 letter says that *Newsweek* had not received a copy of our complaint when *Newsweek* mailed its September 9 letter to us. The explanation is that the way The National News Council received a copy of the September 9 letter was under cover of a September 13, 1983 letter from *Newsweek*. There is no contradiction.

32.　　*Id.* at 2.

33.　　*Id.*

34.　　*Id.*

35.　　*Id.*

36.　　*Id.* at 3.

37.　　*Id.*

38.　　*Id.*

39.　　*Id.*

40.　　*Id.* at 4.

41.　　*Id.* The council also found that there was no intent to distort involved. *Id.* at 3.

42.　　*Id.* at 4.

43.   *Id.*

44.   The Post-Tribune and The Associated Press, "News Group Upholds VU Professors," *The Post-Tribune,* Gary, IN, December 3, 1983, p. 1, col. 1

45.   E.g., Dateline New York, March 22 (AP), "Media Watchdog Votes to Defang," *The Washington Post,* March 23, 1984, p. A–12, col. 3.

46.   *Id.*

47.   *Id.*

48.   *Newsweek* letter, *supra* note 26.

49.   *Id.*

50.   *Id.*

51.   *Id.*

52.   *Id.*

53.   There is a seventh occasion when *Newsweek* may have been, and probably was, referring to the trimester system, but this is not completely clear. In it, *Newsweek* reported that a drawback to relying on amniocentesis for certain diagnoses is that by the time the results are known, "little time [is left] to consider a second-trimester abortion if the fetus is abnormal." By-line Sharon Begley with John Carey and Susan Katz, "The Genetic Counselors," *Newsweek,* March 5, 1984, p. 69, col. 1. It is certainly possible for this sentence to be read erroneously to imply that abortion is not permitted after the second trimester even where maternal emotional or familial health might be adversely affected by the birth of a handicapped child. But the focus is on genetic counseling, not on *Roe,* and the article might also be read as meaning "little time [is left] to consider a second-trimester abortion" which is less risky for the woman than a third-trimester abortion. The article was not included. If the instance was referring to *Roe*'s trimester system, then *Newsweek* got it wrong one more time.

54.   George F. Will, "The Case of the Unborn Patient," *Newsweek,* June 22, 1981, p. 92, col. 1.

55.   By-line Aric Press with Emily F. Newhall in New York and bureau reports, "Abortions for the Poor," *Newsweek,* January 28, 1980, p. 81, col. 1.

56.   *Harris v. McRae,* 448 U.S. 297, (1980) (holding state not required to fund abortion under Medicaid program; federal restriction of funds not unconstitutional); *Maher v. Roe,* 432 U.S. 464 (1977) (holding that the equal protection clause did not require a state participating in the Medicaid program to pay expenses incident to non-therapeutic abortions; the Connecticut statute involved limited benefits to what were called "medically necessary" abortions in the first trimester); *Beal v. Doe,* 432 U.S. 438 (1977) (holding that state funding of nontherapeutic abortions is not required).

57.   Will, *supra* note 54.

58.   By-line Jerry Adler with John Carey, "But Is It a Person?" *Newsweek,* January 11, 1982, p. 44, col. 1.

59. By-line Melinda Beck with Lucy Howard and Diane Camper in Washington and bureau reports, "The Issue That Won't Go Away," *Newsweek*, January 31, 1983, p. 31, col. 1.

60. It is quite clear in *Roe* that the health standard which involves an inquiry into the reason for seeking the abortion is not the second-trimester standard. The introductory language to the second-trimester health standard reads:

> With respect to the State's important and legitimate interest in the health of the *mother,* the "compelling" point, in the light of present medical knowledge, is at approximately the end of the first trimester. This is so because of the now-established medical fact . . . that until the end of the first trimester mortality in abortion may be less than mortality in normal childbirth. It follows that, from and after this point, a State may regulate the abortion procedure to the extent that the regulation reasonably relates to the preservation and protection *of maternal health.*

Roe, supra note 5, at 163 (emphasis added). It is clear from this language that the standard it discusses, the *second-trimester* health standard, is concerned only with protecting the mother, not the child.

Immediately thereafter the court gives second-trimester specifics:

> Examples of permissible state regulation in this area are requirements as to the qualifications of the person who is to perform the abortion; as to the licensure of that person; as to the facility in which the procedure is to be performed, that is, whether it must be a hospital or may be a clinic or some other place of less-than-hospital status; as to the licensing of the facility; and the like.

Id. Plainly, these examples relate only to protecting the mother and involve no inquiry into the reason for the abortion.

By sharp contrast, the introductory language to the *third-trimester* health standard reads:

> With respect to the State's important and legitimate interest in potential life, the "compelling" point is at viability. This is so because the *fetus* then presumably has the capability of meaningful life outside the mother's womb. State regulation protective of *fetal life* after viability thus has both logical and biological justifications. If the State is interested in protecting *fetal life* after viability, it may go so far as to proscribe abortion during that period, except when it is necessary to preserve the life or health of the mother.

Roe, supra note 5, at 163–64 (emphasis added). Here, unlike before, there is concern focused on the child, although it is obvious in the quote that the child's *life* is nevertheless considered less important than the mother's *health.*

61. Adler, *supra* note 58.

62. *Id.*

63.   Press, *supra* note 8.

64.   See *Planned Parenthood of Kansas City v. Ashcroft*, 462 U.S. 476 (1983) (striking down second trimester hospitalization requirement); *City of Akron v. Akron Center for Reproductive Health, Inc.*, 462 U.S. 416 (1983) (striking down: requirement that all abortions after first trimester be performed in a hospital; requirement for parental consent or court order for abortion performed on unmarried minor under age 15; requirement that physician inform patient of status of pregnancy and availability of adoption and other agencies; 24-hour waiting period to ensure "that a woman's abortion decision is made after careful consideration of all the facts applicable to her situation"; requirement for proper disposition of fetal remains); *Colautti v. Franklin*, 439 U.S. 379 (1979) (striking down: requirement that person performing abortion must determine if fetus is viable, and if so must try to save fetus when abortion is performed; and effort to define viability in terms of gestational age or fetal weight); *Charles v. Carey*, 627 F.2d 772 (1980) (striking down: requirement and definition of informed consent; requirement for consultation procedures; rule that fetus aborted alive is an individual). But see *Simopoulous v. Virginia*, 462 U.S. 506 (1983) (upholding requirement that abortions be performed in either a hospital or a licensed clinic); *Planned Parenthood of Kansas City v. Ashcroft*, 462 U.S. 416 (1983) (upholding: requirement of pathology report; requirement that second physician be present in third-trimester abortions to try to save child; requirement of parental consent or court order to perform abortion on minor); *H.L. v. Matheson*, 450 U.S. 398 (1981) (upholding requirement of parental notice in case of minor seeking abortion).

Ohio requires a five-day wait to get married, Baldwin's Ohio Revised Code Annotated, Title 31 Domestic Relations-Children §3101.15 and a 30-day wait to get divorced, *id.* at §3105.64, even though the 24-hour wait to get an abortion was struck down in *City of Akron, supra.*

65.   *Planned Parenthood of Kansas City, supra* note 64; *City of Akron, supra* note 64.

66.   "Sizing up Ms. Justice," *Newsweek*, July 18, 1983, p. 57, col. 1.

67.   Press, *supra* note 8.

68.   *Newsweek* letter, *supra* note 26.

69.   Webster's Seventh *New Collegiate Dictionary* 421–22 (1972).

70.   *Id.* at 952.

71.   Adler, *supra* note 58.

72.   I am reminded of the description of what happens to responsible behavior by individuals when they operate in groups in John K. Galbraith, *Economics and the Public Purpose* (1973).

73.   See note 26, *supra.*

PART TWO

Language and Public Opinion

ADAMEK   Although social scientists have documented changing public opinion on the abortion issue and investigated the correlates of attitudes toward abortion, relatively little information has been available regarding which arguments for and against abortion were reaching the general public. An analysis of two open-ended NORC questions asking respondents to list pro and con arguments was therefore undertaken to determine (1) which arguments are most salient, i.e., which are mentioned most frequently, and (2) what types of respondents give which arguments, i.e., which of eleven sociodemographic and forty attitudinal variables are significantly related to the types of arguments cited. Major findings were: first, Americans are generally knowledgeable about this topic, with only 6.6 percent failing to cite any arguments; second, arguments against abortion seem to be more salient in that a larger percentage of the public volunteers a few key pro-life arguments than volunteers any pro-choice arguments; and third, pro and con arguments are generally equally salient for different types of people.

GRANBERG   Despite the apparent stability of public opinion on abortion over the past twenty years, a contentious struggle has been waged over the custody of the concept of abortion. The conflict has focused on whose definition of the situation, pro-life or pro-choice, will prevail. At issue has been whether abortion is regarded as an absolute evil or a relative good, and whether the focus is on "alpha" or the woman. A comparison is reported of the connotative meaning of four different ways of labeling alpha: embryo, fetus, unborn child, and baby. The person positivity hypothesis is that the more a stimulus resembles a person, the more it will be liked and accorded value.

MALL   In this essay the rhetoric of abortion is analyzed through part of an advertising campaign created by the Hill and Knowlton PR agency for its client, the U.S. Catholic Conference. Essential background material is supplied via a discussion of contemporary consumer research techniques which rely heavily upon value analyses made necessary by increasingly sensitive market segmentation requirements. A value mapping model of persuasion used by a public opinion research company, The Wirthlin Group, is evaluated in detail. Limitations of this model are explained and an alternative and/or supplementary model is advanced. The usefulness of this latter model, described as cognitive moral developmental, is shown by its capacity to illuminate a series of five ads produced by Hill and Knowlton for the U.S.C.C. The essay's rhetorical analysis is placed within the context of the newly emerging specialty of social marketing.

On the Salience
of Abortion Arguments

Raymond J. Adamek

I n previous papers (Adamek, 1986, 1989a, 1989b) we analyzed major national polls dealing with the abortion issue.
In summary form, these analyses revealed that:

1. Attitudes of the American public toward abortion became more
permissive from the early 1960's to 1973, after which they stabilized.

2. Americans are rather evenly divided about the nature and
morality of abortion, about half considering it morally wrong,
and even the equivalent of murder, and half considering it not to
be wrong.

3. A rather large majority of Americans believe that legal
abortion should be available in the first trimester of pregnancy for
what have come to be known as the hard, physical reasons.
These include those cases where the mother's life or health is
seriously threatened, where there is a strong chance of serious
defect in the baby, or in cases of rape or incest. Except for the
mother's life being threatened, however, only a minority of Americans would permit abortion in the second or third trimester, even
for the hard, physical reasons. There is also much less support for
abortion for soft, social reasons, such as not being able to support
another child, being unmarried, resorting to abortion as a means

of family limitation, or having abortion available "if the woman wants it for any reason."

4. Although polls asking general questions about the Supreme Court's pre-*Webster* abortion decisions seem to indicate majority approval of these decisions, more detailed polls asking questions about nine specific issues in the Court's decisions indicate that on eight issues, never more than 38% of the public agrees with the Court. Only on the funding issue are the public and the Court in agreement. That is, Americans do not want their tax dollars to fund abortions and the Court ruled that tax dollars did not have to be used for this purpose.

5. Although a majority of Americans disagree with the Court's pre-*Webster* abortion policies, however, a majority also disagrees with proposals calling for a Human Life Amendment which would make abortion virtually unavailable.

6. Hence, the American public is clearly neither in the pro-life camp nor in the pro-choice camp, although several studies suggest it is closer to the pro-life camp.

7. There is no evidence to support the claim that a majority of Americans are pro-choice, if we define the latter term as advocates of that position would have it implemented in public policy, i.e., abortion-on-demand at any time in the pregnancy.

8. The vast majority of Americans support restrictions on unfettered abortion to protect such rights as the woman's right to informed consent and the right of parents to be informed and to give or withhold consent when their minor daughters seek to have an abortion.

9. Finally, the sociodemographic characteristics related to abortion attitudes have been rather clearly identified. Persons who have relatively permissive attitudes toward abortion are more likely to attend church less frequently, have more formal education, live in the West and East and in larger communities, have higher incomes, be Jewish or have no religious affiliation, be white, younger and male compared to persons whose attitudes toward abortion are more restrictive.

The modern abortion controversy has raged in the United States for some twenty-five years. During this time, increasingly better organized interest groups on either side of the issue have been advancing various arguments for and against legalized abortion. While social scientists have rather extensively documented changing public opinion on the abortion issue, as well as explored the correlates of attitudes toward abortion (for some of the more comprehensive studies and reviews, see Adamek 1986, 1989; Blake 1971, 1977; Blake and Del Pinal 1981; Granberg and Granberg 1980, 1985; Szafran and Clagett 1988; Rossi and Sitaraman 1988), relatively little information has been available regarding which of these arguments were reaching the general public.

An attempt to determine the salience of various abortion arguments was made in 1982, however, when the National Opinion Research Center (NORC) asked a representative probability sample of 1,506 adult Americans the following questions as part of its annual General Social Survey:

a. "As far as you've heard, what are the main arguments in favor of abortions?"

b. "And, as far as you've heard, what are the main arguments against abortion?" (Davis, 1982: 156–157)

Up to three answers per respondent were recorded for each question.

In this paper, we shall analyze the responses to these questions, as well as other data from this survey, and attempt to answer the following:

1. Which of the arguments for and against abortion seem to be most salient to the American public, that is, which are mentioned most frequently by respondents?

2. What types of respondents give which arguments? That is, are the various arguments for and against abortion equally salient to all types of people, or are some arguments more likely to be cited by some types of people than by others?

We should underscore the fact that the wording of the questions limits our analysis to a consideration of the abortion arguments' salience to the respondents, and does not permit us to determine whether the respondent agrees with or is convinced by a particular argument. However, we shall be able to make some inferences about the latter considerations as a result of our analysis.

We should also note that, unfortunately, respondents were not asked to list the main arguments for and against abortion "cold." That is, immediately prior to being asked to list pro and con arguments, the respondents were asked to respond to the standard NORC abortion questions asking under which of seven circumstances they felt it should be possible for a pregnant woman to obtain a legal abortion (Davis, 1982: 218–219). These items undoubtedly reminded respondents of several arguments for abortion, just prior to their being asked to list such arguments.

Method

Utilizing computer data tapes provided by NORC, we first determined the number and percent of the 1,506 respondents who gave particular answers to the two abortion argument questions. Prior to doing this, however, we combined some of the response categories where we felt that respondents were using different words to say essentially the same thing. For example, where the original study coded respondents who said one argument against abortion was that "Abortions are killing or murder" separately from those who said "Abortion is taking a life," we combined these two categories. This was done for two reasons. First, it facilitated economy of presentation. Thus the original 27 arguments given for abortion (including a residual miscellaneous category) were combined to yield 16 arguments, and the original 23 arguments given against abortion (also including a miscellaneous category) were combined to yield 13 arguments. Second, combining categories gave us a larger number of respondents in each category, which facilitated more detailed analysis when we crosstabulated the pro and con arguments with other variables. (In the few instances where individuals originally cited more than one component of the combined category, they were counted only once in the combined category.)

In order to determine whether some types of arguments seem to be more salient with certain types of people, we crosstabulated the pro and con arguments with a large number of other variables in a series of bivariate tables. These variables fell into two broad categories. The first was sociodemographic in nature, and included the respondents' sex, race, age, education, current income, religion, marital status, the number of siblings and children they had, and the geographical region and size of community they lived in. The second set of variables were generally attitudinal in nature, and included items dealing with the economic, political, familial and religious institutions. Although too numerous to list here, they are listed in Appendix 1 by their NORC computer names.

We also crosstabulated the pro and con arguments with a variable which indicated how permissive or restrictive the respondents were on abortion. This variable was constructed by adding together the number of circumstances the respondent believed justified a legal abortion. Those agreeing that no or only one circumstance justified abortion were considered low on abortion permissiveness, those agreeing that two through five circumstances justified abortion were considered medium, and those agreeing that six to seven circumstances justified abortion were considered high on abortion permissiveness.

The crosstabulation procedures generated approximately 1,500 tables, not counting our controls for sex. Given this amount of data, we needed some rules of thumb to determine which of the results were noteworthy. Three such rules were adopted. First, we omitted those pro and con arguments mentioned by less than five percent of the sample from our crosstabulation report. Our reasons were economy of presentation and the fact that the number of respondents in each cell of the tables decreases rapidly when one begins with few respondents, thus producing statistically unstable results. Second, we considered noteworthy only those results which were statistically significant, at at least the .05 level of probability. Therefore, differences between categories of respondents which we report are probably due to real differences between these groups in the population, rather than merely to sampling fluctuation. Third, we considered to be noteworthy only those differences between major categories of respondents which equalled or exceeded ten percent. For example, since 12.8% of the males and 16.8% of the females cited the "It's a woman's right" argument for abortion, this difference would not be reported, even though it is statistically significant ($p < .05$), since it is less than ten percent, and by our rule of thumb, substantively insignificant (i.e., it is a relatively small difference—about the same percent of men and women cite this reason).

Finally, we measured the strength of the relationships between variables utilizing Cramer's V, a statistic whose value can vary from .00 to 1.00. A value closer to .00 indicates a relatively weak correlation or association between two variables, and a value closer to 1.00 indicates a relatively strong correlation.

Findings

General Salience of Abortion Arguments

Following the order in which the questions were asked, we shall first consider the number and percent of respondents who cited various arguments in favor of abortion. These data are given in Table 1. The N column includes all the respondents who cited the argument indicated, regardless of whether they listed it as their first, second, or third argument. On the average, those respondents who cited any arguments in favor of abortion cited two arguments.

Some appreciation of the scope of the abortion controversy can be gained by noting that only 100 respondents (6.6% of the total sample) failed to cite either pro or con arguments. Some of these respondents undoubtedly purposely withheld arguments of which they were aware for personal reasons, so almost all Americans are able to cite abortion arguments. How many people should be expected to mention a particular argument before it can be considered salient is difficult to say. In part, the percent who can be expected to mention a particular argument is a function of the total number of arguments in the population of discourse. In any event, we note that less than one quarter of the respondents mentioned any one pro-abortion argument.

As Table 1 indicates, at least five percent of the respondents cited eight of the arguments given for abortion. Four of these eight (danger to mother's health, rape/incest, child defective, and danger to mother's life) were the hard, physical reasons, and the other four were soft, social reasons. Social reasons also dominated the other seven arguments given by less than five percent of the respondents. The hard, physical reasons therefore constitute half of the most salient reasons for abortion. The other four reasons are the social reasons generally promulgated by the advocates of permissive abortion, including the child being unwanted, and a woman's freedom of choice/right to privacy, which perhaps could have been combined with the woman's right/control over body arguments to constitute a "a woman's personal discretion" argument which would have been cited by a combined 33% of the public. The fourth social reason cited by more than five percent was the argument that parents can't afford/care for a child.

Table 1

Number and Percent of 1506 Respondents Giving Indicated Responses to the Question: *"As far as you've heard, what are the main arguments in favor of abortion?"*

ARGUMENTS	N	%
Danger to mother's health	359	23.8
Rape / incest	355	23.6
Child unwanted	310	20.6
Freedom of choice / privacy	280	18.6
Child defective	269	17.9
Parent's can't afford / care for child	246	16.3
Woman's right / control over own body	228	16.1
Danger to mother's life	106	15.1
Social costs of unwanted / welfare babies	56	7.0
Overpopulation	54	3.7
Prevent illegitimacy / forced marriage	48	3.2
Prevent child abuse	31	2.1
Reduce liabilities / restrictions on women	31	2.1
Avoid illegal abortions	24	1.6
Unborn not persons	18	1.2
Other miscellaneous arguments	27	1.8
No arguments in favor given	259	17.2

Among the less salient arguments, we might note that only 3.6% of the public cites overpopulation, which one suspects was a major concern of some of the architects of the abortion "reform" movement, and only 1.2% cite the unborn is not a person argument, a major justification advanced by the Supreme Court to support its judgment that the unborn were not protected by the Constitution.

Table 1 suggests that the pro-abortion arguments that are most salient to the American public are those which are the most concrete, personal, and immediate in effect, whereas the more abstract, social, and remote reasons tend to be less salient. Table 1 also indicates that 27 respondents gave various other pro-abortion arguments, or unclear responses, and 259 gave no arguments in favor of abortion. We shall look in more detail at the latter below.

Table 2 gives the arguments against abortion that the American public finds to be most salient. On the average, each respondent mentioned 1.7 arguments against abortion. Seven arguments are cited by more than five percent of the public. What is most striking about this table is that fully half the American public cites the it's killing, murder/taking a life argument. If we added the unborn is alive/a person, and the right-to-life arguments, which say the same thing in a more positive way, an even larger

Table 2

Number and Percent of 1506 Respondents Giving Indicated Responses to the Question: *"As far as you've heard, what are the main arguments against abortion?"*

ARGUMENTS	N	%
It's killing / murder / taking a life	758	50.3
Religious beliefs	425	28.2
Unborn is alive / a person	217	14.4
Right to life	178	11.8
It's immoral	159	10.6
Not acceptable as birth control	85	5.6
Not an individual choice	84	5.6
Causes complications for woman	72	4.8
Promotes promiscuity	50	3.3
Should take responsibility for actions	41	2.7
Adoption better alternative	40	2.7
Paid for by taxpayers	29	1.9
Other miscellaneous arguments	53	3.5
No arguments against given	180	12.0

percentage of Americans could be considered to find this argument against abortion salient. Hence, the main message of the pro-life camp seems to have been heard.

About 28% of the public mentions religious beliefs as an argument against abortion, and another 11% mentions moral considerations. About six percent each state that it is not acceptable as birth control, or that it is not an individual's choice to make. Fewer than five percent of the respondents list five other reasons, while 53 list various other reasons. One hundred eighty respondents gave no arguments against abortion.

Let us now take a closer look at the respondents who fell into one of the "no arguments given" categories (see Table 3). One hundred respondents gave neither arguments for nor against abortion. Compared to the rest of the sample, they were characterized by relatively little education (62% had less than 12 years of schooling), and low incomes (48% earned under $10,000). Hence, we might infer that one major reason for their failure to respond was that as a group, they were relatively unknowledgeable and inarticulate. As we may see in Table 3, these respondents tended to be normally distributed across our permissiveness toward abortion index. In contrast, respondents who gave only

Table 3

Percentage Distribution on Permissiveness Toward Abortion Index by Respondent Type

	RESPONDENTS CITING ARGUMENTS			
PERMISSIVENESS TOWARD ABORTION	BOTH PRO AND CON	NEITHER PRO NOR CON	ONLY PRO ABORTION	ONLY CON ABORTION
High	44.1	28.0	51.3	13.8
Medium	46.5	49.0	43.8	51.6
Low	9.3	23.0	5.0	34.6
Total (N)	1167	100	80	159

reasons for abortion, or who gave only reasons against abortion, had more formal education and higher incomes, but were not normally distributed across our permissiveness index. Rather, the 80 respondents (5.3% of the total sample) who volunteered arguments for abortion but none against abortion appear to have been expressing their personal preference. That is, compared to other respondents, they tended to be more permissive toward abortion, and chose not to cite arguments against abortion. Similarly, the 159 respondents (10.6% of the total sample) who cited arguments against abortion but none in favor of abortion also appear to have had their personal preference in mind, since, compared to other respondents, they tended to have more restrictive attitudes toward abortion. Thus, while respondents were asked only to cite the main arguments for and against abortion of which they were aware, some of them were also indicating their personal preferences in responding. This was not necessarily true of all respondents, however.

Besides being concerned about the frequency with which the public cited particular pro and con arguments, the second major task we posed for ourselves was to determine whether there were particular sociodemographic or attitudinal characteristics that were associated with particular pro and con arguments. We shall turn to this question now.

Sociodemographic Variables and Pro-abortion Arguments

Our most general conclusion about the sociodemographic variables is that, together, they do not have much impact on the frequency with which pro-abortion arguments are cited. That is, persons from quite varied socioeconomic backgrounds tend to cite particular pro-abortion arguments in approximately equal proportions. Another way of stating this is to say that pro-abortion arguments are equally salient among different types of people. This general conclusion is illustrated by the fact that with 11 sociodemographic variables and eight major pro-abortion arguments being considered, we potentially could have found 88 significant crosstabulations. However, only 27 significant crosstabulations were found. Moreover, even though each of these 27 relationships was both statistically ($p < .05$) and substantively (difference $> 10\%$) significant, none of them was very strong. Cramer's

V ranged between .08 and .14 in 24 instances, and between .15 and .20 in the other three.

Without losing sight of this general conclusion, then, let us look at the 27 significant relationships in summary fashion to determine which of the sociodemographic factors appear to make the most difference in the frequency with which pro-abortion arguments are cited. Parenthetically, we might first note that sex was the only sociodemographic variable which never made a difference. That is, men and women are likely to cite each of the pro-abortion arguments with about equal frequency.

Education was the sociodemographic variable most consistently (5 of 8 instances) and most strongly (mean V = .15) related to the citation of pro arguments. Two general patterns emerged. With three soft, social reasons, there was a general tendency for the frequency of citation to increase as one went from the respondents with the least formal education (O to 8 years) to the respondents with the most formal education (17 or more years). To illustrate, the respective percentages in these categories citing the following arguments were: child unwanted, 11.7% vs. 32.3%; freedom of choice/privacy, 8.4% vs. 34.4%; woman's right/control over body 2.8% vs. 23.7%. This finding is compatible with those of numerous other studies (Adamek, 1986) which indicate that permissiveness toward abortion and education are positively correlated. If we were to speculate as to the reasons for this association, we would suggest at least four reasons. First, higher education in the United States tends to be nonreligious (if not anti-religious), and religiosity has been found to be a strong predictor of attitudes toward abortion. Second, persons with more formal education are more likely to deal in the abstract, and less in the concrete. Thus, someone with less formal education looking at a picture of a ten-week-old fetus is likely to be convinced that he is looking at "a baby." Someone with more formal education looking at the same picture, however, will be better able to convince himself that he is only looking at "a product of conception." Thirdly, for the same reason, persons with more formal education are better able to assimilate the more abstract, social justifications for abortion, while those with less formal education are less likely to be able to do so. Finally, persons with more education have been found to be more characterized by and concerned about self-

direction and planning for the future, while those with less education are more likely to simply accept things as they happen.
Hence, the "reproductive control" aspect of abortion would be
more attractive to persons with more formal education.

A second pattern emerged when education was crosstabulated with two of the hard, physical arguments for abortion, the
rape/incest and the defective child arguments. Here, although
those with 0–8 years of schooling were again relatively unlikely to
cite these arguments (13.1% and 11.2% did so, respectively),
those with 17 or more years of schooling were also relatively
unlikely to cite them (17.2% and 16.1% did so). Respondents
with intermediate amounts of education were most likely to cite
these two arguments. This pattern may indicate that some of the
most educated respondents are more concerned about the social
arguments than they are about the hard, physical reasons because
they are more controversial and, hence, more salient.

Religion was found to be related to the frequency of citation
of four of the eight most salient pro-abortion arguments. Again,
different patterns were noted for the hard, physical and soft, social
reasons. Persons with no religious affiliation (33.0%) and Jews
(27.0%), who tend to be more permissive toward abortion, were
more likely to cite the freedom of choice/privacy argument than
were Protestants (16.8%) or Catholics (18.9%), who tend to be
less permissive. Those with no religious affiliation (23.9%) and
Jews (37.8%) were also more likely to cite the woman's right/con-
trol over body argument than were Protestants (12.5%) or
Catholics (17.0%). However, Protestants (23.8%) and Catholics
(26.8%) were more likely to cite the rape/incest argument than
those with no religious affiliation (13.8%) or Jews (13.5%).
Protestants (19.3%) and Catholics (17.8%) were also more likely to
cite the defective child argument than those with no religious
affiliation (7.3%) or Jews (10.8%).

The type of community the respondent lived in was also
found to be related to four of the pro-abortion arguments. Persons most likely to cite social justifications for abortion came
from communities found to be characterized by greater permissiveness. Thus, 26.8% of those living in the 12 largest metropolitan areas in the United States cited the woman's right/control
over body argument. This generally decreased across community
size, with only 10.5% of those coming from "other rural" areas cit-

ing it. Similarly, whereas 23.5% of those coming from the 12 largest metropolitan areas cited the can't afford/care for argument, only 10.9% of those from rural areas did so. Once again, the pattern tended to be reversed when two hard, physical reasons were considered. Whereas 36.0% of those from rural areas cited the danger to mother's health argument, only 17.6% of those from the 12 largest metropolitan areas did so. Somewhat similarly, 19.9% of those in rural areas cited the defective child argument, whereas it was cited by only 11.8% of those from the most populous areas. In this instance, however, those from intermediate size areas were most likely to cite this argument (22.8% of those who lived in suburbs of the next 100 largest urban areas did so).

The number of children the respondent had affected the frequency with which three of the pro-abortion arguments were cited. Respondents with five or more children were least likely to cite the woman's right/control over body (7.1%) and the freedom of choice/privacy (9.3%) arguments, while those with no children (18.9% and 21.1%, respectively) were most likely to cite them. The pattern for the hard, physical reasons was again reversed and somewhat curvilinear. That is, while 14.4% of those with no children cited the defective child argument, this increased to 24.7% among those with 3-4 children, but then decreased again to 15.7% of those with 5-8 children.

The size of one's parents' family was also related to citation of two of the social arguments. Not counting only children, the more siblings the respondent had, the less likely they were to cite these two social reasons. Hence, 8.2% of those with seven or more siblings cited the woman's right/control over body argument. This increased steadily to 19.6% of those with 1-2 siblings. Similarly, whereas 12.4% of those with seven or more siblings cited the freedom of choice/privacy argument, 23.3% of those with 1-2 siblings did so. These findings are consonant with those of other studies indicating pro-life attitudes are positively related to family size. Only children did not fit the general family size pattern. Thus, 12.0% of them cited the woman's right/control over body argument, and 22.7% cited the freedom of choice/privacy argument.

Earned income was also related to two of the social justifications for abortion. With minor variations, there was a general increase in the percent citing the freedom of choice/privacy argument from 14.0% of those earning under $10,000 to 26.3% of those earning $50,000 and over. The pattern for the woman's right/control over body argument was more erratic, however. While the lowest percentage citing this argument (7.1%) was found among those with the lowest income (under $5,000), the next lowest percentage (11.4%) was among those earning from $20–$25,000, and the highest percentage (24.1%) was in the adjacent category of those earning $25–$35,000.

Age was also related to the same two social justifications. The freedom of choice/privacy and woman's right/control over body arguments were most likely to be mentioned by those 30–39 years of age (25.4% and 20.5%, respectively). Those under 30 were second most likely to mention them (21.6% and 17.0%), and those 60 and over were least likely to mention them (9.9% and 11.2%).

The frequency with which the freedom of choice/privacy and woman's right/control over body arguments were cited was also related to the respondents' marital status. In both cases, the never-married (24.6% and 17.2%, respectively) and the divorced (22.8% and 19.0%) were more likely to cite these arguments than the married (18.7% and 15.6%) or the widowed (7.6% and 7.0%, respectively).

Geographic region was related to two of the physical reasons. Persons living in the West were most likely to mention the rape/incest (29.3%) and the defective child (26.9%) arguments, while those in the East (18.8%) were least likely to mention the rape/incest argument, and those in the Midwest (15.6%) were least likely to mention the defective child argument.

Finally, by our criteria, race was significantly related to only one of the pro-abortion arguments. Whites (19.3%) were more likely to cite the defective child argument than either blacks (7.7%) or other races (7.4%).

In summary, to the extent that they are mentioned at all, pro-abortion arguments tend to be equally salient among people with diverse sociodemographic characteristics. In those relatively few instances where sociodemographic factors make a difference, two major patterns are observable in the data. First, sociodemographic factors appear to have a greater impact on the soft, social arguments for abortion (17 of 27 significant relationships involve social reasons), than they have on arguments involving hard, physical reasons (10 of 27 significant crosstabulations). In particular, two of the major ideological points proffered by the pro-choice camp, the freedom of choice/privacy and the woman's right/control over body arguments, were susceptible to fluctuation across several sociodemographic categories. The freedom of choice/privacy argument was found to be related to variation across seven sociodemographic variables, and the woman's right/control over body argument was found to be related to variation across eight variables. The only major hard, physical reason which came close to this type of fluctuation in salience was the defective child argument, which was influenced by six sociodemographic variables. This would suggest that the social arguments for abortion are somewhat less convincing to the general public, and that the extent to which they are salient depends more upon the individual's particular circumstances.

The second major pattern discovered was that, with some exceptions characterized by mixed patterns which might be resolved through multivariate analysis, persons from sociodemographic groupings found in previous studies (Adamek, 1986) to be more permissive on abortion are more likely to cite the soft social arguments, while persons from groupings more restrictive in attitude toward abortion are more likely to cite the hard, physical reasons. This again suggests that people tend to cite those arguments with which they agree, although not all do so.

Attitudinal Variables and Pro-abortion Arguments

Previous work (Adamek, 1986) and intuition suggested that some 40 attitudinal variables in the NORC data set might be related to the frequency with which pro-abortion arguments might be mentioned by the general public. Given that we are concerned with the eight most frequently cited pro-abortion arguments, this meant that we had the potential of finding 320 statistically ($p < .05$) and substantively (difference $> 10\%$) significant crosstabulations among these variables. In fact, we found only 56 significant crosstabulations, suggesting that pro-abortion arguments are equally salient among individuals holding diverse opinions regarding a large number of topics.

Focusing now on the few attitudinal variables that were related to the citation of pro arguments, we shall attempt to simplify our presentation by first dividing the variables into institutional areas, as indicated in the appendix, and then by reporting only on those areas where the greatest number of crosstabulations were found to be significant.

The first attitudinal variable we shall report on is our measure of permissiveness toward abortion, which was found to be significantly related to six of the eight most frequently cited pro-abortion arguments. Three of these were soft, social reasons, and three were hard, physical reasons. Persons high on permissiveness toward abortion were most likely to cite the choice/privacy (29.2%), woman's right/control over body (22.8%) and unwanted (29.0%) arguments, while those low on permissiveness were least likely to cite the choice/privacy (10.5%) and woman's right/control over body (7.3%) arguments, and intermediate (17.3%) in citing the unwanted argument. Put another way, we may say that those who cite these three social arguments are much more likely (63.2%, 60.5%, and 56.8%, respectively) to be high on permissiveness than those who do not cite them (35.0%, 36.6%, and 36.0%, respectively).

Individuals moderate on permissiveness toward abortion were most likely to cite the mother's health (28.2%), rape/incest (30.6%), and defective child (23.4%) arguments, followed by those high on permissiveness (22.6%, 18.0%, and 14.9%, respectively), with those low on permissiveness being least likely to cite these arguments (11.5%, 15.2%, and 6.8%, respectively).

The institutional area most consistently related to differences in citing pro-abortion arguments was the familial, including the subareas of attitudes toward sexual matters and toward sex roles. Together, the variables in this set, which constituted 47.5% of the attitudinal variables, accounted for 55.4% of the significant relationships with the pro arguments.

Attitudes toward various sexual matters were more likely (13 of 14 instances) to be related to the frequency of citation of the social justifications for abortion than they were to the citation of physical justifications, with the freedom of choice/privacy and the woman's right/control over body arguments being particularly affected (nine of the 14 instances). Persons who were in favor of the general availability of birth control information for all who wanted it were more likely to cite the major social pro-abortion arguments than those who did not favor open availability. In three of seven instances where respondents were asked to give their opinions about various aspects of sexual behavior (premarital, extramarital, and homosexual), there was a positive relationship between sexual attitudes and citing the social reasons. That is, as permissiveness toward these behaviors increased across a four-point scale ranging from "always wrong" to "not wrong at all," so did the percent citing the social justifications. In four of seven instances, however, although those saying the behavior was always wrong were least likely to cite the social justification for abortion, the relationship was curvilinear, with those saying the behavior was not wrong at all also being relatively unlikely to cite the pro-abortion argument, and those in the middle two categories (almost always and sometimes wrong) being most likely to cite the social reasons. The only hard, physical reason to be related to the sexual items was the defective child argument, which followed the same curvilinear pattern when crosstabulated with attitudes toward premarital sex.

The respondents' attitudes toward sex roles were also more likely (8 of 10 instances) to be related to citation of social arguments in favor of abortion than of physical arguments. Those who had more modern attitudes toward sex roles were more likely to cite the social arguments than those who had more traditional attitudes in each instance. In contrast, in the two instances where sex role attitudes were found to affect the citation of physical arguments, those believing that men are better suited emotionally for politics than women and those opposing the Equal Rights Amendment were most likely to cite the rape/incest justification.

Seven other family items on various topics were also related to the citation of pro-abortion arguments. While those who felt that divorce should be more difficult to obtain were most likely (28.4%) to mention the rape/incest argument, they were least likely (14.5%) to mention the freedom of choice/privacy argument. Expressed ideal family size varied inversely with the frequency of citation of the freedom of choice/privacy argument, from 6.5% of those who mention it thinking five or more children was an ideal family size, to 27.8% of those thinking 0-1 children was the ideal family size. Those thinking two children was the ideal family size were most likely (25.2%) to cite the rape/incest argument, while those thinking 0-1 children was ideal were least likely (5.2%) to cite it. The remaining three items had to do with the importance of family and relatives to the respondent. They were related to three of the physical arguments for abortion, with those indicating that family or kin were of relatively little importance being least likely to cite the physical reasons.

The other major institutional area which yielded fairly consistent patterns was the religious. Of five significant relationships, four involved the social arguments for abortion (either freedom of choice/privacy or woman's right/control over body), and one involved the rape/incest physical argument. Those who tended to be less religious (as measured by church attendance or some subjective evaluation of their own religiosity) were more likely to cite the social reasons, while those who were more religious were most likely to cite the rape/incest argument.

In summary, to the extent that they are mentioned, pro-abortion arguments tend to be equally salient among people with diverse attitudes on a variety of topics. In those relatively few instances where attitudinal factors make a difference, three major patterns are discernible. First, being relatively permissive toward abortion is associated with the citation of soft, social justifications for abortion, while being relatively restrictive in attitude is associated with the citation of hard, physical justifications. Second, as was the case with sociodemographic factors, attitudinal variables are more likely to affect variation in the citation of the social arguments for abortion (39 of 56 significant relationships) than they are in the physical arguments (17 of 56 relationships). Attitudinal factors were also somewhat more strongly related (mean Cramer's V = .12) to the social arguments than they were to the physical arguments (mean Cramer's V = .10), although the correlations were quite weak overall. The freedom of choice/privacy (19 instances) and woman's right/control over body (10 instances) arguments were particularly subject to variation according to other attitudes, accounting for 29 of the 39 significant crosstabulations involving social reasons. Hence, these social justifications for abortion are less generally salient, and depend more for their acceptance upon an individual's other attitudes. The third major pattern observed was that those who tend to have more modern or permissive attitudes in several institutional spheres are again more likely to cite the social justifications for abortion, while those who have more traditional attitudes are more likely to cite the physical arguments.

Sociodemographic Variables and Arguments against Abortion

Sociodemographic factors were found to affect the citation of arguments against abortion even less than they affected arguments for abortion. With seven arguments against abortion being cited by more than five percent of the respondents, and 11 sociodemographic variables, we had a potential of 77 significant crosstabulations. We actually found only 16. Even in these cases the relationships were not very strong, with Cramer's V ranging between .08 and .14 in 13 instances, and between .17 and .18 in three instances. Hence, our most general conclusion is that persons with quite divergent sociodemographic characteristics are likely to cite the various arguments against abortion in approximately equal proportions. Or, we may say that, to the extent that they are cited at all, arguments against abortion are equally salient to different types of people. Indeed, one's sex, race, and the number of children one had made no appreciable difference at all in the citation of arguments against abortion.

Again, without losing sight of this main conclusion, we now focus on the exceptions, i.e., those cases where sociodemographic factors did make a difference. Age was related to four of the con arguments. Individuals over 60 were less likely to mention the killing (42.4%), unborn is alive/a person (10.9%) and right-to-life (4.5%) arguments than persons in the younger age categories. Conversely, those in the under 30 age group were least likely (16.8%) to mention the religious beliefs argument against abortion.

Education was again a relatively important variable, being related to citation of three of the seven major con arguments. As education increased, the proportion citing the arguments also increased in relatively linear fashion. Thus, 39.7% of those with 0–8 years of schooling cited the killing argument, whereas 61.3% of those with 17 or more years of schooling did so. Corresponding percentages for the unborn is alive/a person argument were 3.7% and 19.4%, while for the right-to-life argument they were 2.8% and 22.6%.

Income was also related to three con arguments. Although the pattern was not as well defined as in the case of education, the general tendency was for the unborn is alive/a person and right-to-life arguments to be mentioned more frequently by the upper income groups. Those with more income (37.7% of those earning over $35,000) were also more likely to mention the religious beliefs argument than those with less income (25.1% of those earning under $10,000).

The respondents' marital status was related to two con arguments. Never-married persons were most likely (15.3%) to mention the right-to-life argument, and widowed persons were least likely to mention it (3.5%), with married (12.8%), divorced (12.0%), and separated persons (5.6%) intermediate. The religious beliefs argument was most likely (32.9%) to be cited by married respondents, and least likely (17.5%) to be cited by the never-married, with the other categories ranging between 20.4% and 26.6%.

The remaining sociodemographic variables were related to only one con argument each. Those with no religious affiliation were most likely (56.0%) to cite the killing argument, followed by Catholics (55.6%), Protestants (47.9%), and Jews (37.8%). Only children were most likely (20.0%) to cite the unborn is alive/a person argument, with those having seven or more siblings being least likely (9.2%) to cite it, and those in intermediate categories varying from 12.5% to 18.0%. Persons living in the Midwest were most likely (57.3%) to cite the killing argument, followed by those from the West (49.2%), South (47.4%) and East (46.3%). Finally, the type of community variable yielded no consistent pattern. Respondents living in the central cities of the "next 100 largest" metropolitan areas were most likely (18.3%) to mention the right-to-life argument, while those living in the suburbs of these communities were least likely (7.9%) to mention it.

In summary, to the extent that they are mentioned at all, arguments against abortion tend to be equally salient among people with diverse sociodemographic characteristics. The salience of arguments against abortion appears to be even less subject to sociodemographic variation than was the salience of arguments for abortion. In the few instances where sociodemographic factors were found to affect the citation of arguments against abortion, no clear patterns were observed. That is, there was no clear tendency for categories of persons traditionally permissive or restrictive on abortion to cite any particular arguments against abortion more or less often, with the exception of the education variable. This absence of clear patterns in the relationships between sociodemographic variables and arguments against abortion again suggests that the latter are relatively salient and stable across various sociodemographic groupings.

Attitudinal Variables and Arguments against Abortion

With 40 attitudinal variables and the seven most frequently cited arguments against abortion, 280 significant crosstabulations were possible. However, only 18 significant crosstabulations were found. Moreover, these 18 relationships were quite weak, with Cramer's V varying between .06 and .14 in 15 instances, and between .15 and .20 in three instances.

Our major conclusion again, therefore, is that insofar as they are cited, the arguments against abortion are equally salient to persons with diverse attitudes on a variety of topics. This includes the respondents' permissiveness toward abortion. That is, persons low, medium, and high on our permissiveness index were found to cite each of the arguments against abortion with the same relative frequency, or we might say, no matter what the respondents' attitudes toward abortion, the arguments against abortion were equally salient.

Eight of the 18 significant crosstabulations involved items coming from the familial institutional set. Consistent patterns across the variables were difficult to discern, however. In some cases persons with relatively traditional family values were more likely to cite the con arguments, in other instances they were less likely to do so, and in yet other instances a mixed pattern was observed. Few patterns emerged from the other institutional areas, either, except that in three instances persons who said they followed what was going on in government and public affairs "hardly at all" were least likely to cite the killing, unborn is alive/a person, and religious beliefs arguments, perhaps indicating only a general lack of knowledge on their part. This paucity of consistent patterns again suggests that the arguments against abortion are equally salient among individuals holding different attitudes on many topics.

Keeping in mind that we have found all of the arguments against abortion to be relatively salient and stable across both sociodemographic and attitudinal categories, we note that among the seven most frequently cited con arguments, the right-to-life argument is subject to the most variation. That is, this argument was involved in 13 of the 34 significant relationships involving both sociodemographic and attitudinal variables. A person's sociodemographic and attitudinal characteristics are likely to influence his or her citation of this argument more than any of the other arguments against abortion.

Conclusions

Our review of responses to open-ended questions asking the American public to cite the main arguments pro and con abortion leads us to the following conclusions:

First, the American public is relatively knowledgeable about this topic, with only 6.6% failing to cite any arguments.

Second, twice as many respondents gave arguments against abortion but declined to give arguments for abortion as gave arguments for abortion but declined to give arguments against abortion.

Third, arguments against abortion seem to be more salient to the American public in that (1) a larger percent of the public volunteers a few key pro-life arguments than volunteers any pro-choice arguments, and (2) although, in general, both pro and con arguments are equally likely to be mentioned by persons who differ across numerous sociodemographic and attitudinal categories, where variation occurs, it is most likely to affect the pro-abortion arguments. Thus, whereas 20.3% of the tables involving pro-abortion arguments were found to vary significantly across sociodemographic and attitudinal categories, this was true for only 9.5% of the tables involving arguments against abortion.

Fourth, the pro-abortion arguments may be divided into two general categories: the hard, physical reasons, which are more likely to be cited by persons who are relatively restrictive on abortion, and the soft, social reasons, which are more likely to be cited by those who are relatively permissive on abortion.

Fifth, among the pro-abortion arguments, the freedom of choice/privacy and the woman's right/control over body arguments appear to be the most "unstable," or subject to variation across sociodemographic and attitudinal categories. They account for 31.3% and 21.7%, respectively, of the 83 significant crosstabulations involving pro-abortion arguments. Among the arguments against abortion, the right-to-life argument appears to be the most "unstable," or subject to variation across sociodemographic and attitudinal categories. It accounts for 38.2% of the 34 significant crosstabulations involving arguments against abortion.

Sixth, although arguments pro and con abortion are generally salient in that sociodemographic and attitudinal factors have relatively little impact on their citation, where such factors do have an impact, the sociodemographic factors most consistently related to the citation of pro and con arguments, and the number of significant relationships found, were: education (8), age (6), income (5), religion (5), and type of community (5). By institutional area, the attitudinal factors most consistently related to the citation of pro and con arguments, and the number of significant relationships found, were: attitudes toward sexual matters (16), sex roles (14), the family (9), and religiosity (8).

Seventh, the findings of this study are generally in agreement with previous studies of abortion attitudes.

Eighth, abortion does not emerge as a "woman's issue" in the sense that women cite very different reasons for or against abortion than men do. Rather, the various arguments pro and con have equal salience for the sexes.

Ninth, at the same time, however, as Kristin Luker (1984:244) has pointed out, "How people think about abortion is intimately tied to their thoughts about women, children, and the family," and about sex.

Finally, although we should remember that the questions asked did not measure agreement with the arguments cited, the results suggest that while neither the pro-life nor the pro-choice camps have won over the vast majority of the American people, in terms of the salience of the arguments, the public seems to be hearing the pro-life camp more clearly. Both camps have a considerable way to go to win general agreement with their arguments, however, and the pro-life camp cannot be considered an effective communicator on all counts. A prime example is the public's lack of understanding of the extent to which the U.S. Supreme Court's *Roe v. Wade* and *Doe v. Bolton* decisions (at least as interpreted prior to the 1989 *Webster* decision) made abortion available. The 1973 decisions made abortion available throughout the nine months of pregnancy for virtually any reason. Yet as recently as May 1990, the Gallup Organization (1991) found that only 17.6% of Americans were aware of this fact, with 30.4% believing either that all abortions are illegal, or that they are available only in the first trimester when the mother's life or health is threatened.

Another 12.6% indicated they were not sure what the 1973 decisions allowed. Hence, the pro-life camp will have to do a much better job of communicating with the American public if it hopes to restore legal protection to the unborn.

Appendix

List of Variables Crosstabulated with Pro and Con Arguments by NORC Computer Name

SOCIODEMOGRAPHIC VARIABLES	ATTITUDINAL VARIABLES BY INSTITUTIONAL AREA	
SEX	*Familial:* *General*	*Political*
RACE	SATFAM	POLVIEWS
AGE	ANOMIA6	ANOMIA7
EDUCATION	CHLDIDEL	IMPPOL
INCOME82	DIVLAW	PRIVACY
RELIG	IMPFAM	CIVIC
MARITAL	IMPKIN	CONJUDGE
SIBS		CONLEGIS
CHILDS	*Familial:* *Sex Roles*	
REGION	FEHOME	*Religious*
SRCBELT	FEWORK	FATEND
	FEPRES	RELITEN
	FEPOL	PRAYER
	FEPOLY	CONCLERG
	ERA	IMPCHURH
	ERAIMP	
		Miscellaneous
	Familial: *Sexual*	CONPRESS
	PILL	CONMEDIC
	TEENPILL	CONTV
	SEXEDUC	CONSCI
	PREMARSX	LETDIE1
	XMARSEX	SUIDICE1
	HOMOSEX	ABSUM*
	Economic	* ABSUM was not an original NORC variable. It was our constructed variable measuring permissiveness toward abortion.
	ANOMIAS	
	IMPWORK	

References

Adamek, Raymond J.
  1986   *Abortion and Public Opinion in the United States.* Washington,
              DC: National Right to Life Educational Trust Fund.
  1989a   "The myth of 'pro-choice' America." In Dave Andrusko (ed.),
              The Triumph of Hope. Washington, DC: National Right to
              Life Committee, pp. 31-40.
  1989b   "Public supports protective legislation: part 1." *National
              Right to Life News* 16: 21 (November 16, 1989) 1, 10.
Blake, Judith
  1971   "Abortion and public opinion: the 1960-1970 decade." *Science*
              171: 540-49.
  1977   "The Supreme Court's abortion decisions and public opinion
              in the United States." *Population and Development Review* 1
              and 2: 45-62.
Blake, Judith and Jorge H. Del Pinal
  1981   "Negativism, equivocation, and wobbly assent: public 'sup-
              port' for the pro-choice platform on abortion." *Demography*
              18: 309-20.
Davis, James A.
  1982   *General Social Surveys, 1972-1982.* Chicago: Nation Opinion
              Research Center.
Gallup Organization
  1991   *Abortion and Moral Beliefs.* Washington, DC: Americans
              United for Life, Inc.
Granberg, Donald and Beth Wellman Granberg
  1980   "Abortion attitudes, 1965-1980: trends and determinants."
              Family Planning Perspectives 12: 250-61.
  1985   "Social bases of support and opposition to legalized abortion."
              In Paul Sachdev (ed.), *Perspectives on Abortion.* Metuchen,
              NJ: The Scarecrow Press, pp. 191-204.
Luker, Kristin
  1984   *Abortion and the Politics of Motherhood.* Berkeley, CA:
              University of California Press.

90

Rossi, Alice S. and Bhavani Sitaraman
    1988   "Abortion in context: historical trends and future changes."
                    Family Planning Perspectives 20: 273-301.
Szafran, Robert F. and Arthur F. Clagett
    1988   "Variable predictors of attitudes toward the legalization of
                    abortion." *Social Indicators Research* 20: 271-90.

Struggle for the Custody of the Concept of Abortion

Donald Granberg

I n 1973, the U.S. Supreme Court, through its *Roe v. Wade* decision, caused public policy on abortion to leap-frog public opinion. Prior to 1973, the public may have preferred a policy on abortion that was somewhat less restrictive than what had been the law in most states. However, the Court created a situation far more permissive than what would have been in harmony with public opinion. Since 1973, public opinion appears to have remained remarkably stable. In 1974 *and* 1991, the National Opinion Research Center found that 92% approved of abortion being legally available "if the woman's health is endangered by the pregnancy." Similarly, in both years, 86% approved if the woman "became pregnant as a result of rape." "If there is a strong chance of a serious defect in the baby" evoked 85% approval in 1974 and 83% in 1991.

On the discretionary or "soft" reasons, there may have been a slight diminution in support across these years. Poverty ("cannot afford any more children") elicited 55% approval as a condition justifying abortion being available in 1974, compared to only 48% in 1991. Not wanting to marry the man yielded 50% approval in 1974 and 45% in 1991. Being married but not wanting more children was endorsed by 47% in 1974 and 45% in 1991. These NORC data are the best time series measuring public opinion toward abortion policy. Nonetheless, despite the apparent stability, there has been much activity and perhaps some churning beneath the surface of this facade.

The controversy over abortion in the United States can be understood, in part, as a struggle for the custody of the concept of abortion. Given the flexibility of the human mind and the great variety of social arrangements to which people can adapt, how abortion is to be defined is by no means fixed or given in nature. I am referring here, of course, not to the denotative or dictionary meaning of abortion but rather to the connotative meaning. What image is conjured up by the word abortion, and what associations are linked with it?

I shall review some of the major dimensions on which this struggle occurs, presenting some pertinent evidence. I shall also report, for the first time, the results of a semantic differential study which focused on the object of an abortion, "*alpha*," to use the term chosen by Bernard Nathanson.[1]

Although it took time to develop, the abortion controversy evolved in relation to a social movement which supported a woman's unfettered right to have a legal abortion and a counter-movement opposed to that right. The former sought to have their position designated as "pro-choice," with the implication that their opponents must be "anti-choice." The latter sought to have their preferred position designated as "pro-life" (or "pro-family"), with the implication that their adversaries must be "anti-life."

This technique, seeking to advance a particular cause by trying to associate it as part and parcel of a favorable bundle, is not unusual or unique to the matter of abortion. The Committee for a SANE Nuclear Policy, formed in the late 1950s to oppose the testing of nuclear weapons in the atmosphere, implied that other people might be advocating an INSANE nuclear policy. The various RIGHT-TO-WORK Committees, which opposed requiring membership in a union to hold a job, implied that there could be people out there opposed to an individual's right to work.

The use of the "pro-life" and "pro-choice" definitions of the abortion controversy increased gradually until each gained general acceptance within the respective social movements. One could often infer accurately "which side" people were on by the language they used. By the time I did my survey of the members of the National Right to Life Committee (NRLC) in 1980, fully 97% accepted the idea that *"Pro-life* is an appropriate label for people who oppose legalized abortion." A sizable but slightly smaller majority of NRLC members (77%) accepted the implication that their opponents were *"Anti-life."* NRLC members tended also actively to reject the alternative definition of the situation, with 72% of them rejecting the *"Pro-choice"* label for their opponents and 79% rejecting the *"Anti-choice"* label for themselves.

Not surprisingly, members of the National Abortion Rights Action League (NARAL) expressed views which formed a mirror image to the views of the NRLC. In fact, there was a very strong consensus within NARAL regarding the use of these labels with 96% accepting *"Pro-choice"* as an appropriate label for people who approve of legalized abortion, 87% accepting *"Anti-choice"* as an appropriate label for their opponents, 93% rejecting the label of *"Anti-life"* for themselves and 83% rejecting the label of *"Pro-life"* for their opponents.[2]

That these labels have acquired common usage can be seen in the debate as it occurs among public officials, e.g., in speeches by U.S. Senators prior to the vote on the Hatch-Eagleton Amendment in 1983.[3] Candidates for public office in 1988 frequently used the phrase "I'm pro-life," or "I'm pro-choice" without specifically mentioning the word abortion but with clear implications regarding their position on that specific issue.

There is a second way in which the contending forces have clashed over the context of abortion. Elsewhere I have suggested that the conflict over abortion can be viewed as occurring between those opposing what they regard as an absolute evil and others who are supporting what they regard as a relative good.[4] One might ask how abortion can possibly be viewed as a relative good. If a woman with an unwanted pregnancy views abortion negatively, but if she evaluates abortion less negatively than all the other available alternatives, then she is evaluating abortion as a relative good or as the least undesirable of a set of undesirable alternatives. Technically, she is in what psychologists call an avoidance-avoidance conflict. One can say that people ought to avoid getting into predicaments in which the only alternatives available are viewed negatively, but that is easier said than done.

It is not the case that opponents of abortion simply say abortion is evil or wrong and that's it—without any consideration of the alternatives. In fact, opponents of abortion seek to get others to evaluate and reevaluate alternatives so that abortion is viewed more negatively and other options less negatively. Moreover, it is often the case that pro-life groups alter the possibilities to facilitate the selection of an option other than abortion.

Nonetheless, there seems to have been a tendency for opponents of abortion to be somewhat more absolutistic in their approach and for supporters of abortion to be relativistic. This impression gained support in a survey I did in 1986 of people who had written letters-to-the-editor supporting or opposing legalized abortion. People were asked to choose which of these two statements came closer to their view.

A. Abortion should be judged in and of itself, i.e., is it right or is it wrong?

B. Abortion should be viewed more in the relative sense by asking what are the alternatives and how are they to be evaluated in relation to abortion?

Of the two statements, A was intended to express a more absolute approach and B the relativistic approach. These two alternatives differentiated the two groups of letter writers almost completely. Among the pro-life letter writers, 92% chose A, and 89% of the pro-choice letter writers chose B.

In addition, the person doing the abortion and the place where it is done are labeled differently by the contending forces. The pro-choice movement has sought to "medicalize" the "procedure" of abortion, focusing on the relationship between "the woman and her physician," and referring to the "products of conception," with the "pregnancy being terminated" in a "clinic." This language is, at best, somewhat euphemistic and distorted. For instance, most often the physician performing an abortion has no more than a transitory relationship with the woman having the abortion.

People within the pro-life movement have sought to develop a very different definition of the situation, often explicitly or implicitly trying to employ an analogy to the Jewish Holocaust under the Nazis in World War II. Thus, the place becomes an "abortion chamber." There is an overwhelming consensus within the pro-life movement that abortion involves the murder of innocent victims. In fact, abortion is technically not murder, the latter being a legal category within the more generic category of homicide. Now we can, of course, assert that abortion *should* be regarded as murder, but it is not evident that most Americans are receptive to that message. Nor was abortion regarded as murder in the United States in the days before 1973 when abortion was illegal. While the Holocaust metaphor has great appeal within the pro-life movement, there is no reason to think that it resonates well with the views of most Americans. Apparently, it has fallen flat with the group to which one might suppose it could potentially have the most meaning. Jewish Americans have been one of the most pro-choice groups in the United States public and are very substantially overrepresented in the pro-choice movement.

In Gestalt terms, there is also a very large difference in the focus of concern. Pro-life groups have sought to focus attention and concern on *alpha,* while at the same time not disregarding altogether the interests of the pregnant woman. Pro-choice groups, on the other hand, have sought to focus attention on the needs and wishes of the girl or woman with an unwanted pregnancy with no more than a cursory concern for *alpha*, so long as it has not been born. Which of these is "figure" and which is "ground" is by no means inconsequential.

When *alpha* is referred to as an "unborn or preborn child" or "baby," you can bet the speaker is an opponent of legalized abortion. On the other hand, if *alpha* is referred to by the medical term of "embryo" or "fetus," in all likelihood the speaker supports legalized abortion. Does this language really matter? To examine this, we did a semantic differential study to see how the image conjured up by *alpha* varies according to whether *alpha* is referred to as embryo, fetus, unborn child, or baby.

The semantic differential is a procedure developed by the psychologist, Charles Osgood, to measure the connotative meaning of concepts.[5] A concept, e.g., the NAACP, India, or a Volvo, is presented along with a series of bipolar adjective pairs, e.g., hard–soft. People rate the concept in relation to each adjective pair with seven alternatives, judging, for instance, the degree to which the "U.S. Military Intervention in Vietnam" was necessary or unnecessary, justified or unjustified, legal or illegal, moral or immoral, brief or prolonged, etc.[6] Osgood conducted large-scale studies, measuring the subjective or connotative meaning of concepts in many cultures. In spite of using a very large number of bipolar adjective pairs, he found that the connotative meaning of a concept could usually be reduced to three dimensions or factors, *Evaluation* (exemplified by the good–bad adjective pair), *Potency* (strong–weak), and *Activity* (active–passive).

In the present study, 62 students in a large high school in Missouri each made ratings of four concepts (baby, unborn child, fetus, and embryo) in relation to 17 bipolar adjective pairs. High school students were chosen for this study because we were not interested in the judgments of experts, but rather in the images of people who would have some awareness of the matter but who would also lack detailed knowledge. The order in which the concepts were rated varied from person to person and was randomly determined. Also, as can be seen in Table 1, whether the favorable adjective (e.g., warm, important, sensitive, loveable) was on the left or the right was varied so as to prevent a response set. The instructions were as follows:

> In this survey, you are asked to give your impressions of each of the following terms: BABY, EMBRYO, FETUS, and UNBORN CHILD. We do this by giving a term at the top of a page followed by a series of opposing adjective pairs. Between each set of opposing adjective pairs are 7 blanks. For each adjective pair, put an X on one of the 7 blanks to indicate the degree to which you think the adjective describes the term given at the top of that page. If it seems that neither adjective in the pair describes the term or you can't decide or don't know, you should mark the center blank with an X. It does not matter if you don't know precisely what each term means or the exact distinction between the terms on the different pages. We are more interested in knowing your impressions or images of the terms.

People were told participation was voluntary and anonymous, but they were asked to indicate their age and gender. After the four pages of semantic differential ratings, students were asked to indicate their attitude toward abortion by checking one of six alternatives which varied from extremely anti- to extremely pro-abortion.[7]

The results will be presented two ways, first by examining the ratings of this group of students as a whole and then by look-

Table 1

Semantic Differential Ratings of Four Concepts used in the Abortion Controversy on 17 Bipolar Adjective Pairs by High School Students (N=62)

BIPOLAR ADJECTIVE PAIR		CONCEPT BEING RATED			
(1)	(7)	EMBRYO	FETUS	UNBORN CHILD	BABY
			Average Rating		
Potential---------------Actual		3.7_a	4.0_a	$4.0a$	$6.3b$
Simple--------------Complex		4.4_a	4.7_a	5.5_b	6.0_b
Weak------------------Strong		2.6_a	2.5_a	3.0_a	4.4_b
Passive-----------------Active		3.3_a	3.7_a	4.1_a	5.7_b
Good---------------------Bad		2.4_a	2.3_a	2.3_a	1.6_b
Dependent----Independent		1.9_a	2.0_a	2.0_a	2.0_a
Warm--------------------Cold		2.3_a	2.1_a	1.9_a	1.3_b
Unimportant------Important		6.0_a	5.6_b	6.1_a	6.6_c
Beautiful-----------------Ugly		3.5_a	3.4_{ab}	3.0_b	1.5_c
Unresponsive--Responsive		4.7_a	4.5_a	4.9_a	6.4_b
Developed---Undeveloped		5.0_a	4.6_{ab}	4.3_b	2.4_c
Insensitive---------Sensitive		4.9_a	5.1_{ab}	5.5_b	6.1_c
Moving-----------Stationary		3.6_a	3.3_{ab}	2.9_b	1.8_c
Unattractive-------Attractive		3.8_a	4.1_a	4.6_b	6.0_c
Sturdy-----------------Fragile		5.7_a	5.5_a	5.4_a	5.5_a
Loveable----- Not Loveable		3.7_a	3.5_a	3.0_b	1.3_c
Changeable------Permanent		2.5_a	2.7_{ab}	3.2_b	2.7_{ab}

NOTE: Reading across each row, averages with a subscript in common are not significantly different.

ing at the degree to which ratings made by pro-abortion students differed from those made by anti-abortion students. Table 1 presents the average ratings of the four concepts that were made by these students.

There were only two adjective pairs on which the four concepts were rated similarly. All four concepts were rated about the same and close to the dependent end of the dependent-independent dimension. This is of interest in that it is plausible to argue that an embryo is more dependent on being nurtured by a specific woman than is a baby. The four concepts were also rated similarly on the sturdy–fragile dimension; all of them were rated toward the fragile end.

On each of the other 15 adjective pairs, there was at least some significant difference in the image of baby, unborn child, fetus, and embryo, as revealed in these ratings. However, the pattern of differences was by no means the same from one adjective pair to another. There were six instances in which embryo, fetus, and unborn child were rated similarly, but baby was rated differently from the other three. These dimensions were potential–actual, weak–strong, passive–active, good–bad, warm–cold and unresponsive–responsive. On these, baby was rated more toward the actual, strong, active, good, warm, and responsive end. There was only one dimension (simple–complex) on which embryo and fetus were rated similarly to each other but differently from unborn child and baby. Baby and unborn child were rated similarly, but more complex than fetus or embryo.

There was no adjective pair on which the concepts were each rated significantly different from the others in some orderly progression. In fact, on the remaining adjective pairs, the pattern of differences is not easy to describe succinctly. On all but one of them, however, there is a very big difference between the ratings of embryo and baby. Baby is rated as more important, beautiful, developed, sensitive, moving, attractive, and loveable than embryo. On the changeable–permanent dimension, the only significant difference was that unborn child was rated as less changeable than embryo.

Table 2 compares the average ratings of the four concepts by the pro-life and pro-choice students, grouped on the basis of their attitudes toward abortion. Of 68 comparisons (17 adjective pairs x 4 concepts), the two groups gave ratings that were significantly different on 20 (29%) tests. Interestingly, most of the differences occurred in ratings of embryo and baby, rather than on fetus or unborn child. Naively, one might have expected the smallest differences on ratings of baby, but this was not true.

Table 2

Comparison of Semantic Differential Ratings of Four Concepts in the Abortion Controversy on 17 Bipolar Adjective Pairs by Pro-Choice (N=27) and Pro-Life (N=34) High School Students

BIPOLAR ADJECTIVE PAIR		CONCEPT BEING RATED							
(1) (7)	EMBRYO		FETUS		UNBORN CHILD		BABY	
	Pro-Choice	Pro-Life	Pro-Choice	Pro-Life	Pro-Choice	Pro-Life	Pro-Choice	Pro-Life
Potential---------------Actual	2.9 √	4.4	3.2 √	4.7	3.5	4.5	6.6	6.1
Simple--------------Complex	3.7 √	4.9	4.6	4.7	5.1	5.8	6.1	6.0
Weak-------------------Strong	2.5	2.6	2.4	2.6	2.9	3.1	4.2	4.7
Passive------------------Active	2.7 √	3.8	3.1	4.1	3.5	4.5	5.1 √	6.1
Good----------------------Bad	2.7 √	2.0	2.7 √	1.9	2.6	2.1	1.6	1.6
Dependent----Independent	2.4 √√	1.4	2.4	1.6	2.3	1.7	2.2	1.9
Warm--------------------Cold	2.5	2.1	2.3	1.9	2.0	1.9	1.4	1.3
Unimportant------Important	5.3 √√√	6.6	5.1 √	6.0	5.4 √√	6.6	6.4 √	6.9
Beautiful----------------Ugly	3.8	3.3	3.5	3.3	3.4	2.7	1.7	1.3
Unresponsive--Responsive	4.6	4.9	4.3	4.6	4.4	5.3	6.1 √	6.7
Developed---Undeveloped	5.3	4.9	4.6	4.7	4.6	4.1	3.0 √	2.0
Insensitive----------Sensitive	4.4 √	5.4	4.8	5.3	5.3	5.6	5.7 √√	6.5
Moving------------Stationary	4.2 √	3.2	3.7	3.0	3.0	2.8	2.3 √	1.3
Unattractive-------Attractive	3.4	4.0	4.0	4.1	4.3	4.8	5.4 √	6.4
Sturdy---------------Fragile	5.4	6.0	5.1	5.9	5.1	5.6	5.3	5.6
Loveable-----Not Loveable	4.1	3.4	3.6	3.3	3.4	2.8	1.5	1.1
Changeable------Permanent	2.8	2.3	3.4 √	2.2	3.6	2.8	3.1	2.5

Note: The numbers in this table are the average ratings made by the pro-life and the pro-choice students. The √ indicates that the average ratings by the groups are significantly different at the 95% level of confidence, √√ the 99% level, and √√√ the 99.9 level of confidence.

Compared to pro-choice students, pro-life students rated embryo as more actual, complex, active, good, dependent, important, sensitive, and moving. In relation to the concept of fetus, the only significant differences were that the pro-life students rated fetus as characterized more by actual, good, important, and changeable.

On the concept of unborn child, there was only one significant difference between the groups, with the pro-choice students rating unborn child as less important. Finally, there were seven adjective pairs on which baby was rated differently by the pro-life and pro-choice students. Baby was rated as significantly more active, important, responsive, undeveloped, sensitive, moving, and attractive by the pro-life students.

Conclusion

The semantic differential study demonstrates that the connotative meaning of *alpha* is significantly different if it is labeled embryo, fetus, unborn child, or baby. Moreover, the four concepts clearly had different connotations to students with anti- or pro-abortion attitudes. In the everyday world, there may be a bidirectional relationship between these two psychological phenomena. That is, people may have differing images of *alpha* because of their opposition or support of abortion. However, they may also have different attitudes toward abortion because of holding different images of *alpha*.

The tacit strategy of the pro-life movement has been to direct the focus on *alpha* and *alpha*'s human characteristics with the purpose of directly affecting the image of *alpha* and thereby indirectly affecting attitudes toward abortion. Inasmuch as the two are demonstrably related, this is a plausible strategy. Through pictures, words, sonograms, and other means, pro-life people have sought to provide a "window to the womb," to use Bernard Nathanson's phrase, thereby sensitizing people by making the abstract concrete.[8]

The pro-life movement also has going for it the fact that baby and unborn child are terms of common language which people use and to which they can easily relate. Pregnant women with no connection to the pro-life movement often wear a shirt with the word "BABY" on it and an arrow pointing to the abdomen. His pro-choice position on abortion notwithstanding, Michael Dukakis in his speech accepting the Democratic nomination for President in 1988, made reference to his "first grandchild," using the terms "baby," "new baby," and "he or she," in spite of the fact that his daughter-in-law, Lisa, was only about three months pregnant at the time.[9] Also, women who had abortions and who were not selected because of expressing regret or remorse, often referred to *alpha* as "baby" rather than "embryo" or "fetus."[10] Sears' person positivity hypothesis specifies that the more a stimulus object resembles an individual person, the more the object will be liked and, by implication, valued.[11] Pro-life people have sought to show how closely *alpha* resembles a person. Indeed, their argument is that *alpha is a person,* and, therefore, deserving of affection, respect, and protection.

On the other hand, data from the Gallup poll indicate unmistakably that there are substantial variations in public opinion regarding abortion, depending not only on the circumstances prompting the woman to seek an abortion but also on the stage of the pregnancy. The NRLC and NARAL tend to view the situation as a dichotomy, that is, that all (or nearly all) or no (or nearly no) prenatal life is deserving of protection. Most citizens, however, view it more as a continuum, although developing a policy requires breaking the continuum at some point or points. The NRLC would attach maximum value to *alpha* at conception and make no differentiation along the way. NARAL would attach maximum value at birth or viability with virtually no value attached to *alpha*'s right-to-life before then. Both groups are at odds with public opinion on this, although NARAL's view has been closer to being reflected in public policy. While there is currently not the sort of consensus in the United States that would support a constitutional prohibition on abortion, there has also not been a strong consensus in support of the permissive *status quo.*

In the 1984 election study done by the Center for Political Studies at the University of Michigan, numerous groups were rated on a 0–100 degree affective "feeling thermometer." Although the rating might have been higher had "the pro-life movement" been rated, it is nonetheless of interest that "anti-abortionists" were rated, on average, almost exactly at the midpoint of this scale (50.3). "Anti-abortionists" were rated only slightly higher by Reagan voters (53.7) than by Mondale voters (46.2). Also, the overall rating of 50.3 for anti-abortionists was lower than the ratings of "people on welfare" (52.8), "civil rights leaders" (54.3), "labor unions" (54.5), "women's liberation movement" (58.0), "Hispanics" (59.4), "poor people" (71.8), and several other groups. Of 21 groups rated in the 1984 survey, only the "moral majority" (45.8), "black militants" (32.5), and "gay men and lesbians" (30.0) were rated lower than "anti-abortionists." In the 1960s and 1970s, it was commonly observed that while the United States public gradually came to dislike the Vietnam War, they disliked the anti-war protestors even more.[12]

In closing, the suggestion that the abortion controversy is, in part, a struggle for the custody of the concept of abortion is in no way intended to trivialize the matter. On the contrary, the side that succeeds in having its definition of the situation gain general acceptance will have carried the day. And history may provide a cogent example. In the United States, there was a struggle historically over custody of the concepts of welfare and socialism. Essentially, the conservatives in the United States won that struggle and thus one sees that the concept of welfare has very negative connotations in the United States, especially in contrast to Scandinavia and other European countries where the outcome of that struggle has been very different. Will the concept of abortion meet this same fate?

Notes

1. B. Nathanson, *Aborting America.* Gardcn City, NY: Doubleday, 1979. [In later writings, Nathanson uses the word "child."—Ed.]

2. D. Granberg, "What Does It Mean to Be Pro-life?" *Christian Century,* 1982, 99, No. 17, 562–66.

3. D. Granberg, "The United States Senate Votes to Uphold *Roe v. Wade,*" *Population Research and Policy Review,* 1985, 4, 115–31.

4. D. Granberg and D. Denney, "The Coathanger and the Rose," *Transaction/Society,* 1982, 19, No. 4, 39–46.

5. C. Osgood, G. Suci, and P. Tannenbaum, *The Measurement of Meaning.* Urbana: University of Illinois Press, 1957.

6. D. Granberg and G. Corrigan, "Authoritarianism, Dogmatism, and Orientation toward the Vietnam War," *Sociometry,* 1972, 35, 468–76.

7. D. Granberg, "An Anomaly in Political Perception," *Public Opinion Quarterly,* 1985, 49, 504–16.

8. D. Granberg and N. Faye, "Sensitizing People by Making the Abstract Concrete," *American Journal of Orthopsychiatry,* 1972, 42, 811–15.

9. M. Dukakis, "Text of Acceptance Speech at the Democratic Party's Convention," *The New York Times,* July 22, 1988, p. 8.

10. M. Zimmerman, *Passage through Abortion.* New York: Praeger, 1977.

11. D. Sears, "The Person-positivity Bias," *Journal of Personality and Social Psychology,* 1983, 44, 233–50.

12. M. Rosenberg, S. Verba, and P. Converse, *Vietnam and the Silent Majority.* New York: Harper and Row, 1970.

The Catholic Church and Abortion:

Persuading through Public Relations*

David Mall

O n April 5, 1990, the Office of Media Relations for the U.S. Catholic Conference submitted a press release to the nation's media. The release concerned the implementation of a new "national communications-public information effort to present as persuasively as possible the merits of a determined stand for human rights in all stages of life." The effort was to be coordinated by the Committee for Pro-Life Activities of the National Conference of Catholic Bishops (NCCB).

---

* First presented in a panel "Focus on Abortion: The Role of Public Relations in Guiding Social Discourse" sponsored by the Commission on Public Relations and the Religious Speech Communication Association at the SCA Seventy-seventh Annual Convention, Atlanta, November 1, 1991. The writer wishes to thank the following people who helped shape his thinking prior to the essay's final draft: Robert E. Pitts, a marketing professor at DePaul University; Mary Ellen Jensen, a senior research executive at The Wirthlin Group; Helen Alvaré and Richard Doerflinger of the Secretariat for Pro-Life Activities of the National Conference of Catholic Bishops; and Eugene C. Tarne and Charles R. Pucie, Jr. of Capitoline International. The writer also wishes to extend a special thanks to Lorraine Caliendo and the staff at the Marguerite Kent Library/Information Center of the American Marketing Association for help in researching the topic of social marketing.

Focusing on the rights of prenatal human life, John Cardinal O'Connor of New York, the committee chairperson, was quoted as saying:

> Some organizations have lost sight of fundamental values, such as the sanctity of human life. . . . And to realize their goals they have purchased the advice and assistance of professional communications counselors and public opinion experts. Given the stakes—life itself—we can do no less.

Accordingly, the Cardinal announced that Hill and Knowlton, an international public relations firm, along with The Wirthlin Group, specialists in public opinion research, would be assisting the church's effort. The Cardinal then concluded with a note of cautious concern about the seriousness of the debate. "We want this effort to unfold," he said, "on peaceful grounds, without vitriol, as we work to encourage both within and beyond our faith community serious consideration of moral ends, means and achievable public policy goals."

When this information was released to the media, I was teaching at California Polytechnic State University on California's central coast. I read about it in the pages of the *Los Angeles Times* and heard about it on NBC's evening news. Later the idea that the Catholic Church had hired a PR firm became the subject of editorial cartoon comment. I remember seeing one cartoon which depicted a disappointed Christ, in caricature of Leonardo da Vinci's "The Last Supper," lamenting the intrusion of PR experts to assist what supposedly should have been the exclusive task of the church—the teaching of virtue.

A typical criticism of professional PR involvement in the church's traditional role of public moralizer is summarized in the following editorial comment: "That a prince of the church would no longer trust his own spiritual authority, that the preacher in his pulpit was no longer sure he was reaching his congregation, that the priest needed a public-relations firm—here was evidence of a church that had lost its confidence."[1] Thus is a failure of nerve seen as a primary causative factor in the church's acquisition of professional help to assist its pro-life educational effort. Add this interpretation to the commonly held belief that public relations is a contrived and mostly superficial communication specialty that thrives on cheap gimmicks and media stunts and it may then be possible to understand a little more completely some of the criticism leveled at the church's actions. The reader should bear in mind, however, that these misgivings, though deeply felt, are also advanced by those who wish to offer constructive criticism.

Let me now provide a few words of justification concerning the church's use of a professional public relations agency. The case for professional PR involvement in the abortion controversy on behalf of the NCCB was laid out forcefully by Richard Doerflinger, Associate Director of Policy Development at the Secretariat for Pro-Life Activities. In an op-ed piece for an important diocesan publication, he indicated that the church's use of the most sophisticated communication techniques was prompted by the millions of dollars that had been spent by those favoring abortion to promote their cause following the 1989 Supreme Court decision in *Webster v. Reproductive Health Services*. Doerflinger then quoted from two statements elucidating the church's communication policy: The Second Vatican Council's *Decree on the Means of Social Communication* (1963) and its implementing document, a *Pastoral Instruction on the Means of Social Communication* (1971). In both statements the church is urged to employ the most advanced expertise in preaching the gospel's pro-life message.[2]

Although the church's employment of extensive PR help in the abortion controversy has been only within the last few years, the pro-abortionists saw much earlier the value of this kind of expertise. In 1973, Lawrence Lader, co-founder of the National Association for the Repeal of Abortion Laws (NARAL) which subsequently became, as it is known today, the National Abortion Rights Action League, asserted in his book *Abortion II* that "the best chance to build a movement was through public relations."[3] More recently, professional PR practitioners themselves have asserted that "Public relations is arguably the most effective marketing method for achieving social change."[4] Juxtapose this last claim with the church's eagerness to employ PR expertise and in certain respects the abortion debate in America has increasingly become a battle of PR experts.

With this in mind, what I will attempt to do is analyze and evaluate part of the media campaign put together by the church's recently hired PR experts. My discussion will be confined primarily to the research efforts of The Wirthlin Group. What you read is not intended to be exhaustive. The public relations campaign is still unfolding, and we are much too close to this ongoing event for an exhaustive appraisal. Additionally, and perhaps more importantly, although their contract has officially ended, what we may observe at present is still restricted by the problems inherent in practitioner-client confidentiality.

My interest in studying the PR aspect of the American abortion debate arises from my interest in the cultural transmission of biomedical ethics. I have used the respect life issues of the day such as abortion and euthanasia to flesh out my ongoing investigation of the rhetoric of social movements. Having been a participant-observer of the abortion controversy for many years, I welcome an opportunity to witness the real world of mass persuasion where decisions are made to change human behavior. As a communication scholar, I have always been interested in, drawn to, and fascinated by what practicing rhetoricians do in the context of social movement activism. Justification for my essay then is not only the help it may give other activists like myself but also the insight it may provide other scholars who are exploring the rhetoric of social movements.

The focus of my analysis will be the research model used by The Wirthlin Group to analyze public opinion and to recommend appropriate communication strategies to the PR firm of Hill and Knowlton. Once we have inspected the Wirthlin research tools, I will suggest ways to sharpen and magnify their effects by evaluating five ads generated through the joint collaboration. The analysis will involve two major areas of investigation: Part I, consumer research, which will emphasize market segmentation, and Part II, cognitive moral developmentalism, which will emphasize moral reasoning. For those readers whose background may be in rhetoric and public address, as is mine, what we will be discussing is a new, if not radically different, perspective on the sensitive area of audience analysis. My assumption is that it is only by understanding audiences in the aggregate and ultimately the average individuals who compose them that we can more fully appreciate the role of public relations in guiding social discourse.

We begin our investigation with a brief description of the marketing roots of present day PR techniques, particularly those which are used to enhance the Respect Life Program of the U.S. Catholic Conference. Our journey actually begins forty years ago with the publication of a seminal essay in the journal *Public Opinion*

Quarterly. The author of this article was G.D. Wiebe who at the time was a research psychologist for CBS radio and a lecturer in psychology at the City College of New York. His essay is especially significant to me personally because it appears to have grown out of practical work experience. In short, it was not a product of the ivory tower but of the real world of purposeful, real-time mass persuasion.

Wiebe's thesis was simple: Only when "the essential conditions for effective merchandising exist" can "broad social objectives via radio or television" be fully realized. As the article abstract indicated, "These conditions are primarily that the audience must be forcefully motivated and clearly directed to an adequate, appropriate, and accessible social mechanism."[5] The article subsequently described these factors in order as (1) force, (2) direction, (3) mechanism, (4) adequacy and compatibility, and (5) distance. Then the author applied his analytical instrument to four campaigns, including the CBS Kate Smith Bond Selling Campaign, the campaign relating to Civil Defense Manpower, a juvenile delinquency documentary, and the televised hearings of the Kefauver Crime Committee. We will revisit portions of the Wiebe analysis at the end of the essay. Let it suffice at this point to repeat a question that apparently kindled his approach. Wiebe asked: "Why can't you sell brotherhood and rational thinking like you sell soap?" It took precisely a generation of scholarship finally to produce the beginnings of an appropriate, albeit partial, answer. (See the appendix for a brief description of social marketing.)

Before beginning our analysis, now is a good time to make some important distinctions of a definitional nature to help us get oriented. The reader should not confuse public relations with advertising as is often done. Although both subject matter areas rely heavily upon communication, advertising is related more to economics and business and is usually considered a subset of marketing analysis and is taught primarily in the business curriculum. Public relations, on the other hand, is related more to journalism and speech and is taught in the context of written and oral rhetoric. These distinctions must be kept carefully in mind because the communication models we will examine and the examples I will show you from the Hill and Knowlton campaign are actually the products or outcomes of advertising research and not what are normally perceived as classical public relations activity.

Advertising is a physical entity that is paid for, while the message outputs of public relations are generated by specialists and placed advantageously before their intended audiences without direct cost. Thus public relations works subtly behind the scenes to get a job done for a client, which advertising gets done more openly.[6]

Part I: Consumer Research

To appreciate the work of the Hill and Knowlton PR effort, we must first direct our attention to the theoretical underpinnings of their marketing research. The raw material for their decision making was supplied by their research associates, The Wirthlin Group. The working relationship between the two is such that the completed messages are fashioned from the creative talents of the Hill and Knowlton people assigned to the account. Assisting this creative process were the consumer profiles that The Wirthlin Group researchers had produced.

In the jargon of marketing, one of the first research steps to be taken is to identify the target audience or the consumer segment to be isolated and addressed with appropriate messages. Market researchers speak of demographics and psychographics as consumer characteristics that are important in defining target segments. Demographics involve such characteristics as age, sex, education, income, etc, while psychographics involve such things as personality variables and cognitive styles, as well as attitudes, beliefs, and values. Psychographics are said to "put flesh on demographic bones."[7]

Somewhat similar to this convenient research dichotomy is another that concentrates either on a broad or a narrow focus. Two important scholars write of market segmentation approaches that are macro or micro. The former contains a strong sociological orientation exemplified by survey research of predetermined clusters or groups, while the latter is characterized by the careful in-depth investigation of a small number of people selectively chosen. In contrast to the demographic-psychographic approach which is more content oriented, the macro-micro emphasis is more form oriented.[8]

The jargon of social marketing is perhaps somewhat esoteric for those whose background like my own is more in line with rhetoric and public address. With just a little imagination, however, it is possible to translate one vocabulary into the prevailing or dominant vocabulary of the other. Since communication is obviously the common denominator for both vocabularies, the similarities seem quite easily to outweigh the differences. What really unifies the divergent conceptualizations is the notion of exchange. As one writer contends, ". . . exchange forms the core phenomenon for study in marketing" and "The media of exchange are the vehicles with which people communicate to, and influence, others in the satisfaction of their needs."[9] Thus, as another scholar insightfully observes: "Any object or product is a form of communication . . ." and "our relationship with a product is a series of communications. . . ."[10] With the linkage of an activity or an idea to a product, this definition easily overlaps and even usurps the vocabulary of rhetoric and public address.

The dominant contemporary research paradigm in consumer research is located in the area of personal values. Those marketing scholars who are exploring, exploiting and expanding this area appear to be at the cutting edge of their discipline. This generalization, of course, is made by an outsider on the basis of only a cursory investigation of the number and frequency of related essays in the leading marketing journals dealing with this topic. Pitts and others, for example, consider ". . . personal values as a key consideration in using social marketing techniques to form and change attitudes." Their reasoning is that "Since values are conceived to underlie and determine attitudes and behavior, an appeal directed at values should lead to changes in attitudes and subsequently behavior."[11] And since values are assumed to influence consumer behavior, ". . . one may theorize," as Prakash and Munson do, "that values represent schemata for consumption decisions."[12] It is to this intriguing marketing research area that we now turn.

As a prelude to an investigation of the use and impact of values research on the topic of this essay, we must jump in advance, as it were, to the small end of the funnel to see what has emerged so far at the hands of the professional social marketers. The Wirthlin Group, which as we noted previously did research for Hill and Knowlton on the subject of abortion, has developed a research technique or program for measuring values. They call it VISTA or Values in Strategy Assessment. In an advertising flyer for potential clients, this technique is described as "an innovative, qualitative research program to help our clients understand, communicate with and

motivate their publics more effectively." It is further claimed that
The Wirthlin "experience has clearly shown that effective communication not only persuades with reason, but motivates by tapping
into personal values." Their approach is said to avoid traditional
methodologies that assess communication tactics and concentrate
instead on guiding "your overall communication strategy by uncovering the deeper values which drive all human behavior."

As already noted, a key concept in consumer research, and
one that will appear frequently in our analysis, is segmentation.
In this regard, one writer confesses: "The idea that all markets
can be profitably segmented has now received almost as widespread acceptance as the marketing concept itself."[13] Looking for
predictions to help agencies spend ad money more wisely, market
segmentation strives for a deeper understanding of people, i.e.,
those who consume products, services, or ideas. Presenting any
of the three in its most favorable light means communicating with
the consumer on his or her own terms. And what this also in
essence means is a basic benefits approach to audience analysis in
which products, services, or ideas can be positioned in the market more effectively. "[T]he crux of the problem of choosing the
best segmentation system," writes Haley, "is to determine which
has the greatest number of practical marketing implications."[14]
The shrewd marketing persuader then simply taps into a preexist-
ing benefit system to gain new insights about consumers.

Segmentation is an attempt to eliminate, suppress, or obviate
the confusion and unpredictability of the market place; it is an
attempt to adjust messages to audiences. A key question asked
through segmentation analysis is what are the special wants of
consumers or, more specifically, can these wants be determined
by product attributes? If as one writer notes "The word motivation refers to getting behavior started and giving it direction,"
then a segmented class is in reality a motivation class.[15] And as a
close corollary to this, the idea of how best to identify and satisfy
human wants becomes a search for "opportunity points" in marketing, which is another way to define segment benefits.[16]

With benefits marketing there is a shift in emphasis from the
message itself to the consumer of the message. The old definition
of directing "the flow of goods and services from producer to
consumer," a strictly linear flow, has shifted to a circular and interactive flow that emphasizes consumer needs or social goals.[17]

This ultimately sets the stage for a full blossoming of social marketing and focuses upon which approach to consumer analysis has the highest research and/or creative potential.

Sir Francis Galton once said that "the roadways of our minds are worn into very deep ruts."[18] These ruts, I think, are emblematic of the problems that face some of those in speech communication who are having trouble developing viable theories of persuasion for social movements. We seem to have become deeply grooved into thinking patterns that are sterile and beyond the real world of practical action. So far as such theories go, however, there appears to be some healthy activity in marketing management which has utilized advances in consumer research. What I have discovered in this area confirms my personal belief that important ideas are often generated by those who employ a hands-on approach to their disciplines. What I see now is that the practical world of consumer research can provide rhetoricians with theoretical tools that can possibly add to our understanding of the rhetoric of social movements.

A singular advantage of operating in the real world of communication problems instead of simply hypothesizing about them is that the wall-like ruts of discrete academic disciplines soon come tumbling down. The philosopher Karl Popper perhaps said it best when he dismissed the efficacy of academic studies or disciplines that are differentiated merely by the subject being investigated. According to Popper, these disciplines were originally distinguished in large part for reasons of administrative convenience. "But all this classification and distinction," he said, "is a comparatively unimportant and superficial affair. *We are not students of some subject matter but students of problems.* And problems may cut right across the borders of any subject matter or discipline"[19] (emphasis in citation).

Popper's commonsense message was made quite clear to me as I researched this essay. I choose to believe that it was because I opted to investigate how rhetorical decisions are made in the real world by living and striving communicators that quite possibly I have been able to see how we can extricate ourselves from some of the perceptual ruts we are in with regard to understanding the rhetoric of social movements. What is being done in social marketing management and consumer research holds, I think, an important conceptual key.

Understandably, value analysis really passes beyond psychographics. It has been termed one of the latest marketing tools "to achieve greater precision and effectiveness in market segmentation."[20] It is therefore to value analysis that we must now direct our attention in order to understand more completely the messages on abortion that have emanated from the Hill and Knowlton PR workshop. And in so doing we are compelled to take a close and critical look at the work of Milton Rokeach.

The leading writers on the subject of consumer values have devised a number of investigative approaches. Building on Rokeach's value survey (RVS) and Maslow's hierarchy of needs, Kahle and his associates have developed a list of values (LOV) to assist their consumer research. The values they cite are nine in number: self-respect, sense of accomplishment, being well respected, security, warm relationships with others, sense of belonging, fun and enjoyment in life, self-fulfillment, and excitement. According to Kahle, these values "were selected because of their applicability to all of life's major roles. . . ."[21] It is claimed that each of these values can predict or at least suggest an appropriate behavior.

What is intriguing about the Kahle approach is that it is sympathetic to Piaget's idea of transformation through adaptation to the environment. "Values and attitudes," asserts Kahle, "are abstractions about adaptation." Values differ from attitudes in that they have no objects. "Because the memory capacity of humans is not adequate to remember every instance of previous experience relevant to adaptation, abstractions such as attitudes and values are formed to summarize previous experience. . . ."[22] But what still remains largely unresolved is the correlation between attitudes and actions. This scholarly scandal is one of many that begs to be resolved.

Kahle's adaptive approach to values uncovers some serious shortcomings in the Maslow and Rokeach formulations. Maslow's hierarchy fails to consider the internal and external dimension in values.[23] Kahle claims also that his own LOV formulation relates more intimately to life's major roles such as marriage, parenting, etc. than does Rokeach's value survey.[24] Additionally, many of Rokeach's values "are not directly relevant in a consumer behavior context" (national security and world peace, for example).[25] Actually, to me, *both* the Maslow and Rokeach valuations seem much too arbitrarily drawn. It seems to stretch credulity to believe that there can be such a wide variance between two lists that supposedly all but exhaust the value spectrum. Does the universe of human values contain four or eighteen items? At best, to assign discrete and unimpeachable numbers seems a rather blatant and obviously inconclusive judgment call.

In the evolution of consumer research, it is important to bear in mind that the Rokeach value survey when actually used has had to undergo a pronounced metamorphosis, i.e., when packed into a consumer mold—a design for which it seems never to have been specifically intended. Rokeach appears to have devised his system not with consumerism in mind but as a scholarly project designed to help understand public opinion. It seems intended primarily as a tool in public opinion research and not as a marketing tool. To force it into a consumer mold, therefore, is to distort some of its better features and to go beyond its design parameters.

Perhaps the most innovative development in value research as applied to marketing practices is the work of Gutman and Reynolds. Their rather sophisticated theoretical framework places products and values at opposite sides of a means-end continuum. Even Kahle, an academic competitor of sorts, has something flattering to say about it. "Both their methodology and theory are enormously useful for marketers and others interested in understanding consumer behavior."[26] The Gutman-Reynolds methodology is the latest link in the evolutionary chain of value research prior to the adaptations of The Wirthlin Group. It will be worth our while to look at the latter more closely.

My investigation of this essay topic began in large part with a phone conversation I had with Mary Ellen Jensen, a senior research director of The Wirthlin Group. At the suggestion of Richard Doerflinger of the USCCB's Secretariat for Pro-life Activities, I contacted her regarding The Wirthlin approach to public opinion analysis for sensitive social issues like abortion. During our conversation she directed me to an essay that appeared in the *Journal of Advertising Research*.[27] This essay, I subsequently learned, lays out quite clearly the means-end chain model for consumer analysis. In it, products are no longer treated as objects but as integral parts of people's lives. The researcher concentrates upon the vital linkage between product and value system. In this way, advertising managers are given a powerful new tool in understanding consumers.

The key to or essence of the Gutman-Reynolds means-end chain research model is the linking of product attributes to consequences to personal values, otherwise known as ACV linkages. Starting with a Kelly Repertory Grid, a triadic sorting task uncovers "salient concepts used to discriminate (think about) the stimulus domain" or product.[28] Then using a sample size of 40 to 50 consumers, in-depth interviewing begins to construct a Hierarchical Value Map or HVM. This building block process is called "Laddering," and the result is the accumulation of 3 to 5 ladders from each person. These ladders are then consolidated to produce the HVM. (See diagram.)[29]

What is significant about this value mapping is that it "identifies not only the concepts . . . but the major (most frequent) interconnections. . . ."[30] It describes how a select group of subjects perceives the world as distilled by a particular product or focused by a particular social issue. Used properly, this research technique is said to be "an objective synthesis of what is essentially qualitative data,"[31] and thus it attempts "to bridge the gap between qualitative approaches that can't be quantified and the excessively quantitative models that lack depth of meaning."[32] With this hybrid bridging model, then, the consumer is profiled in relation to a particular stimulus domain.

The laddering process consists of a series of directed probes based on the distinctions uncovered by the triadic sorting technique. As can be seen from the sample, movement up the ladder shifts from what is product specific to what is essentially abstract. The initial distinctions elicited from contrasting three product brands become less brand specific as one moves up the ladder. Gutman and Reynolds point out that "The central idea is to keep the focus of the discussion on the person rather than on the product or service."[33] Using the question "Why is this important to you?" the researcher moves the queried individual from thinking about a product, service, or idea to thinking about the individual.

Results from laddering produce an HVM (or what some also call a value tree) summarizing all the interviews and supplying a panoramic view which can be "interpreted as representing dominant perceptual orientations."[34] As we noted, the rationale for this qualitative and quantitative analytic approach is that products, services, and ideas will be more readily purchased, pursued, or accepted if they are tied to human value structures. Basically, the

Hierarchical Structure Map for Hypothetical Airline Study

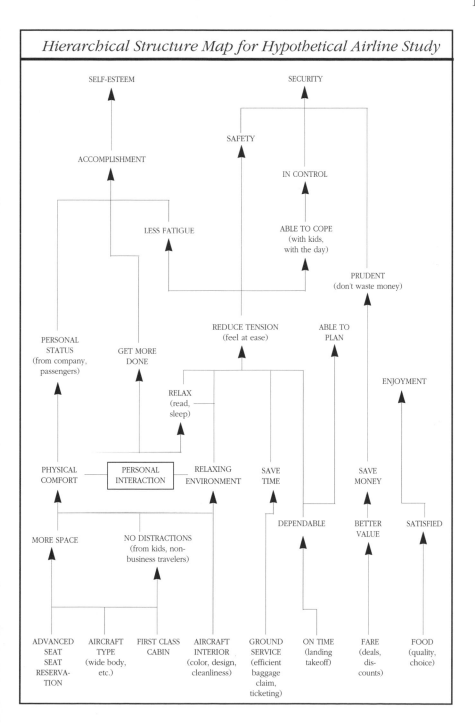

Gutman-Reynolds means-end model is a structuring process which can yield important insights for advertising creatives who can more readily tailor their messages to sensitive areas of the consumer's motivational world. As Gutman and Reynolds describe it, the HVM "can serve as a basis for: (1) segmenting consumers with respect to their values orientations for a product class or brand; (2) for assessing brands or products in a fashion similar to the use of more traditional ratings; (3) evaluating competitive advertising; and (4) as a basis for developing advertising strategies."[35]

It should be obvious just from this brief view of the means-end chain concept that there are a number of fundamental assumptions being made about consumer or audience behavior. Among these assumptions are that values actually do play a dominant role in guiding consumer choice, that values can be best defined in the Rokeachean fashion as desirable end states of human existence, and that consumers are generally not aware that this valuing is actually taking place. It is the job then of the researcher and creative to combine their efforts to determine how best to unlock and activate the motivational power of these unacknowledged end states. And, finally, the means-end chain model makes an assumption that one must understand the individual in isolation before groups or clusters of similarly situated individuals can be understood.

Since the means-end chain focuses upon "the linkages between where a person wants to be and the means chosen to get there,"[36] careful attention must obviously be directed to consequences, which Gutman defines as "a state of being produced by an act of consumption."[37] In this context the product, service, or idea becomes the cause or stimulus that produces the result, effect, or consequence. Gutman summarizes this key terminology with the following: "Values provide the overall direction, consequences select specific behaviors in specific situations, and attributes are what is in the actual products that produce the consequences."[38]

Gutman further defines his system by illustrating how advertising strategies can best be implemented. He posits five levels of tactical activity which he and Reynolds have labeled Means-End Conceptualization of Components for Advertising Strategy or MEC-CAS. A critical element of the strategizing is a leverage point which has the power to unify the entire message and conceptually to simplify it. The levels are (1) driving force, or the value to be appealed to or activated, (2) leverage point, or the key way in which values are linked to the product to provide a single theme, (3) execution-al framework, or the communication vehicle, ad Gestalt, or overall tone, style or plot, (4) consumer benefit, or the positive conse-quence to the recipient conveyed visually and verbally, and (5) message elements, or specific product features or attributes.[39]

One can thus detect a rather complete motivational system in the research efforts of Gutman and Reynolds. It is this system initially developed for products and services that has been utilized by The Wirthlin Group as a social marketing research tool. If good results can be obtained in the commercial marketing sphere, it is reasoned, why can't the same results be obtained in the social marketing arena? In other words, why can't the means-end model with its various strategic and tactical approaches be utilized to sell an idea?

Here we have a tentative answer to the Wiebe question posed earlier: "Why can't you sell brotherhood and rational thinking like you sell soap?" Judging from the present state of research capabili-ty and from what our brief survey of it has disclosed, the answer to the question is *yes*, you probably can. But this answer is tempered with yet another question: Is what we have discussed the best or only answer? In other words, have we gone far enough in our analysis of motivational possibilities, or do we stop here?

The answer to this last question, which we will pursue with vigor in the remainder of our analysis, is *no*; there are other effec-tive ways to generate motivational research data. We will begin with the suggestions of Durgee and end with some of my own. But first we must make some general observations about the rela-tionship between researchers and creatives. And then we will fin-ish by looking at some of the work produced by Hill and Knowl-ton in their contract with the U.S. Catholic Conference.

From the standpoint of a rhetorical analysis that focuses upon the message receiver, the function of the social marketing researcher is to enrich creative insight regarding the basic motiva-tions of the target audiences. They must zero in on or single out the best way to produce the most compelling message. As Durgee indicates, however, this is often difficult to do because "Creatives and researchers have different backgrounds, interests, and perspectives—subjective versus objective, art versus science, qualitative versus quantitative."[40] What is needed then is not just one approach but a combination of approaches that will tap into the richest possible reservoir of meanings. By "rich" Durgee means "that the findings are thought-provoking and that they communicate a lot of information in a parsimonious fashion."[41] "We assume that the work of the researcher," he concludes, "is to identify valid, new product meanings and that the work of the creative is to find novel ways to communicate these meanings."[42]

In explaining the available depth-interview techniques used in creative advertising, Durgee describes the laddering technique as having several weaknesses: (1) "it tends to ground findings in terms of standard perceptions," or what is currently on the market (which tends to produce what is known as "look alike" advertising which occurs when the creative is lulled into using the language of the HVM rather that imaginative alternatives); (2) "there is no certainty that respondents are able or willing to give true answers" (which implies that the researcher can be misled even with good intentions, as when, for example, a businessman justifies a preference for 1st class airplane accommodations, not because there is more room in which to work, but because there are free drinks); and (3) "the questions tend to produce an artificial set of answers" (which may easily be the case with low involvement products, services, and ideas, as when, for example, abortion means very little in some people's lives).[43]

The main criticism to the laddering technique is that it may not give much information about a message recipient's views that is very inspiring. (The cautious respondent gives only the tried and the true.) And without inspiration the creative may have to work overtime to produce something useful or effective. Durgee notes that in a book by Perkins dealing with the problem of creativity, what is prerequisite for the creative person is to immerse oneself in pertinent information about the problem. "Laddering does not appear to provide enough learning for this to happen."[44] Obviously, what the researcher needs is a variety of techniques that induce creativity.

After a lengthy criticism of "laddering," Durgee suggests that advertising creatives could profit by the information gathered by two other research techniques: Hidden Issue Questions (HIQ) and Symbolic Analysis (SA). The former attempts to uncover driving issues of deep personal concern. What is sought is not the socially shared values of the laddering technique but rather, those aggravating "sore spots," as Durgee puts it, in one's life. These include one's most captivating or troublesome hopes and dreams, the anxieties and preoccupations that often drive or circumscribe human conduct. But, of course, HIQ also has its problems. Probing sensitive issues like abortion, for example, requires considerable skill, and the analysis of the findings would obviously require a substantial amount of interpretation. Yet these burdensome drawbacks might be a minor and/or acceptable trade-off to the generation of some novel and highly imaginative campaign ideas.

Less psychoanalytic is the SA approach and one of, perhaps, greater value to those interested in communication. This depth-interview technique derives its core meaning from the research paradigm of cultural anthropologists like Claude Lévi-Strauss. Such anthropologists are said to investigate "the symbolic meanings of cultural artifacts and social structures by comparing them with their opposites."[45] These binary oppositions like Lévi-Strauss' "The Raw and the Cooked" can point to underlying thought structures that can be quite revealing. As every music record usually has a flipside, so also does every product, service, or idea. What, for example, would it be like not to use the product, service, or idea; what would be the attributes of their opposites; or what would be an opposite type of product such as an imaginary non-product, service, or idea. It was this type of symbolic thinking that led to 7-Up's highly successful ads featuring the so-called "Un-Cola."

What the Durgee criticism points out is that laddering simply may not go deep enough to uncover the kind of human motivation that can best assist the advertising creative in optimum fashion. If laddering is to be used, it should be employed with other techniques that in combination will provide maximum motivational insight. And this, it would appear, is as true for social marketing as it would be for commercial marketing for which the laddering technique was originally devised.[46] One important research technique, heretofore overlooked by social marketing researchers and speech communication theorists as well, that can point the way to deeper insight is cognitive developmentalism. It is to this relatively new research tool that we now turn.

Part II: Cognitive Moral Developmentalism

When this essay was first presented to a scholarly audience, the title of the convention panel in which it appeared was "Focus on Abortion: The Role of Public Relations in Guiding Social Discourse." The reader's attention is directed to this title because of its revealing genesis. It was really not the first nor is it the only title that was or could have been selected. The original working title after the colon was, "The Role of Public Relations in the Teaching of Virtue." I mention this because the difference between the two titles lies at the heart of what I think is wrong with the means-end research model used by The Wirthlin Group to provide target audience profiles to the Hill and Knowlton public relations agency. Quite simply, the use of hierarchical value mapping cannot reach its full potential unless it can somehow incorporate the process of moral decision making. For special persuasive problems, special motivational models are needed.

Developmental psychology tells us that moral decision making is a dynamic process that changes qualitatively as the individual traverses the human life span. Failure to recognize this empirically verifiable fact by those who hope to tap the wellsprings of human motivation in dealing with a moral issue is to lose sight of an important characteristic of the human being as a persuadable animal. In short, as helpful as a knowledge of terminal values may be, the social marketing researcher should not lose sight of the fact that these values are treated in the literature as givens or eternal verities. As Rokeach himself puts it ". . . to say that a person 'has a value' is to say that he has an enduring belief that a particular mode of conduct or that a particular end-state of existence is personally and socially preferable to alternative modes of conduct or end-states of existence."[47] What is significant about this definition is that we are left without any knowledge about how the individual arrives at such desirable end states. They have no past but arise full blown, as it were, from the head of Zeus.

Not only does a means-end approach to social marketing analysis fail to recognize the inherently dynamic nature of values, it also fails to make a basic distinction between values which are moral and values which are non-moral. And what this leads to is a seriously confused and watered down understanding of what morality really is. In short, a knowledge of moral reasoning is critical to understanding an issue like induced human abortion. No matter how much we might wish to avoid the matter by disguising the term with euphemisms like social discourse, what we are really talking about is the guiding of moral discourse. And this, in turn, essentially boils down in a classic sense to the teaching of virtue. What, for example, does Rokeach's "a world of beauty" or "a sense of accomplishment" have to do with morality? If we define ethics as the study of morality and morality as the acceptable rules of interpersonal behavior, then the abortion question is at its core unmistakably a moral question. For a social marketer to overlook this uncomplicated fact is to lose a valuable research insight.

Nearly a decade ago, I wrote a book about abortion which deals directly with the dynamics of moral decision making. In this book, which is part of a proposed trilogy exploring the rhetoric of social movements, I attempted to apply a cognitive developmental model to the pervasive moral facets of the abortion controversy. My research led me to the work of Piaget and Kohlberg, both of whom addressed the problem of moral growth.[48]

In 1932, Jean Piaget, the Swiss child psychologist, who considered himself a genetic epistemologist, wrote a book about the moral growth of children.[49] This was a significant departure from his normal research in that it dealt with how maturing humans perceive the socio-emotional world or the world of subjects. Piaget's typical work, of course and in contrast, dealt mainly with how humans perceive the physical world or the world of objects. The Sage of Geneva concluded that a cognitive core ran through both perceptions. In his pioneering study involving the moral judgments of children, Piaget traced this cognitive core through qualitative changes in patterns of thought regarding the virtue of justice. He discovered that there were three dominant stages which each human must traverse in order to mature morally.

A generation after Piaget's path-breaking investigations, a graduate student at the University of Chicago named Lawrence Kohlberg began in his doctoral thesis to elaborate the original Piagetian hypothesis. Kohberg, in what became the beginning of a classic longitudinal study of moral growth, concluded that there was indeed an invariant sequence to moral growth. Using the virtue of justice as a centralizing concept, he expanded and refined the Piagetian scheme into a six stage sequence. In over eighty scholarly essays he explained his system and claimed for it extensive cross cultural support. It is this moral developmental system that a decade ago I used to illuminate the rhetoric of the abortion controversy. Although space precludes here a detailed description of my analysis, a brief description of it may nonetheless enable the reader to compare and contrast it with the means-end model currently employed by social marketing researchers.

A fundamental characteristic of my motivational model in contrast to the Gutman-Reynolds means-end approach is that my model relies upon the empirically based and common sense idea that humans grow into their values—or at least into the value and virtue of justice. What is striking about the RVS, however, is that neither the terminal nor the instrumental values mention specifically the value of justice. Rokeach does posit a world of peace terminal value, but fails to posit its indispensable and inseparable corollary—the search for justice. In this regard there appears to be considerable wisdom in Pope John Paul II's observation "If you want peace, work for justice." The two ends, I would argue, are inextricably related. The Rokeach terminal and instrumental value scales fail to recognize this inherent connection. If, as Rokeach suggests, a value is "an enduring belief that a particular end-state of existence is personally and socially" (and, I might add, rationally) preferable to alternative modes of conduct or end-states, then surely the value and virtue of justice could and should be included in such a definition.

As a desired end state, most people, I think, would prefer to live in a world governed by a vigorous pursuit of justice. Such a pursuit, at least for America, is clearly spelled out in the Pledge of Allegiance: ". . . one nation under God, with freedom and justice for all." In fact, the quintessential American creed seems to be wholly oriented, at least in an ideal sense, to that enduring human value. If this indeed be true, it seems remarkable that the means-end motivational model based upon the Rokeach value list which is used by social marketers omits any direct consideration of the motivational power of the natural human desire for a society governed by justice. To meet this objective, what the means-end model needs is an infusion of cognitive moral developmentalism. Researchers can begin this process by considering values as end states that have a developmental history.

In my book analyzing the rhetoric of abortion, I used the developmental characteristics of justice to evaluate those arguments that represent how the individual views the moral world. In other words, I purposely did not consider the question of when human life begins, which is primarily a scientific question and, considered in isolation, is devoid of moral significance. It is only when one decides to do something about this unborn entity that the question of morality really enters the picture. This, of course, would obviously follow from our previous definition of morality as behavior that focuses upon how one treats others. It seems quite obvious that not to include the virtue of justice as a moral value or attribute is to play games with common sense.

As a neo-Kohlbergian, I have found his developmental system to be ideal in isolating the dominant moral arguments in the abortion debate. The only modification I have made to this system is in changing it from a diachronic to a synchronic one or from a motion picture to a snapshot. And this change can be seen dramatically in a changed set of labels for the major and minor developmental categories. In my modified system Kohlberg's levels and stages become, correspondingly, phases and modes. This substitution allowed me to freeze the Kohlbergian dynamism. Briefly stated, these revised synchronic categories are Phase I, the personal, Phase II, the social, and Phase III, the rational.

Applied to the abortion question, Phase I which begins the cognitive developmental enterprise is divided into two modes of moral discourse: Mode 1, Punishment and Mode 2, Pleasure. These two modes taken together are roughly equivalent to stick and carrot, penalty and reward, disincentive and incentive, as actuators of moral conduct. This suggests that humans begin to act in a moral way by contemplating in a somewhat crude manner both losses and profits, both negatives and positives. As we grow morally, we humans act first to avoid punishment and only then do we feel free to act in accord with the pursuit of pleasure. Both perspectives, of course, are intensely personal and initiated out of fear.

At Phase II the moralizer shifts his or her perspective on justice from a personal to a social sense. And as in the previous phase this again is accomplished in two modes: Mode 3, Peer Pressure and Mode 4, Law and Order. These modes by implication assume the existence of a significant other in determining the content of moral relationships. This significant other at Phase II generates a genuine social sensitivity. At Mode 3 the social awareness helps create a concern for what others think about one's moral activities, while at Mode 4 the social awareness is broadened to include a preference for whatever can keep the social scene in balance. As a result, justification for these patterns of moral reasoning stems, in large part, from an attempt to avoid shame, the controlling emotion of Phase II.

Phase III departs radically from the previous two phases in that the driving force of emotion is replaced by that of the rational. This means that fear and shame give way to guilt and that psychology gives way to philosophy as a source of justification. Modes 5 and 6 clearly indicate this preference for the rational. Mode 5, Utility and Contract, is characterized by due process, while Mode 6, Principle, is characterized by a reliance on universal standards of moral behavior. At Phase III there is less allowance for contrary patterns of moral reasoning because action choices eventually become restricted to a single choice. And this is particularly true with Mode 6.

Obviously, such a highly abbreviated sketch of the moral developmental system leaves out much detail. But as soon as one gains a sufficient grasp of the Kohlbergian paradigm, it is relatively easy to see major characteristics of a developmental progression. On the low side of the upward maturational spiral or at one end of the developmental continuum, to employ a pair of useful metaphors, one will encounter a movement from egocentrism to sociocentrism, from external to internal constraint, from action that is heteronomous and dependent to action that is autonomous and independent, from unilateral decisions based on consequence to interdependent decisions based on intention, from concrete and specific to abstract and general, and finally, from the immature and irresponsible to the mature and responsible. The resulting progression shows that when the moral reasoner moves up the maturational spiral or travels from one end of the developmental continuum to the other, the reasoner's chances of solving complex moral problems increases markedly. The Kohlbergian system strongly suggests that it is only when unsullied principle is vigorously pursued that unresolved problems are truly eliminated. And this is why Mode 6 moral reasoners represent such a considerable deviation from the norm and are so few.

Since the abortion debate in America as presently argued is overwhelmingly conventional in its motivational characteristics, it would be worthwhile to focus our attention on Phase II of the Kohlbergian cognitive developmental scheme. A little reflection shows why most of the contending patterns of moral reasoning in the abortion controversy take place within a matrix of intense social preoccupations. Consider Mode 3, Peer Pressure, for example. It takes little imagination to see the emergence of bandwagon propagandizing when either side to the dispute parades polling data before the public. In moral developmental terms what this says to the uncommitted is that when a decision is made, join the winning side. And assuming that no one likes to be left behind, the psychic pressure might well be decisive in orienting one's moral reasoning.

Mode 4, the Law and Order mode, taps an even greater reservoir of motivational impulse. In fact, a strong case could be made that it is here where most of the current moral argument about abortion takes place. The very presence of abortion clinic demonstrations and counter demonstrations throws the debate rather quickly into the realm of law and order. With the assumption that no one but the anarchist really enjoys social disharmony, threats by both sides to create social disruption are enough to make even the most rigidly indifferent take notice.

When the debate over abortion began in earnest over twenty-five years ago, the moral reasoning frequently advanced by those who favored relaxation of the abortion laws was that in the face of so many illegal abortions taking place, the nation's legal system was being seriously flouted. The pro-abortion suggestion was that if all abortions were made legal, there would no longer be a legal-illegal disparity. Legal chaos can be averted when there is a consistency between what is lawful and what is practiced. "Don't rock the boat" and "slow and steady win the race" are proverbial manifestations of this thinking pattern. Kohlbergian scholars consider law and order moralizing to be modal for western culture.

American cinema and television reflect the conventional in moral reasoning. To comprehend this, one need only peruse the number of new summer releases from the celluloid capital of the world. Most of them seem to have a dominant law and order theme. And to drive home the point, the new fall TV listings and so-called prime time oldies for 1991–92 show an abundant preoccupation with law and order reasoning: Heat of the Night, Matlock, Quantum Leap, Unsolved Mysteries, MacGyver, Top Cops, Good and Evil, FBI, The Untold Stories, American Detective, America's Most Wanted, Cagney and Lacey, Miami Vice, Hill Street Blues,

The Young Riders, Cops, The Commish—need the list be extended? American culture resonates like some gigantic tuning fork to whatever protects the innocent and brings the guilty to justice. (Even vigilantism is a law and order theme.) I submit that in a general sense the cultural evidence is overwhelming, that we are indeed immersed in a sea of law and order thinking. In the 1988 presidential election the law and order saga of Willie Horton rode this mentality all the way to the White House.

Now I would like to share with the reader a cognitive developmental interpretation of some of the educational materials generated by the Hill and Knowlton public relations effort. The samples I have selected are advertisements appearing in the pages of *Columbia* magazine, the official publication of the Knights of Columbus. With a circulation of nearly a million and a half, the potential impact of these materials cannot be taken lightly. I will consider the first five visuals to have appeared in successive issues starting with July and ending with November of 1991. Without being judgmental regarding the quality of these visuals or their potential success or failure, we will consider each in detail.

At first glance, some of the visuals seem more religiously oriented than others in that scripture is quoted. This distinction was made because Hill and Knowlton attempted to create two distinct visual types—one that would appeal primarily to the religiously oriented and the other to more secular viewers. In an instructional sheet to the users, Hill and Knowlton suggested that the religious visuals be used (1) in diocesan newspapers as display ads, (2) as display ads in bulletins and newsletters, (3) as posters or placards to be used in parish and school environments and at meetings and rallies, and (4) as handouts, flyers, and brochures. It was further suggested that the more secular visuals be used in daily and/or weekly newspapers, in mass transit ads, on billboards, etc. Those secular visuals, however, could also serve double duty and be used in religious settings as well. By parcelling out usage in this manner, much of the cost is spread throughout the Catholic diocesan system. And in this way exposure is maximized while cost is minimized.

In comparing the visuals there are some commonalities that need mentioning. The first commonality is the campaign slogan "The Natural Choice Is Life." This slogan was market tested by The Wirthlin Group after its creation in a brainstorming session at

Visual 1

"Anyone who welcomes the little child
in my name, welcomes Me."

Matthew 18:5

1.6 MILLION ABORTIONS A YEAR CAN'T BE RIGHT.

The Natural Choice is Life.

For more information, or if you wish to help the Church provide alternatives to abortion,
please contact your Diocesan pro-life director.

Scripture From The Jerusalem Bible

Visual 2

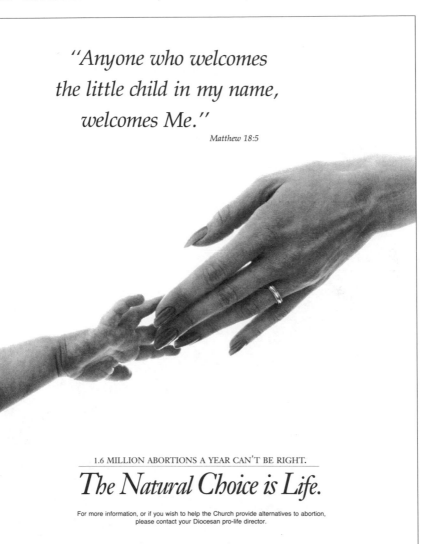

Visual 3

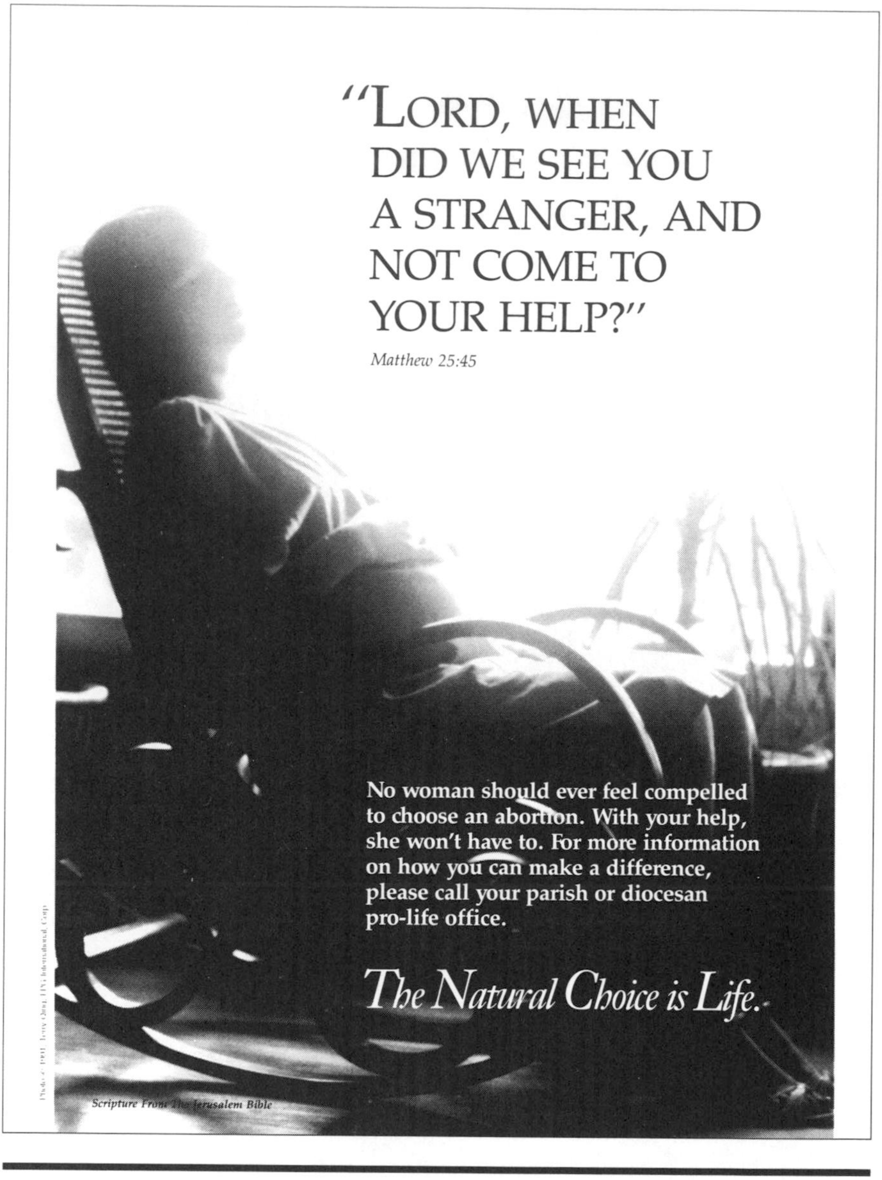
"LORD, WHEN DID WE SEE YOU A STRANGER, AND NOT COME TO YOUR HELP?"
Matthew 25:45
No woman should ever feel compelled to choose an abortion. With your help, she won't have to. For more information on how you can make a difference, please call your parish or diocesan pro-life office.
The Natural Choice is Life.
Scripture From The Jerusalem Bible

Visual 4

To be or not to be
THAT is the question.

The Natural Choice is Life.

For more information, or if you wish to help the Church provide alternatives to abortion,
please contact your Diocesan pro-life director.

Visual 5

Hill and Knowlton. I think it would be possible to see in this slogan an attempt to take back or reconstitute the idea of choice that
has been used so effectively by those who favor abortion. The
word "nature," of course, should resonate well with those who
are conscious about or sensitive to preserving the environment.
This theme would appear to be well adapted to both secular and
religious audiences. But the word "natural" may cut more than
one way. Although it may be a flag word for environmentalists, it
may also be a red flag word for Catholics and their critics. "Natural" might turn on Catholics and turn off others who don't like the
implied association with the idea of natural family planning which
is often confused with rhythm. This mixed message, therefore,
might stimulate some market segments while neglecting or alien-
ating others.

Mode 4 moral reasoning has become a powerful magnet for
attracting considerable anti-abortion argumentation. Visual 1 for
July 1991 is a good example. It employs a picture collage of
endangered species with the caption "Some life is protected . . .
and some isn't." The protected life is obviously symbolized by the
wild animals, while the unprotected life is symbolized in the
lower right corner by a fetal child sucking its thumb. The picture
of the fetus *in utero* is a classic by Lennart Nilsson which has
become quite popular in the visual armamentarium of the pro-life
movement. In Kohlbergian terms this is definitely Mode 4 Law
and Order reasoning. Blatant inconsistencies in legal treatment
are almost always indicative of some kind of cultural disorder. Psychological harmony is likewise disrupted when equal categories
are treated unequally. Also implied is an example of *a fortiori*
reasoning: If these lesser creatures need protection, then all the
more reason to protect the more favored human creature.

Visual 2 employs a compelling picture of Mother Teresa holding a baby. The contrast between young and old adds a certain
dramatic impact—an impact that is intensified by the baby's soft
cheeks and the gnarled hands and lined face of Mother Teresa.
The juxtaposed combination suggests innocence and saintliness—
a combination that is synergetic. This is definitely Mode 3 Peer
Pressure because the commanding presence of Mother Teresa
invites imitation or modeling. Moralizers at this mode wish to be
well thought of and so would likely identify with universally
admired people. Mother Teresa becomes an archetype of what

many would like to become (at least vicariously). Her public persona becomes a powerfully condensed version of an opinion survey, suggesting the human ideal or the collective yearning of humanity. Mother Teresa has become a moral exemplar not only in Judeo-Christian culture but in world culture—a truth that is perhaps somewhat marred by the biblical quotation from Matthew 18:5—"anyone who welcomes the little child in my name, welcomes Me." Arguably, this reference could have been left out to reach perhaps a wider and more secular audience. The "Saint of Calcutta" is everybody's saint.

Yet it could also just as well be argued, and I think with some force, that the use of Mother Teresa as an exemplar could actually be counterproductive. In fact, it might be argued that Mother Teresa's transcendent image could even reinforce inactivity among those who only lukewarmly support the pro-life ideology. Her image might seem beyond the reach of mere mortals or, at best, fearfully inaccessible to the average person. Furthermore, it could be argued that more ordinary people would probably find it much easier to identify with "just plain folks" than with some kind of stand-in saint. Someone of sound character with lofty ideals who appears as a friend or neighbor might well be a better candidate for iconic emulation. In short, there seems to be little if anything in Visual 2 that could counteract or prevent a person's natural inclination not to become overtly involved in the rather bothersome demands of a social movement. Anything more than a tepid involvement might seem only for the saintly or the already anointed. Such rationalizing, of course, is simply the flip side of a spiritual cop out—of letting George do it. Why bother to get involved when such potent saintliness is on our side?

Visual 3 is a subtle exposition of Mode 4 Law and Order moralizing. And here the biblical quotation actually enhances the effect. Again, Matthew 18:5 is cited. There is drama here with the juxtaposition of mother and child—of hands that are new and hands that are not so new. Here is a visually arresting example of one person reaching out to another. The symbiosis of mother and child, or parent and offspring, suggests a little of Michelangelo's act of creation in the Sistine Chapel.

The relationship between the two actors in Visual 3, an example of synecdoche, has been ratified through the convention of matrimony. The woman's wedding ring proclaims this quite vividly.

There is nothing illegitimate here. Everything seems to partake of accepted social practice. Traditional roles and norms are fulfilled when children are born in wedlock. In another context the hands might well have been used to advertise a gentle skin care product, but within a moral setting there is a fulfillment of social expectations. Even though the mother's hands are clearly idealized with their careful manicure and would hardly be typical of the average mother of four with a lot of housework, still the band of silver or gold speaks volumes, making this an accepted Judeo-Christian law and order appeal. This visual is most definitely Mode 4.

Unlike the others, Visual 4 in some respects represents a special case with special problems. It conveys its message primarily by print and not by picture. And the print messages include more than one distinct mode of moral discourse. The picture itself portrays in hazy shades of black and white a pregnant woman in a rocking chair in an attitude of peaceful repose. She gently cradles her swollen abdomen with both hands while looking dreamily into the middle distance. Her thoughts are unknown but suggest something motherly and protective. All this represents more than personal satisfaction; the mother shows concern for the other in anticipation of the future. Already, maternal bonding appears to be taking place.

The printed messages in Visual 4 suggest two modes of moral discourse: Mode 3 and Mode 5. The passage from scripture (Matthew 25:45) which dominates the visual is clearly Mode 3 in sentiment. "Lord, when did we see you a stranger, and not come to Your help?" imposes on the moralizing viewer the attractive role of "good boy, nice girl"—a Kohlbergian way of conveying the subtleties of peer pressure. The implication is I will help the unborn stranger because that is the proper Christian response. In a very important way, however, this message appears to be strangely out of synch with a visual that largely conveys serenity and contentment. Visual 4 does not portray a pregnant woman in distress and so contradicts the written message which suggests someone in need.

Yet Visual 4 exhibits more than what is expected through peer pressure or psycho-social restraints. What it also suggests is the possibility of alternative ways of coping with problem pregnancies. A subtheme speaks directly to this possibility: "No woman should ever feel compelled to choose an abortion. With your help, she won't have to." Such information goes beyond simple maintenance of the status quo which one expects to see at Mode 4; it implies the possibility of another, albeit unspecified, way of handling a problem. This treatment, though muted, is clearly Mode 5 and is the most advanced moral theme developed in the five visuals. Unfortunately, Mode 5 is not where the largest audience segment would likely be. Promoting alternatives is a rational approach to moral decision making which is probably beyond the moralizing capability of most individuals. And when such an appeal does appear in the other visuals it is merely suggested—almost as an afterthought—in the directives for obtaining more information.

A poorly developed moral theme may well be what is wrong with Visual 4, but it points to something that is also wrong with all the visuals, including the one we have yet to discuss. None of them provide an adequate channel to facilitate the desired behavior. Wiebe in his classic study cited earlier advocated the expenditure of a minimum amount of energy to consummate the behavioral goal. Accordingly, he advocated the shortest possible distance between the receiver and the activating mechanism, which in this case is the diocesan pro-life director. The visuals fail to specify didactically not only what needs to be done but also an immediate response channel. Considerable time and effort could be saved with an 800 number to refer interested parties to the appropriate diocesan director. When the public relations campaign gets in high gear, this would appear to be mandatory.

Visual 5 might well have saved the most persuasive appeal for the last. In a dramatic reversal of emphasis, this visual brings the ad sequence to a close. And what is really different about it is that while the first four tended to place the moral world in the foreground, Visual 5 by emphasizing the human characteristics of the unborn places the physical world in the foreground. Thus, the strictly moral is held in abeyance, if not relegated entirely to the background. The reader should note especially how the small picture that originally appeared in the lower right corner of the first visual now consumes over half of the display area of this last visual. Does it not seem fairly obvious what the message makers were trying to accomplish?

The picture tells the viewer that the object of abortion is unmistakably human. The fetus/child sucks its thumb. Its tiny fingers seem perfectly formed and, upon close inspection, peachfuzz-like facial hair appears to be growing above the eyes and nose. These characteristics, too obvious to ignore, suggest to the viewer a rather advanced stage of human development. To any unbiased viewer, such ocular evidence could be decisive in promoting a strong anti-abortion sentiment. More than anything, Visual 5 celebrates the dynamic power of sight in fashioning a persuasive appeal.

Visual 5 also serves as a fitting climax or capstone to the ad series. A famous literary allusion dominates the visual and focuses the abortion issue compellingly. The humanity of the unborn is ratified with perhaps one of the most memorable statements in world literature—the opening lines of Hamlet's soliloquy. In what has become a signature of Shakespeare's genius, we see the fragility of human existence and the stark, uncompromising nature of being and nonbeing—of being and nothingness. How apt is its use in the abortion debate where absolutes of black and white predominate! Even the nuance of typography (the capitalization of the relative pronoun) is evocative and helps attach the quotation's sentiment unmistakably to the abortion issue. So appropriate is the quotation that it could be applied to a fetus/child at any stage of development. The application in this instance, of course, is perfectly arbitrary, but from the pro-life perspective—perfectly apt.

Finally, Visual 5 as a bona fide think piece comes the closest of all the visuals to the purely philosophical. When illuminated and ratified by one of the world's great playwrights, the issue of abortion takes on added significance. Hamlet's brooding question permeates the visual and lingers in the viewer's mind. It cuts to the heart of what it means to be faced with unyielding choices of life and death and reduces the abortion debate to its essence. In Visual 5, quotation and picture become synergetic to sanction the pro-life struggle.

Reviewing the five visuals presented for analysis, there is a minor theme that requires comment. Immediately above the official secretariat slogan, in the first three visuals, there appears the statement "1.6 million abortions a year can't be right." The similarity in typographical size provides a certain continuity. Appended to the very end of the sentence, in almost Ciceronian style, the word "right" throws the statement into the moral realm with a special vehemence. As if borrowed from some word box in central casting, this compelling assertion is stock law and order think-

ing that has been used for years by the American pro-life movement. It was market tested several years before the creatives at
Hill and Knowlton rediscovered it. In 1985 Command Research
concluded for the National Right of Life Committee (NRLC) by
means of extensive polling that a sizable segment of the public—
some 62%—would be opposed to abortion if they knew that
4,000 abortions were performed every day in the United States.
This daily figure was shown to be slightly more compelling than
either 1 1/2 million per year or the notion that 1/3 of all pregnancies end in abortion. (Parenthetically, these statistics also mean
166 abortions per hour, nearly three per minute, and almost nine
by the time it takes to read this paragraph.)

The significance of this subordinate theme (it does not
appear in all the visuals) should be neither underestimated nor
understressed. Too much or too little of something, an excess or
a scarcity, depicts a situation that is unharmonious, that is out of
synch with social expectation. A society that experiences significant imbalances (especially those imbalances which might involve
its offspring) is a society that many would likely consider to be in
disequilibrium. This mode of moral discourse has been evident
throughout the abortion controversy and now dominates much of
the current rhetoric.

Summary and Conclusions

This essay has been an attempt to provide an account of how
public relations can guide social discourse. Using the abortion
topic as a content area, we have placed the commissioned public
relations effort of Hill and Knowlton within the context of social
marketing. And from there we looked closely at the primary communication models used by the social marketers. In doing so it
was found that the consumer segmentation favored by social marketers now relies heavily upon value analysis. We then examined
the Gutman-Reynolds model of value mapping and observed that
limitations of the model appeared significant enough to warrant a
rethinking of the overall approach. A cognitive moral developmental model was thereupon advanced to provide a supplement
or viable alternative. The explanatory power of the new model
was seen in its ability to evaluate materials produced for the
Catholic Church in its continuing campaign to restrict induced
human abortion in America.

Although on the surface this essay has been an attempt to help explain the role of public relations in guiding social discourse, the essayist has shamelessly pursued a secondary agenda which by now should be clearly apparent. The topic has provided him an opportunity to advance a theory of social discourse that should help society to understand and solve some of its most complex and intractable moral problems, particularly those that deal with biomedical ethics. And since specialized issues like abortion demand specialized insights, the following conclusions are offered as suggestions for further rhetorical analysis.

In general, rhetoricians should learn to use the language of the social marketer as a basis for an improved audience analysis. And both can use with considerable profit the segmentation scheme offered by cognitive moral developmentalism. The Kohlbergian paradigm provides a psychic profile of the moral decision maker that can be used profitably in the many controversies in biomedical ethics, including infanticide and euthanasia. As each side to these disputes tries to position its ideology in order to capture the largest segment of the psychological market place, it will be of great help for social marketers and other rhetoricians to study the efficacy of cognitive moral developmentalism in channeling human motivation into acceptable public acts.

When viewed as an important mediating force in the abortion debate, what the cognitive moral developmental paradigm can provide is a potentially useful research technique for determining the contour of the social marketplace. In the marketplace of ideas a competitive edge is given to those ideas that are tailored to appropriate market segments. And in the hands of a skilled interpreter, the modes of moral discourse can become potent criteria for general consumer segmentation and idea positioning.

While values research may be important in segmenting consumers in social marketing, its limitations with respect to moral reasoning should also be acknowledged. It is worth remembering that none of the value categories discussed in this essay actually contain optimally useful moral components, because none of them describe in any detail socially interactive threats to life, liberty, or the pursuit of happiness which are at the heart of moral decision making in America. It is not enough simply to treat products and ideas as parts of people's lives instead of as mere objects; we must go one step further and also make these products and ideas an integral part of people's moral lives. With hope, it should become a commonplace in social marketing research or in studies involving the rhetoric of social movements that issues possessing a direct and intrinsic moral core can be fleshed out more completely when a cognitive developmental model is applied to them. One inevitable conclusion to be drawn from all this, then, is that more flesh can and should be put on psychographic bones.

One of the chief defects of current values research is that such research does not really measure the maturational level of values. When the writer was in graduate school there was an old maxim in quantitative research analysis to the effect that if anything exists in nature, it exists to some degree and can be measured. The best way so far to measure degrees of moral reasoning is through a deepening comprehension of qualitative moral transformations across the human life span. The values analyses of Rokeach and others alone are incapable of doing this but must be assisted by an appropriate moral developmental perspective. Values provide a background or general climate for moral decision making which, in turn, is the indispensable process for maintaining those values. With questions like abortion and other issues with a distinct moral component, behavior is more effectively driven not by a set of permanent end states but by the appropriate mode of moral discourse adapted to the appropriate audience or market segment.

It seems to this writer beyond dispute that those who wish to apply a rhetorical analysis to moral issues must be prepared to take viable theories as starting points before applying them to given cases. And one viable theory is cognitive moral developmentalism. It is a grounded theory generated from qualitative as well as quantitative research data—a theory that can be further developed while it is being utilized. If viable theories do not frame the rhetorical analysis, then social marketers dealing with moral questions will be increasingly victimized by the allure of social gadgetry and the imperialism of facile statistical methodologies. It therefore needs restating that, in the realm of biomedical ethics, rhetorical analyses must be anchored to viable theories such as cognitive moral developmentalism.

The writer wishes to claim neither too much nor too little for his preferred theory. Optimally, it should be viewed not as a substitute but as a supplement to existing segmentation research techniques. And since no simple system may be best for all creative situations, the lead question still remains: What system provides the most congenial framework for creatives in advertising and public relations? It is the writer's firmly held conviction that a cognitive developmental structure may well provide the most heuristic atmosphere for creative endeavor that attempts to resolve serious moral problems. With suitable modifications, the Kohlbergian system can provide a regenerating environment for PR creatives. Again, the lead question remains: If more psychological input produces more creative output, then what system or systems best supports the creative process?

To expand the scope of audience analysis, social marketers and social movement activists must become trained facilitators in the cognitive moral discovery process. This process will place issues like abortion at their deepest and most comprehensive psychographic level. To use a well worn medical designation, cognitive developmental rhetoricians working in the moral sphere are really clinicians or midwives when they apply this innovative scientific construct to an important bioethical issue.

But in a larger and more compelling sense, the overriding metaphor governing our discussion is really that of scout or pathfinder. For in assessing the role of public relations in guiding social discourse, we are forced to ask the ultimate question: Who or what shall guide those who guide others in such hazardous terrain in such trying circumstances? Some will likely say that an ironclad system of professional ethics should be the guide. I will, of course, agree but also add that an equally important approach is to study how the human intellect processes moral information.

One final observation remains. In essence, the purpose of this essay was not to assess the overall effectiveness of the Hill and Knowlton ad campaign. Rather it was to examine the communication model on which that campaign was based. Neither Hill and Knowlton, nor its client, the U.S. Catholic Conference, should be held entirely accountable for what may have transpired. Their joint venture into social marketing was plagued from the start by mitigating circumstances. On the one hand, the Catholic Church was entering virgin territory (a virtual *terra incognita*),[50] while, on the other hand, Hill and Knowlton, even as a full-service PR agency, could not really bring its best talent to bear on the task at hand. As we noted earlier, there is a world of difference between major skills needed by a successful PR program and those demanded by a successful advertising campaign. Advocacy advertising is a specialty that requires peculiar talents that PR agencies may not possess.

More appropriate to the thesis of this essay, however, is the cautionary tale of some recent scholarship that questions the very efficacy of advertising. Social marketers who use advertising would be well advised to make sure that their advertising actually works. According to Syracuse University professor John Philip Jones, who was a senior executive at the J. Walter Thompson agency for nearly 25 years, more than half of the $75 billion spent annually on advertising in America is actually wasted. Advertising, he claims, perpetuates waste when clients are encouraged to continue investing money in campaigns that are not proven to work. "If people are going to spend serious amounts of money on advertising," he suggests, "they should spend serious amounts of money to evaluate it." To help counteract such waste, he urges the ad industry to learn more about the creative process. "We know terribly little about how creative ideas are generated," he says. "It's an enigma surrounded by mystery."[51]

In the final analysis, creativity is really what this essay is all about. The writer's contribution to unravelling the creative mystery is to bring to the reader's attention insights concerning the object of creativity's goal in social marketing which can be no less than truly successful mass persuasion. This essay has been built on the premise that PR creativity in the form of advocacy advertising functions best when those who create it are supplied with the best available information about how moral choices are made and moral discourse is conducted.

In a 1947 movie starring Jimmy Stewart as an ad agency pollster, *Magic Town* was thought to be the ideal American community which at that time most accurately reflected the actual makeup of the nation as a whole. Such a town was obviously a convenient illusion but which nonetheless contained important elements of the real world. To extend this allegory to what we have discussed, if *Magic Town* today can be made to come to grips with complex moral issues like abortion, then the research road that helps us get there becomes doubly important. And while we are looking for that yellow brick road, we might find it in the vicinity of cognitive moral developmentalism. This road to rhetorical knowledge just might contain rich dividends for audience analysis and fresh insights for those in public relations who are asked to create compelling moral messages.

Appendix

Social Marketing

The initial shape of a substantial answer to the Wiebe thesis about the merchandising of ideas first appeared in 1971 in an essay titled "Social Marketing: An Approach to Planned Social Change." The authors, Philip Kotler and Gerald Zaltman, were two marketing specialists who in their revealing essay placed the notion of social change within the framework of marketing management which Kotler described as examining "the wants, attitudes, and behavior of potential customers which could aid in designing a desired product and in merchandising, promoting, and distributing it successfully" (p. 4). While contending that there is really no general agreement on the basic meaning of marketing, the authors established a case for including the concept of social marketing as a vital aspect of a broadened view of marketing.

Kotler and Zaltman contend that "the application of the logic of marketing to social goals is a natural development" (p. 3) or, one might say, an integral part of the evaluation of the total marketing concept. The authors couched their new concept in the following definition: "Social marketing is the design, implementation, and control of programs calculated to influence the acceptability of social ideas and involving considerations of product planning, pricing, communication, distribution, and marketing research" (p. 5). Thus, the concept of social marketing (SM) officially appeared in the academic literature and became recognized as a promising new research area.

Nearly a decade later, in the early 1980's, SM became even more refined with the introduction of a theory of market segmentation by objectives. If social products are to be sold effectively, an attempt must be made to apply consumer segmentation strategies. As Fine indicated in his June 1980 essay in the *Journal of Consumer Research*: "Because markets are heterogeneous, an early step in marketing strategy is to segment the market so that product design and campaign planning may be better individualized" (p. 2). With this essay, the idea of SM is effectively thrown into the domain of consumer research.

It takes little imagination to link the concepts of SM and consumer research with the study of human motivation, of mass persuasion, and, ultimately, with the rhetoric of social movements. Because, as Fennel notes, "a motivational analysis of behavior addresses the conditions under which behavior is activated, triggered, aroused, or instigated" (p. 24) and "is the identification of the conditions that activate brand purchase," (p. 25) consumers of ideas are obviously audiences who decide the outcome of social issues on the basis of successful campaigns of mass persuasion. This fact must not be forgotten in determining the role of public relations in guiding social discourse, particularly that which surrounds controversial topics.

The pervasiveness of SM in today's world can be seen in the large number of issues that have been treated by public service advertising. The print and broadcast media from billboards to thirty-second TV spots have dealt with the following: aging, AIDS, anti-smoking, better hearing, better vision, bicycle safety, breast exams, cancer, car pooling, cholesterol, drug abuse, family planning, 55 speed limit, forest fires, illiteracy, mental retardation, muscular dystrophy, nutrition, osteoporosis, physical fitness, pollution, Red Cross blood drive, seat belts, VISTA. In most people's estimations, these two-dozen examples are all worthy causes. The list could be lengthened considerably, but suffice it to say that when the public needs unbiased information on a problem in the public interest, then advertising is frequently employed.

The subtlety and effort that go into the production of a public service announcement calls for, if not demands, as Mendelsohn says "solid social science research" (p. 61). Market segments, appeals, and media vehicles all figure prominently in social advertising and the research that leads up to it. Fox and Kotler, in their Fall 1980 essay in the *Journal of Marketing*, list three situations calling for SM advertising: "When new information and practices need to be disseminated [cholesterol and AIDS], when countermarketing is needed [cigarettes and alcohol]," and "when activation is needed [water conservation]" (pp. 26-7). In this tripartite context the socially conscious consumer must be identified and addressed through effective communication.

In general, SM is a manifestation and function of, as well as a desire for, planned social change. As such, it helps usher in the modern era of the social planner and subjects the receiver of messages to the status of a consumer of ideas. Therefore, much of the research on consumer decision making comes into widespread use. From the viewpoint of rhetoric and public address then, audience analysis becomes a study of consumption behavior, be that behavior related to a product, a service, or an idea.

The following is a selected bibliography of books and articles dealing in whole or in part with, or useful as appropriate general background for a better understanding of, the social marketing concept. The appendix citations can be found therein.

Articles

Barach, Jeffrey A. "Applying Marketing Principles to Social Causes." *Business Horizons*, XXVII, No. 4 (July-August 1984), 65-69.

Bloom, Paul N., and Novelli, William D. "Problems and Challenges in Social Marketing." *Journal of Marketing*, XLV, No. 2 (Spring 1981), 79-88.

El-Ansary, Adel I., and Kramer, Oscar E., Jr. "Social Marketing: The Family Planning Experience." *Journal of Marketing*, XXXVII, No. 3 (July 1973), 1-7.

Farley, John U., and Leavitt, Harold J. "Marketing and Population Problems." *Journal of Marketing*, XXXV, No. 3 (July 1971), 28-33.

Fennell, Geraldine. "Motivation Research Revisited." *Journal of Advertising Research*, XV, No. 3 (June 1975), 23-28.

Fine, Seymour H. "Toward a Theory of Segmentation by Objectives in Social Marketing." *Journal of Consumer Research*, VII, No. 1 (June 1980), 1-13.

———. "Pet Languages Confuse; Let's Standardize Nonprofit, Social, Societal Marketing Definitions." *Marketing News*, XV, No. 9 (October 30, 1981), 1,15.

Fox, Karen F. A., and Kotler, Philip. "The Marketing of Social Causes: The First 10 Years." *Journal of Marketing*, XLIV, No. 4 (Fall 1980), 24-33.

———. "Reducing Cigarette Smoking: An Opportunity for Social Marketing?" *Journal of Health Care Marketing*, I, No. 1 (Winter 1980-81), 8-17.

Gaski, John F. "Dangerous Territory: The Societal Marketing Concept Revisited." *Business Horizons*, XXVIII, No. 4 (July-August 1985), 42-47.

Guy, Bonnie S., and Patton, Wesley E. "The Marketing of Altruistic Causes: Understanding Why People Help." *Journal of Consumer Marketing*, VI, No. 1 (Winter 1989), 19-30.

Kotler, Philip. "Strategies for Introducing Marketing into Nonprofit Organizations." *Journal of Marketing*, XLIII, No. 1 (January 1979), 37-44.

Kotler, Philip, and Zaltman, Gerald. "Social Marketing: An Approach to Planned Social Change." *Journal of Marketing*, XXXV, No. 3 (July 1971), 3-12.

Laczniak, Gene R., Lusch, Robert F., and Murphy, Patrick E. "Social Marketing: Its Ethical Dimensions." *Journal of Marketing*, XLIII, No. 2 (Spring 1979), 29-36.

Luck, David J. "Social Marketing: Confusion Compounded." *Journal of Marketing*, XXXVIII, No. 4 (October 1974), 70-72.

Marsh, Iders. "Marketing Social Conscience." *Black Enterprise*, XIII, No. 6 (January 1983), 39-41.

Mendelsohn, Harold. "Some Reasons Why Information Campaigns Can Succeed." *Public Opinion Quarterly*, XXXVII, No. 1 (Spring 1973), 50-61.

Mindak, William A., and Bybee, H. Malcolm. "Marketing's Application to Fund Raising." *Journal of Marketing*, XXXV, No. 3 (July 1971), 13-18.

Novelli, William D. "Tremendous Need Is Seen Ahead for More Effective Social Marketing." *Advertising Age*, LI, No. 49 (November 13, 1980), 92, 94.

———. "'Selling' Public Health Programs. How Marketing Applies." *Medical Marketing & Media*, XXIV, No. 5 (May 1989), 36, 38, 40, 42, 44.

Rothschild, Michael L. "Marketing Communications in Nonbusiness Situations or Why It's So Hard to Sell Brotherhood like Soap." *Journal of Marketing*, XLIII, No. 2 (Spring 1979), 11-20.

Samli, A. Coskun, and Sirgy, M. Joseph. "Marketers Can Become Social Activists with These Guidelines." *Marketing News*, XVII, No. 7 (April 1, 1983), 5-6.

Shapiro, Benson P. "Marketing for Nonprofit Organizations." *Harvard Business Review*, LI, No. 5 (September-October 1973), 123-32.

Simon, Julian L. "A Huge Marketing Research Task—Birth Control." *Journal of Marketing Research*, V, No. 1 (February 1968), 21–27.

———. "Some 'Marketing Correct' Recommendations for Family Planning Campaigns." *Demography*, V, No. 1 (February 1968), 504–7.

———. "The Role of Bonuses and Persuasive Propaganda in the Reduction of Birth Rates." *Economic Development and Cultural Change*, XVI, No. 3 (April 1968), 404–11.

Thomas, Michael J. "Social Marketing, Social-cause Marketing, and the Pitfalls Beyond." *The Quarterly Review of Marketing*, IX, No. 1 (Autumn 1983), 1–5.

Zaltman, Gerald, and Vertinsky, Ilan. "Health Service Marketing: A Suggested Model." *Journal of Marketing*, XXXV, No. 3 (July 1971), 19–27.

Books

Bagozzi, Richard P., *et al.*, eds. *Marketing in the 80's: Changes and Challenges*. Chicago: American Marketing Association, 1980. See section on "Social Marketing Issues in the 1980's."

Brown, Lawrence A. *Innovation Diffusion*. New York: Methuen and Co., 1981.

Buell, Victor P., ed. *Handbook of Modern Marketing*. 2nd ed. New York: McGraw-Hill Book Co., 1986. See chapter 7, "Nonbusiness or Social Marketing."

Bush, Ronald F., and Hunt, Shelby D., eds. *Marketing Theory: Philosophy of Science Perspectives*. Chicago: American Marketing Association, 1982. See essay in part 5, "Planned Social Change: Some Implications of Marketing."

Corey, E. Raymond, Lovelock, Christopher H., and Ward, Scott. *Problems in Marketing*. 6th ed. New York: McGraw-Hill Book Co., 1981.

Degen, Clara, ed. *Communicators' Guide to Marketing*. New York: Longman, 1987. See chapter 8, "Marketing in Not-for-Profit Organizations."

Fine, Seymour H. *The Marketing of Ideas and Social Issues*. New York: Praeger Publishers, 1981.

———. *Social Marketing*. Boston: Allyn and Bacon, 1990.

Gaedeke, Ralph M., and Tootelian, Dennis H. *Marketing Principles and Applications*. St. Paul: West Publishing Co., 1983. See chapter 21, "Marketing in Nonprofit Organizations."

Henion, Karl E., II, and Kinnear, Thomas C., eds. *Ecological Marketing*. Chicago: American Marketing Association, 1976.

Kotler, Philip, and Roberto, Eduardo L. *Social Marketing: Strategies for Changing Public Behavior*. New York: The Free Press, 1989.

Lovelock, Christopher H., and Weinberg, Charles B. *Marketing for Public and Nonprofit Managers*. New York: John Wiley and Sons, Inc., 1984. See chapter 2, "Understanding and Contrasting the Public and Nonprofit Sectors."

Nickels, William G. *Marketing Communication and Promotion*: *Text and Cases*. 3rd ed. Columbus, OH: Grid Publishing, Inc., 1984. See chapter 18, "Promotion of Nonprofit Organizations."

Rados, David L. *Marketing for Non-profit Organizations*. Boston: Auburn House Publishing Company, 1981.

Rice, Ronald E., and Atkin, Charles K., eds. *Public Communication Campaigns*. 2nd ed. Newbury Park, CA: Sage Publications, Inc., 1990. See Chapter 4, "A Social Marketing Perspective on Communication Campaigns."

Rogers, Everett M. *Communication Strategies for Family Planning*. New York: The Free Press, 1973.

———. *Diffusion of Innovations*. 3rd ed. New York: The Free Press, 1983.

Rosenberg, Larry J. *Marketing*. Englewood Cliffs, NJ: Prentice-Hall, Inc., 1977. See chapter 4, "Socially Responsible Marketing."

Rothman, Jack, *et al.*, *Marketing Human Service Innovations*. Beverly Hills, CA: Sage Publications, Inc., 1983.

Russ, Frederick A., and Kirkpatrick, Charles A. *Marketing*. Boston: Little, Brown and Co., 1982. See chapter 2, "Environments of Marketing."

Salmon, Charles T. ed. *Information Campaigns*. Newbury Park, CA: Sage Publications, Inc., 1989. See chapter 3, "Family Planning, Abortion and AIDS: Sexuality and Communication Campaigns."

Samli, A. Coskun, ed. *Marketing and the Quality-of-Life Interface*. New York: Quorum Books, 1987. See chapter 13, "Integration of Applied Behavior Analysis and Social Marketing."

Sethi, S. Prakash. *Advocacy Advertising and Large Corporations*. Lexington, MA: D.C. Heath and Company, 1977.

———. *Promises of the Good Life*: *Social Consequences of Private Marketing Decisions*. Homewood, IL: Richard D. Irwin, Inc., 1979. See part 3, section A, "Public Interest Advertising."

———. *Handbook of Advocacy Advertising*. Cambridge, MA: Ballinger Publishing Company, 1987.

Sheth, Jagdish N., and Wright, Peter L., eds. *Marketing Analysis for Societal Problems*. Urbana-Champaign, IL: University of Illinois Press, 1974. See part 1, chapter 3, "Strategies for Diffusing Innovations" and chapter 4, "On the Application of Persuasion Theory in Social Marketing."

Shuptrine, F. Kelly, and Reingen, Peter H., eds. *Non-profit Marketing*: *Conceptual and Empirical Research*. Tempe, AZ: Arizona State University, 1983. See part 2, "Persuasion in Nonprofit Marketing," part 3, "Nonprofit Strategies and Practices," and part 4, "Arts, Government Services and Social Marketing."

Topor, Robert S. *Your Personal Guide to Marketing a Nonprofit Organization*. Washington, DC: Council for Advancement and Support of Education, 1988.

Webster, Frederick E., Jr. *Social Aspects of Marketing*. Englewood Cliffs, NJ: Prentice-Hall, Inc., 1974.

Wentz, Walter B. *Marketing*. St. Paul: West Publishing Company, 1979. See chapter 22, "Consumerism" and chapter 23, "Social Issues."

Windahl, Sven, and Signitzer, Benno H. *Using Communication Theory*. Newbury Park, CA: Sage Publications, Inc., 1992. See chapter 9, "Social Marketing Perspectives."

Zaltman, Gerald, and Bonoma, Thomas V., eds. *Review of Marketing 1978*. Chicago: American Marketing Association, 1978. See part 6, essay N, "Public and Nonprofit Marketing Comes of Age."

Zaltman, Gerald, and Duncan, Robert. *Strategies for Planned Change*. New York: John Wiley & Sons, 1977.

Zaltman, Gerald, Kotler, Philip, and Kaufman, Ira, eds. *Creating Social Change*. New York: Holt, Rinehart and Winston, Inc., 1972.

Zaltman, Gerald, *et al.* eds. *Processes and Phenomena of Social Change*. New York: John Wiley & Sons, 1973.

Zeithaml, Valarie A., ed. *Review of Marketing 1990*. Chicago: American Marketing Association, 1990. See section 6, "Public and Nonprofit Marketing: A Review and Directions for Research."

Zikmund, William, and D'Amico, Michael. *Marketing*. 3rd ed. New York: John Wiley & Sons, 1989. See chapter 22, "The Marketing of Services by Profit-Seeking and Not-for-Profit Organizations" and chapter 23, "Marketing and Society."

Notes

1. Richard Rodriguez, "Losing Faith in Our Own Faith," quoted in *The Chicago Tribune* (February 15, 1992), Sec. 1, p. 13.

2. From the *Pastoral Instruction*: "People today have grown so used to the entertaining style and skillful presentation of communications by the media that they are intolerant of what is obviously inferior in any public presentation. . . . In order to make the teaching of Christianity more interesting and effective the media should be used as much as possible. Every effort should be made to use the most appropriate technique and style in fitting a communication to its medium." (Nos. 130-131) See Richard Doerflinger, "Should U.S. Bishops Use the Media to Defend Life?" *The Catholic Transcript* (July 27, 1990), p. 11.

3. Lawrence Lader, *Abortion II: Making the Revolution* (Boston: Beacon Press, 1974), p. xi. See also "Abortion, Inc." *New Dimensions*, V, No. 9-10 (September/October 1991), p. 15.

4. Thomas L. Harris, *The Marketer's Guide to Public Relations* (New York: John Wiley & Sons, Inc., 1991), p. 281. See also Marvin Olasky, "Engineering Social Change: Triumphs of Abortion Public Relations from the Thirties through the Sixties," *Public Relations Quarterly*, XXXIII, No. 4 (Winter 1988-89), pp. 17-21.

5. See G. D. Wiebe, "Merchandising Commodities and Citizenship on Television," *Public Opinion Quarterly*, XV, No. 4 (Winter 1951-52), p. 679.

6. For a professional's view of the PR-advertising relationship, see Dorothy Levy, "What Public Relations Can Do Better than Advertising," *Public Relations Quarterly*, XXXIV, No. 3 (Fall 1989), pp. 7-9; and Eric J. Bolland, "Advertising vs. Public Relations," *Public Relations Quarterly*, XXXIV, No. 3 (Fall 1989), pp. 10-12.

7. William D. Wells, "Psychographics: A Critical View," *Journal of Marketing Research*, XII, No. 2 (May 1975), p. 198.

8. See the work of Gutman and Reynolds, particularly Thomas J. Reynolds, "Implications for Value Research: A Macro vs. Micro Perspective," *Psychology & Marketing*, II, No. 4 (Winter 1985), pp. 297-305.

9. Richard P. Bagozzi, "Marketing as Exchange," *Journal of Marketing*, XXXIX, No. 4 (October 1975), pp. 32, 35.

10.   William T. Moran, "Why New Products Fail," *Journal of Advertising Research*, XIII, No. 2 (April 1973), p. 11.

11.   Robert E. Pitts, Ann L. Canty, and John Tsalikis, "Exploring the Impact of Personal Values on Socially Oriented Communications," *Psychology & Marketing*, II, No. 4 (Winter 1985), p. 268.

12.   Ved Prakash and J. Michael Munson, "Values, Expectations from the Marketing System and Product Expectations," *Psychology & Marketing*, II, No. 4, (Winter 1985), p. 281.

13.   Russell I. Haley, "Benefit Segmentation: A Decision-oriented Research Tool," *Journal of Marketing*, XXXII, No. 3 (July 1968), p. 30.

14.   *Ibid*, p. 32. See also Nariman K. Dhalla and Winston H. Mahatoo, "Expanding the Scope of Segmentation Research," *Journal of Marketing*, XL, No. 2 (April 1976), pp. 34–41.

15.   Geraldine Fennell, "Consumers' Perceptions of the Product-Use Situation," *Journal of Marketing*, XLII, No. 2 (April 1978), p. 40.

16.   James H. Myers, "Benefit Structure Analysis: A New Tool for Product Planning," *Journal of Marketing*, XL, No. 4 (October 1976), p. 27.

17.   From Committee on Definitions, *Marketing Definitions: A Glossary of Marketing Terms* (Chicago: American Marketing Association, 1960). Quoted in William G. Nickels, "Conceptual Conflicts in Marketing," *Journal of Economics and Business*, XXVI, No. 2 (Winter 1974), p. 140.

18.   Galton, 1879, quoted by Allan W. Wicker, "Getting out of Our Conceptual Ruts," *American Psychologist*, XL, No. 10 (October 1985), p. 1094, who cites H.F. Crovitz, *Galton's Walk* (New York: Harper & Row, 1970).

19.   Cited by Bagozzi, *op. cit.*, p. 37, who quotes from Karl R. Popper, *Conjectures and Refutations* (New York: Harper & Row, 1963), p. 67.

20.   Donald E. Vinson, Jerome E. Scott, and Lawrence M. Lamont, "The Role of Personal Values in Marketing and Consumer Behavior," *Journal of Marketing*, XLI, No. 2 (April 1977), p. 48. See also J. Michael Munson and Shelby H. McIntyre, "Developing Practical Procedures for the Measurement of Personal Values in Cross-Cultural Marketing," *Journal of Marketing Research*, XVI, No. 1 (February 1979), pp. 48–52; and Lynn R. Kahle, Basil Poulos, and Ajay S. Sukhdial, "Changes in Social Values in the United States during the Past Decade," *Journal of Advertising Research*, XXVIII, No. 1 (February/March 1988), pp. 35–41.

21.   Lynn R. Kahle, "The Values of Americans: Implications for Consumer Adaptation," chapter 6, in Robert E. Pitts Jr. and Arch G. Woodside, eds., *Personal Values and Consumer Psychology* (Lexington, MA: D.C. Heath and Co., 1984), p. 78. In this same volume see also J. Michael Munson, "Personal Values: Considerations on Their Measurement and Application to Five Areas of Research Inquiry," chapter 2, pp. 13–33; and Ernest Dichter, "How Values Influence Attitudes," chapter 9, pp. 139–44.

22.   *Ibid.*, p. 77.

23.   *Ibid.*, p. 83.

24.   Lynn R. Kahle, Sharon E. Beatty, and Pamela Homer, "Alternative Measurement Approaches to Consumer Values: The List of Values (LOV) and Values and Life Style (VALS)," *Journal of Consumer Research*, XIII, No. 3 (December 1986), p. 406.

25.   Sharon E. Beatty, Lynn R. Kahle, Pamela Homer, and Shekhar Misra, "Alternative Measurement Approaches to Consumer Values: The List of Values and the Rokeach Value Survey," *Psychology & Marketing*, II, No. 3 (Fall 1985), p. 187.

26.   Lynn R. Kahle, "Social Values in the Eighties: A Special Issue," *Psychology & Marketing*, II, No. 4 (Winter 1985), p. 232.

27.   Thomas J. Reynolds and Jonathan Gutman, "Laddering Theory, Method, Analysis, and Interpretation," *Journal of Advertising Research*, XXVIII, No. 1 (February/March 1988), pp. 11–31.

28.   Jerry C. Olson and Thomas J. Reynolds, "Understanding Consumers' Cognitive Structures: Implications for Advertising Strategy," chapter 4, in Larry Percy and Arch G. Woodside, *Advertising and Consumer Psychology* (Lexington, MA: D.C. Heath and Co., 1983), p. 82.

29.   Adapted from Thomas J. Reynolds and Jonathan Gutman, "Advertising Is Image Management," *Journal of Advertising Research*, XXIV, No. 1 (February/March 1984), p. 34.

30.   Olson and Reynolds, *op. cit.*, p. 85.

31.   Thomas J. Reynolds and Jonathan Gutman, "Laddering: Extending the Repertory Grid Methodology to Construct Attribute-Consequence-Value Hierarchies," chapter 11, in Robert E. Pitts, Jr. and Arch G. Woodside, *op. cit.*, p. 156.

32.   *Ibid.*, p. 166.

33.   Thomas J. Reynolds and Jonathan Gutman, "Laddering Theory, Method, Analysis, and Interpretation," *op. cit.*, p. 18.

34.   *Ibid.*, p. 13.

35.   *Ibid.*, p. 25.

36.   Jonathan Gutman, "A Means-End Chain Model Based on Consumer Categorization Processes," *Journal of Marketing*, XLVI, No. 2 (Spring 1982), p. 68.

37.   *Ibid.*, p. 63.

38.   Jonathan Gutman, "Analyzing Consumer Orientations toward Beverages through Means-End Chain Analysis," *Psychology & Marketing*, I, No. 3/4 (Fall/Winter 1984), p. 25.

39.   *Ibid.*, pp. 41–42.

40.   Jeffrey F. Durgee, "Depth-Interview Techniques for Creative Advertising, *Journal of Advertising Research*, XXV, No. 6 (December 1985/January 1986), p. 29.

41.   *Ibid.*, p. 30.

42.   *Ibid.*

43.   *Ibid.*, p. 31.

44.   *Ibid.*, p. 33. See D.N. Perkins, *The Mind's Best Work* (Cambridge, MA: Harvard University Press, 1981), which Durgee cites.

45.   *Ibid.*, p. 34.

46.   For more information on qualitative marketing research, see Bobby J. Calder, "Focus Groups and the Nature of Qualitative Marketing Research," *Journal of Marketing Research*, XIV, No. 3 (August 1977), pp. 353–64; Richard L. Vaughn, "Point of View: Creatives versus Researchers: Must They Be Adversaries?" *Journal of Advertising Research*, XXII, No. 6 (December 1982/January 1983), pp. 45–48; and Arthur J. Kover, "Point of View: The Legitimacy of Qualitative Research," *Journal of Advertising Research*, XXII, No. 6 (December 1982/January 1983), pp. 49–50.

47.   Milton Rokeach, "The Role of Values in Public Opinion Research," *Public Opinion Quarterly*, XXXII, No. 4 (Winter 1968–69), p. 550.

48.   See David Mall, *In Good Conscience: Abortion and Moral Necessity* (Libertyville, IL: Kairos Books, Inc., 1982).

49.   See Jean Piaget, *The Moral Judgment of the Child*, trans. by Marjorie Gabain (New York: The Free Press, 1965).

50.   While this essay was being written, another church sanctioned venture into big-time social marketing was inaugurated. Called by some "Dial-a-Pope," the program consists of a Vatican 900 number that permits callers to receive a different message from the Pope each day. It is claimed that this social marketing venture could generate as much as $2.8 million each week to help retire the Vatican's annual debt. For more information, see "Calls to the Pope Help Vatican Pay Its Debt," *The Wanderer*, CXXV, No. 10 (March 5, 1992), p. 3.

51.   From an Associated Press account. See "Professor Claims Corporations Waste Billions on Advertising," *Marketing News*, XXVI, No. 14 (July 6, 1992), p. 5. And see especially John Philip Jones, H*ow Much Is Enough? Getting the Most from Your Advertising Dollar* (New York: Lexington Books, 1992).

PART THREE

Lessons from History

SERNETT   The writer examines the analogical appeal made to the fight against slavery in the public debate over abortion in the United States. Those who wish to draw upon the moral capital generated in the abolitionist movement are asked to consider the strengths and weaknesses of the abortion/slavery analogy. The contemporary anti-abortion movement, like the anti-slavery crusade, concerns the fundamental question of how to draw the boundaries of the circle in which constitutional protection is afforded. Though disclaiming a simplistic abortion/slavery analogy, the writer finds important parallels in the 19th-century abolitionist debate to the current one concerning the constitutional rights of the unborn. These include controversy over the religious appeal, the role of government, and social attitudes.

BRENNAN   Anyone who dares to entertain the possibility of connections existing between contemporary abortion and the Nazi Holocaust is likely to be dismissed as an anti-Semitic bigot intent on distorting history for malevolent, far-right religious purposes. There are, nevertheless, some startling parallels that can be legitimately drawn between the killing of the unborn today and the destruction of European Jews during the Nazi era. This article highlights and documents some of these linkages: the nature and scope of the killing, body disposal methods, the invocation of euphemisms and slogans to obscure the concrete horrors of mass destruction, the use of disparaging language to dehumanize the victims, the major role of liberals and the media in perpetuating the violence, and the perversion of the law in the service of genocide. The killing of the unborn and other vulnerable groups will never come to an end until a much wider segment of the public becomes conversant with how the history of inhumanity continues to be repeated in today's society on a massive scale.

Widening the Circle:

The Pro-life Appeal to the Abolitionist Legacy

Milton C. Sernett

A nti-abortion activists frequently draw an analogy with the crusade against slavery in their efforts to overturn *Roe v. Wade*. This appeal to moral capital generated by the antebellum abolitionists deserves an appraisal as to its strengths and weaknesses. When the history of the debate over abortion is written, it will comprise an important chapter in the annals of American reform. The passage of time and cooling of rhetoric on both sides of the abortion controversy will doubtless afford a better comparative perspective than presently possible. Nevertheless, I propose to assess the usefulness of the analogical appeal by examining several similarities and dissimilarities between the anti-abortion and anti-slavery movements.

1. The Analogical Appeal

In any substantive debate, protagonists who invoke analogies run the risk of censure by epistemological puritans. "The chief practical use of history," the English statesman James Bryce wrote, "is to deliver us from plausible historical analogies."[1] David Hackett Fischer reminds us that analogies are only "devices for discovering explanations."[2] An analogical argument seeks to persuade

159

us that if two or more things agree with one another in one or more respects they will probably agree in yet other ways. In its most elemental form, an analogy consists of a set of propositions, best illustrated in a mathematical formula. Historical analogies are not nearly so precise or self-limiting. They are introduced to supplement, sometimes to substitute for, reasoned argument. They carry emotive power, for their purpose is to persuade through an unconscious or inchoate inference by appealing to our collective memory and conscience. These moral claims well up from the ideological springs of our culture.

Analogies function as extended metaphors, and metaphorical thinking is fundamental to the human experience. Just as momentous experiences in an individual's life, times of great personal joy or tragedy, serve as psychological benchmarks by which one measures later experiences, so societies make use of analogical reference points. Despite notions that Americans are a people of short memory in distinction to the Chinese or even Europeans, we too search for moral lessons in the collective past. Who born since the Great Depression has not been reminded of the perils of prosperity learned in lean years? Those who witnessed the devastation wrought by atomic weapons at Hiroshima and Nagasaki will not let us forget the potential for world destruction unleashed by the first wartime use of nuclear fission. The atrocities committed by the Third Reich in Germany are frequently invoked in ethical discussion of biomedical science and technology.

Chattel slavery is the skeleton in the closet of the American past which most haunts the contemporary collective moral conscience. No other moral and political question so bitterly divided the nation or has left as great an imprint upon our social fabric. Black Americans, a people of long memory, are conscious of slavery as the seminal historical experience of their tortuous pilgrimage from Africa to the present moment. Despite the civil rights movement, the pall of slavery lingers in our consciousness and we encounter it in debates over affirmative action and black liberation theology. The African American experience, beginning with the tolerance of slavery by the drafters of the Constitution in 1787, has served as a cautionary moral tale, challenging each successive American generation to fulfill the dream of a truly egalitarian society.

Having said this, we must acknowledge that public sentiment has changed. None but the most misinformed or consciously villainous would now assert that slavery was a positive good, as was maintained in the Old South, or deny the tragedy, both immediate and long-term, of the "peculiar institution." Should an author propose today that slavery either did not exist or that its evils were grossly exaggerated by its victims and its critics, we would dismiss them as readily as one does those who deny the historical reality of the Holocaust. The ratification of the Fourteenth Amendment in 1868, conferring citizenship on the emancipated slaves, was a victory for the abolitionists and is today viewed as an untarnished good.

In the aftermath of the Civil War, social reformers sought to build upon and identify with the moral legacy of the crusaders against slavery. The children and grandchildren of the original abolitionists, as historian James McPherson has shown, continued the battle for black rights after Reconstruction down to the founding of the neo-abolitionist National Association for the Advancement of Colored People in 1909–1910. They transferred similar moral energies into the woman's suffrage and anti-imperialism movements of the 1890s.[3] Howard Zinn subtitled a study of the Student Nonviolent Coordinating Committee of the 1960s "The New Abolitionists."[4] Other historians have drawn parallels between the youthful anti-Vietnam War protesters and the abolitionists of the 1830s.[5]

When appeals to the abolitionist legacy are made by contemporary pro-life writers and speakers, their opponents cry foul. Pro-choice advocates wish to portray themselves as custodians of the liberal, democratic society that prizes individual rights and their adversaries as ideologically conservative and socially retrogressive. Because the abortion/slavery analogy frequently comes from sectors of American society which were not aggressive in the struggle for black civil rights or were noticeably silent, even the friendly critic raises an eyebrow.[6] Who uses what analogies in public debate is often revealing of much more than the speaker may intend, for analogies flood the mind with images and, once introduced, are difficult to limit and control.

Because analogies are embedded in our ideologies and are not given to empirical proof, they cannot resolve core questions such as the evaluation of nascent life. In the strict sense, arguments concerning whether fetuses are truly persons or merely potential persons are not factual or scientific arguments but judgments derived from complex sets of philosophical presuppositions and ethical values.[7] Those who draw an analogy between fetal life and the black slave in the hope of convincing others that the question of the personhood of the unborn is thereby decided have constructed an argument that is a rope of sand. It suffers the fallacy of the perfect analogy, which, as David Hackett Fischer reminds us, is a contradiction in terms, for it "consists in reasoning from a partial resemblance between two entities to an entire and exact correspondence."[8] Though analogies may be useful tools for historical understanding, they serve only as auxiliaries to proof.

The power of analogical explanation is psychological and is sought by protagonists on both sides of the abortion question. Once one has concluded that nascent human life deserves legal protection on other grounds, be they religious or secular, then the analogy with slavery begins to influence the way in which the pro-life argument is framed. Pro-choice advocates are quick to invoke a counter-analogy—that of Prohibition. They argue that a constitutional ban on abortion would result in widespread public disrespect for the law both through a loss of confidence and violation of the letter of the law.[9]

How is it that the pro-life side finds an analogy with the fight against slavery instructive, while the pro-choice side asks us to consider the failures of the Eighteenth Amendment, which prohibited the manufacture, sale, or transportation of alcoholic liquors?

The answer certainly lies in the contrasting ways in which pro-life and pro-choice advocates view the abortion question. Both sides seek to place the debate into a larger scheme of values favorable to their respective points of view. In brief, those who advocate legal protection of the fetus see themselves as defending an individual's right to life, especially in the case of those who are powerless. They see the question as fundamentally one of protecting one defenseless category of human or potentially human life against discrimination. Daniel Callahan observes, "In almost any other civil rights context, the cogency of this line of reasoning would be quickly respected. Indeed, it has been at the heart of efforts to correct racial injustices, to improve health care, to eradicate poverty, and to provide better care for the aged."[10]

Supporters of *Roe v. Wade* view governmental limitations on a woman's right to an abortion as a violation of individual free choice and therefore an invasion of the privacy of moral judgment. The Volstead Act, it is argued, was just such an attempt to enforce morality by governmental intrusion.[11]

We have here a curious convergence, though the contending parties might not see it this way. Both sides appeal to essential parts of the liberal-democratic philosophical tradition as it has developed in American and Western thought. One side seeks to protect the rights of the defenseless at the expense of individual free choice, while the other attempts to preserve the sovereignty of the individual conscience. One side sees the right to life as the most fundamental of civil rights, while the other, having set aside or "bracketed" the question of whether or not the unborn are truly persons and therefore entitled to constitutional protection, focuses on the civil right of privacy in matters of procreation.

The pro-life position that fetal life has intrinsic value apart from any differences or resemblances to adults is the liberal's argument, Roger Wertheimer observes, "turned completely inside out."[12] Civil rights activists echoed the abolitionist argument that blacks were not to be judged by white standards but admitted to the circle of rights-bearers solely on the basis of their kinship with all humanity. We should not be surprised that prominent civil rights leaders, such as the Reverend Jesse Jackson, have drawn parallels between the cultural mentality which disparaged minority rights (because blacks were perceptually categorized as different and thus inferior to whites) and that which stresses differences between prenatal and postnatal life. Indeed, historians will one day have to explain why most public opinion surveys have shown that blacks are less supportive of abortion-on-demand than whites.[13]

Analogical linkages between the struggle for minority rights and that for the rights of the unborn are unavoidable when we consider the historical background of the 1973 Supreme Court decision which precipitated the current controversy. In an exercise of judicial review, Justice Harry A. Blackmun argued that the word "person" in the Fourteenth Amendment does not include the unborn, thereby excluding the previable fetus from protection against deprivation of "life, liberty, or property without due process of law" as afforded blacks in 1868 when the Congress declared the amendment ratified. Blackmun maintained that the fact of widespread legal abortions in the early nineteenth century suggests that Congress did not intend to include the unborn within the purview of an amendment whose purpose was to repudiate the Dred Scott decision. Critics of this point of view were quick to point out that Blackmun inexplicably took a static view of the legal concept of "person" while taking an evolutionary view of the concept of "liberty."[14] Thus, the right-to-life movement seeks to expand the definition of "person" as a "bearer of rights" to include the unborn via a constitutional amendment. We should not be surprised that those opposed to abortion should find an implicit connection with the crusade against slavery in the interpretation and application of the Fourteenth Amendment in *Roe v. Wade*. To put the issue most plainly, the abortion and the slavery debates share the question of how this society is to widen the boundaries of that community whose members are afforded basic constitutional rights.

2. Expressions of the Analogy

The abortion/slavery analogy comes to us in many forms, some of them so simplistic that they are not deserving of extended comment. To argue, for example, that abortion is the modern equivalent of slavery is to strain credibility. Even the most partisan of pro-lifers must recognize that the relationship of a slave to his or her master cannot be precisely equated with that of a fetus to the pregnant woman. The moral conundrum faced by the slave owner is not the same as that of the pregnant woman whose symbiotic relationship to the fetus is much more intense. Slaveholders became such voluntarily and could, as did the abolitionist James Birney, unburden their consciences by freeing their slaves and moving to the North.[15] The vast majority of women who seek abortions have not become pregnant by choice but find themselves in a moral dilemma by virtue of the inexorable laws of reproductive biology. Because the abortion/slavery analogy is used to counter a variety of pro-choice claims, it is constantly shifting. Here, for example, is an excerpt from an anti-abortion newsletter comparing *Roe v. Wade* with *Dred Scott v. Sanford*:

Slavery—1857

Although he may have a heart and a brain, and he may be a human life biologically, a slave is not a legal person. The Dred Scott decision by the U.S. Supreme Court has made that clear.

Abortion—1973

Although he may have a heart and brain, and he may be human life biologically, an unborn baby is not a legal person. The *Roe vs. Wade* [sic] decision by the U.S. Supreme Court has made that clear.

Slavery—1857

A black man only becomes a legal person when he is set free. Before that time, we should not concern ourselves about him. He has no legal rights.

Abortion—1973

A baby only becomes a legal person when he is born. Before that time, we should not concern ourselves about him. He has no legal rights.

Slavery—1857

If you think that slavery is wrong, then nobody is forcing you to be a slave owner. But don't impose your morality on somebody else!

Abortion—1973

If you think abortion is wrong, then nobody is forcing you to have one. But don't impose your morality on somebody else!

Slavery—1857

A man has a right to do what he wants with his own property.

Abortion—1973

A woman has a right to do what she wants with her own body.

Slavery—1857

Isn't slavery really something merciful? After all, every
black man has a right to be protected. Isn't it better never
to be set free than to be sent unprepared, and ill-equipped,
into a cruel world?

Abortion—1973

Isn't abortion really something merciful? After all, every baby
has a right to be wanted. Isn't it better never to be born than
to be sent alone and unloved into a cruel world?[16]

Once premised that the fetus is a person, the parallels here drawn
begin to fall into place, for, as Roger Wertheimer has noted, "the
favored defense of slavery and discrimination, from Aristotle to
the Civil War and beyond, takes the form of a claim that the subju-
gated creatures are by nature inferior to their masters, that they
are *not fully human*"[17] (emphasis in original).

The abortion/slavery analogy is most effective as a means of
focusing the debate on the status and rights of the unborn as
opposed to all utilitarian issues. Just as blacks have been discrimi-
nated against in the past, the argument goes, so the unborn are dis-
criminated against today. Robert M. Bryn writes: "Unfortunately
for the unborn child, even though the law may recognize him as a
human being, he just does not look like the rest of us, and besides,
he is utterly helpless and dependent. He is, in other words, a classic subject for discriminatory treatment."[18] C. Everett Koop, for-
merly Surgeon-General of the United States, has argued that *Roe v.
Wade* subjects the unborn to depersonalization and dehumanization as happened before in history with regard to blacks and Indians in America and Jews in Nazi Germany.[19] Sidney Callahan,
describing herself as a feminist, wrote prior to *Roe v. Wade*: "The
fetus isn't human and has no right to life! But the feminist movement insists that men cease their age-old habit of withholding
human status from women, blacks, Jews, Indians, Asians, and other
helpless or different instances of human life."[20] President Ronald
Reagan lent the prestige of his office to this line of argument:

This is not the first time our country has been divided by a Supreme Court decision that denied the value of certain human lives. The *Dred Scott* decision of 1857 was not overturned in a day, or a year, or even a decade. At first, only a minority of Americans recognized and deplored the moral crisis brought about by denying the full humanity of our black brothers and sisters; but that minority persisted in their vision and finally prevailed. They did it by appealing to the hearts and minds of their countrymen, to the truth of human dignity under God. From their example, we know that respect for the sacred value of human life is too deeply ingrained in the hearts of our people to remain forever suppressed. But the great majority of the American people have not yet made their voices heard, and we cannot expect them to—any more than the public voice arose against slavery—*until* the issue is clearly framed and presented[21] (emphasis in original).

In framing the case against abortion in this fashion, pro-life advocates ask for our sympathetic identification with the unborn. The conservative case, which in the context of the debate over slavery would be considered radical, is to extend the protection of the law to all of human parentage regardless of their secondary attributes and assorted utilitarian arguments. This, or course, begs the question of the personhood of the fetus, the very question which most pro-choice advocates wish to ignore. The debates over abortion and slavery are distinct from public controversies over trade embargoes, taxes, or even prohibition. None of the latter concern the fundamentally important problem of defining the boundaries of human community nor necessitate such a radical and close examination of our basic values.

3. Widening the Circle

Though the slavery and abortion debates turn on a common question, they differ in an important way. In the anti-slavery crusade, the victims of discrimination and prejudice could and did speak for themselves. Blacks participated in the abolitionist movement, influencing its shape and direction by their voices, pens, and physical presence. William Lloyd Garrison's attack on the American Colonization Society's scheme to send blacks to

Liberia was shaped in large part by his awareness of free black discontent with this "surrogate for abolition."[22] By way of contrast, the unborn are incapable of participation in the anti-abortion movement, except by virtue of their very existence as perceived victims. This may be too obvious to need stating, yet the reality of black participation in the antislavery crusade made the abolitionist's task much easier. Blacks and whites interacted even on the plantation in ways that contradicted planter notions that the African slave was not a human being.[23]

Narrowly speaking, the abolition debate dealt with the question of citizenship, whether or not slaves were to be considered as "legal persons" in the constitutional sense. The right-to-life movement is confronted with a prior task. It seeks to convince its opponents that the fetus is a human person bearing the same right to life that society acknowledges postnatally. Thus, it might be objected that the putative analogy with slavery does not hold, as the slave was afforded the right to life, albeit one circumscribed by the power of the master.[24] This is, however, distinction without historical significance. For as Orlando Patterson has argued, slavery is a form of social death. "The slave," Patterson contends, "was natally alienated and condemned as a socially dead person, his existence having no legitimacy whatever. The slave's natal alienation and genealogical isolation made him or her the ideal human tool, an *instrument vocal*—perfectly flexible, unattached, and deracinated. To all members of the community, the slave existed only through the parasite holder, who was called the master"[25] (emphasis in original).

Abolitionists saw this "social death"—this depersonalization of the slave by the master—as the fundamental crime of slaveholding. *Uncle Tom's Cabin*, Harriet Beecher Stowe's antislavery novel, first had as its subtitle—"The Man That Was a Thing." Mrs. Stowe correctly understood the dynamics of the master-slave relationship, despite the protestations of pro-slavery writers that the slaves were well-treated. Southern law recognized the slave as "chattel"—animate property, but property nevertheless. Pro-slavery apologists tried to cloud the issue by painting a picture of an idealized domestic institution, modeled after the patriarchal slavery of the Old Testament.[26] The abolitionists and fugitive slaves countered that whatever ameliorations individual masters granted, the "peculiar institution" robbed blacks of full and free participation in the community of rights-bearers.

Though friends of the slaves, especially those interested in converting them, complained that masters treated the African like a beast, few whites actually thought slaves to be animals. "They are kept only as *Horses* or *Oxen*, to do our Drudgeries," complained the Puritan divine Cotton Mather, "but their Souls are not look'd after, but are Destroyed for *lack* of *Knowledge*. This is a desperate Wickedness"[27] (emphasis in original). Winthrop Jordan cogently argues that by granting that the African possessed a soul worth saving, a manifestation of the inner sameness of all races, "the Christian tradition created a rock-hard shelf below which the Negro could not fall."[28] This proved to be the "thin edge of antislavery" that the abolitionists later used to their advantage.

Having reached a crude consensus on the African's innate nature and membership in the Great Chain of Being, whites then speculated on the place of blacks in the human hierarchy based on physiognomic differences between the races and the African's alleged lack of civilization. Unwilling to admit that the Great Chain of Being originated, as Jordan argues, "in differences in power or social status," whites rationalized slavery by placing themselves at the top of the hierarchical order and blacks at the bottom.[29] Nevertheless, notions of the fixity of the human species derived from eighteenth century rational science and of a single creation, as depicted in the Pentateuch, led to an acknowledgement that the African belonged to the species of *genus homo*. Yet most Southern whites who took the Genesis creation story literally remained racists, for they believed that blacks could only become equal by becoming more like the Anglo-Saxon race.[30] In other words, whites, as adults are tempted to do with regard to the fetus in the abortion controversy, defined the entrance requirements for those who wished to join the circle of rights-bearers with reference to themselves.

When the American abolitionists sought to widen the circle of humanity to include the slave in practice as in theory, they encountered a perverse new appeal to science. During the 1840s and 1850s, the "American school of ethnology" advocated polygenesis, the doctrine that the races had been created as separate and unequal species. Slavery's apologists seized upon the new ethnology because, as George M. Fredrickson writes, it "raised prejudice to the level of science; thereby giving it respectability."[31] Southern churchmen, who resisted polygenesis because it ran counter to the Genesis account, found an alternative justification for slavery in the so-called "Curse of Ham." According to their interpretation of Genesis 9:21–27, the "sons of Ham" were to be identified with the children of Africa and were destined to be slaves because of their ancestor's offense.[32]

In the debate over abortion, some advocates of the species principle assert that being conceived of human parents endows the fetus with the right to life because only Homo sapiens are divine image bearers and the recipients of divine valuation.[33] This echoes the abolitionist argument that the African was inherently meant to be free and responsible before God because the African was a member of the human family, contrary to the pseudoscientific racism of the American ethnologists. The species principle entails the belief that the "image of God" is an inviolable status conferred by a divine act of valuation and is, therefore, fundamentally a theological claim.[34] The abolitionists defended the inclusion of the slave within the circle of humanity on the basis of arguments from Natural Rights and Natural Law as well as from Religion. American scientific thought, until well into the twentieth century, fed the cavernous maw of racist ideology.[35]

In contrast, advances in scientific knowledge in the nineteenth century, especially in a clearer understanding of the process of embryological development, contributed to legislation protecting prenatal life that typifies the period from 1850 to 1890. Regular medical doctors in the period from 1820 to 1850 gradually became more opposed to abortion at any stage in gestation because of new discoveries regarding embryonic development that undercut the older notion that prior to "quickening" a pregnant woman carried within her an inert non-being, or at least something of less value than after "quickening." Historian James C. Mohr summarizes this shift in consciousness as follows:

> If society considered it unjustifiable to terminate a pregnancy after the fetus had quickened, and if quickening was a relatively unimportant, almost incidental step in the overall gestation process, then it was just as wrong to terminate a pregnancy before quickening as after quickening. Regulars believed it immoral, in other words, to make a life or death decision on the basis of a distinction that they could demonstrate to have very little relation to life or death.[36]

Historians of American intellectual and social history have yet to explore the irony that the American Medical Association launched an aggressive campaign against abortion on the eve of the Civil War while scientific attitudes of racial inferiority became institutionalized and further justified by appeals to Social Darwinism after Reconstruction.[37]

The right-to-life movement has capitalized on the tremendous explosion of knowledge gained about embryology since the early 1970s. In arguments from genetic endowment, appeals to potentiality, and emphasis on the biological continuum, much is made of scientific discoveries far more sophisticated than those of the nineteenth century.[38] This appeal to medicine, especially by anti-abortionists who adopt a vitalist approach, involves a historical paradox, for, by and large, the medical profession has abandoned the defense of fetal life against abortion-on-demand, choosing to derive no ethical obligations from biological observations. Having divorced science from questions of ontology, the medical community cannot on the basis of technical information alone be of much help in deciding the issue of whether or not the embryo/fetus is a "human person" vis-à-vis "human life."[39]

This brief overview of appeals to science and social thought suggests that the abortion/slavery analogy has merit in a quite specific sense. If we examine ways in which blacks were perceived by whites in antebellum America, as opposed to viewing them from the vantage point of the present moment, then a parallel can be drawn with fetal life post-*Roe v. Wade*. Just as prenascent life lacks legal protection prior to "viability," so the slave in antebellum America had no rights (according to Chief Justice Roger B. Taney's opinion in *Dred Scott v. Sanford*) which whites needed to respect. In practical terms, the Supreme Court ruled in 1857 that slaves were private property and not "citizens" within the meaning of the Constitution. In 1973, the Supreme Court consigned the unborn to the same category by ruling that the unborn are not to be considered "persons" within the meaning of the Constitution and are therefore excluded from protection as full members of the political community.[40]

Because of the perceptual dehumanization of the slave inherent in the nature of the master-slave relationship, the abolitionists took it as their first priority to change white attitudes toward the slave and his plight. Josiah Wedgwood's widely used cameo portraying an African slave raising his shackled hands in supplication bore the inscription, "Am I not a Man and a Brother?" Daniel Alexander Payne, later a noteworthy bishop and educator of the African Methodists, declared in his ordination address before the abolitionist Franckean Lutheran Synod that slavery's worst crime was its moral not its physical brutalization.

> We have seen that slavery treats man like a brute, therefore slavery brutalizes man! But does slavery stop here? Is it content with merely treating the external man like a brute? No sir, it goes further, and with a heart as brazen as that of Belshazzar, and hands still more sacrilegious, it lays hold of the *immortal mind, seizes the will and binds that which Jehovah did not bind—fetters that which the Eternal made as free to move and act as the breath of Heaven. "It destroys moral agency!"*[41] (Emphasis in original.)

As a strategy to induce empathy from the general public, particularly northern Christians who had not declared themselves for immediate, uncompensated, and universal emancipation, the abolitionists drew attention to how the African American slaves, despite their cruel circumstances, were like the free. Slaves were shown to have feelings of joy and sorrow. They too had families, exhibited the fear of God, and wrestled with the dictates of morality. To use a phrase the historian Kenneth Stampp employed in the preface to his study of slavery published in 1956, the abolitionists sought to prove that the slaves were "white men with black skins, nothing more, nothing less."[42] While this obscures the extent to which African American culture differed from that of European Americans, it does capture the intent of the abolitionists, who, after all, wanted to raise up the slave from the degradation of bondage to the freedom and obligations whites enjoyed.

Since the fetus is truly voiceless in the sense of being unable to express kinship with post-natal life through the powers of sentience, pro-lifers focus on the physical resemblance of the unborn to the newly born. Pictures of the developing fetus are shown to pregnant mothers in the hope that those contemplating an abortion might see anatomical similarities between the fetus and the newborn. Anti-abortionists have brought aborted fetuses into congressional hearing rooms so that the public might see the consequences of abortion. One is reminded of the abolitionist practice of displaying runaway slaves with the scars of the slaveholder's whip on their backs. Most Northerners had no firsthand knowledge of slavery or felt any guilt concerning it.[43] The abolitionists realized that their cause would not gain support so long as slavery was an abstract problem and the victims of slavery were invisible. Pro-lifers too express concern that since the advent of *Roe v. Wade* abortion is conducted behind closed doors in clinics and hospitals, is out-of-sight and therefore out-of-mind to most Americans.

Some of the more perceptive abolitionists realized the weakness in the argument that the slaves were deserving of freedom because they were but "white men in black skins." They feared that such an approach, one that predicated freedom upon character or ability to become white, betrayed a prejudice fundamentally at odds with their ultimate goals. Indeed, African Americans have long suffered from the racist notion that the more one had "white blood" the more one deserved equal treatment. The belief that the mulatto was more enterprising, more intelligent, and therefore better prepared for freedom was persuasive in antebellum, reform circles. Thus radical abolitionists, such as Beriah Green, argued that the slaves merited equal status with whites regardless of any secondary criteria. "We are to exert ourselves," he urged fellow abolitionist James Birney in 1846, "for the enfranchisement of the Slave, not because he is a *Negro*, but because he is a MAN. On the same principle, we are to exert ourselves to secure to ALL our fellow-citizens the free enjoyment of all their rights. Otherwise, lacking consistency, we shall lose our power"[44] (emphasis in original).

Serious advocates of the rights of the unborn will have to educate the public on the need to widen the circle encompassing those to whom society owes constitutional protection. This is tantamount to the revolution in consciousness sought by the abolitionists. For until the slave was perceived as a legal person, in the face of American racism, the public conscience rested easy. Pro-life opponents of *Roe v. Wade* could well become students of that remarkable period in Western history during which, for complex reasons, a dramatic shift occurred in viewing slavery not as a sign of human progress but as a retrogressive institution.[45]

4. Institutional Parallels: Church and State

A retrospective examination of the crusade against slavery in light of the current debate over abortion reveals important institutional lessons, analogues, as well as distinctions. This is especially important since the Supreme Court majority in *Roe v. Wade* established by judicial fiat what had not been resolved by American political and religious institutions. Ironically, the same might be said with regard to the Supreme Court's role in the school desegregation cases of the 1950s. In the 1954 *Brown v. Board of Education of Topeka* decision, Richard Kluger reminds us, the Court "ran ahead" of public opinion and advanced the cause of human rights by severing the remaining cord—of *de facto* slavery.[46] While some pro-life advocates place their hopes on the eventual emergence of a high court majority supportive of their goals, others rightly understand that a fundamental revolution of consciousness must take place in this nation's religious and political institutions.

Having conceived of slavery as a sin and their crusade as essentially a moral enterprise, the abolitionists of the 1830s sought the conversion of the churches as "the earliest and most persistently pursued goal."[47] They urged the various denominations to cleanse their membership rosters of slaveholders, trumpet the immediatist cause from every pulpit, and thereby move America toward the millennial triumph. Abolitionist hopes soon gave way to despair and frustration, for the moral suasion tactic was largely ineffective. The major Protestant denominations were slow in responding. Northern Methodists and Baptists, even after the schisms of the mid-1840s, tolerated the presence of slaveholders in the border states within their communions. The sectional divisions of the great national churches left the abolitionists with no access to southern Christians, except by firing rhetorical missiles against "pro-slavery religion." Conservative denominations and theologians in the North attempted to defuse the abolitionist critique by endorsing the colonization scheme as a patriotic duty in the hope of preserving the Union.[48]

Because of the failure of organized religion in the North and the South to share the immediatist vision of a slavery-free, egalitarian society, many of the pioneer abolitionists began to question the validity of the institutional church. Garrison's anti-clerical views caused, in part, a division within the American Anti-Slavery Society in 1840. More temperate immediatists, such as Arthur and Lewis Tappan and Gerrit Smith, formed the American and Foreign Anti-Slavery Society, which was more willing than Garrison to work within the organized church. Yet many of the non-Garrisonians eventually formed "come-outer" local churches purified of any complicity, even through silence, with slavery. Others went further and adopted a non-creedal rational Christian, humanitarianism.[49] Some historians have concluded that the "war against proslavery religion" hardened sectional sentiment in the South and stimulated a self-righteousness in the North that turned the war for the Union into a holy crusade. This "repressible conflict" thesis implies that had the abolitionists not viewed their mission in such absolutist terms, somehow the nation might have avoided the Civil War.[50] However, from the abolitionist perspective slavery was the epitome of human arrogance and a usurpation of the moral government of God. Given this view, colored as it was with millennial overtones, the abolitionists condemned the churches of their day for being the bulwarks of slavery.

Pro-life advocates who wish to appeal to the anti-slavery crusade must recognize that the religious institutions of the antebellum period were no more able to bring about through internal debate a united front on behalf of the slave than are religious groups of the present moment able to speak with one voice on behalf of the unborn. The late-twentieth century religious landscape is much more complex than that of the abolitionists. The abolitionist crusade was primarily a Protestant enterprise, with the lead taken by the evangelical wing. The evangelicals were heirs of the old Calvinist New England heritage, but were also products of the Second Great Awakening, especially the revivals of such regions as the "Burned-over District" of upstate New York. The abolitionists were not immune to the anti-Roman Catholic bias of their culture, nor were they confronted by the contemporary problem of religious pluralism and legal challenges to exclude religion from the public debate.[51]

The abolitionists quarreled with other Protestants who likewise viewed the Bible as an authoritative guide in every aspect of life. Problems arose in the interpretation of specific texts, and each side sought to make the Bible subserve ready-made positions regarding the "peculiar institution." Robert L. Dabney, a Presbyterian clergyman of Virginia, counseled his brother: "Here is our policy, then, to push the Bible argument continually, drive abolitionism to the wall, to compel it to assume an anti-Christian position. By so doing we compel the whole Christianity of the North to array itself on our side."[52] Southern churchmen found justification for slavery in texts such as Leviticus 25:44–46 and concluded that what was sanctioned in the Old Testament and not explicitly abrogated in the New Testament could not be sinful. The abolitionists countered with an appeal to overriding principles of justice and righteousness, especially as found in the teachings of Jesus, and tried to avoid becoming mired in debates over specific passages, such as those in the Pauline epistles frequently appealed to by slaveholders. The more radical abolitionists eventually shifted away from Scripture as their primary authority because the biblicism of their opponents defined the argument in terms favorable to slavery and the Bible offered no explicit condemnation of the institution.[53]

Christian pro-life and pro-choice writers have also wrestled with the quotation, "What is the biblical witness?" As in the controversy over slavery, differences of opinion and interpretation arise among those who appeal to the same Bible. For example, Exodus 21:22, though appearing to relate to the loss of fetal life, is so complicated by problems of context that neither side has yet convinced the other.[54] Pro-choice authors contend that there is no definitive biblical answer to the question of when the fetus becomes a "person," and, more to the point, no specific passage speaks to the problem of abortion as posed in the contemporary debate. Pro-life advocates generally argue from texts that indirectly affirm the "sanctity of life" within the framework of doctrines concerning divine creation and providence. This parallels the strategy that the abolitionists were forced to take, though, ironically, the pro-life argument generally comes to us today from Protestant traditions which are more conservative in matters of biblical interpretation.

The abolitionists were least successful with the ritualist Lutheran and Roman Catholic and old-line Calvinist denominations of their day. Their strongest allies came from evangelical circles, from among the New School Presbyterians, anti-slavery Methodists, and perfectionist sects.[55] George Huntston Williams observed, even prior to *Roe v. Wade*, that liberal Protestants, who viewed the abortion question as primarily concerning women's right, championed relaxation of the then-existing abortion laws.[56] Conservative Protestants, notably those identified as "evangelicals," have now joined rank with Catholics in the right-to-life movement. In *Abortion and the Politics of Motherhood*, Kristin Luker suggests that among activists on the abortion question, pro-choice people are more apt than pro-life people to rely "upon a subjectively reasoned application of moral principles rather than upon an externally existing moral code."[57] She calls this the "New Testament approach to morality," which was exactly what the abolitionists employed when confronted by quotes from the Old Testament thrown at them by defenders of slavery. They too asked, "What is the *loving* thing to do?," rather than debate the meaning of specific references to slavery in the Bible. There is a historical paradox in all of this that has yet to be fully understood.

In the long struggle for a more racially egalitarian America, conservative Protestants, especially those now claiming to be "the new evangelicals," sought to separate politics and religion. Few took an active institutional role in the civil rights crusade. In contrast, liberal denominations, once thought of as the Protestant "mainstream," tended to favor church involvement in the political arena and advocacy of minority rights. Obviously, problems abound in definitions of "liberal" and "conservative." Nevertheless, if we assume that the abortion/ slavery analogy has merit, then the current attempts of Christian pro-lifers to transform a moral crusade into a political one, as Christian liberals did in the civil rights movement, raises questions of historical congruity. One need only examine the membership roster of the Religious Coalition for Abortion Rights, which takes the position that abortion is a matter of private morality, to note the irony that traditions once favorable to religious activism in political affairs have been caught in a peculiar dilemma regarding the relationship of religion and politics.[58]

The immediatists of the 1830s optimistically believed that slavery's poisonous upas tree would wither and die under an intensive blast of moral suasion. Americans were to be converted to abolitionism, as in the revivals of the day, through preaching and teaching. Garrison shunned politics for fear of tainting the purity of the cause and counseled his disciples to stay away from the ballot box. "The genius of the abolition movement," the iconoclastic reformer commented, "is to have *no plan*"[59] (emphasis in original). By the late 1830s, however, some abolitionists were becoming impatient with Garrison's aversion to practical measures and became involved in the postal and petition campaigns. They organized the American and Foreign Anti-Slavery Society in 1840 and, more importantly, sought to enter directly into the political realm. The Liberty party, devoted to the single issue or "One Idea" of eliminating slavery, never won mass voter acceptance but it contributed to the politicization of the slavery question in the North.

The non-Garrisonians realized that effective political action had to be grounded in adequate political and constitutional theory. Garrison had interpreted the Constitution as a pro-slavery document, a "Covenant with Death and an agreement with Hell," and called for disunion. The political abolitionists, realizing that disunion would abandon the slave to the South, sought to rediscover anti-slavery principles in the Constitution. They resorted to rather convoluted arguments concerning specific provisions, such as the three-fifths clause and that pertaining to the return of fugitive slaves. Finding no clear-cut prohibition of slavery, they had to appeal to the Declaration of Independence and to theories of Natural Law and Natural Rights which they believed to be foundational to any democratic republic. Legal historian William Wiecek has observed that while radical constitutionalism was a failure in the short-run, because Northern opposition to slavery was channeled into sectional politics, it contributed to modern libertarian constitutional thought via the Fourteenth Amendment. He writes, "Ideas of substantive due process, equal protection of the laws, paramount national citizenship, and the privileges and immunities of that citizenship were all first suggested by the radicals."[60]

The Fourteenth Amendment both nullified the *Dred Scott* decision and corrected the defect in the Constitution which tolerated slavery. Pro-lifers today express the hope that a Human Life Amendment of one sort or another will invalidate *Roe v. Wade* and offer constitutional protection to the unborn as the Fourteenth Amendment did for blacks.[61] The analogy with the anti-slavery crusade suggests that such an attempt is inevitable and necessary, since the Constitution was construed in *Roe v. Wade* tolerating abortion-on-demand for the previable fetus. Pro-lifers must recognize, however, that it is an uphill fight. The Fourteenth Amendment was ratified only in the wake of bloody sectional conflict and over strong dissent.[62] "Liberty came to the freedmen," Frederick Douglass perceptively observed, "not in mercy, but in wrath, not by moral choice, but by military necessity, not by the generous action of the people among whom they were to live, . . . but by strangers, foreigners, invaders, trespassers, aliens, and enemies."[63]

Pro-lifers who use the abortion/slavery analogy must recognize that although the Union was saved, moral commitment to the rights of the emancipated slaves, especially after Reconstruction, waned in the North and all but disappeared in the South. Indeed we have yet to witness the fulfillment of the abolitionist vision of a truly egalitarian society. Attempts to link antiabortion with anti-slavery will not be very effective unless those who employ the analogy demonstrate a commitment to the goals of the primitive abolitionists equal to their commitment to the unborn. If the right-to-life movement is perceived, rightly or wrongly, as hostile to the improvement of the social and economic standing of the descendants of the emancipated slaves, then the analogical appeal will appear disingenuous and self-serving. Pro-choice advocates, in turn, must seriously reconsider whether or not they would wish their arguments in defense of abortion to be applied also to the question of black civil rights. William Sloane Coffin, for example, has chided religious liberals who argue that abortion is simply a matter of private conscience: "It's a cop-out to say that abortion is a sin but not a crime. That's like saying slavery is a sin but not a crime, that I personally wouldn't own slaves but I defend the right of others to choose differently."[64]

In 1865, William Lloyd Garrison, noting that the Thirteenth Amendment had become the supreme law of the land, declared, "My vocation as an abolitionist, Thank God, is ended."[65] He urged veteran abolitionists to no longer remain separate from the great mass of the people and to celebrate the victory at hand. Wendell Phillips, however, spoke against dissolution of the abolitionist societies, arguing, "Now, to my mind, an American abolitionist, when he asks freedom for the Negro, means effectual freedom, real freedom, something that can maintain and vindicate itself."[66] Phillips rightly understood that abolitionism involved more than striving for the *de jure* end of slavery. The generation to follow would have to take on the new mission of assisting the freedmen and their descendants so that blacks might enjoy all the rights and privileges of American citizens. Past triumphs would mean little if the newly freed slaves were reduced to "slaves without masters" due to economic and social exploitation. Thus many of the abolitionists who lived into the post-emancipation era devoted themselves to educational and reform efforts among southern blacks and to fighting the emergent "Jim Crow" laws. Here was evidence that they were for a new social order as well as having been against slavery.

The abortion/slavery analogy doubtless appeals to pro-lifers most strongly now in the struggle to overturn *Roe v. Wade*, which, like the *Dred Scott* decision, has cast a pall upon the nation. This appears to be a time for moral absolutism on both sides of the abortion question. But if there is an enduring lesson in this review of the connections between the pro-life movement and the abolitionist crusade, it is that the reformer's task is not done, nor half-done, with legal or constitutional recognition of a given point of view. Those who wish to embrace the abolitionist legacy as their own must recognize that the struggle for a truly egalitarian society is a never-ending one. The campaign for the rights of the unborn should not cease until abortion is deemed a sign of social retrogression not a token of social progress. This demands that the pro-life movement be equally zealous in efforts to mitigate those circumstances, economic or otherwise, which cause some women to seek abortion as the lesser of evils.

Notes

1. Cited by David Hackett Fischer, *Historians' Fallacies* (New York: Harper & Row, 1970), p. 243.

2. *Ibid.*

3. James M. McPherson, *The Abolitionist Legacy: From Reconstruction to the NAACP* (Princeton: Princeton University Press, 1975).

4. Howard Zinn, *SNCC: The New Abolitionists* (Boston: Beacon Press, 1965). Contemporary opponents of nuclear weapons, capital punishment, and racial apartheid have also invoked the abolitionist legacy.

5. See, for example, Bertram Wyatt-Brown, "New Leftists and Abolitionists: A Comparison of American Radical Styles," *Wisconsin Magazine of History*, 53 (Summer 1970): 256–68.

6. The Lutheran Church—Missouri Synod and the Southern Baptist Convention, for example, have been active in the right-to-life movement but were officially quietistic on the race question for many decades.

7. Daniel Callahan discusses this point at length in *Abortion: Law, Choice & Morality* (New York: The Macmillan Company, 1970), chapters 10 and 11.

8. Fischer, *Historians' Fallacies*, p. 248. The philosopher Charles Hartshorne has taken strong exception to drawing a simple analogy. He writes: "Of course the fetus is alive! So are puppies and kittens. Of course it is human (who ever in this controversy has denied this?) if 'human' here means that its origin is in the union, in a human womb, of a human sperm and a human egg cell. To pretend that this settles the question of value is to grossly beg the question. . . . To equate treatment of women or blacks with treatment of fetuses is a gross insult to members of those two groups of undoubted persons." *Omnipotence and Other Theological Mistakes* (Albany: State University of New York Press, 1984), pp. 100–01. Pro-lifers might justifiably respond that the debate over the inclusion of blacks within the circle of rights-bearers was not simply a debate about "facts," for slaveholders admitted that the African was "human" (born of human parents) but one of values, rights, and consequences.

9. For a provocative attempt to undercut the pro-choice use of the prohibition analogy by examining the ideological matrix that gave rise to Prohibition and linking it with that which underlies pro-abortion rhetoric, see David

Mall, "Stalemate of Rhetoric and Philosophy," in *Abortion and Social Justice*, ed. by Thomas W. Hilgers and Dennis J. Horan (New York: Sheed & Ward, 1972), pp. 199–214.

10.   Daniel Callahan, "Abortion: Some Ethical Issues," in *Abortion, Society, and the Law*, ed. by David F. Walbert and J. Douglass Butler (Cleveland: Press of Case Western University, 1973), pp. 100–101.

11.   With regard to the popular slogan, "You can't legislate morality," ethicist Roger Shinn, no apologist for the right-to-life movement, has written, ". . . justice is a moral issue. There are moral reasons for laws against murder, robbery, fraud, denial of civil rights, race discrimination, etc. While no law is ever 100-percent effective, law has some effect in controlling harmful behavior and securing human rights. To some extent there is a possibility and a desirability of enforcing morality. In recent American history the role of law has been *extended* into some areas of racial and economic justice that were once left to personal decisions of the powerful" (emphasis in original). "Personal Decisions and Social Policies in a Pluralist Society," in *Abortion: The Moral Issues*, ed. by Edward Batchelor, Jr. (New York: The Pilgrim Press, 1982), pp. 167–68.

12.   Roger Wertheimer, "Understanding the Abortion Argument," *Philosophy and Public Affairs*, 1 (Fall 1971): 85.

13.   Jesse L. Jackson, "How Shall We Regard Life?," typescript in author's possession, published as "How We Respect Life Is Overriding Moral Issue." Jackson, while a Democratic presidential candidate, reversed himself and, though maintaining a strong personal and religious opposition to abortion, supported "freedom of choice" in a pluralistic and secular society. This caused some critics to wonder how he would respond "if someone deplored black slavery while defending the right of whites to decide for themselves whether to own slaves." See Stephen Chapman, "Jackson's Abortion Surrender," *Chicago Tribune*, February 19, 1984: 8, section 6. See also, Mary Meehan, "Jesse Jackson Changes Position on Abortion," *National Catholic Register*, 59:1 (November 20, 1983): 1, 10. On Jackson's attempts to explain his new position, see Lally Weymouth, "Sticky Questions for Jesse Jackson," *New York*, (January 9, 1984): 34–34, and *"Ebony* Interview with The Rev. Jesse Jackson," *Ebony*, (June 1981): 160. C. Eric Lincoln, prominent black sociologist, has taken a stand against abortion. See his, "Why I Reversed My Stand on Laissez-Faire Abortion," *Christian Century* 90 (April 25, 1973): 477–79. See also the chapter on "Black Genocide" in Betty Sarvis and Hyman Rodman, *The Abortion Controversy* (New York: Columbia University Press, 1973), pp. 185–200. Michael W. Combs and Susan Welch, "Blacks, Whites, and Attitudes toward Abortion," *Public Opinion Quarterly*, 46 (Winter 1982): 510–20.

14.   James J. Kilpatrick, for example, has criticized the Court's nullification of the Texas and Georgia anti-abortion statutes in its interpretation of the Fourteenth Amendment. "But in any fair reading, the Fourteenth contains no such prohibition. In 1868, when the Fourteenth was more or less ratified, 37 states were more or less in the Union. Thirty-six of the 37 had laws limiting or prohibiting abortion. It is nonsense to suppose that the framers of that amendment intended the Fourteenth to nullify these state enactments." "Abor-

tion Decisions: Still Bad Law," *Illinois Right to Life Committee Newsletter*, 2 (January-February 1974). Richard Stith of the School of Law, Valparaiso University, wrote in 1973 concerning the Supreme Court's decision: "I would have thought that the word 'person' indicated a *concept*, which can be reconstructed from the particulars to which it is applied. If we agree that it is applied to the newborn (and even to slaves, as Justice Blackmun points out), we would have to see whether it reasonably applies to the unborn. But Justice Blackmun asserts, in effect, that a word means only the particulars which the speaker is thinking of when he uses it, and that those who used 'person' were probably not thinking of fetuses. Thus south-sea islanders, too, would not be protected by the Fourteenth Amendment unless they were in mind when the Amendment passed" (emphasis in original). "In Response to Those Who Ask Why I Care about Abortion," *The Cresset*, 37 (December 1973): 8.

15.   Except in the Deep South, state constitutions put few obstacles in the way of voluntary manumissions, though only a handful of slaveholders followed Birney's example by placing moral above economic considerations. See Kenneth A. Stampp, *The Peculiar Institution: Slavery in the Ante-Bellum South* (New York: Vintage, 1956), pp. 232–36.

16.   *Marriage and Family Newsletter*, 6 (January-March, 1975): 21.

17.   Wertheimer, "Understanding the Abortion Argument," 73.

18.   Robert M. Byrn, "A Legal View," *Commonweal*, 85 (March 17, 1967): 680.

19.   C. Everett Koop, "Where Is the Abortion Decision Taking Us?" *Eternity* (October 1973): 37.

20.   Sidney Callahan, "Feminist as Anti-abortionist," *National Catholic Reporter*, 8 (April 7, 1972): 11.

21.   Ronald Reagan, *Abortion and the Conscience of the Nation* (Nashville: Thomas Nelson Publishers, 1984), pp. 19–20.

22.   Garrison devoted the second half of *Thoughts on African Colonization* (1832) to extensive citations of black opposition toward removal to Liberia. On black participation in the abolitionist movement, see Jane H. Pease and William H. Pease, *They Who Would Be Free: Black's Search for Freedom, 1830–1861* (New York: Atheneum, 1974). Also, Benjamin Quarles, *Black Abolitionists* (New York: Oxford University Press, 1969).

23.   Winthrop Jordan perceptively argues that white views of blacks in colonial America were significantly altered by interpersonal contact. "Even in the plantations, the Negro walked and hoed and talked and propagated like other men. No matter how much slavery degraded the Negro, every daily event in the lives and relationships of Negroes and white men indicated undeniably that the Negro was a human being. White man [sic] feared their slaves' desires for freedom, they talked with their Negroes, and they slept with them. These were human relationships, continually driving home the common humanity of all." *White over Black: American Attitudes toward the Negro, 1550–1812* (Baltimore: Penguin Books, 1969), p. 234.

24.   Of the codes regarding chattels personal, Kenneth Stampp writes, "Though the slave was property 'of a distinctive and peculiar character,' though recognized as a person, he was legally at the disposal of his master, whose property right was very nearly absolute." *Peculiar Institution*, p. 197.

25.   Orlando Patterson, *Slavery and Social Death: A Comparative Study* (Cambridge and London: Harvard University Press, 1982), p. 337. Patterson observes that slavery originated historically as a "substitute for certain death."

26.   Donald Mathews has drawn a distinction between the slaveholding ethic and a proslavery ideology. The former viewed slavery as a "necessary evil" entailed from previous generations and stressed the moral responsibility of both master and slave, attempting to secure benefits for both. The latter, especially after 1830 and the emergence of the abolitionist critique, defended slavery as a "positive good" on the basis of racist dogma and took no account of the moral character of blacks. *Religion in the Old South* (Chicago: University of Chicago Press, 1977), pp. 172–73. A parallel shift from a "necessary evil" to a "positive good" ideology regarding abortion is evident in some pro-choice sectors of contemporary society. See Marilyn Felix, *Ideology and Abortion Policy Politics* (New York: Praeger Publishers, 1983).

27.   Cited by Jordan, *White over Black*, p. 190.

28.   *Ibid.*, pp. 180, 231.

29.   *Ibid.*, p. 227.

30.   For example, John Bachman, a Lutheran clergyman in Charleston and prominent naturalist, warred against the polygenists but supported slavery as an institution. See William Stanton, *The Leopard's Spots: Scientific Attitudes toward Race in America, 1815–59* (Chicago: University of Chicago Press, 1960), pp. 122–36.

31.   George M. Fredrickson, *The Black Image in the White Mind* (New York: Harper & Row, 1971), p. 89.

32.   For a thorough examination of the shifting ethnic identifications of the "sons of Ham," see William McKee Evans, "From the Land of Canaan to the Land of Guinea: The Strange Odyssey of the 'Sons of Ham'," *American Historical Review*, 85 (February 1980): 15–43.

33.   For a discussion of the species principle as used in the debate over abortion, see Robert N. Wennberg, *Life in the Balance: Exploring the Abortion Controversy* (Grand Rapids, MI: William B. Eerdmans, 1985), chapter 7.

34.   Paul Ramsey writes: "According to religious outlooks and 'onlooks' that have been traditioned to us, man is a sacredness *in* human biological processes no less than he is a sacredness in the human social or political order. This sacredness is not composed by observable degrees of relative worth. A life's sanctity consists not in its worth to anybody. What life is in and of itself is most clearly to be seen in situations of naked equality of one life with another, and in the situation of congeneric helplessness that is the human condition in the first of life. No one is ever more than a fellow fetus; and in order not to become confused about life's primary value, it is best not to concentrate on

degrees of relative worth we may later acquire" (emphasis in original). See "The Morality of Abortion," in *Abortion: The Moral Issues*, ed. by Edward Batchelor, Jr. (New York: The Pilgrim Press, 1982), p. 79.

35.   On the scientific revolt against racism in the 1920s, led by the anthropologist Franz Boaz, see Thomas F. Gosset, *Race: The History of an Idea in America* (New York: Schocken Books, 1965), chapter 16.

36.   James C. Mohr, *Abortion in America: The Origins and Evolution of National Policy, 1800-1900* (New York: Oxford University Press, 1978), p. 36. Those who have argued that the tolerance of abortion prior to "quickening" either in early America or in the earlier Catholic tradition meant an approval of abortion *per se* miss the point. The problem involved determining when a woman was "with child."

37.   John S. Haller, Jr., *Outcasts from Evolution: Scientific Attitudes of Racial Inferiority, 1859-1900* (New York: McGraw Hill, 1975).

38.   For an example of the pro-life appeal to scientific embryology, see the brochure "Abortion: Death Before Life?" distributed by the NRL Education Trust Fund of Washington, DC. It makes frequent reference to Robert Rugh and Landrum B. Shettles, *From Conception to Birth: The Drama of Life's Beginnings* (New York: Harper & Row, 1971).

39.   Edward Manier has put the problem this way: "The status of the fetus is problematic because our awareness of the earliest stages of its development is indirect and technical, and the technical information we have concerning it is not commensurable with our ordinary use of 'human.'" See "Abortion and Public Policy in the U.S.: A Dialectical Examination of Expert Opinion," in *Abortion: New Directions for Policy Studies*, ed. by Edward Manier, William Liu, and David Solomon (Notre Dame: University of Notre Dame Press, 1977), p. 5.

40.   For an extensive, provocative, and eloquent essay on parallels between the *Dred Scott* decision and *Roe v. Wade* and its companion case, *Doe v. Bolton*, see "Eliza and Lizzie Scott, and Infants Roe and Doe: How They Fared," by James T. Burtchaell in *Rachel Weeping: The Case against Abortion* (New York: Harper & Roe, 1984), pp. 239-87. Also, Milton C. Sernett, "The Rights of Personhood: The Dred Scott Case and the Question of Abortion," *Religion in Life*, XLIX (Winter 1980): 461-76.

41.   Douglass Stange, ed. "Document: Bishop Daniel Alexander Payne's Protestation of American Slavery," *Journal of Negro History*, 52 (January 1967): 60-61.

42.   Stampp, *Peculiar Institution*, vii.

43.   Aileen S. Kraditor responds to those historians who have argued that the abolitionists were motivated by psychological guilt. "If slavery was an integral part of the institutional structure of the nation as a whole, the average Northerner had as realistic a basis for guilt feelings as the average German in the 1930s. By the same token the minority of Northerners who were aware of their section's complicity in the crime of slavery and worked in a variety of ways to publicize that complicity and end it were not more pathological than German antifascists thirty years ago. The unrealism was not the abolitionists' for feeling

guilty but their neighbors' for *not* feeling guilty" (emphasis in original). *Means and Ends in American Abolitionism: Garrison and His Critics on Strategy and Tactics, 1834–1850* (New York: Vintage Books, 1969), p. 21.

44.   Beriah Green to James G. Birney, December 17, 1846, in Dwight L. Drumond, ed., *Letters of James Gillespie Birney, 1831–1857*, I (New York: D. Appleton-Century Company, 1938), p. 243. Green was the only American academic moral theologian to join the immediatist ranks in the 1830s, served as president of Oneida Institute (the abolitionist and racially integrated college at Whitesboro, New York), and was widely respected for his radical humanitarianism by African Americans. See Milton C. Sernett, *Abolition's Axe: Beriah Green, Oneida Institute, and the Black Freedom Struggle* (Syracuse: Syracuse University Press, 1986).

45.   David Brion Davis explores this theme in *Slavery and Human Progress* (New York: Oxford University Press, 1984).

46.   Richard Kluger writes: "Every colored American knew that *Brown* did not mean he would be invited to lunch with the Rotary the following week. It meant something more basic and more important. It meant that black rights had suddenly been redefined; black bodies had suddenly been reborn under a new law. Blacks' value as human beings had been changed overnight by the declaration of the nation's highest court. At a stroke, the Justices had severed the remaining cords of *de facto* slavery. The Negro could no longer be fastened with the status of official pariah. No longer could the white man look right through him as if he were, in the title words of Ralph Ellison's stunning 1952 novel, *Invisible Man*." *Simple Justice: The History of Brown v. Board of Education and Black America's Struggle for Equality* (New York: Vintage Books, 1977), p. 749.

47.   John R. McKivigan, *The War against Proslavery Religion: Abolitionism and the Northern Churches, 1830–1865* (Ithaca: Cornell University Press, 1984), p. 13.

48.   John R. Bodo, *The Protestant Clergy and Public Issues, 1812–1848* (Princeton: Princeton University Press, 1954), pp. 126–28.

49.   On the shift away from the conventional churches and orthodoxy to antislavery as a new kind of "church" for heirs of the revivals who Ronald Walters emphasizes had "both a fiercely Protestant morality and a disdain for metaphysics," see his *The Antislavery Appeal: American Abolitionists after 1830* (New York: W.W. Norton, 1978), pp. 52–53.

50.   For a discussion of this historiographical tradition, see Thomas V. Pressly, *Americans Interpret Their Civil War* (New York: The Free Press, 1965), chapter 7.

51.   I have considered this contemporary problem in "The Efficacy of Religious Participation in the National Debates over Abolitionism and Abortion," *The Journal of Religion*, 64 (April 1984): 205–20.

52.   Quoted in H. Shelton Smith, *In His Image, But . . . : Racism in Southern Religion, 1780–1910* (Durham, NC: Duke University Press, 1972), p. 136.

53. For an overview of why Bible-inspired men and women took up the immediatist crusade, their accomplishments, and their failures, see James Brewer Stewart, "Abolitionists, the Bible, and the Challenge of Slavery," in *The Bible and Social Reform*, ed. by Ernest R. Sandeen (Philadelphia: Fortress Press, 1982), pp. 31-57. For examples of those biblical texts about which the abolitionists and their opponents debated, see Caroline Shanks, "The Biblical Anti-Slavery Arguments of the Decade, 1830-1840," *Journal of Negro History*, 16 (April 1931): 132-57; and Ron Bartour, "American Views on 'Biblical Slavery' 1835-1865," *Slavery & Abolition*, 4 (May 1983): 41-63.

54. Evangelicals have differed among themselves over the correct rendering of Exodus 21:22-25. See Jack W. Cottrell, "Abortion and the Mosaic Law," *Christianity Today*, 17 (March 16, 1973): 602-4.

55. McKivagan, *War against Proslavery Religion*, pp. 164-71.

56. George Hunston Williams, "Religious Residues and Presuppositions in the American Debate on Abortion," *Theological Studies*, 31 (1970): 52.

57. Kristin Luker, *Abortion and the Politics of Motherhood* (Berkeley: University of California Press, 1984), pp. 184-85.

58. For an insightful probing of the liberal dilemma, see Richard John Neuhaus, "Hyde and Hysteria," *Christian Century*, 97 (September 10-17, 1980): 849-52.

59. Quoted in James Brewer Stewart, *Holy Warriors* (New York: Hill & Wang, 1976), p. 55.

60. William M. Wiecek, *The Sources of Antislavery Constitutionalism in America, 1760-1848* (Ithaca: Cornell University Press, 1977), pp. 274-75.

61. For example, see John Powell, S.J., *Abortion: The Silent Holocaust* (Allen, TX: Argus Communications, 1981), pp. 163-69. Also, Paul Ramsey, "Protecting the Unborn," *Commonweal*, 100 (May 31, 1974): 312.

62. See Joseph B. James, *The Ratification of the Fourteenth Amendment* (Macon, GA: Mercer University Press, 1984).

63. Quoted in Stewart, *Holy Warriors*, pp. 202-3.

64. Quoted by Richard John Neuhaus, "Speaking Out: Faith and Order Call to Ecumenical Debate," *Christian Century*, 96 (February 18, 1979): 205.

65. Quoted in Lawrence J. Friedman, *Gregarious Saints: Self and Community in American Abolitionism, 1830-1870* (Cambridge: Cambridge University Press, 1982), p. 265.

66. *Ibid.*, p. 268.

Specifying the Abortion-Holocaust Connections

William Brennan

The Wrath of the *Times*

O n March 14, 1984, *The New York Times* stooped to a new low in its relentless campaign to discredit anyone who dares challenge the contemporary abortion juggernaut. The target of the *Times*' wrath was New York Archbishop John J. O'Connor because he linked abortion with the Nazi Holocaust. For this, Bishop O'Connor was subjected to a severe tongue-lashing and thrust into that time-worn caricature of a shadowy religious zealot bent on imposing his narrow sectarian morality onto everyone else. An insidious inference was also made that the Bishop's remarks smacked of anti-Semitism.[1]

On this occasion the "Catholic strategy" backfired badly. Bishop O'Connor stood by his analogy, refused to be intimidated by the bullying tactics of the mega press, and rightly responded with outrage at the blatantly false and offensive insinuations drawn. Letters to the *Times* reflected considerable support for the Bishop. Former U.S. Supreme Court Justice Arthur J. Goldberg wrote: "Any inference in your editorial that Bishop O'Connor in any way minimized the tragedy of the Holocaust is in my view entirely without foundation and constitutes an unwarranted aspersion on Bishop O'Connor's total dedication to human rights and his total abhorrence of anti-Semitism in any form."[2]

But why single out Bishop O'Connor? After all, he is not the only prominent individual to portray abortion as a modern-day Holocaust. Congressman Henry Hyde, former U.S. Surgeon General C. Everett Koop, and English author and social critic Malcolm Muggeridge are among the growing list of notables who have publicly compared abortion to the Nazi war against the Jews. In his historic article, "Abortion and the Conscience of the Nation," President Ronald Reagan quotes a passage from *The Abortion Holocaust: Today's Final Solution* which underscores a basic principle related to both abortion and the Nazi Holocaust: "The cultural environment for a human holocaust is present whenever any society can be misled into defining individuals as less than human and therefore devoid of value and respect."[3]

What got Bishop O'Connor into hot water with the opinion shapers on the *Times* editorial staff is his disconcerting habit of calling things by their rightful names, a characteristic quite foreign to a media elite so thoroughly indoctrinated into a pro-abortion mindset saturated with slogans, euphemisms, and linguistic distortions. And, even more to the point, the Bishop draws parallels between past and current atrocities with a degree of precision and specificity unmatched by any public figure in recent memory. He zeroes in on a number of significant connections which are rarely if ever given any coverage by the secular press. A closer examination of some of them will reveal why the gatekeepers of public information at the *Times* were so upset.

Abortion as a Holocaust

It was in a television interview on WNBC's "Newsforum" (March 11) that Bishop O'Connor highlighted a series of parallels between abortion and the Nazi Holocaust. He emphasized that "I always compare the killing of 4,000 babies a day in the United States, unborn babies, to the Holocaust."[4]

In this statement alone he violates two sacrosanct principles of abortionspeak: Never call abortion "killing" and never refer to the victims of abortion as "unborn babies." In today's abortion culture where destructive activities have been technologically and semantically transformed into minor medical procedures, the Bishop's style of expression is considered downright tasteless, much too graphic, and a grave threat to the very credibility of the abortion establishment and the media elite which play such an indispensable role in disseminating pro-abortion rhetoric.

Despite the pervasive efforts to malign anyone who employs such words as "kill" and "destroy" when referring to abortion, these are perfectly legitimate terms to describe what abortion actually does to the unborn child. When the abortionist invades the sanctuary of the womb, the passenger within is by all scientific criteria alive, growing, and developing. After the abortionist accomplishes his lethal task, the intrauterine victim is definitely no longer alive, and therefore dead. And it is the abortion procedure which brought about this death.

To call abortion anything less than killing is, as so cogently pointed out by former abortion clinic director Dr. Bernard N. Nathanson, "the crassest kind of moral evasiveness."[5]

There are some other remarkably revealing insights into the real essence of abortion that provide a solid factual foundation for the comparisons stressed by Bishop O'Connor. As far back as 1859, the American Medical Association House of Delegates, in a historic policy statement against abortion, referred to abortion as "the slaughter of countless children" and "such unwarrantable destruction of human life."[6] In 1871, the AMA reiterated its opposition to abortion in the strongest terms, calling it "the wholesale destruction of unborn infants."[7] Periodically, even some contemporary abortionists and abortion supporters acknowledge the true nature of abortion. Fetal research advocates Drs. Willard Gaylin and Marc Lappe describe abortion procedures as "unimaginable acts of violence."[8] According to veteran abortionist Dr. Warren E. Hern, D and E abortion is "an act of destruction" in which "the sensations of dismemberment flow through the forceps like an electric current."[9]

Not only does Bishop O'Connor call abortion what it is, he also points out that the killing of the unborn is comparable in scope to the Nazi extermination of European Jews. The number of unborn lives extinguished by abortion is staggering: 4,000 on a daily basis, over 1.6 million annually, and over 30 million in a 20-year span since the U.S. Supreme Court rendered its pro-abortion decision in 1973. On a worldwide annual basis the abortion toll has reached astronomical proportions: 50 to 60 million. And there is no letup in sight! During the 12 years of the Third Reich the Nazis did away with 6 million Jews, 275,000 German handicapped, a quarter of a million Gypsies, and untold numbers of unborn children in the occupied Eastern territories.

Body Disposal

Bishop O'Connor also focused on the strikingly similar methods employed to get rid of past and present victims defined as problems: "Now Hitler tried to solve a problem, the Jewish question. So kill them, shove them in the ovens, burn them. Well, we claim that unborn babies are a problem, so kill them. To me it really is precisely the same."[10]

Burning in crematory ovens and huge ditches constituted the predominant means of body disposal in the Nazi killing centers. Huge numbers of aborted bodies today are likewise disposed of by burning in hospital furnaces and city incinerators.

At the Treblinka death camp a major controversy erupted over whether the bodies of victims should be buried or burned. Odilio Globocnik, an SS officer consumed with Nazi ideals, defended burying the bodies and placing bronze plaques over the mass graves with the inscription: "It was we, we who had the courage to achieve this gigantic task." Dr. Herbert Linden, a realist, countered with the observation: "But would it not be better to burn the bodies instead of burying them? A future generation might think differently of these matters."[11] Reality won out over idealism and the order was given to burn all bodies, including those previously buried.

A similar debate raged over what to do with more than 16,000 aborted babies discovered in a huge metal storage container outside of Los Angeles in 1982. Pro-life groups were in favor of at least according these victims the dignity of a Christian burial. The American Civil Liberties Union, a staunch proponent of burning the bodies, conjured up that all-too predictable concoction—violation of separation of church and state—to block the burial.

One cannot help but conclude that the ACLU, like the Nazi realists, favors burning not because of legal principles or ideals, but because this particular method of disposal permanently removes all telltale traces of mass destruction. Burial, especially Christian burial, is doubly threatening: not only does it bestow upon the victims a transcendent value intolerable to civil libertarians, it also draws attention to a disturbing truth which abortionists would prefer to keep hidden from public view—the existence of actual human bodies.

Euphemisms in the Service of Destruction

Nazi perpetrators and contemporary abortionists share another important attribute: a persistent habit of calling what has been done to their respective victims something other than killing.

Nazi semanticists avoided the word "kill" like a plague and manufactured an unprecedented list of code words, slogans, and euphemisms to cover up their destructive actions. According to the Nazi lexicon, people were simply "removed" from ghettoes and "evacuated" to "the East" for "resettlement," "special treatment," or "rehabilitation" in the "bathhouses" and "wash and disinfectant rooms" of "labor," "concentration," or "resettlement" camps.

Abortion linguists are equally adverse to using any unpleasant terms, especially "kill," when referring to their deadly procedures. They too have created an extensive vocabulary of euphemisms and abstract phrases to conceal horrendous realities. In the sugar-coated abortion versions, "products" or "contents" are merely "removed" or "evacuated" from the womb in the antiseptic settings of "reproductive health centers," "clinics," or "preterm institutes."

Much of the inoffensive language fabricated by past and present perpetrators has taken on a strong medical flavor. A study of former death camp doctors conducted by American psychiatrist Robert Jay Lifton in 1979 revealed that medical involvement in the Holocaust was projected not as killing, but as a "medical operation."[12] This is exactly how abortion doctors justify their assaults on the unborn: as "medical procedures" or "minor medical operations."[13] At the Hadamar euthanasia hospital, patients about to be killed by lethal injections were told that the substances administered were for "treatment of their lung disease."[14] In 1976, Dr. Willard Cates presented a paper before a meeting of Planned Parenthood Physicians entitled: "Abortion as a Treatment for Unwanted Pregnancy: The Number Two Sexually Transmitted 'Disease.'"[15]

These malignant metaphors are manifestations of a process best characterized as the medicalization of destruction. As such, they symbolize the most radical of transformations: the redefinition of killing as a type of medical treatment, and the reconceptualization of the victims as disease entities.

Choice Slogans

For those politicians who continually maintain that "I person-ally am opposed to abortion, but, after all, we must have a choice," Bishop O'Connor had some pertinent observations to convey: "You show me the politician who is prepared to say, 'I personally am opposed to bombing cities with nuclear weapons, but we have to have free choice,' 'I personally am opposed to killing Blacks or Jewish people or Methodists or Lutherans or Catholics, but we have to have a choice.' That's—you know—that's to me, sheer absurdity."[16]

Here the Bishop confronts the most sacred cow of abortion rhetoric: "choice" or "the right to choose." Those who rely on these slogans rarely specify the right to choose what for whom. Beneath this democratic facade lurks an especially reprehensible form of oppression: the right to choose to kill innocent human beings who cannot defend themselves.

The Nazi medics utilized almost identical designations—"selection," or they were "selected"—to cover up death camp atrocities. They never elaborated upon the true nature of their selections. Such seductive semantics were intended to obscure a particularly deplorable type of tyranny, namely, the right to select helpless victims for mass extermination.

"Pro-selection" and "pro-choice" semantics have proven to be enormously effective weapons in helping facilitate past and contemporary holocausts. Toward the latter part of July 1944 women who contracted scarlet fever were gassed to death at Auschwitz. This destruction process was classified as "a selec-tion."[17] In June 1981 doctors at New York's Mount Sinai Hospital announced they had pierced the heart and extracted half of the blood from an unwanted unborn twin afflicted with Down's syn-drome. *Newsweek* dubbed this destructive procedure "a choice in the womb."[18] Thus, Nazi doctors had "the right to select" who perished in gas chambers, just as today's abortion doctors in col-laboration with women insist on "the right to choose" who will expire in abortion chambers.

Dehumanizing the Victims

One other significant feature common to both Nazi and abor-tion rhetoric is the pervasive pattern of dehumanizing victims through the imposition of derogatory labels. As Bishop O'Connor so aptly put it, "The abortion mentality that has swept the country, that has simply declared the unborn to be nonhuman—that is what I compare to the Holocaust."[19]

Again, the Bishop draws a compelling analogy. A study of the disparaging language leads inevitably to the conclusion that abortionists and their most ardent supporters deny the humanity of the unborn as vociferously as the Nazis denied the humanity of the Jews.

Situation ethics professor Joseph Fletcher frequently refers to the unborn, especially if afflicted with a handicap, as "subhuman life in utero."[20] Sociologist Amitai Etzioni favors the development of "procedures and criteria for determining who and what shall live or die and which fetuses are tissue and which are human." He contends that most people view the "previable fetus" as "not alive, not human." He therefore defines the unborn during the first four and one-half months of pregnancy as "subhuman and relatively close to a piece of tissue."[21]

Paradoxically, Etzioni, a Jew, resorts to the same terminology against the unborn as the Nazis used against his ancestors. His preoccupation with such demeaning categories as "subhuman" bears an alarming resemblance to the Nazi approach toward determining who would survive and who would not. On many an occasion Adolf Hitler asserted that "Jews are not human."[22] University of Strasbourg anatomy professor Dr. August Hirt, whose research consisted of trying to demonstrate the inferiority of the Jewish race through an examination of skulls severed from gas chamber victims, referred to his subjects as "a repulsive yet characteristic subhumanity."[23]

Liberal Input

The images of Jews as "nonhuman" and "subhuman" did not originate with Hitler and his cohorts. One of the most significant but least publicized facts is that many of these depersonalized perceptions emanated from liberal intellectual circles. Professors Jacob Katz in *From Prejudice to Destruction* and Alfred D. Low in *Jews in the Eyes of the Germans* indicate that numerous demeaning stereotypes foisted on Jews were the handiwork of German intellectuals, many of whom possessed impeccable liberal credentials. As early as 1819 Christoph Heinrich Pfaff, described in

Katz's book as "an individual of high intellectual standards and genuine liberal convictions," compared Jews to "a rapidly growing parasitic plant that winds round the still healthy tree to suck up the life juice until the trunk, emaciated and eaten up from within, falls moldering into decay."[24]

Similarly, the members of today's American liberal community are among the most steadfast promoters of subhuman semantics directed against the unborn. Liberals repeatedly proclaim how much they care about an ever burgeoning list of oppressed groups, including blacks, women, the poor, homosexuals, and endangered animals. At the same time they remain completely oblivious to the existence, let alone plight, of the most thoroughly oppressed minority group in contemporary society: unborn children. In a style strikingly reminiscent of the German anti-Semitic liberal Pfaff, today's radical feminists, foremost puppets of ultra-liberal propaganda, frequently reduce the unborn to "a parasite" or "a parasite within the mother's body."[25]

Contemporary liberals commonly cite opposition to nuclear weapons as proof of their magnanimous concern for the largest possible constituency: humanity itself. Simultaneously, however, they play an instrumental role in support of the most awesome global slaughter in history: 50–60 million unborn children destroyed annually. A typical example of how pejorative stereotypes lead to such a schizophrenic type of mentality is evident in the comments of a rabbi interviewed on ABC's "Nightline" in 1984. Host Ted Koppel asked him how he could reconcile his pro-abortion position with his anti-nuclear defense posture. The rabbi replied that, according to over 2,000 years of Jewish tradition, "a fetus is not a human being."[26]

It is supremely ironic that years of Nazi tradition asserted just as emphatically that "a Jew is not a human being." Despite claims to the contrary, the American liberals' notion of who deserves to be defined as a legitimate member of the human community, like that of their German counterparts before and during the Nazi era, is an exceedingly selective, elitist, and constricted one.

The Legalization of Killing

Killing at the level of a holocaust is enhanced enormously when the derogatory mentality toward the victims becomes embedded in the legal structure. Regarding the legalization of destructive attitudes, Bishop O'Connor had this to say: "I very sincerely believe that an abortion mentality, structured and legalized in this country, does not differ in essence from that mentality that legalized putting Jews to death in Nazi Germany."[27]

A brief history of the word "nonperson" illustrates the process involved in moving from the private level of personal prejudice to the public level of legal definition. At first the designation "nonperson," along with "nonhuman," "subhuman," and "parasite," functioned to dehumanize those so labeled. Later the term "nonperson" was transformed into a legal construct which had the effect of stripping away rights from the victims and elevating their destruction to the exalted level of legality. In *The Dual State: A Contribution to the Study of German Dictatorship*, legal scholar Ernst Fraenkel revealed that the German Supreme Court in 1936 "refused to recognize Jews living in Germany as 'persons' in the legal sense."[28] In 1973, the U. S. Supreme Court declared that "the word 'person', as used in the Fourteenth Amendment, does not include the unborn."[29]

Political scientist Hannah Arendt considered the "nonperson" concept a crucial cornerstone of the victimization process intrinsic to totalitarian governments. In *The Origins of Totalitarianism*, she indicates that the hallmark of a totalitarian state, whether communist or fascist, is to declare those deemed stateless and expendable as "legal nonpersons."[30] According to this criterion, the United States qualifies as a totalitarian society because unborn children, chiefly through the device of "legal nonpersonhood," have been rendered stateless and outside the law's protection where doctors can inflict unimaginable acts of violence on a massive scale with full-fledged legal support.

Once a practice is legalized, even one so repulsive as large-scale killing, it is endowed with incredible respectability. Then the law itself becomes a prime justification for participation in destructive activities. And the practitioners of malevolent deeds can be expected to invoke the law relentlessly.

"What is legal is moral" is an astoundingly effective slogan utilized to vindicate all types of atrocities. Abortionists exploit the law to justify their involvement in feticide as extensively as the Nazis called upon the law to rationalize their participation in genocide. At the Nuremberg Doctors' Trial in 1947, defendant Walter E. Schmidt projected responsibility for the Nazi Holocaust onto the legal system. "The jurists in Berlin," he testified, "told us that this was a legal matter . . . quite legal."[31] In 1980, Dr. Michael Jackson invoked the law to defend his flourishing abortion business. "I just go by what the courts say," he explained. "I only do what's legal."[32]

Penetrating the Tip of the Iceberg

Bishop O'Connor has focused on some highly disquieting realities. They are far from subtle. And they reveal just the tip of the iceberg.

The New York Times and other members of the media elite are in much the same position as those in Hans Christian Anderson's fable who maintained that the starkly-naked emperor was fully arrayed in the most splendid finery. The bishop, like the boy who put an end to all the pretenses by announcing that the emperor had no clothes, has dealt a serious blow to the very core of pro-abortion ideology and semantics. The alarming parallels between past and current atrocities will not go away no matter how much the *Times* denies them or attempts to discredit anyone who risks bringing them to the fore.

Instead of castigating Bishop O'Connor for calling things by their proper names, the mega press would do well to start probing the corruption of language and thought that masks the medical execution of millions inside the womb. For too long the watchdogs of public perception in the mainstream secular media have functioned as agents of destruction-inducing propaganda by accepting at face value the euphemistic and dehumanizing rhetoric circulated by the abortion establishment. Today's gatekeepers of public information need to abandon their selective, schizophrenic brand of reporting morality and start covering the contemporary medical war on the unwanted unborn at least as directly and graphically as they have covered the Vietnam War, the massacre in Beirut, the horrors of capital punishment, and the slaughter of seals, dolphins, whales, and eagles.

George Orwell warned that the semantics of tyrants throughout history invariably stray "away from concreteness" toward the realm of abstractions where "defense of the indefensible"[33] can be more readily accomplished. Bishop O'Connor's manner of expression—direct, forthright, noneuphemistic and factual— should go a long way toward helping to prevent the concrete horrors of abortion from melting into remote abstractions. His ability to articulate an indispensable historical perspective and a profound moral vision with a refreshing sense of clarity, vigor, and consistency provides a model of discourse with great potential for seriously disrupting an abortion mentality which dominates the mind-sets of so many individuals.

Notes

1.   Ari L. Goldman, "Bishop Defends Holocaust Analogy," *The New York Times*, March 14, 1984, p. 17.

2.   Arthur L. Goldberg, "When Admiral O'Connor Went to Dachau," *The New York Times*, March 23, 1984, p. 26.

3.   Ronald Reagan, "Abortion and the Conscience of the Nation," *The Human Life Review*, 9 (Spring 1983): 12; William Brennan, *The Abortion Holocaust: Today's Final Solution* (St. Louis: Landmark Press, 1983), p. 5.

4.   Goldman, *loc. cit.*

5.   Bernard N. Nathanson, *Aborting America* (Garden City, New York: Doubleday, 1979) p. 165.

6.   Horatio R. Storer *et al.*, "Report on Criminal Abortion," *Transactions of the American Medical Association*, 12 (1859): 75-78.

7.   D.A. O'Donnell and W.L. Atlee, "Report on Criminal Abortion," *Transactions of the American Medical Association*, 22 (1871): 239-58.

8.   Willard Gaylin and Marc Lappe, "Fetal Politics: The Debate on Experimenting with the Unborn," *Atlantic*, May 1975, p. 66.

9.   Warren M. Hern and Billie Corrigan, "What about Us? Staff Reactions to the D & E Procedure," Paper presented at the Annual Meeting of the Association of Planned Parenthood Physicians, San Diego, California, October 26, 1978, p. 9.

10.   Goldman, *loc. cit.*

11.   Extract from the Field Interrogation of Kurt Gerstein, 26 April 1945, Describing the Mass Gassing of Jews and Other "Undesirables," *Trials of War Criminals before the Nuremberg Military Tribunals, The Medical Case*, 2 vols. (Washington DC: U.S. Government Printing Office, 1947-1949), 1: 866-67 (hereafter referred to as *Medical Case*).

12.   Howard Wolinsky, "War and Holocaust are Focus of His Work," *American Medical News*, June 13, 1980, p. 15; "Doctors of the Death Camps," *Time*, June 25, 1979, p. 68.

13.   Carl O. Rice, "Operation on Demand?" *Minnesota Medicine*, 36 (May 1973): 412.

14.   Earl W. Kinter, ed., *The Hadamar Trial: Trial of Alfons Klein and Others* (London: William Hodge, 1949), p. 176.

15.   Willard Cates, David A. Grimes, and Jack C. Smith, "Abortion as a Treatment for Unwanted Pregnancy: The Number Two Sexually Transmitted 'Disease,'" Paper presented at the Annual Meeting of the Association of Planned Parenthood Physicians, Miami Beach, Florida, November 11, 1976, pp. 5-6.

16.   Goldman, *loc. cit.*

17.   Raymond Phillips, ed., *The Belsen Trial: Trial of Josef Kramer Defendant and Forty-four Others* (London: William Hodge, 1949), p. 73.

18.   "A Choice in the Womb," *Newsweek*, June 29, 1981, p. 86.

19.   Goldman, *loc. cit.*

20.   Joseph Fletcher, "Ethics and Euthanasia," in *To Live and to Die: When, Why, and How*, ed. Robert H. Williams (New York: Springer-Verlag, 1973), p. 116.

21.   Amitai Etzioni, "A Review of *The Ethics of Fetal Research*," *Society*, March/April 1976, p. 72.

22.   C.C. Aronsfeld, "The Nazi Design Was Extermination, Not Emigration," *Patterns of Prejudice*, 9 (May-June 1975): 22.

23.   Letter from Sievers to Rudolf Brandt, 9 February 1942, and Report by Hirt Concerning the Acquisition of Skulls of Jewish-Bolshevik Commissars, *Medical Case*, 1:749.

24.   Alfred D. Low, *Jews in the Eyes of the Germans: From the Enlightenment to Imperial Germany* (Philadelphia: Institute for the Study of Human Issues, 1979); Jacob Katz, *From Prejudice to Destruction: Anti-Semitism, 1700-1933* (Cambridge, MA: Harvard University Press, 1980), pp. 149-50.

25.   See Boston Women's Health Book Collective, *Our Bodies, Ourselves: A Book by and for Women* (New York: Simon & Schuster, 1973), p. 144; Rosalind Pollack Petchesky, *Abortion and Women's Choice: The State, Sexuality, and Reproductive Freedom* (Boston: Northeastern University Press, 1984), p. 346.

26.   "A Moral Paradox: Abortion and the Freeze," *Nightline*, Transcript, Show #712, January 31, 1984, pp. 9-10.

27.   Goldman, *loc. cit.*

28.   Ernst Fraenkel, *The Dual State: A Contribution to the Theory of Dictatorship*, trans. E.A. Shils with Edith Lowenstein and Klaus Knorr (New York: Oxford University Press, 1941), p. 95.

29.   *Roe v. Wade*, 410 U.S. 158 (1973).

30.   Hannah Arendt, *The Origins of Totalitarianism* (New York: Harcourt Brace Jovanovich, 1973), p. 290.

31.   Extract from the Testimony of Walter E. Schmidt, *Medical Case*, 1: 890.

32.   Thomas G. Gulick, "Even Some Abortionists Having Second Thoughts," *Human Events*, April 12, 1980, pp. 20-21.

33.   George Orwell, "Politics and the English Language," in *The Orwell Reader: Fiction, Essays, and Reportage by George Orwell* (New York: Harcourt Brace Jovanovich, 1956), pp. 355–66.

PART FOUR

Insights from Rhetoric and Philosophy

DeMARCO   It is commonplace in our consumer-oriented, advertising-mediated world for words to be severed from their link with reality. Words arouse, but do not enlighten. Advocates of abortion use words rhetorically, not to shed light on what abortion entails, but to win people over to a "pro-choice" position. This article shows in detail how pro-abortionists subject words to the processes of: (1) deification, (2) devaluation, (3) devitalization, (4) deterioration, (5) deception, and (6) doublethink in order to dissociate words from their relationship with truth. In contrast, pro-life advocates rely on words to reveal clearly and unequivocally what abortion involves. The first commandment of the educated person is *respect for the word*.

GILLESPIE   In this essay, the writer offers a model of abortion rhetoric by plotting opposing terms in the controversy on four dimensions of the cognitive system—arousal, relationship, reality, and goal. Then, applying a key concept in Kenneth Burke's dramatistic theory, the principle of victimage (our desire to seek and destroy, or identify with, a victim) is shown to shape how the fetus is perceived by participants in the completing dramas.

HUNT   Building on the thought of Jacques Ellul, the writer identifies six technological themes which make it difficult for contemporary people to act morally or think ethically about public policy issues. The themes are: (1) preoccupation with means, (2) efficiency, (3) problem, (4) artificiality, (5) facts, and (6) inevitability. These themes undercut our exercise of freedom as the power to choose the good versus the power to choose what is useful: freedom based on truth rather than on power; freedom as creativity; freedom to accept reality as a gift; and freedom as resistance to evil. Understanding the power of technological themes enables us to respond more critically to the rhetoric surrounding issues of public policy such as abortion.

McCLERREN   Abortion rhetoric both pro and con is analyzed by criteria abstracted largely from the writings of the late Richard M. Weaver. Emotive language is identified as "ultimate terms" or "god" terms and "devil" terms. Modes of argument are identified and classified according to the philosophical stance of the rhetorician. Neuter, evil, and noble types of rhetoric are viewed from a Platonic framework.

Grace and the Word

Donald DeMarco

W *ords* (*Les mots*) is the title of Jean-Paul Sartre's autobiography. It could just as well be the countersignature of our present age. Just as Sartre's "words" present an image of alienation from the flesh and blood existence of their author, so too, much of the verbiage that floods our civilized landscape exists without bearing any discernible connection with the substantial world it is meant to signify. Words have lost their link with the world. They have become little more than momentary stimulants for the unthinking masses whose apparent need for stimulation is limitless. Words are processed, circulated, consumed, absorbed, and then forgotten—a pattern whose endless repetition is best typified by the daily press and commercial advertising. Words influence, but fail to nourish; they arouse, but do not enlighten.

Thus, when a major moral controversy arises, such as abortion, a numbing war of words prevents any true discussion concerning which view is more moral or realistic. A formidable impasse has existed for some time, precisely because words no longer direct us toward a common reality or a common moral vision, but lock us in a futile verbal struggle which prohibits understanding and perpetuates division.

On one side of the abortion issue is the organization that identifies itself as "pro-life." This identification label rankles the opposition for two fundamental reasons: (1) it insinuates that the opposition is not fully sensitive to the value of life, an insinuation the opposition vehemently rejects; and (2) it suggests that "pro-lifers" are in full support of all life, an unconvincing claim in the light of their perceived attitudes on issues involving war, capital punishment, and the rights of animals.

The "pro-life" group identifies the opposition as "pro-abortion," a label which the opposition also rejects, maintaining that it does not promote abortion in individual cases, but merely its availability. Once the availability of abortion is secured, individual women are then free to choose abortion for themselves.

Those labelled as "pro-abortionists" are understandably emphatic in identifying their position as "pro-choice," and strongly disavow the "pro-life" charge that they are "anti-life." "Pro-choice" advocates take pride in their rhetoric of choice, for it conveys a liberal frame of mind which is neither dogmatic nor judgmental, and suggests a compassionate and humanitarian disposition that is fully accepting of the pregnant woman and whatever choice she makes concerning her pregnancy. Moreover, it allows them to intensify their negative portrayal of their opposition from "anti-abortion" (a source of annoyance to the opposition which prefers to be viewed by the more positive sounding expression, "pro-life") to "anti-choice," which carries the rhetorically strategic implications of being anti-freedom and virtually anti-human.

Both sides have adopted a rhetoric that casts themselves as being in favor of something good and their opposition as being against something good. This verbal stand-off is confusing to those not committed to either side. Such a stalemate, however, plays into the hands of the "pro-choice" allegiance, for, if it is impossible to determine which side has the superior moral vision, fairness would seem to mandate allowing women to choose for themselves. When there is genuine doubt in a moral issue, moralizing or legislating takes on the appearance of authoritarianism. If it cannot be decided what is moral, then it must be moral not to decide. This victory by default for the "pro-choice" side effectively makes irrelevant any discussion of real issues such as the nature of the unborn, the physical and psychological sequelae to induced abortion, the trivialization of sex and procreation, and the effect abortion has on the integrity of the family.

A purely rhetorical debate, which does not get beyond words, is a victory for "pro-choice" because "pro-choice" seems more neutral than either "pro-" or "anti-abortion." But a "pro-choice" position is not really neutral. As a matter of fact, it is decidedly inclined toward abortion. Whenever a pregnant woman makes her "conscientious" choice, which is also said to be "anguished" or "agonizing," it is invariably for abortion. Although "pro-choice" rhetoric logically implies that a woman's conscience or her anguished or agonizing choice is equally disposed toward birth as well as abortion—the myth of neutrality—in actual practice it is not. André Hellegers makes the point that "any such 'agonizing decision' which results so consistently in the death of the fetus should not be described as an 'agonizing choice'."[1] And Joseph Sobran asks the question that he says "never gets answered": "Why it should be the decision to kill the child, rather than the decision to let it live, that is represented as the triumph of conscience?"[2] The answer, of course, is that "pro-choice" is a rhetorical ploy that covers the reality of "pro-abortion." And this is precisely why "pro-choice" advocates want to keep the discussion away from reality and permanently on the level of verbal rhetoric.

By insisting that the discussion remain on a purely verbal plane, "pro-choice" enthusiasts adopt the curious position that reality actually interferes with moral decision making. Their belief that a position of "moral neutrality" is really morally neutral and does not affect their decision betrays an ignorance of the most fundamental law of the cosmos, namely, that nothing stands still. Existence abhors neutrality more firmly than nature abhors a vacuum. A log in the water is carried downstream. Untreated silver tarnishes, unprotected iron rusts. Muscles that are not exercised, atrophy. And moral indifference is not a virtue but a vice. Indecision and ignorance are liabilities. Nowhere in the physical world or in the moral sphere are there any points of neutrality. Everything is either developing or decaying; nothing is at rest. In the absence of a positive effort there is a negative slide. The Law of Entropy describes a cosmic fact and offers a parable by which we gain insight into the dynamics of our own moral condition. Without grace, gravity reigns. If one takes a neutral stand on the abortion issue, one becomes—by force of gravity—drawn toward abortion. That is the reality of it. And as long as words are kept disconnected from reality, this fundamental axiom which describes the inherent dynamism of all things, remains ignored.

Physicians have called attention to the fact that showing a pregnant woman the image of her fetus on an ultrasound screen, even before quickening, can help complete the bonding process between that mother and her child, and influence her against abortion.[3] In such cases, the real image of the fetus is like grace acting against the gravity toward abortion that sets in when such forms of grace are withheld. Nonetheless, the question has arisen as to whether ultrasound viewing would give an unfair advantage to those who represented the interests of the fetus. Ultrasound would seem an unfair maneuver since it violates a context of "neutrality." As doctors have reasoned: "Ultrasound examination may thus result in fewer abortions and more desired pregnancies."[4] The truth of the matter, of course, is that ultrasound provides what words should ordinarily provide, that is, an insight into reality. And the more one knows about the reality of the issue, the better able one is to make the right decision. Reality does not interfere with moral decision making, it is merely indispensable if the moral decision is going to be a wise one. The criticism that ultrasound is unfair because it violates neutrality is made by those who try to conceal their pro-abortion bias under a camouflage of "pro-choice" neutrality, realizing that if all positive realities were withheld, abortion would eventuate just as surely as the release of one's supporting grip will cause a ball to drop to the ground. By keeping the abortion debate on a verbal level and thereby excluding the pertinent realities, "pro-choice" rhetoric—under the guise of neutrality—effectively promotes abortion.

But abortion is more than a verbal issue that is to be fought the way sales wars are waged between competing brands of soft drinks and laundry detergents. Abortion is a real issue, involving flesh and blood people and far-reaching consequences. Tradition knew this well, and its prohibitions and restrictions of abortion reflected a stubborn realism. "Pro-life" people evidence their sensitivity to this tradition in their fondness of citing Edmund Burke's remark that in order for evil to triumph all that is necessary is that good people do nothing.

The "pro-choice" insistence on severing rhetoric from realism reveals the inherent weakness in its position, but it also reveals culture's woeful lack of respect for the real, truth-communicating function of the word. And the "pro-choice" movement is taking full advantage of this lamentable state the word has reached. Words fulfill their proper function when they are subordinated to and measured by the things they name. "All education," writes Richard Weaver, "is learning to name rightly, as Adam named the animals."[5] When words are no longer measured by the truth of things, they become instruments of deception. "The rectification of names," said Confucius, is perhaps the main business of government: "If names are not correct, language will not be in accordance with the truth of things."[6] The sentiment is by no means uncommon and we find it echoed throughout Western history from Heraclitus to Hammarskjöld. Heraclitus, anticipating John the Evangelist's lofty use of the Word, stated: "One ought to follow the lead of that which is common to all men. But although the Word is common to all, yet most men live as if each had a private wisdom of his own."[7] And Dag Hammarskjöld, former Secretary-General of the United Nations, remarked:

> *Respect for the word* is the first commandment in the discipline by which a man can be educated to maturity—intellectual, emotional, and moral (emphasis in original).
>
> Respect for the word—to employ it with scrupulous care and an incorruptible heartfelt love of truth—is essential if there is to be any growth in a society or in the human race.
>
> To misuse the word is to show contempt for man. It undermines the bridges and poisons the wells. It causes Man to regress down the long path of his evolution.[8]

For Hammarskjöld, words, when properly employed, represent avenues to grace; when they are misused, they serve the cause of gravity. The first responsibility of the writer involves an uncompromisable integrity in the use of words, an insistence that there must always be a fidelity between the word and the reality it signifies. This is why Alexander Solzhenitsyn, who knows a great deal about the misuse of the word in the hands of a totalitarian regime, says that he studies the words in his Russian dictionary "as if they were precious stones, each so precious that I would not exchange one for another."

The function of the word is to mediate the world. Language is a bridge that connects the mind of humans with the extramental world that lies beyond words. The fact that one does not always use words in a way that is commensurate with what they signify is only too evident. Blasphemy is a case in point. As Chesterton has remarked: "Blasphemy is not wild; blasphemy is in its nature prosaic. It consists in regarding in a commonplace manner something which other and happier people regard in a rapturous and imaginative manner."[9]

Blasphemy is a lie inasmuch as it speaks of grace in terms of gravity. The public may have come to associate blasphemy with excitement, but that is because they have lost their sense of proportion between the word and the reality it represents. "Our words have wings," George Eliot reminds us, "but fly not where they would." Chesterton's intention in asserting that blasphemy is not wild—when everyone knows it is—is to startle people in the hope that they might rectify their use of words and better align them with reality.

The ideologue offers another example of trying to give the word more importance than the reality it is supposed to mediate. His aim is to substitute the word for the world and his strategy is an expression of faith in verbal magic: "I want the world to be a different way than it is. I will insist that people speak as if it is that way—this will bring it about." For the ideologue, the word does not mediate the created world; rather, the world is created by the word.

When the late Dr. Alan Guttmacher, former president of the Planned Parenthood Federation of America, was involved in preparing a series of television programs on physical and mental health for teenagers, he urged that in at least sixteen of these programs the word abortion be employed in such a way as to "detoxify the viewing audiences from cultural shock at the word."[10]

Similarly, a moral theologian once complained that "adultery" is a "negative" word that should be replaced by the more positive sounding "flexible monogamy" in order to invest marital infidelity with a more positive reality. Man's belief in the magical properties of words notwithstanding, Limburger has the same disagreeable odor no matter what appellation it receives.

Disrespect for the Word

In general, the dissociation of the word from the world follows a diversified pattern. Of particular interest among these forms of dissociation include the following: (1) deification, (2) devaluation, (3) devitalization, (4) deterioration, (5) deception, and (6) doublethink. In each of these forms there is a failure of the word to unite the mind with the truth. To the extent that these forms are prevalent in culture, a fruitful debate on abortion, or any other moral issue, becomes increasingly unlikely. Fruitful debate presupposes a link between word and world.

Deification

The story is told of a woman from Siam who decided to abort when she learned that she was carrying twins; she could not face the prospect of giving birth to Siamese twins. The woman, needless to say, was reacting to the word rather than the reality. Another story centers around a Canadian farmer who lived close to the American border. When authorities surveyed his property for legal purposes, they discovered that the actual site of the farm was in the United States. Upon learning this, the farmer was greatly relieved, commenting that he didn't think he could take another one of those Canadian winters! Needless to say, one does not make the winters any colder by calling them "Canadian" anymore than one makes them any warmer by calling them "American." Nonetheless, as the word becomes mightier than the reality it signifies, it becomes increasingly difficult to separate fact from fiction. A television weatherman solemnly predicts "rain tonight in some official areas."[11] An anxious mother decides to bed her infant in a playpen in order to prevent "crib death." A youngster stitches a Levi label on his Brand-X jeans to gain the acceptance of his peers.

The folly of mistaking words for things, of abandoning the world for the word, is perfectly exemplified in commercial advertising, an enterprise whose annual budget in the United States alone is estimated at $50 billion. Advertising can be, as George Orwell has remarked, "the rattling of a stick inside the swill bucket," but the rattling itself is often hypnotic. "Sell the sizzle, not the steak," is a sacrosanct first principle in the advertising industry. When ad men identify a certain shade of lipstick as "Pizzicato Pink," they are banking on verbal magic to sell their product. "Pizzicato," in this case, has nothing to do with the plucking of stringed instruments; it is exotica, pizzazz, intoxication, romance, sensuousness, frivolity, and pseudo-elegance. Likewise, "Apricot

Shimmer" is not a lipstick color but the lushness of tropical fruit or surrender to sexual passion. Advertising uses words not to convey meanings but to create illusions.

The philosopher Usener, alluding to the capacity of words to overwhelm people, speaks of them as "momentary deities." Literary critic George Steiner has pointed out in his book, *Extraterritorial*, that eleventh century theologian Peter Damian believed men fell into paganism through a grammatical flaw: "Because heathen speech has a plural for the word 'deity,' wretched humankind came to conceive of many gods." The very existence of the word "deities," for Peter Damian, was enough to convince people that it must denote a reality. Words can be as large, if not larger, than reality itself. The United States government plays on the assumption that the word itself is the reality when it recruits comic strip character Snoopy to exhort the public to "savEnergy."[12] By allying the two words together, an entire "e" is saved. Presumably, we can savEven morEnergy if we bind more words together.

The modern writer who is perhaps best identified with dissociating words from the world in order to make them into "deities" unto themselves, is Gertrude Stein. A brief excerpt from her book, *Tender Buttons*, is sufficient to illustrate the point: "The care with which the rain is wrong and the green is wrong and the white is wrong, the care with which there is a chair and plenty of breathing. The care with which there is incredible justice and likeness, all this makes a magnificent asparagus, and also a fountain."

Stein uses words not as windows that open to the world, but as walls that exclude the outer landscape. Her experiment in separating words from the world strips words of meaning and leaves her reader with a profound sense of alienation—between author and language, language and reality, author and reader. Stein's deified language decomposes into a loose assortment of atomic units—reminiscent of the cubism of her close friend, Picasso—that no longer has the capacity to convey an integrated meaning.

"Pro-choice" rhetoric continues this modern penchant for deifying words and abandoning reality. "Pro-choice" is like "Pizzicato Pink"; it sounds good. And there it rests its case. In addition, it is consistent with the modern process of fragmentation which reduces organic structures to collections of discontinuous bits and pieces. In the "pro-choice" world of abortion, society is reduced to a collection of private and isolated individuals.

It is fatal in art as well as in thinking to abandon the world for the word; but it can also be fatal in life. Some "pro-choice" supporters have proposed the deification of words as a "possible solution to the abortion situation." This "solution" consists in substituting the letters "MR" (for "menstrual regulation") for the more problematic word "abortion." Professor Luke Lee and John Paxman write: "MR can be performed with or without confirmation of pregnancy, an important difference between MR and conventional abortion. . . . For many women, not knowing whether amenorrhea is a result of conception may be of great psychological value."[13] The reality of abortion can be conveniently obscured by calling it MR. But the fact remains that a blanket of words is not an adequate protection against the force of reality. Words should reflect reality. If they are to have psychological value, that value should be grounded in the truth they convey. Psychological value uprooted from truth is fraudulent and, at best, can confer only temporary and superficial benefits. We are not fair to people if we are concerned about their psychological comfort and nothing more. The deification of words makes the preposterous claim that the word is more important than the world and that ideology is more real than reality.

Devaluation

The deification of words elevates them to a greater importance than reality itself. The devaluation of words, on the other hand, reduces them to less importance than what is naturally due them as conveyors of meaning. Nonetheless, the two processes are closely related. It is axiomatic that whenever something is elevated above its nature, it is, in the final analysis, degraded; for, in trying to make something fulfill a function for which it has no aptitude, one makes a mockery of it—like the horse which tried to sing like a nightingale and lost its ability to whinny like a horse. People invariably lose faith in what appears ridiculous. Hence, the deification of words leads to their devaluation.

The facile use of superlatives to advertise mediocre commercial products illustrates the point. Not only does such a practice empty the language of words to express true excellence, but it devalues the superlative. If all movies are "great," the word "great" loses its credibility, becomes devalued, and finally means nothing. If every experience is "fantastic," the word soon becomes bankrupt.

News reporting is often as irresponsible as commercial advertising in its use of words. A few years ago, in 1979, the media created a sensation out of a malfunction that occurred at a nuclear power plant at Three Mile Island in Pennsylvania. No one was killed and public-health damage, if any, was unmeasured. The New York *Post*, however, ran banner headlines on its front page: One day it was, NUKE LEAK GOES OUT OF CONTROL; the next day, RACE WITH NUCLEAR DISASTER.[14] Even after the hydrogen bubble began to dissolve, one network referred to the incident at Three Mile Island as a "calamity," a description which prompted George Will to ask the question: "What language does the network reserve for events that kill people?"[15] In 1984, a group of people held a candlelight vigil on the site of the "calamity" to commemorate its 5th anniversary.

When the cry of "wolf" is made too often, it ceases to alarm people. In becoming devalued, words lose their capacity to arouse. As our faith in language diminishes, our faith in more graphic means of making a point increases. Since we are a technological society, we inevitably put additional faith in technology. According to one writer: "Part of the devaluation of language results from a feeling that somehow it is no longer effective. Samuel Johnson's society pinned its faith on language; Americans attach theirs to technology. . . . Man does not ascend to heaven by prayer, the aspiration of language, but by the complex rockets and computer codes of NASA."[16] But our loss of faith in language is also, and out of desperation, an invitation to violence. The poet W. H. Auden has warned us that when language is "corrupted, people lose faith in what they hear, and this leads to violence." Words, once believed to be grace that counteracts the human gravitational pull toward violence, seem impotent against the impressive weight of technology and violence. Abortion, needless to say, is one of many points where technology and violence intersect.

Given the current devaluation of words, it is easy for many to, dismiss "pro-life" expressions such as "Stop the Killing," "Abortion Kills," "Save a Human Life . . . Fight Abortion," "Death Before Birth," and so on, as just another wave of irresponsible rhetoric. The cry of "wolf" falls on deaf ears.

Devitalization

British literary critic David Holbrook has observed that ours is a time when "the capacities of English-speaking people to contemplate the mysterious and metaphysical through the word are weakened and unexercised."[17] His observation warrants thoughtful attention. As words are devitalized to accommodate bureaucratic, ideological, or political needs for more neutral expressions, language begins to lose its capacity to evoke feelings of awe, wonder, or reverence. "Awesome" is currently the antithesis to "gross" in the two-word vocabulary of today's teenager. "Wonder" is routinely applied to brassieres and antibiotics. And to call someone "irreverent" is not to suggest impiety, but to confer praise.

One enterprising hospital has translated and tranquilized the word "death" into "negative patient care outcome." And California Governor Edmund Brown, Jr., during his term of office, established a council on "wellness." The combination of these two instances of newspeak inspired language ombudsman Edwin Newman to quip that couples may soon be marrying each other "for better or for worse, in sickness and in wellness, until negative patient care outcome do us part."

"Vanity of vanities, saith the Preacher. . . ." But in one new translation the words become, "A Vapor of vapors! Thinnest of vapors! All is vapor!"—moving one critic to decry the "turning of the most passionate cry in the literature of nihilism into a spiritual weather report."[18]

In order to devitalize the word "recession," the United States government, according to William Safire, has experimented with more tepid alternatives such as "a mild downturn" and a "soft landing."

The poet, on the other hand, being more attuned to the pulse of truth and tragedy, assumes the important task of preserving language's vitality. In his hands, words evoke a presence, make their subject live in the listener's imagination. His contribution to restoring life to language becomes all the more urgent as the subordination of words to various political and practical needs continues to erode their power. American poet Robert Penn Warren sees the poet as a sublime gadfly, an ever-vigilant ombudsman who keeps what Santayana called "the prestige of the infinite," the boast of technology, from overshadowing the prestige of the intimate, which is the business of poetry.[19]

In the abortion discussion, however, "pro-choice" defenders regard the neutralization of language as an ideal. A child that is developing in its mother's womb, therefore, becomes a "fetus," or a "product of conception," or simply a "conceptus." Even Bernard Nathanson, now an apologist for the right-to-life of the unborn, prefers the word "alpha," in the interest of what he calls "neutralizing the discussion." In addition, "life" becomes "potential life," and abortion becomes the "termination of pregnancy" (which is also what birth is) or the "interruption of pregnancy" (as if the pregnancy were to be resumed after a brief pause). "VIP" is a canonized code word for "Voluntary Interruption of Pregnancy."

When words are devitalized, bled of their life substance, their power to elicit an awareness of the value they signify weakens. The neutralization of words in the abortion debate, therefore, is a capitulation to the "pro-choice" position. Words that no longer convey objective values present the image of a world without values that can be subjectively altered. A neutral discussion is tantamount to an inducement to interpose one's own values. M.J. Sobran writes:

> To say that woman is "with child" is to affirm that what she carries in her womb is a member of the human family, akin to all of us: it is to speak not with the forceps of analysis, but with the embrace of metaphor. But to call the child a "fetus" is to pickle it in a kind of rhetorical formaldehyde, and to accept the burden of proving what cannot be proved by empirical methodology: that the pickled thing had a right to live.[20]

A dead language cannot evoke live values. Words ought not to be devitalized—in the interest of fairness—because reality itself is vitalized. Martin Heidegger spoke repeatedly of language as "the house of Being." We cannot get to Being, to the reality of things, through a language whose relationship with Being has been dissolved. Philosopher Ludwig Wittgenstein alluded to the same dilemma when he remarked that "The limits of my language are the limits of my world."

The word "life" itself loses at least some of its denotative meaning in a mental climate which accepts that it is a popular soft-drink which "adds life,"[21] or makes one "come alive." And what tragic implication can the word "murder" have for Magda

Denes who says that "Abortion is murder of a most necessary sort?"[22] If there is more "life" in a soft drink than in a developing fetus, and if murder is "a necessity" whereas protection for the unborn is a "violation of a woman's rights," it is only because words have undergone a process of devitalization whereby they have lost their capacity to direct the mind to a world of objective values that transcend one's arbitrary will or private dispositions, a truth Shakespeare expressed when he stated that "Value dwells not in particular will."[23]

Since there is nothing neutral in reality, neutrality should not be an ideal when it comes to using language in order to discuss real moral values. There can be no poetry that defends or celebrates abortion because poetry, in respecting the vitality of words, unites us with the vitality inherent in existing things. To treat something which is vital as if it were neutral is to relinquish care for it and allow it to be overtaken by the force of gravity—a neutral language must ultimately become a dead language. And a dead language cannot inspire moral action.

Deterioration

"STIX NIX HIX PIX" is a famous newspaper headline and a prime example of newspaper-speak. Translated into "normal" English it means that the citizens of a certain rural community (STIX) have rejected (NIX) a particular motion picture (PIX) that deals with a pastoral (HIX) subject. The French version—*"Morceau de bois nient paysans au cinéma"*—was no doubt met with bewilderment since it literally means: "Pieces of wood disown farmers in the cinema." This unorthodox and even unnatural use of language illustrates the extent to which newspapers are prepared to go in order to accommodate themselves to space limitations and the need to catch the reader's eye. In this regard, a newspaper has something in common with the wild proliferation of commercial signs customarily found in a city's shopping district. Both truncate and glamorize language for the purpose of competing more successfully for their readers' attention. Traffic signs, product labels, thirty-second commercials, billboards, skywriting, T shirts, and bumper stickers are a few more of many instances in which language must be severely altered in order to fit space, time, and attention needs. The binary language of the computer forces upon us its own dipolar rhythm: feedback, input, output, legwork, sit-in, and so on. Police prose offers an amusing burlesque of administration jargon: "I apprehended the alleged perpetrator." A United States handbook refers to a shovel as a "combat emplacement evacuator" and the CIA uses the expression "non-discernable micro-bio-inoculator" to describe a poison dart.

We are all familiar with political blather, bureaucratic gobbledygook, the surreal boobspeak of commercial advertising, the sludge of academic writing, sledgehammer slogans, medical officialese, and the yahoo erudition of Howard Cosell ("I am impressed by the continuity of his physical presence"). These exemplify practices that contribute to the growing deterioration of words, rendering language dense and confusing, robbing it of its artistry and grace. Much of what passes for education, complains one educator, takes on the rhetorical form of "para-sense"[24]—verbal constructions that sound like sense but are devoid of sense as well as reference. "The English language is dying," moans another educator, "because it is not being taught."[25]

In J.M.G. LeClézio's novel *The Flood*, the anti-hero succumbs to the deluge of words he encounters in his daily life. Even while strolling down the street minding his own business, words assault him from every direction: instructions (Walk—Don't Walk), threats (Trespassers Will Be Prosecuted), and newsstand alarms (Plane Crash at Tel Aviv). All words blur together and become a meaningless buzz in his ears. Finally, in self-defense he suffers what might be called semantic aphasia—a numbness to the meaning of words. His malady is symbolic of a cultural epidemic of semantic aphasia that results from a prolonged and ubiquitous deterioration of words.

Semantic aphasia may be best associated with the use of acronyms, word initials that do not even hint at what they conceal. At some abortion clinics, aborted fetuses are routinely called P.O.C.s (standing for "products of conception"). In some hospitals, the term for patients believed to have no hope of recovery is "GORK," the acronym for God Only Really Knows.[26]

Neuro-surgeon Harley Smyth decries the use of medical officialese to justify abortion, such as "therapeutic," which treats no disease and cures no symptom, or "reactive depression in pregnancy," which he says "must represent one of the most serious of all prostitutions of psychiatric diagnostic language."[27]

One of the most inventive expressions of medical officialese is related to an abortion performed in 1981 at New York's Mt. Sinai Hospital. In this case, an expectant mother was carrying twins, one of whom was diagnosed to have Down's syndrome. Doctors offered her the unusual option of destroying the Down's syndrome fetus in the womb by drawing out its blood through a needle. The prenatal procedure was performed and the mother delivered one healthy baby and one papery vestige of the fetus that had been.[28] The expression coined to obscure the purpose of the procedure was "selective delivery of discordant twins," an expression that omits reference to the selective killing, and fabricates a "discordant" relationship between twins who are merely different from each other.

The deterioration of words represents a linguistic counterpart to Newton's Second Law of Thermodynamics—a Second Law of Verbal-dynamics according to which words drift downward toward a sea of incomprehension. The character in LeClézio's novel is a victim of this downward drift and represents the predicament of many others who suffer from the same phenomenon.

"Pro-life" writers consistently complain about the deterioration of words, and many ardently seek to restore them to a condition of grace. "Pro-choice" writers have a different complaint: not that words are deteriorating, but that "pro-life" people are trying to impose their own values on others. The "pro-life" position recognizes clearly that the values pro-lifers uphold are not "their values," but objective values that extend to all human beings. In order to make this point in a cogent and convincing way, however, demands a language that is healthy. At a certain point in the deterioration of words, it is no longer possible for language to communicate values that are universal and objective. At this stage, the only values that language can communicate are those of the individual. The deterioration of words, then, is necessary in order to allow the "pro-choice" position to survive as a cultural force, for a deteriorated language provides an effective barrier against all moral values that transcend those of the mere individual.

Deception

The processes of deification, devaluation, devitalization, and deterioration by which words are dissociated from their proper meanings facilitates deception. Although deception involves an intent to mislead, it is relatively easy to conceal such an intent when using words whose popular usage is already misleading. While "pro-life" writers and speakers are trying to restore language to health, their adversaries are taking advantage of the weakness of language in order to deceive the public even further. And because language is currently in so weakened a state, there seems to be no limit to the amount of deception that is possible.

American abortion entrepreneur William Baird, in a documentary produced for closed-circuit television and shown to thousands of college students, explains in reassuring tones to a young woman who is nine weeks pregnant how her "pre-fetus" will be removed and how she will feel strong enough by that evening to dine with her boyfriend.[29] The "pre-fetus" is a precursor to the fictitious "pre-embryo" which Professor Jérôme Lejeune exposed during the Maryville, Tennessee trial in 1989 involving seven frozen embryos. Canadian abortionist Henry Morgentaler complains to a news reporter that, "People who say the heart starts beating 18 days after conception are crazy. At 10 weeks, the embryo still only weighs one ounce, so how could it have a fully formed heart?"[30] It is a matter of scientific fact that at four weeks the embryo's skin is so transparent that one can observe blood pumping through its heart. At eight weeks the heartbeat is sufficiently strong and clear that it can be taped and played on an inexpensive cassette recorder. Can Baird, Morgentaler, and others be as ignorant about their career specialty as they claim?

The abortionist is sometimes called a "health care provider," and the clinic where he works is a "health care facility." Such appellations suggest that pregnancy is *unhealthy* when, in actuality, the pregnancy is merely *undesired*. Dr. Elizabeth Connell, president-elect of the Association of Planned Parenthood Physicians and associate director of the Rockefeller Foundation, told her audience at an APPP conference that "pregnancy is a kind of nasty communicable disease, too."[31] Her remark had been buttressed by the opening paper at the conference—prepared by three employees of the United States Department of Health, Education, and Welfare at the Centers for Disease Control in Atlanta— entitled, "Unwanted Pregnancy: A Sexually Transmitted Disease." To blur the distinction between pregnancy and the developing fetus, and then associate the fetus with venereal disease is nothing less than willful deception. (Presumably the male has the venereal disease, or pregnancy, first and then transmits it to the woman.)

Some victims of "pro-choice" rhetoric discover the deception, but too late. In July of 1977, *Good Housekeeping* ran a feature called "Are You Sorry You Had an Abortion?" The fact that emerges most clearly from the article is how women were deceived. One woman recalls her experience in these words: "Oh, my God, I thought, I've just killed my baby and *all it was supposed to be was some bloody tissue.*" Another woman, who had been told that her three-month child was "a clump of cells," exclaimed: "When I saw that a three-month old 'clump of cells' had fingers and toes and was a tiny perfectly formed baby, I became really hysterical."

Bernard Nathanson has amply documented the pattern of "pro-choice" deception in his two books: *Aborting America* and *The Abortion Papers*. On the other hand, no one realistically accuses "pro-life" supporters of deception. The great task of "pro-life" writers and speakers is to use words, already weakened through misuse, to describe accurately what any honest and competent fetologist describes when referring to the developing human fetus.

Doublethink

Sir William Liley, the father of modern fetology, found it a bitter irony that just when scientific observation greatly enlarged our appreciation of the importance of human intrauterine life there should arrive such sustained pressure to reduce it to a biological triviality and a social nonentity. "In this Orwellian situation," wrote the late Dr. Liley, "where so much semantic effort and logical gymnastics are expended in making a developing human life into an 'unperson,' modern anatomical, genetic, immunological, endocrinological and physiological facts are a persistent embarrassment."[32]

The Orwellian situation to which Dr. Liley refers is "doublethink," an ultimate state in the degeneration of language and thinking in which people annunciate bald contradictions without the slightest suspicion that what they are saying makes no sense whatsoever. Orwell defined "doublethink" in *1984*, his immensely successful description of a totalitarian anti-utopia, as "the power of holding two contradictory beliefs in one's mind simultaneously, and accepting both of them."[33] It was the hope of Orwell's Party intellectuals that eventually all people would speak directly from the larynx without thinking at all.

Orwellian doublethink has been a normal strategy for "pro-choice" rhetoricians since the earliest days of the debate when they sought to identify abortion with contraception. Surgeon General C. Everett Koop has alluded to the terms "postconceptive contraception" and "postconceptive fertility control"—promulgated as synonyms for abortion—as "doublethink of the highest magnitude."[34] As abortion became more accepted in society, the attempt was made to identify infanticide with abortion. A physician and member of the University of Virginia Medical School asserted three times in a brief article in *The New York Times Magazine* that parental refusal to allow a lifesaving operation on a Down's syndrome baby is "a woman's second chance to have an abortion."[35]

Once the human fetus had been dehumanized through an assortment of "verbal abominations,"[36] to use Gordon Zahn's expression, "test tube" babies and fetal experimentation provided new reasons to rehumanize him. If a human being was conceived in a woman and subsequently aborted, even as late as the third trimester, it was described in a variety of ways ranging from "an inch of tissue" to "garbage." But if a human being was conceived in a petri dish and spent no more than six days there, it metamorphosed into a human being—a "test tube" baby! The need for experimentation on human fetuses because knowledge so gained would have direct applicability to other human beings, also required the verbal rehumanization of the fetus. The subject that *was* and then *was not* human became human once again, perhaps outdoing doublethink with a new violation of thought and language—triplethink!

By using the word "doublethink," Orwell's characters were admitting that they were tampering with reality, but by a fresh act of doublethink, they could erase this recognition, the lie always being one step ahead of the truth. Although Orwell has aroused people to oppose doublethink in theory, he has not been nearly so successful in helping them to recognize it when it appears. Thus, many instances of doublethink, particularly in the case of "pro-choice" rhetoric, go unnoticed while statements that are not contradictory are taken as prime examples of doublethink. From the file of a university language professor comes this presumed paragon of doublethink: "The U.S. navy has a warship, the Corpus Christi." The name, however, was taken from the town in Texas and not from its Latin signification. In this instance, political ideology is one step behind the truth, the very verbal imprisonment which Orwell warned against. A similar victim to political myopia is a U.S. group called the Committee on Public Doublespeak of the National Council of the Teachers of English. Its annual Doublespeak award for 1983 went to President Reagan for his quote: "A vote against MX production today is a vote against arms reduction tomorrow."[37] The award could have been conferred posthumously to America's first president who said: "To be prepared for war is one of the most effectual means of preserving the peace." Of course, Washington was merely echoing a maxim that is at least as old as the Roman Empire—*Si vis pacem, para bellum.*

Reagan is hardly guilty of authoring that year's most perfect example of doublethink. He was simply reiterating an ancient belief that an arms buildup can be a deterrent to war, and couching that belief in modern terminology. The belief may be paradoxical, but it is not illogical. Opponents may disagree on political or tactical grounds, but the remark, innocent as it is of logical or semantic contradiction, is no example at all of doublethink, let alone the best example of its kind for the year.

The English Committee's official Doublespeak Award for 1984 went again (as did its first award in 1974) to the U.S. State Department, this time for its replacement of the word "killing" in its official reports on the status of human rights in countries around the world by the phrase "unlawful or arbitrary deprivation of life." The State Department, however, is merely clarifying the meaning of "killing" in a specific context by saying that it is unlawful or arbitrary (not all killing is unlawful or arbitrary). What results is a clarification, not a contradiction.

Consider a few other references to killing which were passed up by the Committee. The head of the crisis-intervention unit at Toronto East General Hospital has gone on record as saying that "If someone is confronted with certain knowledge that he or she is going to die a painful, undignified death through terminal illness, then suicide can be a viable option."[38] Canadian abortionist Henry Morgentaler has argued that "abortion is necessary to protect the integrity of the family." On a more recent occasion, he admonished Cardinal Carter for objecting to "the killing of innocents" by describing the Cardinal's words as "the rhetoric of violence."

Also, consider University of Alberta law professor Ellen Picard's assertion that parents who interfere with their minor daughter's (under the age of sixteen) attempt to obtain an abortion, would run the risk of being charged with "child neglect" and face the possibility of losing custody of the child to provincial child care authorities.

It may be impossible to imagine a better candidate for the 1984 doublethink award than the brainchild of Drs. Chervenak *et al.*, which appeared in the prestigious *New England Journal of Medicine*.[39] In buttressing their "argument" for third-trimester abortions, the doctors state: "prenatal death does not constitute a harm, nor does the prenatal termination of the fetus' life through induced abortion constitute an injury." Could someone in any other field than medicine get away with such undiluted doublethink? Imagine a scout carrying the following message back to his company: "We are happy to report that neither General Custer nor any of his men were either injured or harmed at the Battle of Little Big Horn. Incidentally, they were all killed."

Conclusion

When words are dissociated from the world and from truth in order to provide a neutral discussion, or to promote a particular ideology, or to further some private interest, genuine communication between opposing parties becomes impossible. In the abortion discussion, this communication stalemate represents an advantage to the "pro-choice" position and abortion, since failure to communicate a world of objective values leaves people unaided and without the inspiration that is needed to choose the more difficult path of protecting life. "Man is born broken," writes the playwright Eugene O'Neill. "He lives by mending. The grace of life is glue." Words are a mending grace, providing life with the possibility of higher levels of integration, but only when their connection with the world of truth and values is preserved.

The proper use of words is indispensable for the proper functioning of society, a truth well understood by the ancients. A Confucian maxim states with unarguable simplicity: "If language is incorrect, then what is said is not meant. If what is said is not meant, then what ought to be done remains undone."

The use of words constitutes a moral action, and a person is as accountable for his words as he is for his deeds. The Bible offers stern warnings against the abuse and careless use of language, such as in Matthew 12:36: "Every idle word that men shall speak, they shall give account thereof in the day of judgment." Recalling his days as a journalist with the *Manchester Guardian*, a now chastened Malcolm Muggeridge confesses:

> It is painful to me now to reflect the ease with which I got into the way of using this non-language; these drooling non-sentences conveying non-thoughts, propounding non-fears and offering non-hopes. Words are as beautiful as love, and as easily betrayed. I am more penitent for my false words—for the most part, mercifully lost for ever in the Media's great slag-heaps—than for false deeds.[40]

The way we use words reveals our concern for truth as well as our concern for our fellow man. The abortion debate provides what appears to be an ideal opportunity—for anyone who can be objective about the matter—to assess which side of the debate is more faithful to these concerns. We cannot but be judged by our words, for they make all too clear, as much as do our actions, the kind of people we are.

Notes

1.   André Hellegers, "Abortion and Birth Control," *The Human Life Review*, Vol. 1, No. 1, Winter, 1975, p. 22.

2.   M.J. Sobran, "The Abortion Ethos," *The Human Life Review*, Winter, 1977, p. 16.

3.   J.C. Fletcher, Ph.D. and M.I. Evans, M.D., "Maternal Bonding in Early Fetal Ultrasound Examination," *New England Journal of Medicine*, February 17, 1983, p. 392.

4.   *Ibid.*

5.   Richard Weaver, "The Power of the Word," *Ideas Have Consequences* (Chicago: University of Chicago Press, 1948), p. 149.

6.   Quoted by Henry Fairlie in "The Language of Politics," *The Atlantic*, January 1975, p. 25.

7.   Heraclitus, Fragment 2.

8.   Dag Hammarsjöld, *Markings*, tr. Leif Sjöberg and W.H. Auden (New York: Knopf, 1964), p. 112.

9.   G.K. Chesterton, *William Blake* (London: Duckworth, 1910), p. 178.

10.   Quoted in *Alliance for Life National Newsletter*, Vol. 10, April 1974, p. 4.

11.   *Time*, August 25, 1975, p. 57.

12.   Edwin Newman, *Strictly Speaking* (New York: Warner, 1974), p. 2.

13.   L.T. Lee and J.M. Paxman, "The Population Council," *Studies in Family Planning*, Vol. 8, No. 10 (quoted in *Lifelines National*, Vol. 7, No. 3, Fall 1978, p. 8).

14.   "Covering Three Mile Island," *Newsweek*, April 16, 1979, p. 93.

15.   George Will, "As I Was Saying," *Newsweek*, April 16, 1979, p. 100.

16.   "Can't Anyone Here Speak English?" *Time*, April 25, 1975, p. 56.

17.   David Holbrook, "Letters to the Editor," *Spectator* (London, March 24, 1961), p. 400.

18.   Melvin Maddocks, "The Limitations of Language," *Time*, March 8, 1971, p. 20.

19.   Robert Penn Warren, *Democracy and Poetry* (Cambridge: Harvard University Press, 1975).

20.   M.J. Sobran, "Rhetorical and Cultural War," *The Human Life Review*, Vol. 1, No. 1, Winter 1975, p. 93.

21.   See Karl G. Schmude, "Redeeming the Word," *Communio*, Summer 1980, p. 159.

22.   Magda Denes, *In Necessity and Sorrow: Life and Death in an Abortion Hospital* (New York: Basic Books, 1976).

23.   *Troilus and Cressida*, I, iii, 52.

24.   J.M. Cameron, *On the Idea of a University* (Toronto: University of Toronto Press, 1978), p. 33.

25.   Leon Botstein, president of New York's Bard College, quoted in *Time*, August 25, 1975, p. 56.

26.   A former nurse on trial in the death of a patient allegedly confessed she had discontinued the respirator of several patients but only if they were "gorks"—hospital slang for patients who showed no signs of life except breathing and heartbeat. See *Pro-Life News/Canada*, Vol. 4, No 2, April 1979, p. 7.

27.   Harley S. Smyth, M.D., D. Phil. (Oxon.), F.R.C.S.(c), "Motive and Meaning in Medical Morals," Alliance for Life Annual Conference, University of Toronto, June 1976, p. 6.

28.   "The Unborn Patient," *LIFE*, April 1983, p. 44.

29.   Edwin A. Roberts, Jr.,"What Others Say: About Destruction Called 'Abortion'," *The National Observer*, n.d.

30.   Lynda Hurst, "Pro-Abortionist: Decision Is Woman's Abortion Doctor Says," *The Toronto Star*, Thursday, November 29, 1973, E1.

31.   *Love, Life, Death, Issues*, Vol. 2, No. 4, December 15, 1976 (newsletter, Human Life Center, Collegeville, MN).

32.   Sir William Liley, "The Development of Life," in *Quality of Life*, edited by D.K. Bonisch (Dunedin, New Zealand: The Guild of St. Luke, 1975), p. 80.

33.   George Orwell, *1984* (Middlesex, England: Penguin, 1954), p. 171.

34.   C. Everett Koop, M.D., "A Physician Looks at Abortion," *Thou Shalt Not Kill* (New Rochelle, NY: Arlington House, 1978), p. 9.

35.   Paul Ramsey, "Abortion: A Review Article," *The Thomist*, Vol. 37, No. 1, January 1973, p. 201.

36.   Gordon Zahn, "Abortion and the Corruption of Mind," *New Perspectives on Human Abortion*, eds. Hilgers, Horan, and Mall (Frederick, MD: University Publications of America), p. 335.

37.   "1984, Newspeak Doesn't Call a Spade a Spade," Kitchener-Waterloo *Record*, Saturday, December 31, 1983, E1.

38.   William Safire, *William Safire on Language* (New York: Avon, 1981), p. 288 (quoted from Toronto's *Globe and Mail*).

39.   Frank Chervenak *et al.*, "When Is Termination of Pregnancy during the Third Trimester Morally Justified?" *New England Journal of Medicine*, Vol. 310, No. 8, p. 502.

40.   Malcolm Muggeridge, *Chronicles of Wasted Time*, Vol. 1 (London: Collins, 1972), p. 171.

Abortion as Symbolic Action:
Fetal Victimage in
Pro-choice and Pro-life Rhetoric

Gary Gillespie

Abortion is a nasty thing, but our society deserves it.
Margaret Mead[1]

T he battle over abortion is more than the most hotly contested social issue of our times[2]—more than a partisan fight over policy. Where we stand on abortion and how we speak about it is a cultural mirror. The values reflected in this most fundamental of debates dramatize who we are and what we will become as a society. At issue are such psychologically volatile concepts as the meaning of human life and death, motherhood, sexuality, and the limits of individual freedom and governmental control. The study of how and why we think and feel the way we do about abortion is, therefore, significant.

First, this essay offers a comprehensive model for categorizing the basic language and arguments in the abortion controversy. The persuasion theories of Stephen Littlejohn are combined with dramatistic analysis to show how opposing facts, values, themes, and metaphors ascend on four dimensions of the cognitive system. Second, applying the dramatistic methodology of Kenneth Burke, the arguments and language will be interpreted as an outplaying of the rhetorical principle known as victimage.[3]

The Cognitive System and Abortion Rhetoric

In explaining the process of persuasion, Littlejohn proposes that each person develops a cognitive system for interpreting the world. Messages will be persuasive if they are salient with the individual's system in four dimensions. The first dimension is reality. Reality concerns what a person believes is objectively true. It includes beliefs, rational thought, and socially transmitted assumptions about the real world. The second, goal dimension, concerns what an individual considers good or desirable and is influenced by values, needs, and motives. The third, arousal dimension, deals with emotion and emotional intensity including the effects of pleasant and unpleasant feelings. Dominance, or the sense of being in control, is one of the strongest factors in arousal. Fourth and finally, the relational dimension functions to help the person develop a self-definition and achieve identification with others as a member of a larger group. We are often most influenced by the political or ethical positions of our reference groups or opinion leaders. In short, people will be persuaded by arguments for or against abortion if messages appeal to their sense of reality, are congruent with their value systems, touch them emotionally, and are endorsed by their reference groups.[4]

In order to apply the four dimensions to abortion rhetoric, we can identify four levels of argument in the controversy: arguments over facts, values, themes, and metaphors. We will limit our discussion of the nature of abortion and the fetus to these levels and place them in ascending order on the four dimensions to achieve a graphic model or matrix of abortion rhetoric. (See Diagram.)

Four Levels of Abortion Rhetoric

The Level of Fact

The first level of abortion rhetoric deals with the basic facts of the issue—the nature of the fetus and of abortion itself. At the bottom of the model, factual disputes are closest to the reality dimension, low on emotional arousal, and are the least influenced by personal identification with reference groups or opinion leaders.

Drawing on the fields of biology, genetics, and fetology, anti-abortion advocates argue that abortion is the killing of a unique human organism and is not merely the removal of tissue from the

Abortion Rhetoric Matrix Diagram

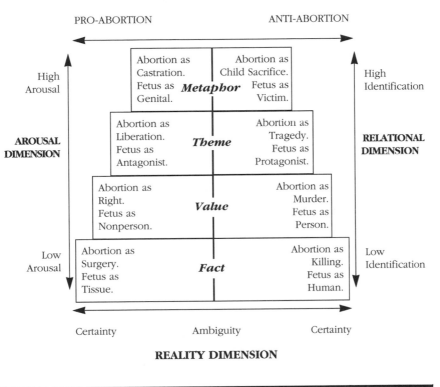

woman's body. Fetal development is detailed and abortion methods are described to show that abortion is distinct from other forms of surgery in that it is primarily non-medical. Abortion kills rather than heals. When the scientific term "fetus" is not used, "unborn child" or "pre-born child" are employed. One author, Bernard Nathanson, sought to avoid pejorative or emotive terms and offered the fetal label, "alpha," in his first book *Aborting America*. (In later writings, however, he uses "child.")[5]

Abortion advocates see reality differently. Turning to the fields of medicine, especially gynecology, they hold that a woman's decision to abort is protected by the physician-patient relationship. Abortion is one of many surgical procedures the physician offers to help a patient. Unwanted pregnancy becomes a maternal complication with abortion the morally neutral treatment. The fetus is too small and rudimentary to be of concern and is described in scientific or factual sounding terms: "zygote," "embryo," "a specialized collection of cells," "a spot of blood," "contents of the pregnant womb," "birth matter," "uterine contents," "fetal tissue," or "pregnancy tissue." The fetus is essentially part of the woman's body—a bit of tissue indistinguishable from other kinds of pathology refuse left after surgery.

One apparent anomaly, however, concerns those abortion advocates who admit the fetus is a human being. These proponents accept the traditionally anti-abortion factual premise that abortion kills a living human individual, but argue that this killing is a justified lesser evil. When confronted by the scientific evidence, many pro-choicers will privately shift to this position, even though it leads to a troubling conclusion. A few will do so openly. A *New Republic* editorial argues in support of abortion but does not try to avoid perceiving the fetus as a human being. While "there clearly is no logical or moral distinction between a fetus and a young baby," say the authors, abortion is still justified because the "social cost" of protecting fetal life is too great.[6] Another example of an advocate who defends abortion as the justified killing of a human being is pro-choice writer Magda Denes, who, while supporting legalization, describes abortion clinics as "death factories" in her book *In Necessity and Sorrow: Life and Death in an Abortion Hospital*.[7]

The Level of Value

The position of defending abortion as justified killing is clarified on the second level of abortion rhetoric. Here we move closer to the goal dimension in applying value assumptions. Field dependent arguments—or arguments that according to Stephen Toulmin have special meaning in the field where they are developed[8]—are taken from normative ethics, philosophy, and law. Advocates here are more apt to feel emotions of pity, disgust, and rage and will more likely look to reference groups for guidance.

Proponents evaluate the choice for abortion positively, arguing that even if the fetus is more than tissue (something most will not admit), it is certainly not a person worthy of legal protection. Abortion is part of a woman's fundamental right to self-determination and privacy. Laws limiting abortion are unjustified interference and abuses of governmental power.[9] The fetus is perceived as a nonperson; therefore, its destruction, when necessary, is not a concern of social policy. One popular pro-choice slogan says, "A Fetus Is Not a Person." On this level labels are used to emphasize the impersonal nature of the fetus. Besides the factual-sounding terms already mentioned, we can add other, slightly more emotive, words taken from a review of pro-choice literature: "products of conception," "devitalized tissue," "feto-placental unit," "potential life," "abortus," "the-child-that-would-be," "ovum," "conceptus," or "fertilized egg." Each of these labels suggests the fetus is unworthy of protection or consideration as a human agent in the abortion drama. Focus is given to the woman and her rights. She is the agent who has value and should be the recipient of our sympathy.

The difference between the factual term "human being" and the value term "person" is an often overlooked distinction in the abortion debate. Personhood is a philosophical concept. Some philosophical ideas have been debated for 4,000 years without a clear consensus. This does not mean there are no right answers, only that in the realm of values answers will lack scientific certainty. Personhood is also a legal term. Corporations and ships can be considered persons under the law. Pro-choicers argue that even if the fetus is in fact a human organism, society should not grant it the legal and moral status of personhood.

The value system for pro-lifers is more inclusive. For them all human beings should be considered persons. They point out that any set of criteria—self-awareness, ability to communicate, viability—cited to deny the fetus personhood, equally apply to newborn babies as well as to many other groups we would hesitate to strip of rights. They do not see any convincing arguments that the fetus is not a person. If there is uncertainty, the fetus is given the benefit of the doubt. Just as it is illegal and immoral to drive over a heap of clothing on a dark roadway when we are unsure if the object is a person or not, so we should treat fetal life with respect.

Using deduction, anti-abortionists reason that since the fetus is a human being, since all human beings should be considered persons, and since killing a person is murder, therefore, abortion is murder. Evidence is presented showing that by eight weeks gestation, and perhaps before, the fetus is quite sensitive to pain. Because abortion dismembers the fetus, it is an act of cruelty violating the ethical imperatives of nonviolence and respect for others. It also violates the Hippocratic "do no harm" ethic of medicine. On the level of value, then, abortion is portrayed as a crime against the fetal person. When arguing these points, opponents use terms stressing the human worth of the fetus. Besides "unborn," "pre-born," or "child," anti-abortion literature refers to the "baby," "developing baby," "fetal child," "tiny passenger," or even "intrauterine being."

The Level of Theme

On the third level of abortion rhetoric—theme—we find the human tendency to dramatize social conflict. We are storytellers. Much persuasive discourse is based on narratives that are generated to portray a social drama between good and evil or right and wrong. Narrative structure leads to the perception of morally good dramatic agents or protagonists who are faced with some problem that is usually caused by or associated with the opposing antagonist. The story tells how the dramatic conflict is resolved or the antagonist overcome. Every narrative follows this simple pattern. This level is obviously more highly emotive. Thematic arguments are also more relationally dependent. Many groups define themselves by the stories that they tell. In other words, the language and arguments on the level of theme are closely tied to the self-definitions and group identity of advocates.

Abortion advocates emphasize the freedom to choose abortion as a necessary step toward the liberation of women from the "biological imperative" of being forced to bear unwanted children by chance. Feminism holds that no woman is free who cannot decide if and when to become a mother. Those who oppose this freedom of choice are antagonists who threaten to enslave women by unreasonably protecting the life of the fetus. Opponents are vilified as the "enemies of choice," "friends of the fetus," "right-to-life zealots," or "the anti-choice forces."[10] Narratives are told of suffering women who were denied choice before legalization.[11] Thousands of women once died at the hands of illegal back-alley abortionists, we are told. Abortion-on-demand has solved this problem and represents significant progress in the quest for a just and equal society.

When proponents refer to the fetus on this level, often emotive, negative terms are used. These labels suggest the fetus is

being taken as a central antagonist in the drama.   It is the existence of the unwanted fetus that is the cause of the problem.
Thus the fetus is referred to as "parasite," "aggressor," "unwelcome invader," "worm," "thief," "rapist tissue," "glob of cells,"
"ejaculated leavings swelling up *in utero*," "blob," "fetal wastage,"
"venereal disease," "cancer-like cells," or the "sexually-transmitted
condition." Destroying the fetus is a subtle means of defeating a
menacing antagonist.

The theme of anti-abortion advocates, however, is tragedy.
Abortion is the equivalent of child killing. It is a modern example
of the age-old problem of people with power exploiting and dehumanizing weak and vulnerable groups. Narratives are told of
women who were pressured to abort by boyfriend or parents, or
who chose abortion and later came to regret it. Examples of emotional and physical hardship, even death, caused by legal abortion
are given. Testimonies report that rather than solving the
woman's problem, abortion actually caused far worse ones.[12]

But the central protagonist is the fetus who is portrayed as
an "innocent victim," "abortion victim," "victim of the abortion
mentality," "helpless baby," "little one," or "tiny boy or girl." One
highly emotive technique is to compare the fetus to Jesus Christ
and identify it with God. Here the field-dependent language of
theology is used, and abortion is said to violate the "sanctity of
life," since the fetus is "made in the image of God." The biblical
command "thou shalt not murder," New Testament narratives of
Mary pregnant with Jesus, and certain Hebrew poems are applied
to show that the fetus is protected by divine sanction.[13] Some
pro-lifers claim that the fetus falls under the category of the
oppressed people Christ referred to when he said, "As you have
done to the least of these my brothers, so you have done to me."[14]

The Level of Metaphor

The final rhetorical level in the controversy is representational metaphor. The metaphors rank highest for arousal and relational identification and tend to sum up or represent each of the dramas. The argument form is vilification—each metaphor is a stunning rebuke of the hidden motives of the opposition.

Drawing on the theme of women's liberation, some pro-
choice proponents theorize that male anti-abortionists oppose
abortion because they fear it as a form of castration. The fetus is

implicitly perceived as the male genital—a symbol for masculine control over women. Referring to the problem of male hegemony, Mary Daly in *Gyn/ecology: The Metaethics of Radical Feminism* suggests that an unconscious motive for the anti-abortion position is the desire of men to subjugate women. By identifying with the fetus, the male is expressing his need for sexist power. Both the fetus and the male must be permitted to control the bodies of women, and outlawing abortion is one way to symbolize female subservience to the wishes of men. "Males do indeed deeply identify with 'unwanted fetal tissue'," she writes, "for they sense as their own condition the role of controller, possessor, inhabitor of women. Draining female energy, they *feel* 'fetal'"[15] (emphasis in original). For Daly, men resent abortion because the destruction of the fetus represents the killing of their power over women.

Feminist author John Stoltenberg likewise points to the symbolic meaning of the fetus when he writes:

> Men control women's reproductive capacities in part because men believe that fetuses are phallic that the ejaculated leavings swelling up in utero are a symbolic and material extension of the precious penis itself. This belief is both literal and metaphoric, both ancient and modern. The mythology of the fetus as a purely male substance harbored inside the body of a nonmale host reaches back at least as far as fifth century B.C. Greece.[16]

Stoltenberg argues that the concept of personhood itself is sexist, since historically only men were considered persons. Thus, to say the fetus is a person is to say it is an extension of male identity. Radical feminist Andrea Dworkin agrees, "To abort a fetus, in masculinistic terms, is to commit an act of violence against the phallus itself."[17]

Anti-abortion advocates offer an equally disturbing metaphor. Abortion is the modern equivalent of ancient child sacrifice. A kind of modern blood rite, abortion is perceived as a horrible means of securing collective redemption in exchange for the lives of unborn humans. Proponents gain the same psychological benefit from killing the fetus that ancient societies did in sacrificing children. A *Christianity Today* editorial laments that "millions of lives are sacrificed on the pro-abortionist altar of the 'right to choose'."[18] Jean Garton observes: "The unwanted child is the victim . . . in a society attempting to solve its social, economic, and personal problems by the sacrificial offering of its children."[19] "Motherhood," David Granfield exhorts, "can never justify despotic dominion over fetal life and death. An innocent life should never be sacrificed on the altar of expediency."[20] John Powell urges: ". . . let there be no human sacrifices on our altars—beseeching the great gods of science to create for us a pain-free world."[21] The abhorrent connotations of associating abortion with child sacrifice is a revealing facet of the way anti-abortionists think and may be taken as a prototype for this entire perspective.

An overview of the matrix shows two competing rhetorical dramas—one portraying the fetus as a helpless sacrificial victim and the other casting it in the role of an inhuman (and sometimes human) agent without intrinsic worth. An application of the model would suggest that an uninitiated or relatively uninformed audience would be most persuaded by fact and value issues, while a more informed and committed audience would find theme and metaphor more persuasive. Communication research indicates that extremely high levels of arousal tend to be less persuasive for a general audience. Therefore, most people would probably find the level of metaphor least persuasive for either side of the controversy.[22]

Now that we have reviewed the language and arguments and ranked them according to the dimensions of the cognitive system, let us turn to an interpretation of the data by applying a key concept in Kenneth Burke's methodology known as the principle of victimage.

Victimage: The Desire for a Scapegoat

Like many dramaturgical sociologists, Burke believes that society is best understood as drama. Human relations, according to Burke, should be analyzed like works of drama.[23] In the same way a playwright has a certain number of dramatic themes to work with, social dramas also have basic themes which influence behavior and determine how people interpret reality. One of the most common of these themes in the drama of human relations is the desire of groups to see a victim punished and destroyed. Just as tragic plays have protagonists and antagonists, so in every social drama people are driven either to identify with a beloved martyr or lash out and destroy a subhuman enemy. When it comes to the fabric of the abortion controversy, Burke's concept of victimage becomes a handy analytical thread we can pull to begin unraveling the meaning of mass abortion for our society.

Burke observes that society's demand for "perfection" places all people under a burden of "categorical guilt." A kind of secularized version of original sin, categorical guilt is defined as alienation among humans which results in feelings of anxiety over perceived imperfection or disorder. The most basic reason why people communicate is to rid themselves of guilt. By identifying with a group and sharing common values, individuals overcome estrangement and achieve identification with one another. Burke interprets all human relations as "essentially a purgative-redemptive drama,"[24] in which "innate forms of the mind" lead to "forms of symbolic action" that emerge in society to strengthen the bonds of unity between individuals and reduce feelings of alienation. Victimage is one of these universal symbolic forms people act out to purge themselves of evil and achieve redemption.

Burke defines victimage as "purification by sacrifice, by vicarious atonement, unburdening of guilt within by transference to a chosen vessel without."[25] Victimage occurs when the guilt of individuals or groups is projected on a scapegoat, which is then symbolically or physically destroyed. In destroying the victim, the persecutor is purged. Burke insists the scapegoat principle is not primarily a memory from ancient times, but a device "natural to language here and now."[26] It is, in effect, imprinted on the structure of language because all linguistic activity is substitutional in nature. Just as a symbol represents an object or concept, so the despised victim is made to represent the inner guilt of the righteous oppressor; and thus, as Burke says, "one character may be redeemed through the act or agency of another."[27] Put otherwise, the guilt of one character may be resolved by projecting it vicariously onto another.

In *Civilization and Its Discontents*, Freud maintains that the psychoanalytic technique of uncovering subconscious motives can by applied to society as a whole. Freud says that guilt emerges in society much as it does in individuals. In fact, guilt is the "most important problem" facing civilization. Without symbolic outlets, civilization may begin to demonstrate neurotic symptoms. Naturally, then, members of societies develop mechanisms for guilt reduction. One of these mechanisms, says Freud, is to distinguish sharply between one's own society and that of one's enemies. Aggressive tensions are thereby relieved by singling out and punishing a symbolic victim.

> The advantages which a comparatively small cultural group offers at allowing this [aggressive] instinct an outlet in the form of hostility against intruders is not to be despised. It is always possible to bind together a considerable number of people in love, so long as there are other people left over to receive the manifestations of their aggressiveness.[28]

Here, Freud describes the same principle Burke calls victimage: The abuse of scapegoats serves as a catharsis to expiate guilt, reduce estrangement between individuals, and finally unify a society. Like mortar for bricks, the drama of the victim's destruction cements people together by giving them a common identity.

In the *Rhetoric of Religion*, Burke defines two kinds of victimage: the destruction of a polluted agent because it is polluted and the destruction of a pure agent because it is pure. Two examples are given: the Nazi Holocaust and the Crucifixion of Christ. The death of Jesus on the cross is the supreme archetypical example of purgation through the sacrifice of the principle of good. When the crucified Christ bearing the sins of the world died, the power of sin died with him. "Behold the Lamb of God who takes away the sins of the world."[29] Christians who pattern their lives after the drama of Christ's life, death, and resurrection take on a new identity and become "reborn."

The Nazis, in contrast, sought unification through a common enemy which symbolized the principle of evil. Hitler depicted the Jews as the embodiment of all evil, justifying their destruction as a purgative act to cleanse Germany of its sins. "Hitler's 'idealizing' of the Jew as a perfect enemy . . . provides the most drastically obvious instance of the ways in which such 'cleansing' operates. . . ."[30] In his analysis of *Mein Kampf*, "The Rhetoric of Hitler's Battle," written while World War II was still being fought, Burke explains Hitler's rise to power as the result of anti-Jewish victimage.[31] Perhaps the dual nature of victimage could be described as pure and impure victimage, i.e., pure when the community identifies with the victim, which is perceived as a suffering martyr (the Crucifixion) and impure when people unite *against* the victim, which is perceived as a profane and subhuman enemy (the Holocaust).

Advocates in the abortion controversy appear to be motivated by pure and impure victimage. Anti-abortionists speak out on behalf of the suffering fetus and see its death as a tragedy, while abortion proponents defend a women's choice to be purged of the problematic fetus and of what it represents.

Frustrated Vengeance: Reasons behind the Reasons

In the pro-choice castration metaphor we see that the fetus is perceived as a phallic symbol. Fear of being denied sexist control is supposedly the motivation for anti-abortion activism. However, in using the metaphor, abortion advocates may be saying more about their own motives than about the opposition. If the term "fetus" is unconsciously associated with male control, then we cannot help but assume that abortion has a similar symbolic meaning for the radical feminist. The right to abortion stands as a symbol for female self-determination and the rejection of male dominance. The ability of women to obtain abortions is taken to represent everything the feminist is fighting for. Abortion is therefore revered as "a civil right for every female person," nearly allied to "her right to be." Perhaps each termination of pregnancy is implicitly perceived as a kind of ritual of liberation.

Even writers who advocate abortion-on-demand recognize the presence of discrete psychological desires which motivate women to abort their pregnancies. Helene Arnstein, in *What Every Woman Needs to Know about Abortion*, explains the widespread problem of "repeaters," or women who abort again and again, by suggesting that a repeating woman "is motivated by strong irrational forces of which she is unaware." Two unconscious "reasons behind the reasons" to explain why women seek multiple abortions, she says, may be:

> A need for punishment and self-injury to atone for guilt feelings, possibly connected with having had sexual relations [and] a need to discharge hostility—against herself, her husband or lover, or the unborn child, or to "get even" with her own mother or father for some real or imagined injury or lack of love.[32]

In other words, some women seek abortions in order to purge themselves of feelings of guilt and alienation.

Daphne de Jung, a feminist writer who describes herself as pro-life, similarly believes abortion is an expression of women's "frustrated vengeance," a way of striking out against men, and that "the unborn is the natural scapegoat for the repressed anger and hostility of women." She says:

> Even while proclaiming "her" rights over the fetus, much liberationist rhetoric identifies pregnancy with male chauvinist "ownership". The inference is that by implanting "his" seed, the man establishes some claim over a woman's body ("keeping her barefoot and pregnant"). Abortion is almost consciously seen as "getting back" at the male. The truth may well be that the liberationist sees the fetus not as a part of her body but as part of his.[33]

When Arnstein and de Jung speak of the unborn child as a woman's "scapegoat" and abortion as a way "to atone for guilt feelings," they are using the language of victimage.

As we have seen, abortion advocates argue that abortion restrictions victimize women. The victimage of women is stressed by Randall Lake in his dissertation analyzing the abortion controversy using Burke's methodology.[34] However, statistics show that women denied legal abortion have never died by the millions—as opposed to fetuses who die at a rate of four thousand each day in the United States. Dramatistic structure might motivate advocates to imagine that large numbers of women have died, but unbiased government statistics show otherwise. The Centers for Disease Control reported that in 1972—a year before legalization—thirty-nine women died, not the 10,000 maternal deaths asserted by NARAL.[35] Comparatively few women have ever died from abortion. Similarly, when abortion was illegal in the United States, few women were ever prosecuted. Laws against abortion in the nineteenth century were directed against abortionists, not women. Moreover, women are not given dehumanizing labels by pro-lifers in the way the fetus is vilified by pro-choicers.

Pro-abortion rights advocates attempt to dramatize the woman as a suffering victim and ignore the fetus as much as possible, delegating it to the status of "unwanted tissue." However, the euphemistic language meant to draw our attention away from the fetus, reveals a kind of contempt for intrauterine life which may be interpreted as impure victimage. To refer to the fetus as "the contents of the pregnant womb," or to label the unborn child a "blob," or a "fetal-placental unit," or to compare an unwanted pregnancy to venereal disease and call the human fetus a "sexually transmitted condition," is similar to the same kind of terms used to dehumanize despised racial groups or the enemy during war. The Nazis not only labeled Jews "subhumans," "bacilli," and "parasites," but concentration camp authorities referred to "loads" and "consignments" of human research "material." Wardens talked of handling so many new "pieces of prisoner per day." S.S. record clerks at Dachau sought the name of a new prisoner's mother by asking the standard question, "Which Jew-whore shit you out?"[36] Holocaust victims were not perceived as human beings, and labels used to describe them carried neutral or negative connotations. Communication scholars and others have shown that dehumanizing labels for the victims are historically and cross-culturally a prerequisite for genocidal violence.[37]

Although the most common pro-choice strategy is first to avoid speaking of the fetus at all and second, if necessary, to use terms which make it appear part of the woman's body, as we have seen, some abortion proponents openly attack the fetus as a subhuman enemy. The unborn is described as a polluting agent. Joseph Fletcher, father of situation ethics, justifies abortion in rape cases by making the unborn and rapist equally guilty: "The embryo is no more innocent, no less an aggressor or unwelcome invader!"[38] In the same way a woman is justified in killing an attacking rapist, so she is justified in killing the "aggressor" embryo.

Still another technique is to call the fetus a "parasite." Bernard Nathanson reports that in his experience of the abortion rights campaign in New York, fellow pro-choice advocates often referred to the fetus as "parasite" and "aggressor."[39] (Curiously, attributing guilt to the fetus contradicts the argument that it is part of the woman's body. How, we might ask, can part of a woman's body be an "invader" or be guilty of "aggression"?)

After learning that in order to save a pregnancy she must remain in bed, radical feminist Oriana Fallaci wrote a novel based on her experience. In *Letter to a Child Never Born* she speaks of the fetus as both nonhuman and "thief."

> No one is human by natural right, before being born. We become human afterward, when we're born, because . . . someone teaches us to eat, to walk, to speak, to think, to behave like humans. The only thing that joins us, my dear,

is an umbilical cord. And we're not a couple. We're persecutor and persecuted. You the persecutor and I the persecuted. You wormed your way into me like a thief, and you
carried away my womb, my blood, my breath. Now you'd
like to steal my whole existence. I won't let you.[40]

The labeling of unborn children as dispensable nonhumans
or attacking them as dangerous enemies, clearly characterizes pro-
choice rhetoric as impure victimage—destroying a polluted agent
because it is polluted. For the radical pro-abortionist, the destruction of the fetus is made to symbolize the liberation of women
from sexist oppression and is offered as a solution for a host of
social and economic problems. The life of the fetus is exchanged
for individual and collective redemption. Abortion frees women
from the profane "biological imperative." Advocates thereby
establish bonds of group unity out of a shared belief that a subhuman victim must sometimes be dispatched and that this procedure has enormous practical and symbolic benefits.

Right-to-life advocates, on the other hand, seek unity out of a
common concern for the "children never born." Their rhetoric is
characterized by a pure victimage, and their goal is to confer sanctity on society. The anti-abortionist identifies with the fetus as a
fellow human being. The fetus is an innocent and pure victim.
Its death is a tragedy. Prenatal killing is made a symbol of all that
is bad in our world, and mass abortion is dramatized as a violent
ritual of death.

One of the most obvious ways in which pure victimage is
achieved is through the metaphor of human sacrifice. Burke suggests that one method for uncovering the basic values and
motives of a group is to single out for study "representational
anecdotes," which embody or sum up the group's vision. Just as a
fragment of pottery has great significance for an archeologist, or a
spectrum of light carries worlds of meaning for an astronomer, so
an outstanding metaphor can mean much for the critic of social
discourse. In *A Grammar of Motives*, Burke maintains that predominant figures of speech, such as a recurring metaphor, may
represent whole systems of thought, and that by isolating these
key terms we can explain what motivates people to take action
for a cause.

The Sacrifice of the Unborn Child

The negative connotations of human sacrifice run deep in Judeo-Christian culture. Abraham's offering of Isaac and God's intervention to stop it is a central story in Jewish biblical history. When Israel entered the land of Canaan after the exodus and desert wandering, the prophets told of God's hatred of child sacrifice, and the practice was forbidden. Likewise, the terrible image of Christ dying on the cross—God offering his Son as a human sacrifice for sin—is central to the Christian drama.

Right-to-life advocates who identify abortion as sacrifice tap these negative religious connotations, sometimes by making biblical allusions. Francis Schaeffer and C. Everett Koop, in *Whatever Happened to the Human Race?*, depict abortion as a modern form of the ancient rites. Instead of the god Moloch, the current victims are offered up on behalf of the god of Self—the selfish desire for individual freedom and material prosperity:

> In Old Testament days, God expressed special abhorrence for the Canaanite practice of infant sacrifice. With heathenism, this was not confined to the Canaanites. For example, the ancient Europeans also offered up their offspring to the gods. These people killed their offspring *in order to purchase from the gods, they hoped, their own personal peace and affluence.*
>
> Today, indiscriminate abortion, infanticide, and euthanasia are also performed *for the personal peace and affluence of individuals.* People who destroy their own children and others, so that they can maintain their lifestyles, are also sacrificing to the gods—the gods of a materialistic world view . . .[41] (emphasis in original).

Versions of the metaphor sometimes appeal to the New Testament when abortion is associated with the Crucifixion. Here victimization is taken to the highest level—the fetus is identified with God. To kill the fetus is to kill Jesus all over again. Jean Garton writes: "He is hidden, he told us, in the hungry, the thirsty, the outsider, the naked, the sick and the imprisoned. Could He be hidden in the unborn? Could Jesus himself be hidden in each fetal child who 'came unto his own, and his own received him not'? (John 1:11)"[42] Likewise, Paul Vitz, in *Psychology as Religion: The Cult of Self Worship*, notes the connotative similarities between abortion and the Gospel story: "Recall that the young Mary was pregnant under circumstances that today routinely terminate in abortion. In the important theological context of Christmas, the killing of an unborn child is a symbolic killing of the Christchild."[43]

The image of abortion as human sacrifice provides strong motivations for anti-abortion activism. Whenever the metaphor is presented—Abraham's offering his son, the killing of the Son of God, and pagan child sacrifice—the emotional appeal of these and other biblical dramas is recollected. Much of the persuasiveness of the right-to-life case may be explained as the tugging of these volatile taproots of the religious mind. In the same way, since the majority of people continue to drift from the traditional Judeo-Christian value system, the failure of anti-abortion rhetoric to influence public opinion and policy may also be traced to society's secularization. As the memory of these values fade, we revert to the rhetorical forms of our pre-Christian roots, and the deeply structured impulses for impure victimage begin to emerge. The result is the widespread acceptance of abortion as "a necessary evil."

Burke's theories seem to suggest that the sacrifice metaphor applied to abortion is in fact sociologically valid—that our current policies and attitudes supporting abortion-on-demand are shaped by unmet desires for redemption. In contrast with most anthropologists, Burke believes that all social acts are ritualistic, possessing deeper symbolic relevance. If collective behavior is always to some extent ritualistic, then the practice of abortion may actually be a contemporary expression of the ancient need to search out and destroy a victim. Finally, a review of the pervasive role human sacrifice played in the ancient world may reveal how this form of symbolic action is structuring social reality today.

Ancient Sacrificial Victimage

Burke argues that the desire to achieve redemption by destroying a victim is an innate cognitive structure by pointing to the universal examples of victimage in ancient and primitive societies. Aboriginal peoples often devise sacrificial systems to purge themselves or the tribe of offenses against the ideal order. Tribes in Africa, for instance, burn sacrificial fires to placate the forest while hunting. Moreover, most ancient cultures have been known to practice some form of sacrificial victimage.

The ancient Hebrew system of sacrifices is one of the best documented examples. In addition to the sacrifices for the sins of individuals which could be offered year round, once a year at the Feast of Dedication the high priest would lay his hands on the heads of two goats and confess over them "all the sins of Israel." One goat would then be killed, its blood used in ritual, the other —the "scapegoat"—would be driven into the wilderness, banished from the people. In this way, the lives of the goats were substituted for the guilt of the community. Correspondingly, another rite involved the sacrifice of two doves. The neck of the first dove would be cut by the priest. The second would receive a sprinkling of blood and then be released into the air, carrying with it various infirmities.

The Hebrews are only one ancient culture which practiced expiatory sacrifices. The Hindus also had a complex system of ritual killings which is a central theme of Vedic scriptures. Ancient Vedic creation myths, for instance, tell of the sacrifice of the Primal Man, in which the world was created from the torn pieces of a cosmic sacrificial victim. Objects and people in the world are hierarchically ordered depending on what part of the man they were made of (i.e., the lower castes were made from the feet and legs, the Brahman priests from the head, etc.). Historian of religion, Mircea Eliade, points out that certain sacrificial rites (such as the horse sacrifice) were performed annually to "regenerate the entire cosmos and, at the same time, to establish all the social classes and all the vocations in their paradigmatic excellence."[44]The importance of sacrifice in the Vedic Hindu system is seen in the fact that "every sacrifice repeats the primordial act of creation and guarantees the continuity of the world for the following year."[45]

The experiences of the Hindus and Hebrews are the most well known and studied examples of ancient victimage. However, the desire for psycho-dynamic cleansing through the destruction of a victim was apparently universally expressed in ancient times. In fact, human sacrifices were common in most parts of the world. Although animal victims were always identified with their human counterparts, often human beings themselves were chosen for the kill:

Human sacrifices were known in ancient India and survived till late in the 19th century; . . . both Greeks and
Romans practiced them, no less than the wilder races of
ancient Europe. Semites and Egyptians, Peruvians and
Aztecs, slew human victims; Africa, especially the West
Coast, till recently saw thousands of human victims perish
annually; in Polynesia, Tahiti and Fiji were great centers of
the rite—in fact, it is not easy to name an area where it has
not been known.[46]

The ancient Baal worshippers in Carthage are infamous for
their rites of human sacrifice. These people believed that the
most powerful method for proving their sacred allegiance and
influencing the gods was in killing their own children. Baal (also
called Moloch) demanded the blood of newborn babies in
exchange for his protection and blessing. The result was that
thousands of children "passed through the fire"—a euphemism
for burning the infants alive in the arms of the bronze statue. One
of the most noted ritual killings occurred when the Carthaginians
were attacked by the enemy general Agathocles. Attributing their
misfortune to religious negligence, in a single expiatory holocaust
they sacrificed five hundred children chosen from among the
noblest families. Dozens of giant urns containing the ashes and
charred bones of babies have been unearthed near the site of the
ancient city.[47]

Anthropologist Angelo Brelich studied Greek myths of
human sacrifice and notes that ritualistic reenactments of the
myths involved the substitution of nonhuman victims. When the
myth was retold, goats were dressed in clothes and slaughtered as
if they were human. Sometimes the substitution of animals for
human victims was present in the myths themselves. The sce-
nario of these myths went as follows: (1) a sacrilegious crisis
results in the community suffering certain disasters; famine,
plague, earthquakes; (2) the oracle orders a human sacrifice as
payment to the gods; (3) a human sacrifice is identified with a
nonhuman victim, which is substituted as its equivalent and
killed; (4) the rite solves the crisis, brings order, moral restora-
tion, and spiritual redemption to the community.[48] Sacrificial
myths such as these were a common and important element of
Greek religion.

Burke sees all of these ancient rites, Jewish, Hindu, Greek, and others, as evidence for the sacrifice principle as a universal symbolic form of the mind. In the modern world he argues that the form is still actively present, though relegated to the recesses of consciousness. There, in the "night side of language" it lingers on as a discrete yet powerful demon.

Victimage and Technological Society

According to Burke, failure to expiate guilt through some form of victimage can result in serious consequences. Technological society has created a radical dissociation between the rational and emotional categories of the mind, stressing the scientific and denying the mythic. We ignore what Burke calls "hidden offenses against submerged processes," and suffer from "the loss of a definite, generally recognized technique for cancelling off these hidden offenses."[49] Without a symbolic "lightning rod," the blasts of social discontent become lethal. Burke sees the symptoms of a modern "technological psychosis" in racism and other forms of social violence, especially war, and hopes his ideas may contribute to the cause of peace.

Writing just before World War II, Carl Jung also warns of the likelihood of mass violence when a society has forgotten how to mythically expiate guilt:

> One thing is certain—that modern man . . . has lost the protection of the ecclesiastical walls carefully erected and reinforced since Roman days, and on account of that loss has approached the zone of world-destroying and world-creating fire. Life has become quickened and intensified. Our world is permeated by waves of restlessness and fear.
> . . . There are not a few people, nowadays, who are convinced that mere human reason is not entirely up to the enormous task of fettering the volcano.[50]

Shortly after Jung expressed these words, Hitler's rhetoric triggered the predicted eruption. The Nazi "death factories," described vividly by literary critic George Steiner as reconstructed "medieval hells,"[51] were scattered across Europe, and six million victims were condemned to die in the genocidal upheaval of the Holocaust, so inexplicably perpetrated and permitted by the highly civilized German people. According to Burke, the same kind of

psychological processes which led to the Nazi mass extermina-
tions may still threaten us today. Because "technological psychosis" drives the modern world on a frantic search for acceptable means of purification, the frightening possibility of "the holocaust of total war" is a constant menace.

The implications of Burke's theories for abortion are unmis-
takable. It would seem that because the desire to find a scapegoat
has been permanently written into the script of human relations,
part of the appeal of the pro-choice case must be traced to the
symbolic action associated with killing the fetus. This appeal
would be especially strong for abortion proponents who consciously perceive the fetus as a human being. Whether killing the
unborn child is psychologically denied or rhetorically covered up,
it has a powerful effect in satisfying the "frustrated vengeance" of
pro-choicers.

"Abortion is a nasty thing," quipped Margaret Mead, "but our
society deserves it." Gauged at four thousand a day, totaling 1.5
million a year or one third of all pregnancies, with 17,000 performed after 21 weeks gestation, we can wonder if our society
really deserves abortion, or whether we are merely expressing a
primeval need for violence. Have we come so readily to accept
abortion as an inevitable part of modern life, not because a world
without it is impossible, but because in killing the children never
born we are striking at our own fears and guilt?

Notes

1. Charles Hartshorne, "Concerning Abortion: An Attempt at a Rational View," *The Christian Century* (21 January 1981), p. 45.

2. Abortion in the United States is virtually unlimited. It is legal anytime before birth (as long as an abortionist considers it necessary to preserve a woman's health—including her "emotional health"). Abortion can be performed for sex selection or birth control. Yet polls show that a significant majority of Americans support abortion only for the hard cases. The liberal *Boston Globe* reported in April 6, 1989 (p. 1) a random, nationwide survey of 1,002 registered voters on the question of the acceptability of abortion. The study revealed that the vast majority of Americans would ban most abortions. "While seventy-eight percent of the nation would keep abortion legal in limited circumstances, according to the poll, those circumstances account for a tiny percent of the reasons cited by women having abortions," said the *Globe*. The limited circumstances were the classic hard cases: rape, incest, when the mother's physical health is endangered, and when the baby will have a "definite genetic deformity." A 1990 Gallup poll of 2,174 adults nationwide reported a similarly high percent of the population are opposed to the vast majority of abortions: 66% disapprove of abortion for financial reasons, 77% disapprove when pregnancy would interrupt a woman's career, 88% are opposed to it as birth control, and 91% oppose its use for sex selection. [Melodie S. Gage, "AUL Releases Major Survey," *Life Docket* (March 1991), p. 1.]

3. Burke's major works include: *Counter Statement* (New York, 1931); *Permanence and Change* (New York, 1935); *Attitudes toward History* (New York, 1937); *A Grammar of Motives* (New York, 1945); *A Rhetoric of Motives* (New York, 1950); *The Philosophy of Literary Form* (Baton Rouge, 1951); *A Rhetoric of Religion* (Boston, 1961); and *Language as Symbolic Action* (Berkeley, 1966).

4. Stephen W. Littlejohn and David M. Jabusch, *Persuasive Transactions* (Glenview, IL: Scott, Foresman, and Company, 1987), p. 44.

5. Bernard Nathanson, *Aborting America* (Garden City, NY: Doubleday and Co., 1979), p. 179.

6. "The Unborn and the Born Again," an editorial, *New Republic* (2 July 1977), p. 5.

7. Magda Denes, *In Necessity and Sorrow: Life and Death in an Abortion Hospital* (New York: Basic Books, 1976).

8. Stephen Toulmin, *The Uses of Argument* (Cambridge: Cambridge University Press, 1958), pp. 13-15.

9. Rosalind Pollack Petchesky, *Abortion and Women's Choice: The State, Sexuality and Reproductive Freedom* (Boston: Northeastern University Press, 1984).

10. Andrew Merton, *Enemies of Choice: The Right to Life Movement and Its Threat to Abortion* (Boston: Beacon Press, 1981).

11. *The Voices of Women—Abortion: In Their Own Words*, NARAL booklet (Washington, DC: The NARAL Foundation, [1986]).

12. David Reardon, *Aborted Women Silent No More* (Westchester, IL: Crossway Books, 1987).

13. Deuteronomy 5:17; Luke 1; Psalm 139.

14. Matthew 25:40.

15. Mary Daly, *Gyn/ecology: The Metaethics of Radical Feminism* (Boston: Beacon Press, 1978), p. 59.

16. John Stoltenberg, "Fetus as Penis: Men's Self-Interest in Abortion Rights," *Refusing to Be a Man, Essays on Sex and Justice* (Portland, OR: Breitenbush Books, Inc., 1989), p. 96.

17. Andrea Dworkin, "Sexual Politics of Fear and Courage," *Our Blood: Prophecies and Discourses on Sexual Politics* (New York: Harper and Row, 1976), p. 55.

18. *Christianity Today*, an editorial (16 November 1979), p. 13.

19. Jean Staker Garton, *Who Broke the Baby?* (Minneapolis, MN: Bethany Fellowship, 1979), p. 30.

20. David Granfield, *The Abortion Decision* (Garden City, NY: Doubleday and Co., Inc., 1969), p. 166. (The clothbound edition is cited.)

21. John Powell, S.J., *Abortion: The Silent Holocaust* (Allen, TX: Argus Communications, 1981), p. 117.

22. "Bower's conclusion was that '. . . a metaphor nearly always communicates a stronger attitude than does a conventional expression.' He goes on to suggest, however, that to conclude that metaphor usage will be effective in attitude change is not to conclude that such emotional language usage will necessarily be in a direction desired by the source. For the receiver who holds relatively moderate views toward the topic, a message that uses very extreme language is likely to have a boomerang effect. It may cause him to change his attitude less than a more moderate speech would. Highly emotional language in a message directed toward an audience that already is inclined to side with the source may serve to strengthen those attitudes, but receivers in general tend to react negatively toward extremely intense language." [Erwin P. Bettinghaus, *Persuasive Communication*, Second Edition (New York: Holt, Rinehart and Winston, 1968), pp. 133-34.]

23.   See Kenneth Burke, *The Philosophy of Literary Form: Studies in Symbolic Action* (Baton Rouge: Louisiana State University Press, 1941).

24.   William H. Ruechkert, ed., *Critical Responses to Kenneth Burke, 1924-1966* (Minneapolis: University of Minnesota Press, 1969), p. 348.

25.   Kenneth Burke, "Postscripts on the Negative," *The Quarterly Journal of Speech* (April 1953), p. 216.

26.   Hugh Duncan, *Symbols and Social Theory* (New Oxford University Press, 1969), p. 260.

27.   Kenneth Burke, *The Rhetoric of Religion* (Boston: Beacon Press, 1961), p. 176.

28.   Sigmund Freud, *Civilization and Its Discontents* (New York: Norton and Co., 1961), pp. 61, 81.

29.   John 1:29.

30.   Burke, *The Rhetoric of Religion*, pp. 217, 224.

31.   Burke, *The Philosophy of Literary Form*, p. 191.

32.   Helene S. Arnstein, *What Every Woman Needs to Know about Abortion* (New York: Charles Scribner's Sons, 1973), p. 89. Public health statistics indicate that, in 1990, more than 40% of all women seeking abortions already had one or two before.

33.   Daphne de Jung, "The Feminist Sell-Out," (Campus Pro Life, P.O. Box 14, Student Union Building, University of British Columbia, Vancouver, British Columbia, Canada), p. 1.

34.   Randall Lake, "Order and Disorder in Anti-Abortion Rhetoric: A Logological View," *The Quarterly Journal of Speech* (November 1984), p. 425.

35.   See the 1978 *Abortion Surveillance* annual summary of the Centers for Disease Control, Public Health Service, U.S. Department of Health and Human Services, p. 61.

36.   Richard Grunberger, *A Social History of the Third Reich* (London: Weidenfeld and Nicolson, 1971), p. 330.

37.   P. Zimbardo and F. Ruch, *Psychology and Life* (Glenview, IL: Scott, Foresman, 1977), p. 647.

38.   Joseph Fletcher, *Situation Ethics* (Philadelphia: The Westminster Press, 1966), p. 39.

39.   Bernard Nathanson, M.D. and Richard Ostling, *Aborting America* (Garden City, NY: Doubleday and Co., 1979), p. 220.

40.   Oriana Fallaci, *Letter to a Child Never Born* (New York: Simon and Schuster, 1976), p. 79.

41.   Francis Schaeffer and C. Everett Koop, M.D., *Whatever Happened to the Human Race?* (Old Tappan, NJ: Fleming H. Revell Co., 1979), p. 112.

42.   Garton, p. 72.

43. Paul C. Vitz, *Psychology as Religion: The Cult of Self Worship* (1977), p. 89, cited in J.W. Montgomery, *Slaughter of the Innocents* (Westchester, IL: Cornerstone Books, 1981), p. 10.

44. Mircea Eliade, *A History of Religious Ideas: From the Stone Age to the Eleusinian Mysteries* (Chicago: The University of Chicago Press, 1979), p. 219.

45. *Ibid.*, p. 229.

46. *Encyclopedia Britannica*, Eleventh Edition (see "sacrifice"), p. 984.

47. Gilbert and Colette Charles-Picard, *Daily Life in Carthage* (New York: Macmillian Co., 1961), p. 67.

48. Angelo Brelich, "Symbol of a Symbol," in Joseph Kilagawa and Charles Long, eds., *Myth and Symbols* (Chicago: The University of Chicago Press, 1969), pp. 195-99.

49. Kenneth Burke, *Permanence and Change: An Anatomy of Purpose* (Los Altos, CA: Hermes Publications, 1954), p. 74.

50. Carl Jung, *Psychology and Religion* (New York: Yale University Press, 1969), p. 59.

51. George Steiner, *In Bluebeard's Castle* (New York: Yale University Press, 1971), pp. 54-55.

Technological Themes
in the Abortion Debate

William C. Hunt

I n 1975, an ecumenical group of theologians issued "The Hartford Appeal for Theological Affirmation." It was a brief declaration in which the scholars identified thirteen themes in modern thought which they felt undercut the whole theological enterprise.[1] People influenced by these themes do not necessarily deny God or attack religion. Often they are regular churchgoers. However, they perceive questions about God and religion as basically private and, at best, marginal to public affairs.

One of the identified themes asserts: "Religious statements are totally independent of reasonable discourse." If that theme dominates a person's approach, theology is on a par with stamp collecting; there is no accounting for one's passion for the practice, and it is useless to consider any truth claims it happens to make.

The authors of the Hartford Appeal identified other themes which either cut religion off from "the real world" or reduce religious issues to strictly secular terms.

It is my contention that a similar phenomenon is taking place in the technological world with regard to morality and ethics. Just as the themes identified in the Hartford Appeal undermine religion and theology, so also some of the major technological themes make it difficult, if not impossible, for contemporary people to act morally and think ethically about public policy issues. I hope to identify a few of these technological themes and show how they affect argument on both sides of life issues with particular attention to the abortion controversy.

Worlds in Conflict

It is difficult to analyze one's own world.[2] There is no place to view it "from the outside" since the world always goes along with the viewer. Moreover, people move in different, interacting worlds of home, work, leisure, politics, etc.

The technological world seems to pervade the other worlds. It is very definitely *our* world. We are caught up in it. More and more, it is seen as characteristic of contemporary consciousness. This blurs our awareness and appreciation of other worlds and conditions them in subtle but powerful ways.

Though difficult, critical reflection on one's own world is possible. One can at least identify themes that are more or less taken for granted such as the notion of a free market by people in the world of commerce or the positive attitude toward play by people in the world of leisure.

Conflict can be helpful here. Although some worlds can coexist in the same person without conflict, others cannot. It is hard for a person from the world of work who places a negative value on wasting time to enter into the world of leisure and really enjoy a game of golf. In the process, however, that person might well become more aware of some of the dimensions of the worlds of work and leisure.

It is my contention that the dominant themes of our technological world are in conflict with what we have hitherto known as our moral world. This stems mainly from a tendency to look upon human organizations in terms of machines and to understand human interactions primarily by way of a mathematical methodology. As a result, it is difficult, if not impossible, for someone immersed in the technological world to act morally in any traditional sense of the word. Quite literally, technological themes demoralize decision making and diminish responsibility.

Some Technological Themes

In order to understand our technological world better, it is helpful to reflect on a number of pervasive themes which all too often are taken for granted. Hopefully, this will throw some light on the debate over life issues, particularly abortion. It is important to be aware that these themes creep into the rhetoric on both sides of the debate. Living in a technological world, one is sorely tempted to avail oneself of the persuasive power of technological lines of argumentation.

1. Preoccupation with Means[3]

Essential to ethical discourse is the balance between ends and means. Usually we denounce those who pursue ends with no regard for the means taken to achieve them. However, the reverse is a problem too. One can become so fascinated with the means at hand that the end in view becomes obscured.

Our technological world seems preoccupied with means and neglectful of ends. Think of the number of offices where computer hardware has been installed without previous analysis of data processing needs. Such a significant investment of money and prestige makes it necessary to adjust the purpose of the operation to the capabilities of the new computer.

On a much larger scale the space technology which enabled the United States to place a man on the moon was so popular with the general public that it obscured the essentially military purpose of the space program and undercut the discussion of alternative uses of the public funds involved. America's love affair with the automobile and freeways has blinded us to the negative effects on urban neighborhoods and made it very difficult to address public policy issues relating to mass transit.

We are like the enthusiastic young American visiting England for the first time who blurts out, "You know, sir, I guess the whole of England could be fitted into one corner of Nebraska," only to have his companion on the train, an English parson, reply, "But to what *end*, young man?"[4] (Emphasis in original.)

Preoccupation with means does overcome the paralysis of indecision. If we debate about ends endlessly, nothing gets done. However, neglect of ends "demoralizes" the choice of means. When the end in view is taken seriously, usually there are a number of alternate ways to get there and some freedom of choice in the selection. When there is little attention to the purpose or goal of an activity, fascination with sleek lines or prestigious name brands often preempts moral considerations.

The application to life issues is apparent. The advent of the vacuum aspirator and the technological capability for safe abortions at a very early stage in pregnancy distracts moral attention from the purpose of the procedure. The Supreme Court's 1973 abortion decision focused on means, requiring only that abortion be performed by a licensed physician. The implicit and largely unchallenged argument seems to have been that if the procedure is carried out by the technological specialist (the physician) in accordance with recognized medical practice there is no need to be concerned about the purpose of the operation.

Preoccupation with means has had a similar effect at the end of life. The technology of intravenous feeding, medication, respirators, heart simulators, etc., has made it more difficult to face issues of useless treatment, precisely because the spontaneous tendency is to treat first and ask questions later. Right now the means are at hand and something can be done. Whether it ought to be done is put off until later or never asked.

2. Efficiency

The technological world is consumed by a restless passion for efficiency. Efficiency is its golden rule. However, it is a peculiar kind of efficiency which takes a machine for its model. Each component is judged for its usefulness, and the ultimate criterion is whether or not it works.

How often have we been swayed by the assertion: "It works!" How often has it been used to set aside moral scruples! Administrative costs for some charitable fund-raising consume more than 50% of the total amount raised, but "It works!" No other scheme has netted the same amount. Chemical fertilizer pollutes the water supply, but "It works!" Crops have never been so abundant. A crash diet might have dangerous consequences, but "It works!" It helps people lose weight quickly where everything else has failed.

This is the other extreme of the ends-means dialectic. Here the end justifies the means which will achieve it with the least expenditure of time and energy. Once again, freedom of choice is the casualty because a single criterion predetermines the selection of a particular means.

This has had a particularly serious effect upon our legal system which is increasingly ordered to efficiency instead of to justice. Understandably, this is due, in part, to the enormous complexity of modern life, but the result is an increasingly narrow focus on enforceability. It has become axiomatic among us that a law which cannot be enforced should be stricken from the books. The notion that the role of law in society is to enable virtue to flourish gives way to the notion that its role is to coordinate societal subsystems in the most efficient fashion. The educational or hortatory function of law suffers as well. Witness the opposition to mandatory seat belt laws with no penalty for violation. Many oppose such laws, not because they question the contribution of the laws toward saving lives, but because they have no teeth. They cannot be enforced.

The theme of efficiency has affected the abortion debate. Opponents of laws restricting abortion claim that an extremely large number of illegal abortions were being performed before changes in the law began around 1967. The rhetorical force of this largely unsubstantiated claim is that the law wasn't working then and won't work in the future if legal protection of the unborn is restored. The law, they say, is not an efficient way to prevent abortions.

When the focus is primarily on enforceability it is difficult for the question of justice to arise. The passion for efficiency and control renders questions of right and wrong irrelevant. Even people who are personally opposed to abortion on moral grounds feel helpless when captured by this argument. Regardless of the merit of a restrictive law, regardless of its justice, it cannot be enforced. It is inefficient; it just doesn't work!

On the other side of the abortion debate stands the claim supported by the technological wizardry of ultrasound imaging that an unborn child undergoing a first trimester abortion experiences pain and even terror in the process. The rhetorical impact is powerful; it has persuaded thousands, perhaps millions, of the evil of abortion; unquestionably, it works![5] Given that fact, it is difficult to give full weight to the counterclaims of neurologists that the fetus's nervous system is not sufficiently developed to sustain the subjective experience of pain. The technological argument has been so successful that it sweeps aside moral scruples about its use.

3. Problem v. Dilemma

The term "problem" has a particular meaning in a technological context. Basically, it is derived from mathematics and mechanics where a problem, by definition, is capable of being solved in the same terms in which it is stated. Problem solving consists of reducing the matter to its simplest terms, examining the relationships, and restructuring the components to achieve the desired outcome. Coupled with a statistical methodology, this technique is applied to everything from studying the effects of gamma rays to assuring enough ducks for hunters in the fall.

It is important to note that the solution to this kind of problem is a matter of intelligence and technique. It has nothing to do with moral goodness.

When technological problem solving is applied to human affairs there is a tendency to ignore individual differences and the uniqueness of the human person. There is an emphasis on interchangeability of parts rather than on interrelationships between people. For purposes of analysis, individual human beings become units in a statistical continuum, and there is a tendency to disvalue intermediate groupings between the individual and the state.[6]

Quantitative analysis can be a useful instrument for understanding the human phenomenon and organizing society. However, to the extent that it is absolutized it becomes a procrustean bed, excludes a holistic approach, and is destructive of both individual uniqueness and community.

In the technological approach to things it is easy to see abortion as the solution to a problem pregnancy. The technique is available to any woman who is smart enough to take advantage of it. So called eugenic abortion also fits the technological mold. If a fetus is "defective" it can be replaced by another later on. After all, it is argued, one fetus is pretty much the same as another. Similarly, a person with a handicap is a problem, a substandard part of the social mechanism, whether born or unborn.

Vindictive approaches to a woman's problem pregnancy also belie a technological attitude. Often the woman is looked upon as more stupid than bad. "She should have known enough to use contraception. In any event, it's her problem." The problem theme also accounts, at least in part, for the naïve confidence in contraception as a solution to problem pregnancies.

A human dilemma, by contrast, cannot be resolved in the terms in which it is originally posed. Resolution requires an act of human creativity and freedom. If someone in your family faces a financial problem, usually the solution is quite obvious—increase income or decrease spending. If that were the extent of the response, most of us would consider it rather heartless. Only a decision to share the burden in some way would serve to resolve the dilemma in a humane fashion.

Similarly, the humane resolution of the dilemma a woman faces in a difficult pregnancy requires that someone say: "I will help you. I will make a difference in what you face. I will share your burden with you so that together we can find the right way to act." Only then does a fully moral response to her dilemma become possible.

4. Artificial v. Natural

The technological world is an artificial world with a difference. At one time the goal of art was to imitate nature. The goal of modern technology is to learn from nature so as to modify, improve upon, and replace it.

It is already nearly impossible for modern people to get in touch with nature. City children visit zoos to see cows. For the most part campers haul a highly sophisticated artificial environment with them on their nature treks. Artificial illumination eliminates the basic rhythm of light and darkness. Even the blueness of the sky is judged by its conformity to a Kodachrome prototype.

It is true that mechanization has reduced the destructiveness and fluctuations of capricious nature. It is also true that, in theory at least, machines neither grow up nor die. The possibility of repairs and the interchangeability of parts assures them of a kind of immortality. To the extent that we attempt to modify nature at will and create a wholly artificial world, we are involved in the denial of death—a refusal to acknowledge any radical givenness or limits in reality. Reality or nature becomes totally malleable. It is not surprising, then, that when the operative model of society is a machine rather than a living organism, there seems to be no limit to our tinkering with the social fabric.

In some respects the ecological crisis results from this mentality. The development of nuclear power plants without adequate concern for the problems of the disposal of radioactive waste materials illustrates the point, as does the effect of petrochemicals on the air we breathe. Still, there is a confidence in technological circles that it is only a matter of time until these things can be worked out. Technological solutions will be found to any conceivable technological problem.

All this affects how we deal with "defective" human beings before and after birth. If society is viewed in mechanical terms, elimination of defectives can contribute to the well-being of the state, its efficient functioning, and ultimately to its immortality.

On the other hand, there is the unquestioning confidence that one day medical technology will be able to rectify any physical disability. The results of prosthesis have been astounding, and major advances have been made in the treatment of genetic disorders. However, that is no reason to disregard genetic counseling or to fail to take action before conception occurs.

5. Facts v. Truth

Technique has worked its way into our very method of communication and notion of truth. The invention of writing was both a facilitator and a limitation of communication. It enabled messages to be conveyed across boundaries of space and time, but it was not able to capture the subtle nuances of face-to-face conversation or story telling.[7]

Techniques of communication tend to define what is worth communicating by what they communicate best. Modern electronic media are no exception. The computer, for example, is a powerful instrument for processing information which can be reduced to binary notation or yes-no responses. It does amazingly well with quantifiable data, so well, in fact, that computer users are tempted to discount other types of information as unscientific.

Likewise, television is capable of transmitting factual information so effectively that by a subtle shift the impression is left with the viewer that everything television communicates is factual. The possibilities for propaganda are significantly expanded by this change of attitude.

Prior to 1973 and to a lesser extent since the Supreme Court's decision, the assertion was made over and over again in all the different media that 10,000 women died each year in the United States from illegal abortions. Accepted as factual, this information had a profound effect on people who were opposed to abortion. Operating in conjunction with other themes, especially the theme of efficiency, the presumption that what the news media asserted was factual led many to acquiesce to permissive abortion even though they opposed it on moral grounds. The media was telling them that the situation was out of control, that thousands of women were needlessly dying, and that a million or more illegal abortions were being performed every year anyway. By legalizing abortion at least the slaughter of pregnant women could be stopped, so the argument went.

Of course, none of this was true in the sense that it conformed with reality or that it was based on scientific observation. However, few had the resources to challenge the flood of information supplied by the media industry with its bias against laws restricting abortion.

This theme affects both sides of the abortion debate. Once a piece of information appears in print it takes on the aura of fact. Perhaps a trivial example will suffice to illustrate the tendency. Some years ago I ran across the quotation attributed to Dante: "The hottest places in hell are reserved for those who in time of crisis choose to do nothing." A great one-liner, and who should know more about hell than Dante? Although quoted widely in pro-life literature, the best verification I could discover was that someone had taken it from the parish bulletin of a church in Florida. I doubt very much that Dante said it because in his *Inferno* the worst sinners are encased in ice!

The point is that moral decisions must be based on truth. Unquestioning acceptance of media information as factual undermines the ethical enterprise. There is no substitute for critical judgment.

6. Inevitability

Another powerful theme is the technological imperative: What can be done will be done! Under the influence of this theme history is seen as a uniform, unidirectional continuum in which later developments are better and only the best survive. History becomes the arena of inevitable events which cannot be resisted without personal self-destruction. The trick is to get on the band wagon or go with the flow.

In this sort of world it becomes increasingly evident that superior technology wins out in the end. The only way to survive is to become more efficient, more organized, in a word, more technological. Moreover, there is nowhere to hide, and we cannot return to the past except by dropping out of the mainstream and relinquishing any influence, however minimal, on the course of events.

The technological imperative is approaching a law of nature. It is no longer a question of morality any more than a sunset is a question of morality. In fact, as technology becomes second nature to us we tend to approach the technological world in much the same way as ancient people approached the natural world—with a sense of worshipful reverence and absolute submission.

It is really questionable whether morality is possible in such a world. There is no question that the theme of inevitability makes it extremely difficult to mount resistance to current trends. When people say that it is a waste of time to work for a human life amendment, it is difficult to argue the contrary. Once a new practice has been approved by the American Medical Association and affirmed by the highest court in the land, there is little likelihood of reversal. If one is also captured by the theme of technological irreversibility, there is no hope at all.

A mirror image of the technological theme of inevitability lies in the confidence of some people that what they consider to be good will win out in the end. John T. Noonan, Jr. has brilliantly shown that evil works to its own destruction by overreaching itself,[8] but this is not an argument that goodness will ultimately prevail without the creativity and activity of free people. There is nothing automatic about human history.

Perspectives on Freedom

These themes which are constitutive, at least in part, of our technological world provide us with a contrast to a world in which morality is possible. By reappropriating the tradition of creativity and freedom we can fashion a moral response to issues such as abortion.

Each of the themes challenges our understanding of freedom. By collapsing the necessary tension between ends and means, the themes of preoccupation with means and efficiency undermine freedom of choice. It is only by keeping ends and means separate that one can address alternative courses of action and face realistic choices.

The theme of efficiency also highlights the contrast between the understanding of freedom as the power to choose the good versus the notion of freedom as the power to choose what is most useful in attaining one's end.

The problem theme stands against the understanding of freedom as creativity, and the factual theme opposes the idea that freedom is based on truth rather than on power.

The theme of artificiality conflicts with the freedom to accept reality as a gift, to accept oneself and others with limitations, including the necessity of death, and to affirm and appropriate one's own humanity with all its limitations.

Finally, the technological imperative or the theme of inevitability opposes the notion of freedom as resistance to evil— the determination to do no harm, regardless of the consequences of success or failure in one's resistance. This is one of the highest forms of freedom, whether it be in the form of Christian martyrdom, protest against the absurdity of existence, opposition to tyranny, or the practice of soul force (*ahimsa*, non-violence) after the fashion of Gandhi.

When we recognize that the technological world is our world and when we appreciate the power of some of its major themes, we will be able to reflect more critically on the tradition of freedom which is constitutive of our truly humane world. Then, perhaps, we will be better able to deal with the rhetoric surrounding issues of public policy such as abortion—to appreciate its force, to understand its distortions, and to counter it with moral arguments.

Notes

1. See Peter L. Berger and Richard John Neuhaus, eds., *Against the World for the World*, The Hartford Appeal and the Future of American Religion (New York: Seabury, 1976).

2. The English word "world" seems to have been derived from the Latin *vir* (pronounced "were"), meaning "man," and the Germanic *alt* or *ald* (related to the English word "old") referring to age or experience. Hence, "world" conveys the meaning of "human experience " or, more properly, "the experience of being human." Its meaning is primarily psychosocial rather than spacial or geographical.

   The English term "worldview" which frequently translates the German *Weltanschauung* does not capture the same reality. It is more abstract than "world." At least in common parlance, it seems to separate the subject from the reality being observed as though one could be an independent observer. It has less of a social dimension. On the contrary, one enters a "world" and, in turn, one's perception of oneself and one's outlook are aspects of that world. One tends to be immersed in one's world, and it is very difficult to find a place to stand to view one's world "from the outside."

   See *The Compact Edition of the Oxford English Dictionary*, 2 vols. (New York: Oxford University Press, 1971) s.v. "world;" *Webster's New World Dictionary of the American Language*, David B. Guralnik, Editor in Chief, Second College Edition (New York: The World Publishing Company, 1970) s.v. "world."

3. The impetus for my approach to technology comes from the work of Jacques Ellul, especially his *The Technological Society*, John Wilkinson, trans. (New York: Vantage Books, 1964). For a briefer presentation of some of the main ideas, see *The Presence of the Kingdom*, Olive Wyon, trans. (New York: Seabury, 1967) especially chapter 3, "The End and the Means," pp. 61-95. With regard to technology, as Ellul put it, "The real problem is not to judge but to understand." See *The Technological Society*, p. 190.

4. Alistair Cooke, *America* (New York: Alfred Knopf, 1973), pp. 14-15.

5. See Dave Andrusko and Richard Glasow, "'High Tech' Educational Outreach Builds Pro-Life Momentum," *National Right to Life News*, Vol. 13, No. 1 (January 9, 1986), pp. 1, 16, with reference to the film "The Silent Scream" narrated by Bernard N. Nathanson, M.D., and distributed by American Portrait Films, 1695 W. Crescent Ave., Suite 500, Anaheim, CA 92801.

6.   See the comments of Jacques Ellul about "social plasticity" in *The Technological Society*, *loc. cit.*, p. 126. See also Peter Berger and Richard John Neuhaus, *To Empower People: The Role of Mediating Structures in Public Policy* (Washington: American Enterprise Institute for Public Policy Research, 1977) and my review in *ACCL Update*, Vol. 3, No. 2 (July 1977), p. 12.

7.   See Lucien Deiss, C.S.Sp., *God's Word and God's People* (Collegeville, MN: The Liturgical Press, 1976), pp. 91-93, "Greatness and Limitation of the Written Word."

8.   See John T. Noonan, Jr., *A Private Choice: Abortion in America in the Seventies* (New York: The Free Press, 1979) and my review in *ACCL Update*, Vol. 6, No. 1 (January/February 1980), p. 6.

The Rhetoric of Abortion:
A Weaverian Method of Analysis

B. F. McClerren

All things considered, rhetoric, noble,
or base, is a great power in the world. . . .[1]

O ne of the most intense rhetorical wars being waged in the
United States is between pro-abortion and anti-abortion
advocates. The January 22, 1973 *Roe v. Wade* decision by the
Supreme Court gave the legal victory to proponents of abortion,
but the battle continues.[2] Both sides realize that the ideological
victory must still be won.

How may the rhetoric of abortion be analyzed? This paper
offers a method for analysis based on a synthesis of selected
essays by Richard Weaver. The method is the focus of this essay,
and readers are invited to apply it to other social issues. Indeed
the application of the method to an entire speech or series of articles should yield more meaningful results than the necessarily
brief examples given.

The Weaverian method provides criteria for three basic identifications: (1) emotive language; (2) modes of argument, including definition, similitude, cause-effect, and testimony; and (3)
types of rhetoric, including neuter, base or evil, and noble.

Emotive Language

Abortion rhetoric, both pro and con, carries persuasive force
with overt and concealed "should" and "ought" propositions.
Appropriately, Weaver instructs:

The condition essential to see is that every speech, oral and written, exhibits an attitude, and an attitude implies an act. . . . Your speech reveals your disposition first by what you choose to say, then by the amount you decide to say, and so on down through the resources of linguistic elaboration and intonation. All rhetoric is a rhetoric of motives, as Kenneth Burke saw fit to indicate in the title of his book.[3]

Weaver's "Ultimate Terms in Contemporary Rhetoric" invites us to identify significant words and phrases and to classify them as "god terms" or "devil terms."[4] Some of the primary "god terms" of our society are "progress," "American," "freedom," "science," and "modern." For every "god term" there is a corresponding "devil term." Most powerful among the latter are "un-American" and "prejudice."[5]

The terms discovered by Weaver pertain to the society in general, but those that follow were found in the rhetoric of abortion.[6]

The ultimate "god term" which pro-abortion advocates call themselves is "pro-choice people." Describing pregnancy, they use generally innocuous "god terms" such as "tissue," "products of pregnancy or of conception," and "contents of the uterus." Anti-abortion proponents are said to have a "fetus fetish," or they are "fetus lovers." Both are "devil terms."

Among the most euphemistic pro-abortion terms we find "therapeutic," "safe and legal," "humane," and "liberalized." Also heard are "contraceptive back-up," and "termination of pregnancy." Anti-abortionists are labeled as favoring "illegal abortions," "coat-hanger abortions," and "discrimination in health care."

Some of the most poignant ultimate terms center on freedom and rights. "God terms" invoked include "supporters of free choice," "pro-choice," "freedom of conscience," "reproductive freedom," "American right," "right of privacy," "right to control the body," "right to control reproductive lives," and "right to meaningful humanhood." "Devil terms" directed to the opposition include "anti-choice fanatics," "anti-choice zealots," "extreme right wingers," "abortion prohibitionists," "forced pregnancy people," "mandatory motherhood people," and those who "discriminate against the poor."

Ideological acceptability of abortion often seeks "god terms" in various applications of "separation of church and state." The opposition, in turn, is accused of "restricting religious liberty," "establishing theological presuppositions," and "imposing morality."

Anti-abortion proponents call themselves "pro-life" or "right-to-life people." Other "god terms" include "prenatal child," "preborn baby," and "smallest youngster." Abortion "devil terms" include: "lynching in the womb," "life-lifting," and "front street quackery."

Revealing their opinions about those who support abortion, they speak of "liberty-hogging," "pro-choice to kill," "abortion pushers," "anti-life campaign," "compulsory death people," "baby terminators," and "compulsive copulation people."

Modes of Argument

In two essays, Weaver presents a hierarchy of modes of argument, including definition, similitude, cause and effect, and testimony.[7]

Definition

From Weaver's perspective, definition is the highest form of argument. It is based on the nature of a thing and helps "people to see what is most permanent in existence or what transcends the world of change and accident."[8] Definition, then, reveals a metaphysical position. Weaver offers the example that "if a speaker should define man as a creature with an indefeasible right to freedom and should upon this base an argument that a certain man or group of men are entitled to freedom, he would be arguing from definition."[9]

Much of the abortion controversy proceeds from definition. By definition of the Supreme Court, all the unborn are not persons. From that definition flows other definitions. For thirty years prior to the Court's decision, a mother could receive aid for her unborn child through the Social Security Act. HEW and the Court redefined "child" to exclude the unborn.[10] Now medical personnel and anti-abortion advocates define the unborn as not being a part of the mother's body, while some pro-abortionists reverse that definition.

Weaver advises sensitivity to changes in definition because they portend ideological changes. From 1937 through 1961, for example, the works of Alan Guttmacher, M.D., explicitly identify his belief that a baby is conceived at the time of fertilization. During

that time, his works reject abortion. By 1968, Dr. Guttmacher, head
of The National Medical Advisory Council of Planned Parenthood,
changed his position and affirmed, "My feeling is that the fetus,
particularly during its early intrauterine life, is merely a group of
cells that do not differ materially from other cells."[11]

This Weaverian analysis also identifies that the Supreme
Court's definition of human life in *Roe v. Wade* differs from
explicit and implicit definitions found in the Hippocratic Oath,
The World Medical Association of Geneva, The Nuremberg Code,
and the Declaration of Helsinki.[12]

Identifying name-calling as a "perversion of the argument
based on definition," Weaver warns that when the propagandist
"desires us to accept something, he applies a good name to it; if
he desires us to reject it, he applies an evil one."[13] Only if the
term is true or exact may the argument be viewed as honest, but
the "propagandist applies a name that is speciously good."[14] Certainly some perversions of definitions that Weaver eschewed can
be found in the "god terms" and "devil terms" identified earlier.

Similitude

Similitude, and its related forms, is favored by those with a
creative sort of mind and may tactfully lead to generalizations. In
anti-abortion rhetoric, the slavery-abortion analogue seems to be a
favorite. David Mall observes that "in a very important sense, any
decision which affects the alleged humanity of intrauterine life is
in essence a second Dred Scott Decision, for it defines a human
being."[15] André E. Hellegers, M.D., points out that "to discuss
abortion only in terms of the mother but never the fetus is like
discussing slavery only in terms of the owner but never the
slave."[16] John T. Noonan, Jr., predicts: "It is only another age than
ours which will be able to pronounce on the pro-abortionists the
judgment history eventually recorded on the slaveholders—that
they were blind to what they did."[17]

Pro-abortion speakers and writers demonstrate a fondness
for the blueprint-baby analogy. Garrett Hardin asks us to "consider the case of a man who is about to begin to build a fifty thousand dollar house."[18] The blueprints are burned by a joker and
the owner sues for the price of the house. The decision is, of
course, that the prints are not of equal value to a house. In like
manner, says Hardin, "it is recognized that all life is not equally

valuable, and that the value of the life of a few-days-old embryo is only a tiny fraction that of the value of an adult life."[19]

In all, Weaver warned that we must be wary of misleading or false analogies.

Cause and Effect

Cause and effect function in the realm of becoming instead of being, and this mode of argument is used primarily by pragmatists. Weaver reports: "It is not unusual today to find a lengthy piece of journalism or an entire political speech which is nothing but a series of arguments from consequence—completely devoid of reference to principle or defined ideas."[20] Also, they play on the emotions of their audience "by stressing the awful nature of some consequence or by exaggerating the power of some cause."[21]

Within pro-abortion rhetoric many cause-effect arguments are found. First, we heard that back-alley abortions would stop if abortion was legalized, and that if abortion was not legalized, many poor women would die. After abortion was legalized, the argument shifted to: If abortions are not funded by the government, many poor women will die.[22]

Anti-abortion forces declare that legalized abortion will lead to legalized euthanasia. Dennis J. Horan, with others, writes: "The position that our law takes on abortion indicates the position it will take on euthanasia, genetic engineering, cloning, and all of the difficult human life problems facing our society in the years ahead."[23]

Other cause-effect relationships involve child abuse and family relationships. Philip G. Ney, M.D., says, "There is no convincing evidence that liberalized abortion has reduced child abuse; in fact the evidence indicates the opposite."[24] Continuing, Dr. Ney describes shattered family relationships as a consequence of abortion.

Argument from circumstance is a subvariety of cause and effect that, says Weaver, "amounts to a surrender of reason."[25] In this type of argument, no explanation is offered. One is simply urged to step lively, change rapidly, or be destroyed. For example, the pro-abortion advocate may urge that we adapt ourselves to a fast changing world.

Testimony

Testimony or arguments based on authority are only as good as the authority. Weaver warns that we may be misled when we are "not sufficiently critical of the authority being used."[26]   In a more subtle way we are misled "when an argument is expressed in language that distinctly echoes some famous or dear document. . . ."[27]

Both pro- and anti-abortion rhetoric lean heavily on authority.   Persuaders quote medical personnel, sociologists, psychiatrists, judges, lawyers, and others.   Acceptance is courted with quotes from the Bible, the Constitution, and respected literature.

Weaver concludes his discussion of the modes of argument with an indication of their value as a critical tool. He advises:

> Follow utterances of some public figure, past or present, in
> whom you have a strong interest and know what he seems
> to prefer as the basis of his appeal. . . . Does he like to
> define things and argue deductively, does he like to dwell
> on results, is he fond of analogies, or does he prefer to fall
> back on authority and argue from the prestige of some great
> name? You will find that this examination will be both
> instructive and entertaining, and it may give you an under-
> standing of the figure, the kind of understanding . . . that
> you did not have before.[28]

Here we find an index to the character and intentions of the rhetorician not only by what is asked for but by the mode of argument used.

Types of Rhetoric

Weaver compares the three speeches on love in Plato's *Phaedrus* to: (1) neuter rhetoric (non lover), (2) evil or base rhetoric (evil lover), and (3) noble rhetoric (noble lover).[29] Plato's central idea, according to Weaver, "is that all speech, which is the means the gods have given man to express his soul, is a form of eros in the proper interpretation of the word."[30] The problem that plagues Plato may be stated in this way: "If truth alone is not sufficient to persuade men, what else remains that can be legitimately added?"[31] The three speeches attempt to answer that question.

Neuter Rhetoric

In Socrates' speech on neuter rhetoric, "Plato is asking whether we ought to prefer a neuter form of speech to the kind which is ever getting us aroused over things and provoking an expense of spirit," says Weaver.[32] Here we have a semantically purified speech which may be compared to scientific notation where meaning is transferred from mind to mind without passion.

The advocate of this type of rhetoric praises objectivity, simple realism, and unprejudiced relationships. Of course such a logical positivist faces a dilemma. In order to gain acceptance of his "neutral" speech he must use urgent persuasion. Weaver admits that the idea of neutrality is "ridiculous" and concludes that "expression purged of all tendency rests upon an initial misconception of the nature of language."[33] Plato also admits that the practitioner of neuter rhetoric may follow a policy of enlightened self interest. Lysias, for example, while praising the nonlover (neuter rhetoric), "had concealed designs upon Phaedrus, so his fine speech was really a sheep's clothing."[34] Today, we too may suspect that behind a facade of neutrality may lurk urgent persuasion and a cleverly concealed self-love.

Obviously, pro-abortion and anti-abortion rhetoric cannot be neutral. Even the most scientific discourse purged of semantic tendencies carries implicit value judgments as shown by subject, method, and source of publication. Placing abortion rhetoric on a continuum from the most violent name-calling to the most neutral denotations, some of those who speak of biology would fit the latter category. Dr. Bart T. Heffernan's "The Early Biography of Everyman," and Dr. Albert W. Liley's "The Foetus in Control of His Environment," serve as examples.[35]

Ideological and moral arguments often wear the mask of neutrality. The watchword of abortion advocates is "freedom of choice." This assumes neutrality and invites the opposition to assume a neutral stance. John T. Noonan, Jr., observes that "the dedicated defenders of choice were dedicated to making everyone else agree with the choice of abortion."[36] Pointing to a federal court decision in New York, the facade of neutrality crumbles: "Judge Dooling adopted the argument of Planned Parenthood that, as the morality of abortion was disputed by 'God-fearing people,' the government would be required to be neutral. And 'neutrality' meant the government should be on Planned-Parenthood's side and pay for abortions."[37] George F. Will puts the "choice" and "neutrality" relationships in perspective:

The idea that "freedom of choice" is necessarily neutral as regards social outcomes is the characteristic pretense of liberal societies. But liberal societies do not provide "freedom of choice" without having certain expectations about which choices will be made. And they try to shape choices by shaping attitudes. All societies do this. Only liberal societies pretend to be neutral.[38]

Evil or Base Rhetoric

Socrates' second speech introduces the evil or base rhetorician, whose purpose is exploitation; he fears dialectic and uses whatever means are necessary to conceal or overcome truth. Noting that the base rhetorician today has vastly augmented power of propagation through the media, Weaver points to politics and journalism as areas where they function. "What he does," says Weaver, "is dress up one alternative in all the cheap finery of immediate hopes and fears. . . . By discussing only one side of an issue . . . he often successfully blocks definition and cause-and-effect reasoning."[39]

"Rhetorical substitution" and "rhetorical prevarication" are semantic changes finding their source in false reasoning or objectionable motives.[40] To illustrate "rhetorical substitution," Weaver examines the word "liberalism." "In the nineteenth century," he says, "this word referred to an ideal of maximum individual liberty and minimum state interference. . . . Today, it is being used to refer to something like the ideal of the welfare state which involves many restrictions upon liberty."[41] Although the ideas are discrete, proponents of the new idea of liberalism would argue that the old meaning is no longer possible because circumstances have changed. They really prefer the new circumstances and make the substitution.

Rhetorical prevarication is committed in an attempt to "impose a change in the interest of ideology."[42] For example, the word "sick," we have thought, applies to a victim of disease who deserves assistance and sympathy. Now, says Weaver, "We mark a growing tendency among certain groups of people to refer to alcoholics, moral delinquents, and even criminals as 'sick people'."[43] Through rhetorical prevarication, moral responsibility is removed from crime, and the criminal has become the victim of society who should have kept him from getting "sick."

In summary, the base or evil rhetoricians victimize and possess. Interested in personal aggrandizement, or getting desired results at any cost, they are self-lovers of the worst sort.

Indeed, pro-abortion or anti-abortion advocates would not want to be identified with base or evil rhetoric, although some embrace the methods as necessary to accomplish their purposes. The Weaverian method may be rejected by some defenders from either camp, but the method cannot be bent or redefined.

The methods used by the base rhetorician must be viewed from an ideological position. Rejecting situation ethics and defending the covenant of language from rapid change, Weaver was a conservative. He wished to conserve the Constitution and metaphysical first principles.

Both pro- and anti-abortion rhetoric is base or evil when emotive language is used without responsible relationships to modes of argument. When the National Abortion Rights Action League advertises that "Your American right of choice is under attack—protect your right to choose," the most powerful "god terms" of our time are employed.[44] "Rights," a most charismatic term, is closely related to "freedom of choice." The terms torn from their etymological anchorages urge one to react rather than to think.

Finally, I offer examples of base or evil abortion rhetoric including rhetorical prevarications and substitutions. Because the Supreme Court declared abortion to be a private act, the other rights claimed flow from that decision. An analysis of abortion, however, will reveal that it is not a private act. As John T. Noonan, Jr., has pointed out, abortion bears on marriage, family, children, community, medical profession, and government.[45] In "Coercion in Liberation's Guise," by Victor G. Rosenblum we find:

> There is no setting of privacy for decision-making when fear of being labelled unpatriotic or subversive of ecological factors leads a woman to remit the life within her. There is no setting of privacy when fear of a husband's job layoff impels a pregnant wife to seek abortion. There is no setting of privacy when fear of being removed from the rolls of Aid to Dependent Children . . . compels a pregnant woman to destroy that child.[46]

Next, consider the argument that a woman has the right to control her own body. This, too, seems to be a very American argument based on the ideals of self determination and respect. Dennis J. Horan, with others, admits that "the claim of freedom over one's body is, of course, a self-evident right if it means that a woman should be free to refuse sexual intercourse or free to practice contraception."[47] Robert A. Hipkiss identified the real intent of the argument, saying, "The assumption here is that the fetus is really part of the woman's body, not a separate body in itself."[48] Therefore, the "right to control our own bodies" argument must be seen for what it is—a rhetorical prevarication, because medical authorities agree that the life of another body begins at conception.[49]

From the "own body" argument there flows a change in language designed to "hide the baby." In "Abortion and the Cognitive Foundation of Dehumanization," David Mall observes: "Efforts by the abortionist to make the unborn baby disappear . . . can be seen in the language often used in the abortion debate to describe this unborn entity. . . ."[50] John T. Noonan indicates the extent of change:

> To make the abortion liberty stick, the language would be revised. The unborn "children" of the law of torts and of wills and of trusts had become the "fetuses" of the law of abortion. The child of the Social Security Act no longer meant "unborn child." The dead unborn child had become "fetal wastage." A living baby not expected to live had become a "fetus *ex utero*."[51]

Although the rhetoric of abortion hides the baby, common usage does not. Noonan again speaks to the issue.

> Baby is the most usual way to refer in ordinary speech to the being a particular woman is carrying. "How is your child?" is slightly jocular. "How is your embryo" will not be asked. "How is your fetus?" is absurd. "How are your products of conception?" is beyond absurdity, as is a similar question about "your ovum." "How is your baby?" is the way a relative, a close friend, or even a doctor will inquire about the mother's perceptions of the being within. "How is my baby?" is what a mother will ask when the physician listens to the new heartbeat within her.[52]

Noble Rhetoric

The third speech by Socrates presents the noble rhetorician who answers Plato's basic question by combining truth with an artful presentation. "What Plato has prepared us to see is that the virtuous rhetorician, who has a love of truth, has a soul of such movement that its dialectical perceptions are consonant with those of divine mind."[53] The noble rhetorician is first interested in dialectic, a discovery of truth, and from that base he speaks of actuality and potentiality. Adding language that stirs the soul, without wanton sensationalism, noble "rhetoric at its truest seeks to perfect men by showing them better versions of themselves. . . ."[54] The noble rhetorician lacks selfishness and to that extent differs from the evil rhetorician in moral purpose. Weaver said: "Responsible rhetoric, as I conceive it, is a rhetoric responsible primarily to the truth. It measures the degree of validity in a statement, and it is aware of the sources of controlling that it employs. As such, it is distinct from propaganda, which is the distortion of the truth for selfish purposes."[55]

Reminding us of the metaphysical starting point for noble rhetoric, Weaver adds: "As rhetoric confronts us with choices involving values, the rhetorician is a preacher to us, noble if he tries to direct our passion toward noble ends and base if he uses our passion to confuse and degrade us."[56] Undoubtedly, Weaver agrees with Charles Sears Baldwin that what makes a man a sophist is not his method but his moral purpose.[57]

How can abortion rhetoric be identified with noble rhetoric? By Weaverian criteria, the garland of approval goes to the anti-abortion advocates. Why? Weaver's concern, overshadowing any considerations of responsible uses of language and of argument, is with metaphysical starting points. One of the first principles in which he believed was a reason for being. Pro-abortion rhetoric assumes a different metaphysical stance, a multi-valued definition of life.

The victory, due to effective use of rhetorical methods, continues to belong to pro-abortion forces. Why is that happening? A more noble rhetoric is not given an equal chance. Judges upon whom the pro-abortion persuasion is plied lack the courage or wisdom to be definers and defenders of first principles found in the Constitution and in the metaphysical traditions of our society.

Being bombarded with relativism and situation ethics, the American public is also gradually losing awareness. "A million abortions a year," says George F. Will, "proves that the movement has achieved its primary goal, which is to transform attitudes."[58]

Dynamic language and argument shall not cease until complete agreement or acquiescence is won. Perhaps Marshall McLuhan is prophetic in saying that "when the mechanization of death occurs on a vast scale, the minds of civilized people are numbed."[59] Agreeing with that perspective, Charles Carroll speaks of "the wanton destruction of life and the anesthetization of a nation's conscience. . . ."[60] Of course we cannot forget the title of Weaver's famous work —*Ideas Have Consequences*.[61]

Summary and Conclusion

In this paper, a Weaverian rhetorical method is developed and applied to the rhetoric of abortion. The method provides criteria in three categories. First, emotive language is identified. Weaver calls terms and phrases carrying emotive force "ultimate terms" and further classifies them as "god terms" and "devil terms." Second, modes of argument are identified. Here a hierarchy is established as follows: definition, similitude, cause and effect, and testimony. Third, based on Weaver's interpretation of Plato's *Phaedrus*, three types of rhetoric are identified: neuter, base or evil, and noble, revealing an ideological stance.

The Weaverian method of analysis is unique in providing a distinct treatment of language, argument, and metaphysical starting points of discourse. This method should be of value to serious students of rhetoric who may wish to test it further with applications to other social and civil rights problems. Those who wish to improve their own critical evaluation of what is spoken and written will find the method useful.

Notes

1. Richard M. Weaver, "Language Is Sermonic," Richard L. Johannesen *et al.* (eds.), *Language Is Sermonic: Richard M. Weaver on the Nature of Rhetoric*, (Baton Rouge: Louisiana State University Press, 1970), p. 80. Richard M. Weaver was, until his death in 1963, Professor of English at the University of Chicago.

2. See Robert E. Ratermann (ed.), *Oral Arguments in the Supreme Court Decisions* (St. Louis: Gateway Press, 1976).

3. "Language Is Sermonic," p. 221.

4. "Ultimate Terms in Contemporary Rhetoric," in *Language Is Sermonic*, pp. 87-112.

5. *Ibid.*

6. The terms cited are based on an extensive review of the literature.

7. Richard M. Weaver, "A Responsible Rhetoric," *The Intercollegiate Review*, (Winter 1976-77), pp. 81-87; also see, "Language Is Sermonic," pp. 201-25.

8. "Language Is Sermonic," p. 212.

9. *Ibid.*, p. 213.

10. John T. Noonan, Jr., *A Private Choice: Abortion in America in the Seventies* (New York: The Free Press, 1979), pp. 146-47.

11. Alan F. Guttmacher, "Symposium: Law, Morality, and Abortion," *Rutgers Law Review*, 22 (1960), pp. 415-16. For a discussion of the Guttmacher change of definition, see Noonan, pp. 35-37.

12. Noonan, pp. 120-25.

13. "A Responsible Rhetoric," p. 86.

14. *Ibid.*

15. David Mall, "Stalemate of Rhetoric and Philosophy," Thomas W. Hilgers and Dennis J. Horan (eds.), *Abortion and Social Justice* (New York: Sheed and Ward, 1972), p. 209.

16. André E. Hellegers, "Fetus, Not Just Mother, Part of Abortion Debate," *Ob. Gyn. News* (November 1, 1974), p. 2.

17.   Noonan, p. 88.

18.   Garrett Hardin, "Semantic Aspects of Abortion," *Etc.: A Review of General Semantics*, (September 1967), p. 279.

19.   *Ibid.*, p. 281.

20.   "Language Is Sermonic," p. 214.

21.   *Ibid.*, pp. 214-15.

22.   See Noonan's discussion, pp. 64-68.

23.   Dennis J. Horan *et al.*, "The Legal Case for the Unborn Child," in *Abortion and Social Justice*, p. 106.

24.   Philip G. Ney, "Infant Abortion and Child Abuse: Cause and Effect," David Mall and Walter F. Watts, eds., *The Psychological Aspects of Abortion*, (Washington, DC: University Publications of America, 1979) p. 25.

25.   "Language Is Sermonic," p. 215.

26.   "A Responsible Rhetoric," p. 87.

27.   *Ibid.*

28.   *Ibid.*

29.   "The Phaedrus and the Nature of Rhetoric," in *Language Is Sermonic*, pp. 57-83.

30.   *Ibid.*, p. 83.

31.   *Ibid.*, p. 30.

32.   *Ibid.*, p. 60

33.   "Language Is Sermonic," p. 221. Also see, "Concealed Rhetoric in Scientistic Sociology," in *Language Is Sermonic*, pp. 139-58.

34.   "The Phaedrus and the Nature of Rhetoric," p. 79.

35.   See both essays in *Abortion and Social Justice*.

36.   Noonan, p. 64.

37.   *Ibid.*, p. 109.

38.   *Chicago Sun-Times*, August 21, 1979, p. 36.

39.   "The Phaedrus and the Nature of Rhetoric," p. 67.

40.   "Relativism and the Use of Language," in *Language Is Sermonic*, p. 131.

41.   *Ibid.*, p. 132.

42.   *Ibid.*, p. 133.

43.   *Ibid.*, p. 134.

44.   *Daily Eastern News*, Charleston, IL, September 5, 1979, p. 15.

45.   Noonan, pp. 1-2.

46.   *Abortion and Social Justice*, p. 155.

47.   Horan, *et al.*, p. 108.

48.   Robert A. Hipkiss, "Abortion Language and Logic," *Etc.: A Review of General Semantics*, (June 1976), p. 209.

49.   Horan *et al.*, p. 112.

50.   Mall, *The Psychological Aspects of Abortion*, p. 146.

51.   Noonan, p. 151.

52.   *Ibid.*, p. 155.

53.   "The Phaedrus and the Nature of Rhetoric," p. 73.

54.   *Ibid.*, p. 82.

55.   "A Responsible Rhetoric," p. 82.

56.   "Language Is Sermonic," p. 225.

57.   Charles Sears Baldwin, *Medieval Rhetoric and Poetic* (Gloucester, MA: Peter Smith, 1959), pp. 2-7.

58.   Will, *Chicago Sun-Times*, August 21, 1979, p. 36.

59.   "Private Individual vs. Global Village," in *Abortion and Social Justice*, p. 247.

60.   "Abortion without Ethics," *ibid.*, p. 255.

61.   Chicago: University of Chicago Press, 1948.

PART FIVE

Strategies for Persuasion

FRANZ   An educational message must be evaluated and interpreted by each person who receives it. The effectiveness of the message will be determined by the level of cognitive functioning of the person. Piaget's theory of cognitive development provides guidelines for the assessment of the cognitive abilities of individuals. This essay applies the theory to the way in which people receive and interpret information on abortion. Recommendations are then made for presenting pro-life arguments so they are most apt to be received and understood by people at different developmental levels.

MIGLIORINO MILLER   This article is an examination of abortion from a civil rights perspective in terms of prejudice. The writer argues that prevailing attitudes toward the unborn, i.e., that they are less than human, non-human, non-persons, etc., are the fruit of a centuries old and deep seated ignorance and fear regarding who the reborn are in relation to us. Respect for human rights will never be complete unless society's misconceptions about and prejudice toward the most vulnerable members of the human family are abolished.

WILLKE   The battle over abortion is being fought to a large extent over semantics. Pro-abortion forces and the heavily biased public media know this well and have been using it to promote the pro-abortion cause. Because of this, it is important that the pro-life side uses its language wisely and effectively. The writer explores in depth the semantics used by both sides. To a considerable degree, the side that finally prevails will have done so through the proper use of semantics.

JOYCE   "Be crafty as serpents and innocent as doves," the Gospel says. As doves, pro-lifers have the truth, but lack the rhetorical weapon and skill to defend the truth effectively. They need to sharpen their verbal art with shrewdness and focus on the spot where the opposition is vulnerable. Uniting the serpent with the dove, they can develop the kind of language power that actually silences the opposition. Silence gives the truth a chance to change hearts.

Abortion through the Eyes of the Beholder:
A Cognitive Analysis

Wanda Franz

T he major goal of the pro-life advocate is to educate the public-at-large about abortion and its evils. We know that if people really understand the horror of what abortion is that they will join us in opposing it. Whether we speak publicly to large audiences or chat quietly with our neighbor over coffee, we are educating others.

We have all had the experience of saying words that were completely meaningful to us, but finding that our audience just didn't seem to understand what we were saying. There are many reasons for these misunderstandings. A portion of this problem might be ascribed to the fact that some people simply want to have "abortion-on-demand," and they are working as hard as they can to justify their own position. In these cases, almost nothing that is said will really make a difference at the moment, although it might in the future. Other blocks to communication include fear of the truth and psychological repression due to guilt, inadequate education in the fields of basic biology and psychology, personal experiences of family and friends who have had abortions or who can't have children, etc.

Cognitive Reasoning

This essay will deal with only one kind of communication problem, the one based on cognitive reasoning ability. That is, people may not be affected by the arguments we are using because they do not think about the problem in the way it is being formulated to them. Their method of reasoning about problems is different from ours, so they fail to follow us to our conclusion that abortion is wrong.

In these instances, it is possible to find a better way to present our position, a different argument that will drive home the point to that particular audience. I had such an experience when giving a talk to a group of university students in a health class on human sexuality. I knew from previous experience that they were not impressed by arguments that dealt with complex principles, involving the inviolable rights of the infant. On this occasion, I chose to talk only about health issues and to emphasize the damage that abortion does to the woman, physically and emotionally.

On this occasion, those arguments really "grabbed" the audience. It got them "where they were" and touched on realities that they simply couldn't ignore. Of course, there were still many skeptics when I had finished, but they saw the entire problem in a new light and a few of them were moved to positions of opposition to abortion. I had found the arguments that were most likely to move them to think differently about the problem.

It is obviously to our advantage if we can do this with an audience. We want to provide the arguments that are most apt to attract their attention. The first step in doing this is to understand how people think, to recognize the various levels of understanding that people move through, and to learn the ways to use this knowledge to create the right arguments that will be most effective for each person. I will focus my discussion on the evaluation of thinking processes proposed by Jean Piaget (See Ginsburg & Opper, 1969).

Piaget has been asking entirely different kinds of questions than those of traditional psychologists. Rather than asking "What can one know," he has asked, "How does one come to understand?" From this question have come some suggestions on how one helps to provide understanding to others.

Piaget believes that the kind of knowledge we acquire is directly related to the way in which we acquire it, that is, the strategies, procedures or methods we use to get information from our environment. Piaget observed that these strategies change with age. He identified four major stages people use to extract information from their environment. From birth to two years, the child uses sensory and motor skills; during the preschool years, the child develops representational competencies and language, but is still not able to use logical processes; during the elementary school years, the child acquires logical abilities, but can only apply them to concrete situations. It is not until the high school years that the child begins to be capable of using logical systems in truly abstract situations. However, we have evidence that this last stage is not fully developed until well after high school, and may never reach full development.

The four stages have been referred to as the sensorimotor stage, pre-operational stage, concrete operational stage, and formal operational stage (See Table 1).

Table 1

I - Sensorimotor Stage	0- 2 years
II - Pre-operational Stage	2- 6 years
III - Concrete Operational Stage	6-12 years
IV - Formal Operational Stage	12 years and up

The stage of formal operations is dependent on cultural and educational factors, and unlike the other three, is not manifested universally in all cultures. It is associated with technologically advanced societies and higher educational levels.

Justification

What application does this approach have for the right-to-life movement? It provides a framework in which to ask the right kinds of questions. The question, "What does one need to know in order to be pro-life," cannot be asked first. Rather, one must ask, "What can this particular person or group understand about the issues?" Because people will acquire different knowledge at different developmental levels, it is necessary to apply the question to each group separately so that a functional approach can be taken. Although these stages supposedly are age-related, in reality, many adults are functioning at levels lower than the formal level.

General Developmental Principles

The object of Piaget's interest is knowledge. There are any number of different ways that knowledge can be defined, for example, as accumulated pieces of information, or as the complete result of everything we have learned. Piaget defines knowledge in a different way. He emphasizes the internal characteristics. Knowledge is something we have inside of us. Piaget views knowledge not as a fact or a thing, but as a function. It is a process or a strategy, a method of understanding. Thus, he defines knowledge as the internal function of creating understanding of a particular concept. Piaget distinguishes between understanding and memorization. A fact, such as 2+2=4, can be memorized. However, to really understand this simple equation, the child must be able to apply a number of mathematical processes, including associativity, sequentiality, equality, etc. It is possible for the child to give the correct answer through memorization; however, if he does not know how to get the correct answer by applying the correct principles, he has no knowledge and will not be able to go on to more advanced application of these principles. Thus, Piaget distinguishes between learning, based on memorization, and knowledge, based on the application of correct principles to a given environmental problem.

It is common in the pro-life movement to emphasize the principles underlying our belief in the sanctity of each human being and the rights of all under the Constitution. However, these are meaningless phrases to someone not functioning at the highest levels of intellectual knowledge. He or she has heard them all before and can use them in casual conversation (that is, they have been memorized); but they have essentially no real value to the person, if he or she does not fully understand them and how to apply them to life's problems (that is, knowledge).

It is very likely that most of our audiences are incapable of such principled thinking. When we make our pleas, they fall on deaf ears and are lumped by our opposition into a general collection of "religious ideas" that they can then ignore. It is at this time, we must be prepared to fall back on arguments that our audiences can understand.

In order for knowledge to be acquired, it is necessary for the person to be actively involved in his own learning. There must be behavior of some sort, whether it is grasping with the hand or the mind. The process of coming to know something can be carved out by the hand or the mind; each one can be an action of knowing. It is these actions which change with age and constitute the differences that Piaget describes in each of his four stages. He emphasizes that although internal representational abilities begin during the preoperational period, logical and analytical abilities are not available until formal operations are developed in early adulthood.

Piaget has argued that we can only come to know through the process of mental adaptation. As living organisms we must be adapted to our environment. We must be able to use our internal, structural knowledge to solve the problems presented to us by our environment. If we observe that we can handle the challenges adequately, then we feel comfortable, or, in Piagetian terms, equilibrated. If we act on the environment and fail to solve the problem adequately, then we feel uncomfortable and confused, or disequilibrated. In this latter state of poor adaptive functioning, we are most susceptible to changing our structures so as to learn. This change in structures is called accommodation (See Table 2). That is, the person accommodates himself to the demands of the environment. The opposite of this is the process of assimilation, in which the environment is taken in, acted upon, and no change occurs in the organism.

Table 2

Environment touches person:
1. Assimilation = Person distorts the environment.
2. Accommodation = Person changes to match the environment.

Assimilation is the application of structures to given problems in the environment. For example, a baby rolls a ball under the table. He can find the ball if he can apply his structures for spatial organization and trajectory of moving objects to the problem. That is, he assimilates the situation to his structures. Or, the college student answers the test question correctly because she assimilates a new math problem to already existing structures for calculus. Assimilation is a process by which a newly acquired structure is generalized to all the possible variants of the situation. The child playing with moving toys, including balls, trucks, cars, etc., in a wide variety of environments, assimilates each one to his existing structures in order to find the objects (See Table 2).

However, the structures we use are necessarily limited. None of us has perfectly formed mature structures. Therefore, when we take in the environment, we must distort or limit it in order to make it fit our structures. Thus, all assimilation involves some change in the environment. The environment is always distorted to some extent; but the younger the child, the greater the distortions.

Using Piaget's model, the person is perceived as a dynamic system of active, changing perceptions. In order to help people to know something, we must first evaluate the structural level, introduce disequilibrating experiences and then give the person an opportunity to actively seek the solution.

The Meaning of Life

Since we in the pro-life movement are dealing with human life, it is important to realize that one's perception of what life is, is controlled by structural development. There isn't just one clear-cut answer. People will have a different answer depending on their level. In fact, biological life is a fairly complex notion, and most young children do not understand it.

To begin, ask yourself the question, "How do you know that something is alive?" If you have children, you have probably had to deal with that at a time when the children were not really able to fully understand your answers. I overheard a conversation between my daughter, aged four, and my son, aged six. They were discussing the nature of the plastic flower attached to a bottle of room deodorant at the supermarket. My daughter was unsure as to whether or not it was alive, but my son was certain that it was not. In an effort to explain to his structurally limited sibling the meaning of life, he said, "It's not alive, because it can't die." There is certainly a lesson in this explanation that we have been trying repeatedly to teach to pro-abortionists. That is, of course, "If you have to kill it, it must be alive," when referring to the fetus.

However, inherent in this basic assumption are some very important pieces of knowledge about life. Let us examine what these are. Some of this knowledge has been arrived at by asking subjects to categorize a list of items according to whether they are living or not. By studying the characteristics of each group, it is possible to identify the concept common to each member and to infer the characteristic used by the subject to separate the objects (see Maurer, 1970).

Very young children tend to assume that life is present when the object resembles something living or whenever the item moves. Thus, all animals and people fall into this category. However, such living elements as seeds, eggs, and dandelions, which don't move, are categorized as nonliving. In addition, the nonliving things, which are moved, such as airplanes, are also viewed as being alive by the very young child. In studying this, Maurer (1970) found that the majority of five- and six-year-old children stated that the following were alive: the sun, human statues, cartoons, dolls, airplanes, and a halloween skeleton.

By age seven, most children recognized when an object was only an image of a living thing. They did not ascribe life qualities to these nonliving items. However, young children clearly do not understand the vitality of the biological organism. They do not conceptualize living organisms as dynamic organizations of growth processes that reorganize themselves into more advanced units in an orderly process. They tend to equate food with general intake that makes the "machine" move much like gasoline powering a car. Consequently, the organism takes on the static character of a machine, whose output is more important than the process of growth.

Pro-abortionists often talk this way about organisms, as though they were made to produce products that have a human quality, such as speech and art. However, they do not value the growth process itself as contributing to the way the organism behaves. As one said to me in a debate: "There is no organized growth process. It is just a mass of tissue that gets bigger." This attitude makes a discussion of the origins of life very difficult.

Unfortunately, this problem is not limited to young children. In the Maurer study, most disconcerting was the finding that adolescents and even adults retain such primitive concepts. Only 1/5 of adolescents had completely correct scores. But fewer than 1/2 of the teachers and nurses were able to distinguish correctly all items. It would appear that any introduction to the idea of pro-life issues would have to begin with a review of the biological organism and the functioning and growth which characterizes it.

Without this basic knowledge, a discussion of pro-life concerns about protecting the developing organism is essentially wasted. That is why the pictures of the growing organism *in utero* are so important to the pro-life cause. However, it is not simply to show the form, but to emphasize that biological growth is the process of the unfolding of a particular organism whose form has been established from the beginning. That is, the mature form is inherent in the seed. Everything is present in the conceptus that will make growth and development possible. The growth then proceeds in an orderly and systematic way.

Beginning at age 7, at the origin of the concrete operational period, the child can begin to apply these notions to the concrete reality of the living person. However, it is quite possible that the child has difficulty making the application to the hidden fetus, which does not have any real concrete reality for the child.

It is not until formal operations that the young person can begin to make the application to a completely unknown entity, such as the fetus. However, as we have stated, many adults are not functioning at such an abstract level; and most adults probably need help making a concrete reality out of the fetus (See Franz, 1981). That is another reason why the pictures help us to bring reality to the unborn human baby. Once they have seen the pictures, it is hard to ignore the reality of the baby. Indeed, this is the point that Bernard Nathanson has made in emphasizing such new technology as ultrasound, which allows us to visualize and identify the humanity of the unborn.

Uniqueness of Human Life

One day my daughter and I were standing at the window looking at the snowy landscape, and my daughter suddenly said,"Isn't it fantastic that everyone of those snowflakes is different?" I felt she was placing value on the individuality of all living things. And I was struck by the important pro-life message she was communicating. Unless we really care about the value of each individual person, we can never truly argue for their individual rights. In order to make that important judgement, we need to understand and value the fact of the totally unique character of every single fetus.

Mr. Rogers on PBS-TV says, "You are special, and you are special to me." Our abortion laws make this statement a hollow mouthing of words. How can we truly value the uniqueness of every living child if we deny that uniqueness during the youngest period of their lives?

Moral Development

Kohlberg (1964), in elaborating on Piaget's original theory, has identified a number of stages of moral reasoning. For simplicity, we shall discuss three that correspond to the Piagetian stages already discussed. These are: (1) egocentric, (2) socialized, and (3) principled (See Table 3).

Table 3

COGNITIVE STAGES	MORAL STAGES
II - Pre-operational	Egocentric
III - Concrete Operational	Socialized
IV - Formal Operational	Principled

The egocentric stage is one of self-involvement with an overriding concern for personal needs. This stage is common among preschoolers. The socialized stage is one of concern for social rules and responsibilities. It is the most commonly found way of dealing with moral issues in the general population. The principled stage is represented by an altruistic appreciation of the needs and rights of others, even when these are not part of one's own personal experience. This stage only begins in the late teen years or young adult period, if at all. Many people never acquire this last stage of moral reasoning; and there are many egocentric adults in our society.

Moral stages, unlike other cognitive stages, can be found at every age level. Infantile egocentrism can occur at every stage of the human life span. In young children this represents a normal, natural condition. In an adult, the same condition becomes aberrant and dysfunctional. The egocentric adult is immature and responds to problems in an inappropriate way.

Let us examine the way in which people at each stage of moral development will respond to the message we give.

The Egocentrism Argument

The egocentric child tends to see in the innocent, defenseless baby a person much like himself. He tends to feel concern for the fetus, because he does not want to be abused in painful ways and so he puts himself in the place of the fetus. He feels sorry for the poor, damaged child.

But what of the egocentric adult? She is no longer small and defenseless. She finds it difficult to put herself into the place of the fetus. She is interested in protecting herself as an adult. Any empathy such a person possesses is likely to be directed toward the adult who has a problem, particularly the pregnant woman. Seeing pictures of developing fetuses will not have much impact on such a woman because she is overwhelmed with her own images of the dead woman—the victim of a "back-alley butcher." In addition, the egocentric adult can find it easy to ignore both the baby and the mother in the face of the sexual self-gratification that is possible when abortion offers the "easy way out" of an unplanned pregnancy. This is the position most apt to be held by the egocentric male.

How can we reach such a person? For the person functioning at the egocentric, self-involved stage, we must appeal to their own sense of self-preservation. We need to convince women that abortions are not entirely safe or free of any damaging side effects. For these people, the data on side effects and medical and emotional problems need to be emphasized. From their perspective, abortion is supposed to free women from the pain of suffering from the social and emotional damage of carrying the child to term and giving it up for adoption, as happened traditionally. In that system the man got off scot-free, usually without even being censured.

We are rightfully angered at this double standard. And yet, nothing has really changed. Women are still the ones who pay with the physical and emotional risks inherent in the abortion. The man involved still gets off easily; and he is even applauded for helping to provide his partner with the choice of avoiding pregnancy and delivery. This is a message that we need to sell much more effectively than we have, that is, that we are not providing the woman with a better solution. She is still the one who pays the price. The price is simply different, consisting of guilt, emotional disruption, risk of infection, etc., and the long-term risk that she may be sterile or have complications of miscarriage when she wants to become pregnant at a later time.

The Socialization Argument

Those functioning at the second level are concerned primarily with social responsibility. If they define the fetus as a member of society, then their sense of social responsibility will extend to the unborn child. However, the Supreme Court has formally declared that the unborn are not recognized as persons under the law.

Many people have simply ignored the Supreme Court. But for most people, the Supreme Court action undermines the sense of responsibility they have for the unborn child. How would a person at this stage react? They would tend to see the needs and problems of the adult woman as much more important than the needs of the immature fetus. Even the fetal pictures cannot help with this type of person, because they argue in their own minds that the adults are more worthy of support and abortion is necessary for them.

People who are concerned about social factors are apt to think in terms of something that is "cost" effective. Abortions clearly are cheaper and easier than helping a pregnant teenager come to grips with her problems and finding a solution for both mother and child. These people are apt to be impressed with the long-term benefit of simply getting rid of the problem. Even a child who has been placed for adoption can come back to find the missing parent. It leaves open the possibility of problems developing later. It is "messy."

This type of person does not hear our message because he is willing to put social concerns above the needs of individuals. The plight of the individual baby is not important to this type of person, because the baby's needs are small compared to the problems of society. This distorted moral orientation creates great difficulties for the pro-life advocate, who can empathize so easily with the baby. What approach would work for this individual?

I believe that we can make a case for the social destruction caused by the abortion mentality. For example, each of the supposed social benefits of abortion is offset by long-term problems. The current population problem will be replaced by long-term population imbalances. The problem of unwanted pregnancies will be replaced with the problem of infertility. Women prepared to abort their unborn children today will be more inclined to abuse their born children at a later time. Doctors who have participated in the abortion mentality today will be more inclined to recommend infanticide and euthanasia tomorrow. Children who see abortion as a convenient method of birth control will be more inclined to experiment with sex before they are emotionally and socially ready to accept the consequences for their behavior. The social devastation of increases in VD and emotional problems in children have already shown themselves through increases in alcoholism and suicide among the young.

Thus, the supposed social benefits of uncontrolled abortion simply do not exist. This type of argument is very persuasive for the person who takes pride in being socially responsible. When one really examines the facts, it is difficult to make the case for abortion as an act of social responsibility and maturity. Our opponents need to be informed of these facts.

The Principled Argument

I believe that it is in the nature of the pro-life movement that we are asking people to function at the highest level. We are asking for a completely altruistic response based on principles of the Golden Rule and human rights. Saving unborn babies does not provide much personal benefit to those who work in the area. The infant is unseen and not experienced by the pregnant woman at the time that most abortions take place. Furthermore, because we have already safely escaped the womb, we will not benefit directly from any efforts to save unborn children. Unfortunately, Level 3 people make up a smaller percentage than the other two levels. Even they can be distracted from this issue by the pressures of other needs in our society. These people need the facts to shock them into an awareness of the enormity of the abortion problem. They are, ultimately, the easiest to convince.

For principled persons, there are different ways of formally structuring the abortion argument. Perceptions of the way it causes an impact on our lives are molded by assumptions which guide our thinking. I believe that there are at least two such model assumptions.

The first is an "adversarial" model in which pregnancy is represented by an "adversarial relationship" between the pregnant mother and her child. The presence of the unborn child creates a crisis of rights in which the mother's rights come into opposition with those of the child. This is the position most used by the pro-abortion advocate to argue for the rights of the mother over those of her child. Those people using this model generally agree that it is more appropriate for the small unborn child to be the victim when comparing his rights to those of the adult woman.

The pro-life position, on the other hand, is based on the "naturalistic" model. This position recognizes the fundamental naturalness of the pregnant condition which is inherently beneficial to both the mother and child. Using this assumption the pro-lifer takes the position that the solution for the unplanned pregnancy most apt to benefit the mother is one that also benefits the child (See Mall, 1983, for a discussion of moral development and natural law).

Thus, at the formal operational level, there can be more than one way of structuring our responses to the environment. The nature of these structures will determine to a large extent whether one argues a pro-life or a pro-abortion position. In debates, pro-lifers must focus on these model differences to highlight our position of a compassionate view of both mother and child. Ultimately, the pro-life position is the one which most clearly benefits both the mother and the child, unlike the position taken by the pro-abortionists.

Summary

In summary, it is important to realize that people pass through stages in their ability to receive and understand information. We must be attentive to the differences in people, based on the questions they ask and the kinds of statements they make. Once we realize "where they are coming from," then we can more effectively answer the real concerns they have, which may not be directly voiced. We must be prepared to educate about the most basic aspects of human life, including the unique nature of the conceptus, the presence of our unique person during our entire lives from conception to natural death, and the unfolding of our development from the plan established at conception. We must continue to use the fetal pictures and to emphasize the humanity of the fetus. We must also recognize the importance of the arguments that abortion does great damage to the mother, as well as to society at large. Policies which protect the well-being of the child inevitably are also the ones which are most beneficial to the mother.

We must also recognize the limitations in the value judgments that many people make. We must be prepared to argue with them in a way that meets their needs. This may mean that we emphasize issues of basic self-interest, which may not be a high value to us. However, if a woman is moved by the fact that abortions could make her infertile, then we must use this type of argument to begin the process of building up knowledge about this issue. We must use every method we can find, because the lives of too many children depend on our effectiveness.

References

Franz, Wanda. "Fetal Development: A Novel Application of Piaget's Theory of Cognitive Development." *New Perspectives on Human Abortion.* Edited by Thomas W. Hilgers, M.D., Dennis J. Horan, and David Mall. Frederick, MD: University Publications of America, 1981.

Ginsburg, H. and Opper, S. *Piaget's Theory of Intellectual Development.* Englewood Cliffs, NJ: Prentice-Hall, 1969.

Kohlberg, Lawrence. "Development of Moral Character and Moral Ideology." *Review of Child Development Research.* Edited by D.A. Goslin. New York: Russell Sage Foundation, 1964.

Mall, David. *In Good Conscience: Abortion and Moral Necessity.* Libertyville, IL: Kairos Books, Inc., 1983.

Maurer, Adah. "Maturation of Concepts of Life." *Journal of Genetic Psychology,* 116 (1970), 101–11.

The Preborn and Prejudice

Monica Migliorino Miller

O n May 10, 1980, five pro-life activists stationed themselves outside an abortion clinic on Michigan Avenue in
Chicago in order to persuade women entering the clinic not to
abort their children and to offer them alternatives. The pro-lifers
had brought a poster with them which read in simple block letters: "Human Life Is Sacred." They propped the poster up against
the building which housed the clinic. On this day the sidewalk in
front of the clinic was more crowded than usual with people pass-
ing to and fro because a massive rally for the Equal Rights Amendment was taking place in Grant Park, located nearby. A young
woman, heading for the rally, passed by and having read the
poster commented aloud, "Why of course, human life is sacred."
One of the pro-life activists struck up a conversation with the
woman stating that unfortunately most women who support the
Equal Rights Amendment are also pro-abortion. The woman
immediately became very angry and defended what she believed
was her right to abortion—the same woman who not one minute
previously had said, "Why of course, human life is sacred."

One must therefore ask a crucial question: What is the basis
of the discrepancy between the woman's belief that human life is
sacred and her belief in the right to abortion? Undoubtedly, the
woman, like so many of those who share her view on abortion,

really does believe that human life is sacred. However, this belief seems not to apply to human life which is still in the womb.

It must be noted, additionally, that many who advocate legalized abortion are quite open-minded and liberal concerning rights for themselves, and for those in socially or politically disadvantaged positions. However, they vehemently withhold those same rights from those who are certainly living but not yet born. Many people who advocate abortion would not favor killing in any other type of situation, some not even in war, others not even in punishment for heinous crimes. Yet they promote the "right" to kill when it comes to the preborn child.

The reason for this discrimination between those who are born and those who are not lies, I believe, in the fact that supporters of legal abortion actually harbor a form of prejudice—that human attitude that forms the basis of so much persecution and suffering in the world. In order for us to understand more clearly how the preborn are victims of prejudice we will compare attitudes toward the fetus to several kinds of active discrimination.

One of the first writers to place abortion within the context of prejudice was the philosopher Germain Grisez when, in the epilogue of his book *Abortion: The Myths, the Realities, and the Arguments*, he compared the pro-abortion mentality to racial prejudice. Racial prejudice, of course, is defined as the active discrimination of one race against another based upon the differences between them. Another form of prejudice is sexism, with differences in sex forming the basis for discrimination. Obviously, the preborn are not a race or a particular sex. Rather, they are a class of individuals composed literally of all races and both sexes who are in a prenatal existence. Nevertheless, the principles of racism and sexism form the basis of prejudice against the preborn.

First, instead of a race such as whites discriminating against, say, blacks, abortion involves the discrimination of a class of individuals, the born, against another class of individuals, the preborn.

Second, just as discrimination leads to a denial of equal opportunity for blacks when they are denied the equal opportunity for a decent job, a decent education, etc., in a similar way, the preborn are denied equal opportunity to the right-to-life.

Third, prejudice usually involves an element of expediency for those maintaining the discrimination. For example, it is expedient for whites to discriminate against blacks because of the economic benefits whites will derive, i.e., there will be more jobs for whites, better housing, etc., and, generally speaking, a position of social dominance and superiority. Indeed, the enslavement of the black man was exceptionally expedient for the white slave owner in that slavery provided a cheap form of labor which contributed to the wealth of the white class. As it was and is expedient for whites to discriminate against blacks, there are several reasons why it is expedient for the born to discriminate against the preborn via abortion. Discrimination against the preborn allows men and women, but most particularly women, to avoid the responsibilities of child care—freeing them from the innumerable sacrifices connected with bearing and rearing a child.

Fourth, as Grisez points out,

> People who are racially prejudiced do not like to be shown facts and have a hard time following arguments that might dislodge their prejudice. This resistance is always surprising, especially when it is encountered (as often happens) in persons who are extremely perceptive and logical in other matters. When intelligent people perform a discriminatory act, they always seem to have a perfectly plausible excuse that conceals the attitude of prejudice. However, the shifting of excuses tends to reveal to an unprejudiced observer that there is an attitude of prejudice underlying a consistently discriminatory pattern of behavior.[1]

All of these insights, of course, hold true with regard to those prejudiced against the preborn.

Fifth, prejudice, whether it be racial or against the preborn, is almost never consistent in its logic. An example of inconsistency in racial prejudice is that while many blacks fought in the American War of Independence along with whites, they were nevertheless regarded as an inferior race in the Dred Scott decision and subject to slavery. Similarly, as Grisez indicates:

> Physicians publish articles about methods of treating the "unborn patient" in the very medical journals in which other physicians describe the latest techniques for removing "fetal material" from the uterus. One judge declares an unborn individual a child and orders his illegitimate father to provide support while another denies a legitimate father a court order to prevent an abortion.[2]

While prejudice against blacks and the preborn share many principles, Grisez notes that many of those who favor abortion are strongly opposed to other forms of prejudice. He states:

> The fact that those who approve abortion and who advocate its legalization show characteristic signs of prejudice has misled some into wondering if the prejudice might be racial in its basis. However, many of the strongest advocates of abortion are also opponents of racism. I therefore believe that the prejudice against the unborn is an independent factor. It is merely coincidental if one person is the subject of both prejudices. A new name is needed for prejudice against the unborn; I suggest it be called "prenatalism" since it is based on the fact *we* are already born while *they* are unborn (prenatal)[3] (emphasis in original).

The Roots of Prejudice

The roots of all prejudice, whether it be racism or prenatalism, lie in ignorance and fear. The prejudice of whites against blacks is rooted in the false or "ignorant" notion that black skin causes the negro to be an inferior human being when compared to people with white skin. This notion is then clung to *out of fear* by whites that their higher social status will be threatened if the black is recognized as a human being with equal rights. Similarly, prejudice against the preborn is rooted in the "ignorant" notion that prenatal life is *subhuman*. This notion is clung to out of fear that the benefits of abortion will be threatened if the preborn are recognized as human beings with equal rights.

Ignorance against the preborn is pervasive in our culture, but it is an ignorance which can be explained. Not until very recent history has mankind been able to uncover the truth concerning the development of human life in the womb. In the twentieth century the life of the preborn child has been revealed as never before. Without the aid of modern technology the truth about the preborn could not be fully discovered. Because the preborn's humanity was hidden from human sight in the darkness of the womb, what I call an "innocent prejudice" against the preborn child prevailed.

The life of the preborn has been subject to myriad speculations and misconceptions. Even the greatest thinkers of their day, such as Aristotle in the third century B.C. and St. Thomas Aquinas in the thirteenth century A.D., believed that the male fetus developed faster than the female and therefore became totally human with the infusion of a rational soul at forty days gestation, while the female fetus did not receive a rational soul until ninety days gestation. Aquinas believed further that a female was the result of conception only when there was some "defect in the semen or in the matter," and speculated further that "extrinsic forces may also be influential, for example, the southwind."[4]

The Roman Catholic Church has always condemned abortion as a terrible sin against God and man. However, for centuries theologians speculated as to the time of ensoulment marking the point when the fetus became fully human. While theologians, such as St. Bonaventure, certainly regarded abortion prior to ensoulment as a serious sin, they did not regard it as a homicide, or the killing of a human being, until ensoulment had occurred.[5] This distinction between the formed (ensouled) and unformed (unensouled) fetus was also made in private penance prescribed in the penitential books. For example, the Penitential of Theodore, Archbishop of Canterbury (668–690), "provides that before forty days of fetal development, the penance will be one year or even less, but after that the penance increases to three years . . . yet the penance for killing an infant already born is fifteen years. . . ."[6] Other penitentials, however, especially those of Burgundy, Spain, and France, did not make a distinction between formed and unformed fetuses. Rather, the penance for abortion was generally considered to be the same as for any act of homicide.[7]

The historical development of Roman Catholic theology and Canon Law teachings demonstrates that the abortion of very young fetuses was not consistently regarded as true homicide from the Middle Ages to the nineteenth century, though it must be emphasized that even such abortions were regarded as mortally sinful.[8]*

---

* According to *The Catholic Catechism* by John Hardon, S. J., in the practical order no Christian could treat the fetus otherwise than a human being (p. 106). Furthermore, Hardon states that "if some jurists later on invoked the distinction to assess different canonical penalties, based on the accepted civil codes of their day, the Catholic Church itself never altered its permanent moral judgment that direct abortion is always gravely offensive to God because it is willingly homicidal in intention." (p. 338)

Finally, the lack of scientific knowledge concerning the development of human beings in the womb led Leonardo da Vinci to conclude that the heart of the baby did not beat until birth. We now know that the heart of the preborn child begins to beat as early as eighteen to twenty-four days after conception. And we must consider also how those who supported Darwin's theory of evolution in the nineteenth century claimed that the embryo actually had a tail and gills—for the purpose of illustrating humanity's very primitive beginnings with other creatures. Any study of those ideas of centuries past regarding human life before birth would reveal that attitudes toward the preborn have been shrouded in the deepest ignorance, giving birth to crippled and false theories concerning who the preborn really are. It is time we shed these false theories and enter the twentieth century.

The question must now be asked, why do modern people cling steadfastly to antiquated views regarding the preborn when every means is now available to go beyond such false conceptions and assert the true humanity of the preborn child? Why?

Most people still do not know the basic biological facts of fetal development and do little or nothing to educate themselves on the subject. I have had conversations with many individuals who embrace what da Vinci believed five hundred years ago. Others have stated to me that the fetus is simply in a vegetative, passive stage of existence not active until six months, when the mother feels movement. Then there are those who fail to see reality altogether and believe that in the early months of pregnancy there really is "nothing there." Others simply believe that the embryo is too small to be human. With such ignorance regarding the preborn child there is little wonder why society is generally prejudiced against them.

Since the Supreme Court decision of 1973, some pro-abortionists have continued to promulgate false theories regarding the preborn, thereby sustaining the prejudice against them. In addition to believing in antiquated theories, the abortion advocates have even created new false theories of fetal development, some of which deny that the preborn even exist. Some pro-abortionists have referred to the fetus as a "blob of cells" or a "clump of tissue" with no recognizable humanity whatsoever. Other pro-abortionists rationalize that the preborn are not fully human until viability. Others believe that only when fetuses manifest self-consciousness can they be considered fully human. Still others believe that not until fetuses are a certain size, a certain weight, or a certain age in their gestational period can they be considered fully human. Of course, we must include here the Supreme Court's own peculiar theory of life, which states that the "fetus, at most represents the potentiality of life."[9] Finally, there is the perspective of such groups as the National Organization for Women (NOW), the National Abortion Rights Action League (NARAL), the Planned Parenthood Federation of America, and assorted journalists who never tire of referring to the preborn child as a mere "fertilized egg."

In addition to all of the above, several euphemisms have been created specifically to conceal the reality of the preborn for the purposes of abortion. These medical-sounding euphemisms refer to the preborn as "products of conception," "contents of the uterus," or as "uterine tissue." The creation of such terms illustrates that prejudice against the preborn has gone so far as to deny the preborn's existence in order to ensure their destruction.

Those who are inclined to acknowledge the humanity of the fetus, even if unconsciously, refer to the fetus as an "unborn baby" or "baby" or "child." This *language of recognition* is not a contrivance but flows from the inherent human bond between ourselves and the intrauterine person. The language discloses this bond and affirms it. Language that "humanizes" fetuses reveals the truth about them and us. They, along with us, are members of the human family. When we want to reject the preborn we first reject them from the human family by *naming* them as something other than human.

The Help of Science

The perpetuation of false theories regarding the preborn is partly due to the failure to objectively recognize and accept the humanity of the fetus as presented by the biological facts of fetal development. In October 1971, 220 physicians, professors, and fellows of the American College of Obstetricians and Gynecologists submitted an *amicus curiae* brief to the Supreme Court. This brief was a detailed scientific analysis of fetal development. It testified that from conception the child is a complex, dynamic, rapidly growing organism. By the end of the first 33 days of life, the child's major organs have begun to develop, including the heart and the brain. By the end of the seventh week the fetus looks like a well proportioned small-scale baby bearing all the familiar external features and internal organs of the adult. In the third month the child shows a distinct individuality in his behavior with facial expressions similar to those of his parents.[10]

Many experts in the field of embryology testify to the humanity of the preborn child:

> *The unborn offspring of human parents is an autonomous human being* (emphasis in original). (Bart T. Heffernan, M.D., in *Abortion and Social Justice*.)[11]

. . . .

> The majority of our group could find no point in time between the union of sperm and egg, or at least the blastocyst stage, and the birth of the infant at which point we could say that this was not a human life. (Statement from the First International Conference on Abortion, October 1967.)[12]

. . . .

> When does the embryo in a human mother become a human being?
> It has been one all the time, since the moment of conception. (Axel Ingelman-Sundberg and Claes Wirsen in *A Child Is Born*.)[13]

. . . .

> It is the penetration of the ovum by a spermatozoon and the resultant mingling of the nuclear material each brings to the union that constitutes the culmination of the process of *fertilization* and marks the initiation of the life of a new individual. (Emphasis in original.) (Bradley M. Patten in *Human Embryology*.)[14]

One of the most significant statements ever made concerning the humanity of the fetus was provided by the late Sir William Liley, who is known as the Father of Fetology.

We know that he moves with a delightful easy grace in his buoyant world, that foetal comfort determines foetal position. He drinks his amniotic fluid, more if it is artificially sweetened and less if it is given an unpleasant taste. He gets hiccups and sucks his thumb. He wakes and sleeps. He gets bored with repetitive signals but can be taught to be alerted by a first signal for a second different one. Despite all that has been written by poets and songwriters, we believe babies cry at birth because they have been hurt. In all the discussions that have taken place on pain relief in labour, only the pain of the mother has been considered— no one has bothered to think of the baby.

This then is the foetus we know and indeed each once were. This is the foetus we look after in modern obstetrics, the same baby we are caring for before and after birth, who before birth can be ill and need diagnosis and treatment just like any other patient. This is also the foetus whose existence and identity must be so callously ignored or energetically denied by advocates of abortion.[15]

Finally, we end these quotes with a statement from the California State Medical Association issued in September, 1970. This statement explains why, though science demonstrates that the preborn are human, this knowledge fails to liberate the supporters of abortion.

The reverence for each and every human life has also been a keystone of Western medicine and is the ethic which has caused physicians to try to preserve, protect, repair, prolong, and enhance every human life. . . .

. . . .

Since the old ethic has not yet been fully displaced, it has been necessary to separate the idea of abortion from the idea of killing, which continues to be socially abhorrent. The result has been a curious avoidance of the scientific fact, which everyone really knows, that human life begins at conception and is continuous whether intra- or extra-uterine until death. The very considerable semantic gymnastics which are required to rationalize abortion as anything but taking a human life would be ludicrous if they were not often put forth under socially impeccable auspices. It is suggested that this schizophrenic sort of subterfuge is necessary because while a new ethic is being accepted, the old one has not yet been rejected.[16]

Thanks to modern scientific technology, people have the unprecedented opportunity to break down the barriers of their ignorance concerning the preborn child; and yet so many, especially those in favor of legal abortion, dehumanize the fetus as never before.

The Source of Our Fear

A major reason for this refusal to accept the truth is fear. The roots of prejudice lie not only in ignorance, but in fear as well. The refusal of the supporter of abortion, and of society in general, to acknowledge the preborn as human beings is a refusal founded in fear of the preborn child. Yes, we fear them! In some sense the preborn are regarded as a threat. But how can this be? How can a small, helpless human life confined to the womb with neither voice nor weapon ever be a threat? The answer lies certainly not in that they have any physical power over us. No—this is not what is feared about the preborn. I will suggest that what we fear about the preborn is their very humanity. Their humanity has psychological power over us—and it is a power we would prefer the preborn did not possess. Their humanity places demands on us to care for them, to nurture them, to respond to them *humanly*. This response is perceived as a great task, a great burden. To admit that the preborn are human beings threatens the use of the only weapon we have to relieve us of their humanity—the "liberty," "freedom," and "right," of abortion.

The preborn are feared because if they were accepted as human beings much would have to be sacrificed in order to make room for them. Prejudice and discrimination against the preborn are expedient. In other words, modern society has found that denying the preborn their humanity, and thus the rights which are consistent with that humanity, has many benefits for those who are born. Thus, we see a pervasive utilitarian ethic which says that human life is not sacred in itself, but only sacred when it serves a useful purpose. Once a people has reduced others to nonhuman or subhuman status in order to be relieved of the burden they represent, the utilitarian ethic puts moral rectitude into killing. If it is more useful to exploit, enslave, or kill those for whom we do not wish to be responsible, society, accepting the utilitarian ethic, will do so because of the benefits derived.

The Benefits of Abortion

Consider the many benefits of abortion. It allows men and women to avoid the responsibilities of child care. Abortion frees them to pursue education and career plans unhindered. Abortion saves the spoiling of one's reputation from a pregnancy conceived out-of-wedlock and lessens the strain on a couple who find it economically difficult to bring another child into the world. Abortion allows couples to have only the number of children they want and have planned for. It allows for greater sexual freedom in eliminating the responsibility of pregnancy. It unburdens the woman from the psychological stress that may accompany pregnancy. It eliminates the problems of caring for physically and mentally handicapped children, ends poverty thus lessening the welfare burden, decreases the number of children born to teenage mothers, and is a means of combating overpopulation. This list could go on and on.

In order to maintain these benefits the preborn must be suppressed. Society, for the most part, however, cannot accept the idea of killing innocent people. Therefore, the humanity of the fetal child must be denied, lied about, left unstudied, and covered up in favor of a false conception that the preborn are subhuman, *out of fear* that their humanity will place demands upon us.

Whether we are talking about enslaving blacks, exterminating Jews or preborn children, these types of injustices are based on an ignorance concerning the true humanity of the victims. It cannot be denied that before the Jews could be systematically destroyed they first had to be denied their status as fellow human beings. Of course, there are many differences between the persecution of the Jews and legalized abortion. For one, the Jews suffered greater psychological and physical torment than do most preborn children killed in abortion. Nevertheless, the principle of prejudice as the root of oppression is active in both cases. The Jew was viewed as a subhuman creature by the Nazi regime. The fetal child is viewed as a subhuman creature by the abortion industry and its advocates. The Nazis destroyed the Jews out of fear—viewing them as a threat to the unity and strength of the German nation and Aryan people. Similarly, those who advocate abortion destroy preborn children out of fear because they threaten personal liberty and the social benefits allegedly derived from their destruction.

Of course, it is entirely possible that the oppressing group simply does not know that it views another class or race as sub-human (or at least inferior), because it has no access to further enlightenment. Nevertheless, justice demands that the barriers of ignorance, however maintained, be broken in order to free the victims of oppression. Those who have overcome their ignorance and their fear have a social responsibility to educate those still carrying on the oppression. The pro-life cause sees in the pre-born a victim of violent oppression and discrimination. Because the pro-life cause seeks to eradicate injustice against the preborn it is a movement of liberation on behalf of the weakest and most vulnerable member of the human family.

The abortion advocate's view of the preborn child is actually a very conservative one—conservative in a bad sense. The abor-tion advocate holds to ignorant notions about the preborn which have been codified over the years, but which are restrictive of true justice and liberty. Abortion causes a whole segment of the human race to be denied its rightful place within society. The view of some abortionists is so extremely conservative that the preborn are excluded by them from the human race altogether.

In contrast to this type of conservativism, the pro-life move-ment embraces a very broad-minded and liberal attitude concern-ing the right-to-life. The movement's perspective, based upon the Judeo/Christian ethic and the facts of fetal development, leads pro-lifers to adopt an unprejudiced, objective, and generous defin-ition of what constitutes human personhood and meaningful life. Unable to ignore the humanity of fetuses, the pro-life movement struggles to end discrimination against them and all other human beings whose lives are considered by the abortion ethic as unwor-thy of living.

In essence, the view of the pro-life cause is liberal and pro-gressive because it seeks not to restrict, but to broaden the pre-sent boundaries of social justice. Those boundaries will then include without prejudice even those conceived and living, but not yet born, members of the human family. Abortion, rooted in despair, has enshrined a new human liberty which, wrapped in a rhetoric of compassion, hides the nihilism beneath it. Victor G. Rosenblum articulated well the contrast between the abortion and pro-life ethic:

> Let us rid ourselves of the false pieties with which we have often invaded human freedom while pretending to expand it. I urge that we reaffirm simple but crucial choices. I urge that we choose compassion over indifference, affection over gratification, sharing over insularity, giving over demanding, life over death. The technical skill to provide fuller and more meaningful lives for all is within our grasp. Let the quest be our priority, our prayer and our act.[17]

Breaking the Prejudice Habit

In order for prejudice against the preborn to be overcome, much must be overcome within ourselves. We must first break down preconceived ideas about what human beings are supposed to be, supposed to look like, supposed to do. We must then encounter and accept the *apparently* subhuman being, the preborn child, as a fellow human person. But change does not come easily. It is not done without pain. But, if the preborn are ever to be liberated, change within ourselves is crucial. And as it was not easy for many to overcome their prejudice against blacks, so it will not be easy to overcome our prejudice against the preborn child.

To overcome prejudice means that we must see with more than the eye; it means seeing with an open mind and an open heart as well. Science tells us the preborn are human beings. Common sense and reason also tell us that they are human beings. To cling to some theory that says they are not human is to avoid reality in order to remain in the narrow confines of one's subjective opinion. Avoiding reality would not be so tragic except that when we avoid the reality of another's humanity this inevitably leads to injustice.

If the preborn are to be treated as human beings, pro-life rhetoric must help society to rethink and change its attitude toward human life in the womb. The first step in breaking prejudice against the preborn is to realize that relevant lifetime does not begin at birth, but a full nine months prior to birth—at conception.

Germain Grisez, after studying the work of anthropologist Ashley Montagu, concludes:

> Even before birth a human being is never an individual iso-
> lated from the patterns of culture. Because the mind and
> body are not distinct entities, but only aspects of a unified
> human being, socialization is a psychosomatic process.
> Because the embryo develops by interaction with the
> maternal organism, socialization has its beginnings in the
> most fundamental modes of biological communication.[18]

The conception of a new human being is a historical event that can alter the course of human history, though no one (except conceptions that occur in test tubes which are hailed by the world as historical events) sees the event or is immediately affected by it.[19]

Long before a child is born, the world is having a relationship with him, and he with the world. Germain Grisez noted that prior to birth we affect and are affected by the environment around us. For years psychologists in the field of primal therapy[20] have researched the effects of intrauterine experiences on the preborn child. Dr. Leni Schwartz in her book *The World of the Unborn* presents research suggesting that a fetus is capable of reacting to movement, light, and sound, with the implication that these intrauterine experiences shape future perceptions and preferences.[21] Other primal therapists, such as Thomas Verney of New York University, argue that, in a number of ways, a woman's psychological well being during pregnancy is vital to the future healthy development of her child.[22]

Clinical psychologist Dr. Andrew Feldmar believes that human beings are affected by their environment from the very moment of conception. He states:

> From the moment of conception I am exposed to danger.
> My encounters with the environment may not lead to
> death, but far from optimal stress seems to leave its
> imprint deep inside my cells. If my first interpenetrating
> contact with the host tissue (endometrium) is conjunctive,
> i.e., I am welcomed, accepted as if into a "bed of crimson
> joy," this positive first impression of how I am received
> may color all my subsequent impressions of entering with
> anticipation, hope, and excitement. If, however, that first

contact turns out to be disjunctive, i.e., I am resisted and attacked as an invading tissue by my mother's immune system, and I have to enter by force, like the marines landing at the enemy's beachhead, this negative first impression may color subsequent entries with fear, hostility, and grim determination.[23]

In order to understand that time in the womb is not irrelevant, we need to become aware that some of the most dramatic events in a person's life may occur prior to birth. For example, a child who suffers injuries while yet unborn may very well be affected physically and psychologically for the rest of his life. A preborn child having undergone fetal surgery in order to correct some illness or defect has certainly experienced one of the most important experiences of a lifetime. Without such surgery a live birth may not occur at all!

Human beings are also dramatically affected while yet unborn by events that do not necessarily have a direct influence upon their bodily existence. For example, if a pregnant woman is abandoned by her husband, this event not only influences her life but will forever alter the life of the child as well. The woman has lost a husband and the preborn child has lost a father. It must be realized that such an event is not external to the fetal child but *takes place in the personal life history of the child.*

The conception of a new human individual will dramatically alter the lives of many people. Consider how pregnancy changes the lives of married couples. The first to be affected is the mother who very soon detects changes in her body which signal that a new human being has been created. It is when a woman conceives that her role as a mother begins, and thus it is a mistake to call women who are pregnant "mothers to be." A pregnant woman is *already* a mother, caring, nurturing, and even worrying about the child within her. When this new mother notifies her husband, he is drawn into this new reality, becoming more aware of his new role as a father. Together, their attention is focused on the preborn child who has come into their lives.

The preborn child is the cause of many emotional reactions ranging from joy to despair. The couple desiring the child will greet the conception with an embrace of fondness and love. The couple not desiring a child many possibly lament and curse the fact of that child's existence. Couples faced with the conception of a new human being must now begin to exhibit care even before birth. The mother may have to watch her diet, the father to do more of the physically demanding chores, etc., while making preparations for the child's birth. Doctors must be seen, budgets watched more closely, and sacrifices made. Even the couple who seek to abort their child must make plans, except their plans will center on the presence of an unwanted child they plan to eliminate. Whatever route is taken, the conception of a new human being will often in some way alter the lives of other persons.

Recognition of the preborn child as a human person requires that we become extremely conscious of the living reality of the child prior to birth. The pre-born must be recognized and treated for what they are—fellow human beings. To think they are not members of society until emergence from the womb is a mistake. I have often heard pro-abortionists argue that it is permissable to kill the pre-born because they are not yet here! It is true that fetuses may not be born, but they certainly do exist *in the world* and their presence will impact many lives.

Prejudice can be eliminated by altering our awareness, by seeing ourselves in relation to intrauterine human life. Subconsciously, when we are not influenced by Planned Parenthood slogans, *we do* treat the preborn as members of the human family. When this treatment becomes *conscious* it informs society that its prejudice against the preborn is utterly unfounded; it is a product of injustice that feeds on ignorance and fear.

To consciously recognize that relevant lifetime begins at conception and that the preborn are members of society is a revolution in thinking. To realize these things is to leap beyond our current prejudice against the preborn in order to treat them as civilized people ought to treat all human beings—with respect, dignity, and love. Prejudice against the preborn causes us to sink into human degradation. We become less than we were meant to be— creatures who dominate and oppress the weak rather than liberate the weak from the chains we can so easily place upon them.

When prejudice against the preborn and discrimination against them are eliminated, the cause of justice in society will be served, another class of human beings will be free, and society will, in turn, liberate itself from an ignorance and fear that binds it to a prejudice that kills.

Notes

1.   Germain Grisez, *Abortion, the Myths, the Realities, and the Arguments*, (New York: Corpus Books, 1970), pp. 467-68.

2.   *Ibid.*, p. 469.

3.   *Ibid.*, p. 470

4.   John Connery, S.J., *Abortion: The Development of the Roman Catholic Perspective*, (Chicago: Loyola University Press, 1977), p. 110-11.

5.   *Ibid.*, p. 109.

6.   Grisez, p. 151.

7.   *Ibid.*, p. 152.

8.   *Ibid.*, p. 181.

9.   *Roe v. Wade*, 410 U.S. 113 at 162 (1973).

10.   Dennis J. Horan, Jerome A. Frazel, Thomas M. Crisham, Dolores V. Horan, *Motion and Amicus Curiae of Certain Physicians, Professors and Fellows of the American College of Obstetrics and Gynecology in Support of Appellees*, No. 70-40.

11.   Bart T. Heffernan, M.D., "The Early Biography of Everyman," in *Abortion and Social Justice*, ed. by Thomas W. Hilgers and Dennis J. Horan, (New York: Sheed and Ward, 1972), p. 3.

12.   Dr. and Mrs. J.C. Willke, *Handbook on Abortion*, (Cincinnati: Hayes Publishing Co., Inc., 1975), p. 9.

13.   Axel Ingelman-Sundberg and Claes Wirsen, *A Child Is Born*, (New York: Dell Publishing Co., 1965), p. 50.

14.   Bradley M. Patten, *Human Embryology*, (New York: McGraw-Hill Book Co., 1968), p. 43.

15.   "The Termination of Pregnancy or Extermination of the Foetus," speech delivered by Dr. A.W. Liley before the Wellington Chapter of the Society for the Protection of the Unborn Child, Nov. 18, 1970, in New Zealand.

16.   Willke, p. 37.

17.   Victor G. Rosenblum, "Coercion in Liberation's Guise," in *Abortion and Social Justice*, ed. by Thomas W. Hilgers and Dennis J. Horan, (New York: Sheed and Ward, 1972), p. 156.

18.   Grisez, p. 278.

19.   That conceptions are historical events is certainly the Christian perspective in view of the conception of Jesus Christ, an event called the Incarnation, in which the world was embraced by God in His saving act for mankind which ever since has altered the course of human history. Many Christian churches celebrate this event each year in the Feast of the Annunciation.

20.   Primal therapy is a treatment of mental illness through the healing of a patient's earliest life experiences, including prenatal and the birth experience.

21.   Charles Spezzano, "Prenatal Psychology: Pregnant with Questions," *Psychology Today* (May 1981), p. 49.

22.   *Ibid*.

23.   Andrew Feldmar, "The Embryology of Consciousness: What Is a Normal Pregnancy," in *The Psychological Aspects of Abortion*, ed. by David Mall and Walter F. Watts, M.D., (Washington, DC: University Publications of America, 1979), p. 18.

The Battleground of Semantics

John C. Willke

V ery early in the abortion controversy some unknown but extremely wise people began to use a name to describe those who would protect the unborn. It turned out to be a smashingly successful semantic coup. The title they chose was "right-to-life." Without question, this has been startlingly effective in the battle to protect the unborn and to stop the killing. In response, pro-abortion people came up with "pro-choice." The instant semantic retort to pro-choice is to ask them to finish the label. It then becomes "pro-choice to kill." The slogan, "Abortion, A Woman's Right-to-Choose," becomes "A Woman's Right-to-Choose to Kill." Properly publicized, often and forcefully used, when we add that proper ending the "pro-choice" label loses most of its effectiveness. To date, the pro-abortion people seem to have nothing comparable to the "right-to-life."

They have, however, quite successfully engaged in semantic gymnastics. They have told us that we are for "compulsory pregnancy." Our answer is they are for "compulsory death." Of course they are for a "woman's right to choose." They use the phrase "termination of pregnancy," which is interesting, for each of us once naturally terminated our mother's pregnancy, most of us at nine months, and no one presently reading this is dead. "Termination of pregnancy" refers only to the mother's condition. It completely ignores her passenger. Worse yet is the phrase "interruption of pregnancy." "Interruption" means a temporary cessation and then resumption, as when I interrupt your speaking and you then resume. "Interrupting" a pregnancy is rather permanent and is of course a complete misuse of the word, a misuse that a wise debater should certainly point out.

Pro-abortion people speak of abortion as being "as simple as pulling a tooth." All it does is to gently remove the "products of pregnancy," "the fetus," "the embryo," "the fetal placental unit," and other dehumanizing terms. Our response is that we never use the words "the fetus" or "the embryo," for these terms strike the listener as nonhuman, denoting only a clump of cells or a glob. Pro-lifers, therefore, should prefer to use "baby," "developing baby," "unborn baby," "he or she" rather than "it," "unborn child," "the little guy," etc.

One totally specious use of terms is to ask the pregnant woman if she "wants her periods restored." This is a thinly veiled semantic falsehood for an early abortion. The woman, often desperate not to admit to herself that she will be "killing her baby," may eagerly take part in this deception. It works for a while, but the price is paid later in psychic trauma, guilt, etc.

One of the accusations against pro-life people is that they want to "impose their morality on women." The answer to that is very simple. Pro-lifers must point to the fact that there are two patients, one of whom is being killed, and isn't it about time for us to prevent mothers from imposing *their* morality on their helpless babies—fatally?

She has a "right to her own body." The baby is "part of her body." Again, how silly. Our five-year-old boy answered that once. He was sitting on the kitchen counter and asked his mother, "Hey mom, what's this bit about the baby being part of the mother's body?" "Well, Tim," she said, "Some mothers don't want to have their baby. They say that the baby is part of their body and that they can therefore get rid of that part of their body." The little redhead wrinkled his freckled nose, thought a minute and then said, "But aren't half the babies born boys?" "Yes, Tim, that's true." "Well, who ever heard of a woman with two testicles"? Of course this was the son of a doctor and a nurse who talk about abortion at home, but—"out of the mouth of babes. . . ." It is clear that the baby within her is not part of her body, being a genetically distinct human being and half the time of the opposite sex.

The pro-abortionist claims that she has a right to "reproductive freedom." As a matter of fact, except for the rare case of assault rape pregnancy, she has already exercised her reproductive freedom. Now she is confronted with a new and different situation, a living human baby growing within her.

Many politicians claim that they are "personally opposed, but. . . ." All right-to-life people hope that everyone will some day personally oppose. But for the political servants, what matters is not whether they are personally opposed or personally in favor. That is quite irrelevant to their role in the public arena. The only thing that matters is how they will vote. Will they vote pro-abortion or will they vote pro-life? Sadly, most who claim to be "personally opposed" also consistently vote pro-abortion.

The pro-abortionists fear a return to "back-alley butchery." We must constantly point out that what they have today is often "front-alley butchery."

They emphasize the problems of unwanted pregnancy. It produces an unwanted child. The answer is to ask "Since when does anyone's right to live depend upon someone else wanting them?" Then, we must pursue the argument and prove that unwanted pregnancies produce no more unwanted children than wanted pregnancies do.

After showing that battered children were more planned and more wanted prenatally than the average child, we conclude, "We don't understand all of the sick psychology of battering children, but one thing is clear. These were not unwanted pregnancies. These were super-wanted pregnancies."

What of the title "pro-life"? This is an excellent title, but not the best one. Others have used "pro-life" in many other ways and thus have changed its original meaning to some extent. Some use it who labor against poverty, against war, against capital punishment, against nuclear arms. Even pro-abortionists at times claim to be "pro-life." We must use "pro-life" of course. It is a more generic term, i.e., it can more readily be applied in a variety of contexts. It is also an excellent bit of semantics, for its opposite is "pro-death." Even so, as mentioned above, the name "right-to-life" is the best of all.

What of being "anti-abortion"? Let's always be positive if possible. We are *for* the protection of the unborn. We also seek equal protection under the law for the handicapped, the aged, and others unable to protect themselves. Is the protection of innocent, helpless, and tiny human life a negative? We think not. Therefore, we never accept the title "anti-abortion," for being against killing is not at all negative. Sometimes in a debate, in order to balance the presentations, the moderator will ask that we agree on the titles to be used. It is best to use the titles "pro-life" and "pro-abortion." Oh yes, of course, but they will not accept this. More likely the moderator will suggest "pro-life and "pro-choice." That certainly is better than "anti-abortion" and "pro-choice." If we had our way, we would call them "anti-life." Since that will never be allowed in a debate, our best bet is "pro-life," and "pro-choice." Then during the debate, call ourselves "right-to-life" while adding to their "pro-choice" the words "to kill."

Who does the procedure? Never, never call him or her a "doctor" and certainly never a "surgeon." There is a certain dignity to these words and the person doing the abortion does not deserve that stature or dignity. We should always call this person an "abortionist." I cannot think of a single time or place in my lifetime where there was a necessity to deviate from that title. The word "abortionist" is one of derision, of criminality, of killing, and that is the label that they deserve. Use it always, use it consistently.

The other word to use constantly is the word "kill." It should be used repeatedly and in every context. As mentioned above, "termination of pregnancy" is a pro-abortion phrase. What of the word "murder"? A much stronger word? Certainly, but let's remember one cannot murder a dog or an insect. One can only murder a human being. "Murderer" clearly implies that the abortionist knows that this living being is human and kills anyway. Therefore, we must use the word with caution. Sometimes it may be too inflammatory. Sometimes it may even be counter-productive. "Kill," however, is always in order. It is a non-judgmental, accurate, biologic description of what happens. We use it when we step on a roach. We use it when we spray crabgrass. We use it anytime we specifically and directly end the life of a living being. There is no question but that this being within the mother is living. There is no question that what happens is to kill. Always use the word "kill."

Pro-abortion people use the word "woman" or "pregnant woman." It is important that pro-lifers make this point very clear. Once she is pregnant, she is already a mother. We should always call her a "mother." Pro-abortion people become very upset at this, and well they should. The word "mother" is one to respect, a soft term. It clearly means "with child." In addition, do we use the word "uterus"? Yes, often enough this technical word is needed. The word "womb" however, is much better when talking to the average person and also in lecturing. The word "womb" carries a message of love, of warmth, and of security. It, of course, ties closely to the word "mother." It also can lead to certain phraseology such as "the womb has become a tomb," and "the womb until the last few years, the safest place in the world for a tiny baby, has become a free-fire zone and is now the most dangerous place." One of every three babies conceived today in America is killed in the womb.

Sometimes we hear the phrase that a woman has the "right to control her own body." One might facetiously ask, since when has it been out of control? Perhaps that would not always be in order, however. Another thought on the "right to her own body" is that if this were honestly accepted as a feminist credo, would it not serve to protect the almost 800,000 tiny women whose mothers kill them annually in the United States?

"Place of residence" is a catchy and accurate way of remembering that the killing of the unborn in America is legal as long as the baby still lives in the womb, which is her first place of residence. We also use "place of residence" when speaking of the basis for other discrimination. We list discrimination on the basis of race, color, age, handicap, and place of residence. We note that if the little child can move out of his first place of residence the night before his scheduled execution, then all of the civil rights protecting you and me become operative and should protect the life of that child (unless, of course, his name is Baby Doe and he has Down's syndrome).

Where is the procedure done? Sadly, most pro-life people still use the phrase "abortion clinic." We would like to point out that this is strong and consistent pro-abortion propaganda. "Clinic" is a place where one goes to be healed. There are even automobile transmission clinics. *Please*, do not use the word "clinic." The word "abortion" is a negative, but the word "clinic" softens it and tends to neutralize that negative. What should be used? Use "abortion mill." If you must be neutral, use "abortion facility." Some would say "abortorium," but that is a mouthful. Best of all is "abortion chamber." Chamber? That reminds us of gas chambers, of Nazi Germany, of extermination centers. Yes, and properly so. Every second human who goes into an abortion chamber is exterminated. But we should remember, of course, that sometimes this is too strong a word in the context of a discussion or speech. "Abortion chamber" is so strong that sometimes it can even be counterproductive. In such a case, don't use it. However, *never* use the word "clinic," but rather "facility."

When speaking of the United States Supreme Court decision of 1973, we have the opportunity to use adjectives. Let's then use "the tragic," "the savage," "the unfortunate," etc., to describe it.

Planned Parenthood is a name that should be an object of attack every time a pro-life speaker talks. There are times when "Planned Barrenhood" may be in order. The group can always be labeled "the largest baby killing conglomerate in America." They can be accused accurately of being not merely anti-life but anti-child and anti-family. One should always mention their 60 plus abortion chambers and the over 120,000 "body count" per year in those "kill centers." The American Civil Liberties Union is accurately described as the legal defense and legal attack arm of the anti-life movement. Since it is so selective of whose right to live it defends, many now call it the "Anti-Civil Liberties Union."

"Liberalize abortion." Never use this term. For many people, to be liberal is to be concerned about those who need help the most. Some of the strongest right-to-life leaders in the movement are out of a true liberal background. Rather, we must speak of "permissive abortion laws" or "radical abortion laws." In the same vein, one should never use "reform" to describe the killing that is now permitted. To reform is to allow killing? Let's think that one over.

"Rape pregnancy" is not specific enough. The right-to-life speaker must always use "assault" rape pregnancy. This is very rare and this *is* what we are talking about. The most important single thing to say about assault rape pregnancies is that abortion for this reason is "killing an innocent baby for the crime of the father." And, finally, we should always talk about support for the rape victim who deserves all our compassion and help.

Never say "saline" abortion. Never say "salting out." These are pro-abortion terms. They really do not face what happens. The mechanism of death is saline hypernatremic poisoning, in short, "salt poisoning." Why not say it? There is never a time when this is not appropriate. We would suggest always and without exception using the phrase "salt poisoning." And what of "date rape"? The answer is that rape is rape is rape, whether behind the bushes or on a date.

The abortion curette is not a "spoon-shaped" instrument. That is an incorrect description. It is rather a "loop-shaped steel knife." Best say those words rather slowly. They tend to cut through one's consciousness. Furthermore, the abortionist doesn't "gently scrape" the placenta (afterbirth) away. Rather, the abortionist "cuts and slices" it away.

What of the word "person"? This word is defined in one dictionary in 14 different ways. In the field of theology, it usually means when the soul is created. In philosophy, it has as many meanings as there are philosophers. In law in the United States, personhood begins at birth. In other nations, it begins at the times that their parliaments or high courts have set. In medicine and science, it tends to mean when alive and complete. Therefore, when pro-abortionists speak of "being a person" or "when a person is present," ask them to define the word "person." Only then can you engage in rational discourse.

Life begins at conception! Yes, that is a fact of biological science and the cornerstone of the pro-life message. But what of the word "conception"? It always used to mean the event of union of sperm and ovum. Overwhelmingly, the public still understands it to be that event.

Some years ago, however, the American College of Obstetricians and Gynecologists, along with the U.S. Food and Drug Administration, redefined the word "conception." They stated that henceforth it would mean nidation or time of implantation (at one week of life). That made it possible, for example, to label the intrauterine device, a "contraceptive," when in fact it is an abortifacient. In 1981, during the U.S. Senate hearings on the Helms Human Life Bill and later on the Hatch-Eagleton Human Life Amendment, the Senate reports clearly defined "conception" as union of sperm and ovum. Since neither of these became law, however, this had no legal force. So, what should right-to-life speakers say? "Fertil-ization" and "fecundation" are exact terms and can always be used. To a lay audience "conception" is a softer, almost holy, term and is probably better if one bears the above information in mind.

Other terms demand our attention. "Unwanted pregnancy," for example, is a somewhat negative word. Often it is better to speak of "untimely" pregnancy or "problem" pregnancy. "Abor-tion" as a word continues to have a very negative context in America. Some have suggested "feticide" to match "homicide, fratricide, infanticide, etc." This is questionable because for too many, the "fetus" is not yet human.

"Single issue" is a charge that has been used to discredit the right-to-life movement. This is rather interesting when one thinks back to single issue groups in the past. Single issue groups and their influence on the political scene are a well established and hallowed tradition in American politics. To mention but a few examples, think of civil rights in race relations, think of price sup-ports or other vital issues to a farmer, think of certain important issues to a union member. What of those advocating or disagree-ing with gun control, nuclear energy, capital punishment, the Vietnam War? The list is lengthy. All of these issues, in turn, have been the single focus that has aroused voters and determined for whom they voted. However, after the right-to-life movement gained strength and it became evident that (on this issue alone) from three to ten percent of voters would actually cross party lines to vote for a candidate of the opposite party, the pro-abor-tion press raised a tremendous hue and cry. They have to some extent succeeded in making "single issue" voting a bad thing to do. Is the "right-to-life" a single issue? Yes, of course, it is, in that it limits its purview to human life from the time of conception until natural death. More pertinent, however, is the issue of can-didacy or of political viability. Here it is better to use the term "disqualifying issue." "Disqualifying issue" is what it is all about. What that says is that a pro-lifer is not a "single issue" voter, but rather holds the abortion issue as the toweringly central issue of our time.

If a person running for public office is actually in support of the continuing destruction of every third baby conceived in Amer-ica and, worse yet, would have us pay for this killing with our taxes, that person is disqualified from holding public office. Comparisons with capital crime, stealing, bribery, abuse of power, sexual aberration, etc., are all available for use, since highly placed government officials have been disqualified from public office for each of these reasons.

"Therapeutic Abortion." This is an interesting term. All through history it meant an abortion needed to save the life of the mother. Then came the original permissive California law which was titled the "Therapeutic Abortion" Law. When the Canadian law changed, hospitals in that nation appointed "therapeutic abortion committees," and the adjective became even more meaningless. Pro-abortionists have, for all practical purposes, totally destroyed its original meaning. Conclusion? Never use the term "therapeutic abortion."

A question sometimes thrown out is that since men cannot get pregnant, they should have nothing to say about abortion. If that were true, no doctor could treat a disease unless he or she had had it first. How could morticians be trained unless they had died first? In any case, men do have something to say, because each child has had a father. Furthermore, almost 52% of all unborn babies are boys.

"Potential Life"? Even sperm have actual life, but they share that life with the body of the father. They do have the potential for producing a brand new, unique, alive, sexed, and complete human life. This life growing within the mother is not "potential human life," but rather "human life with vast potential." A more catchy way to define potential human life is "millions of eager sperm chasing one ovum—actual human life is when one catches it."

Did you "come from" a young woman, a teenager, a small girl, an infant, a female fetus, a female embryo, a female fertilized ovum? No, you once *were* a young woman, a teenager, a small girl, an infant, a female fetus, a female embryo, a female fertilized ovum. You were all of these in turn. These are just names for different stages of life's development. You were totally there as a single cell. All you have done is grow up.

"Health" is a word that is important to us in the right-to-life movement. As defined by the United States Supreme Court, and as interpreted in law almost universally, it means "social, economic, and physical well being" as defined by the mother herself. The word is no longer confined to physical or mental health; it has far broader implications.

The media constantly speaks of the unborn child who is not perfect as a "deformed fetus" with even a "horrible deformity." How does that word fall on the human ear? Well, who wants to look at something or someone who is deformed? We tend not to want to look or to turn away. There is perhaps even some revulsion. It should be obvious that for many listeners it is easier to permit the killing of a "deformed fetus."

Another word is also used. That word is "defective." Again, what does our culture do with defective merchandise? Commonly we return it for credit or even throw it away. And so it is with "defective" unborn babies. The abortion establishment would have us "throw them away" also. Curiously, however, when the child is born and has a problem, we then do not use the word "deformed," nor do we use the word "defective." Rather, we use the word "handicapped." We also then speak of "special" education. Everyone agrees with these terms.

It is interesting to examine the semantic impact of the term "handicap." It tends to call from the listener a sense of compassion, a sense of wanting to help. Let us then be very conscious of the semantic impact of these words. Pro-life people should never use the word "deformed" or "defective" when speaking of the unborn. They should always use the word "handicapped."

Abortion of handicapped preborn babies should be spoken of as "killing the patient to cure the disease." Remember, before birth and after birth, it is the same patient and the same handicap. Some are willing to "solve the problem" before birth by the violence of direct killing. But tests are sometimes not done, or sometimes return false answers. What if this handicapped baby is born? Same patient. Same handicap. Same solution? And so we start down the "slippery slope" from abortion, to infanticide, to euthanasia.

"Violence" is a good word to use against the abortion promoters. They are the violent ones. We are a "people of peace." Our abortion chamber picketers are basically nonviolent. The violence occurs *inside* the doors of the abortion chamber, not outside.

"Who decides" is a newer pro-abortion catch phrase. It can be answered by Lincoln's words in the Lincoln-Douglas debates: "No one has the right to decide to do what is wrong."

And finally "civil rights." We are the "civil libertarians." Ours is a "civil rights," a "human rights" movement. We are for equal protection under the law for all Americans (or Canadians, or . . .), whether they live in or out of the womb, are perfect or handicapped, male or female, etc. Abortion is indeed a "civil rights issue."

We haven't yet won the war of semantics, but with wisdom, education, and continuing alertness, the use of proper language should go a long way to insuring that ultimately we will again protect the little ones.

The Dove and the Serpent

Mary R. Joyce

W hen the abortion issue began to surface in our society, I experienced a change in my way of communicating with others. As a teacher and writer, I was involved in a kind of communication and persuasion that was peacefully interested in the truth. The world seemed relatively safe and secure for Christian values. Then ominous voices began attacking the value of life. Soon I found myself challenging and fighting those voices, and learning, from practice, a different kind of language art.

Since 1968, I have been writing letters to various papers on the abortion issue. One of them was titled by the editor "Doctors Who Perform Abortions Are Quacks" and appeared as follows:

> What does your doctor think about medical quackery? Has he or she done anything to rid the medical profession of false and regressive practices?

> Quackery is dealing in falseness and promoting it as a true solution to a problem. Doctors who treat normal, healthy physical conditions as if they were diseased are practicing quackery. An example is abortion, a "procedure" approved by the American Medical Association (AMA) and the U.S. Supreme Court.

Quack doctors are treating thousands of pregnancies a day as if they were unwanted growths such as malignant tumors. But no conceived child is anything like a cancer of the uterus. The real cancers are the killing attitude and the use of medical quackery to destroy the child—social malignancies that need to be removed from the social body and the medical profession.

There are good, noble doctors who act on the fact that better ways of responding to an untimely pregnancy exist. These ways might not be easy or lucrative for doctors. But, as everyone knows, quacks deal in the easy and the lucrative instead of the wise and the true.

I appeal to all physicians and to the AMA to abolish this blight. Though the Supreme Court, in a regressive move, approved of medical quackery, it did not command the medical profession to get involved. Doctors are still free to clean up their act.[1]

Though there are many vocal pro-abortionists in town, no one sent a reaction to the paper. At least, no reaction was printed. Letters written like this rarely receive rebuttal. However, if someone sees a chance to challenge a writer's use of facts, the opportunity to discredit a pro-lifer is usually taken. When that happens, a prompt reply to the challenge is necessary. Credibility always depends on documentable facts.

The letter above could have said that doctors who perform abortions are murderers. This would be more faithful to reality than saying that these doctors are quacks. But doctors can argue themselves out of the greater of the two truths. They can say, "The law does not define abortion as murder. Besides, medically performed abortion prevents women from killing themselves." So, doctors are not as vulnerable to the truest thing that could be said about abortion. But they are quite vulnerable to a lesser truth. No doctor likes to be called a quack. This word demeans their professional competence. The other word attacks their moral credibility. In an age that values professional competence, while it relegates so much of morality to private opinion, a critique of abortion based on what the abortionist values most is the more effective critique.

In other words, approach the abortionists where their values are. Otherwise they regard you as irrelevant. If they are vulnerable in the area of lesser truths about abortion, it is best to approach them there. One can bring in the greater truths through the back door of a lesser truth. For example, in the letter about quackery, the point about killing is tied into the definition of quackery. The lesser truth is made to *carry* the more important point.

In May of 1978, the local pro-abortionists began to attack the Catholic Church. Speaking to an audience that packed the cathedral on that Pentecost Sunday, the Bishop of the Diocese referred to one such statement saying, "We have been attacked." I made up my mind, hopefully inspired by "the dove," to fight back. Knowing from experience the power of sublimated ridicule, I wrote a letter to the editor about the puritanism of the pro-abortionists, referring to the Yale scholar, Sidney Ahlstrom, who said that if the Puritans were anything they were anti-Catholic. Since that time, the pro-abortionists in town have not mentioned the Catholic issue again.

In this case, I did not waste any time defending the teaching of the Catholic Church on abortion. Instead, I looked for the spot where the attacker was vulnerable, and simply put my point into clear-cut, straight-forward language. The result was like throwing a spear into the heart, without having a spear or a desire to throw one. Words can be our most powerful weapons.

This is something the pro-abortionists knew instinctively all along. They won their cause faster, and to a greater extent, than any of them dreamed possible at the time they began their movement. And they won not with money or political power, but with their cunning, clever use of words.

Over the years, I have wondered why pro-lifers have not shown such an instinctive awareness of the power of language. It has reminded me of the gospel story where Jesus seemed to be regretting that the children of darkness are so clever, while the children of light are not. He seemed to be encouraging the children of light to be, also, crafty and clever.

In another situation, Jesus said, "Be cunning as serpents and innocent as doves"(Matt. 10:16). In this statement, he was actually combining opposites: craftiness and simplicity. I believe the Lord Jesus means to tell us that the children of light should learn how to be clever and loving at the same time—how to be like a serpent as well as a dove.

Like the moon, a human person has a dark, as well as a light side, even if that person is a good Christian. We are much more like the moon than like the sun. A good Christian is one who knows how to integrate the dark side of human nature with its bright side, and how to use the energy of anger and shrewdness to the advantage of good, creative purposes. This is what I believe that Jesus, the great psychologist, means when he tells us to be like the serpent and the dove together. Far from developing a split personality, this integration of the dark with the brighter side of the human person releases the unity of singleness of heart.

When we hear the children of darkness talk so persuasively about "freedom of choice," "compulsory pregnancy," "products of conception," and "fetal tissue," we should feel the dark side of our own selves touched and mobilized. As long as we fear this dark side; as long as we think we should not even feel it, we are cutting off a valuable source of creative energy. We are rendering ourselves much less effective than we otherwise could be.

A large part of the problem is that we do not know how to live well with our feelings of anger, and how to receive these "dark" feelings as *energy* for creative action. We do not realize that all of our spontaneous feelings are good, that all provide energy for goodness, including our feelings of anger. These feelings challenge us to make decisions according to life-enhancing values. In making these decisions, we are given the opportunity we need to develop as persons. If, on the other hand, we suppress or even repress our feelings of anger, we deny ourselves the opportunity for further human development and also for creatively responding to and correcting the social evils around us.

The main reason why we fear our feelings of anger is that resulting impulses to act in destructive ways scare us. We think that angry feelings might cause us to strike or otherwise harm someone else. This causes us to think that angry feelings are bad for us and bad for other people around us. But feelings, though they often lead to impulses to act out these feelings, do not have to be expressed in behavior. We need to *feel* our angry feelings and receive them as energy for creative action, but we do not have to express any of our feelings of anger.

The following story shows how valuable our feelings are to our lives, and also, how feelings can be sources of power even when we do not express them. The late Dr. Conrad W. Baars, a psychiatrist, tells of his experience with anger, a feeling which he constantly allowed himself to feel, but could not express in any way, for two years. He was caught and imprisoned by the Nazis during World War II when he was helping downed Allied flyers escape from Europe. He was shipped by train with one thousand prisoners from France to Buchenwald, a concentration camp. "Next to my faith in God," he says, "it was my constant anger at the Nazis for having deprived me of my liberty and their inhuman treatment of their prisoners that stimulated my determination to survive and to deny them the satisfaction of seeing me die."[2]

Dr. Baars explains that he could not show his anger outwardly without meeting certain death at the hands of his captors. He experienced his angry feelings as energy to keep himself alive, while others succumbed to apathy and despair. Having lost their will to live, they died from minor illnesses and infectious diseases. In the end, only six of the original one thousand prisoners survived the ordeal.

If angry feelings can supply so much valuable energy to survive an almost impossible situation like two years in a Nazi concentration camp, what else can these feelings help us accomplish? The fact that we do not have to express our anger in violent actions gives us the chance we need to find ways of directing the energy of our anger into creative action. I guess there is nothing in the world that makes me angrier than abortion and the rhetoric used to defend and promote this act. Instead of telling myself not to be angry, I use this valuable energy to turn words into weapons, and to combine the serpent with the dove. Hopefully, I really love my enemies (the abortionists and their defenders), while I fight them.

Finally, an aspect of the pro-life cause that interests and challenges me the most is one that seems to have been all but ignored by the pro-life movement. This is the matter of the so-called sexual revolution. It seems clear to me that as long as this revolution is in full swing, it will not be possible to end abortion-on-demand in this country.

Are pro-lifers ready to take on the sexual revolution and win?

The first premise of this revolution is that there is no connection between sex and morality. Pro-lifers know this premise is false. Their first inclination is to try to show how sex is, indeed, connected with morality. That would be working on the highest level of the truth involved. But it would be almost totally ineffective. Ears filled with the clichés, slogans, and sophisticated lines of the sexual revolution are unable to hear anything about the connection of sex with morality. Such talk by pro-lifers would be an exercise in futility. It would be a waste of time.

Moving into the dark side of our nature, or turning on the serpent, so to speak, we can begin to look for the point of vulnerability in the children of darkness. Where is their version of sexuality vulnerable? In other words, what are its greatest values?

Sexual competence is high on the list. Freedom of choice is another top value. Since January 22, 1973, as a result of the awful shock of that terrible day, I have been looking at these areas of vulnerability in the sexual revolution and slowly but steadily trying to devise the most stinging attack.

One thing that must be shown is that sexual competence is a matter of total man-woman competence, not just a matter of genital potency. In this context, one can see that it takes more sexual potency to conceive another person than to start the growth of a blob of protoplasm. Indeed, abortion is a result of sexual impotence and frigidity in the broader and deeper dimension of human sexuality. Showing the connection of abortion to sexual incompetence throws a verbal spear into the very heart of the sexual revolution's performance ideology and freedom of choice. And this can be done without any disquisition on the relation between sex and morality.

Besides learning how to confront our opponents where they are vulnerable, we need to learn how to love them. We need to combine the serpent with the dove. Besides attacking the sexual revolution where it hurts, we need to elucidate the real sexual revolution that is so badly needed. And we cannot do this simply by explaining, at length, the connection between sex and morality.

First, we need to find out more about human sexuality, more about sexual feelings and their value as energy for human development, and more about the inner connection between feelings and values. We need to find an answer to the problem that started the false sexual revolution in the first place.[3] Unless we find that answer, I'm afraid no exercise of pro-life language power will be fruitful.

At the same time, if we do not become angry at the evils in this world, and if we do not use the energy of this anger to fight injustice with forcefulness and shrewdness, innocence and truth are threatened with extinction.

Notes

1.   *St. Cloud Times*, January 19, 1984.

2.   Conrad W. Baars, M.D., *Feeling and Healing Your Emotions* (South Plainfield, NJ: Bridge Publishing Inc., 1979), p. 149.

3.   One book that deals with the sexual revolution in this manner is my *Women and Choice*: *A New Beginning* (St. Cloud, MN: LifeCom, 1986).

Contributors

Raymond J. Adamek, Ph.D., is a Professor of Sociology and Coordinator of Graduate Studies in the Department of Sociology, Kent State University, Kent, Ohio. He teaches courses in the family, research methods, and statistics. Adamek has published numerous articles and chapters in both sociological and more general sources. He has been a student of U.S. public opinion polls on abortion since 1976 and is currently working on a review of major polls from 1986 through 1991.

William Brennan, Ph.D., is a professor in the School of Social Services at St. Louis University. His major teaching areas include social psychology, human development through the life cycle, sociology of the family, family interaction under stress, communicating with children, and social theory. He has written articles for both professional and popular journals and is a specialist on the relationship between the Nazi Holocaust and the contemporary abortion, infanticide, and euthanasia movements.

Keith Cassidy, Ph.D., is an Associate Professor in the Department of History at the University of Guelph in Ontario, Canada. His principal field of research is the social and intellectual history of the United States in the twentieth century. He obtained his doctorate from the University of Toronto and initially focused on the Progressive Era. In recent years, he has begun work on a history of the right-to-life movement in the United States.

Donald DeMarco, Ph.D., is a Professor of Philosophy at the University of St. Jerome's College in Ontario, Canada. He obtained his doctorate from St. John's University in New York and is Associate Editor of *Child and Family Quarterly*. An extensive lecturer in the United States and Canada, DeMarco has written a number of articles and books which deal with family values. One of his better known books is *Abortion in Perspective*.

Wanda Franz, Ph.D., is a developmental psychologist and a professor of child development in the Division of Family Resources at West Virginia University in Morgantown, West Virginia. She has been involved in the right-to-life movement since 1971 and is the current president of the National Right to Life Committee. She is also president of the Association for Interdisciplinary Research in Values and Social Change and trustee of the National Right to Life Educational Trust Fund. Her area of specialization is adolescent development and abortion decision making.

Gary Gillespie is an Assistant Professor of Communication and Interdisciplinary Studies at Northwest College in Kirkland, Washington. He wrote his graduate thesis, "The Rite of Abortion: Forms of Victimage in Abortion Rhetoric, a Dramatistic Social Movement Study" at Western Washington University. Gillespie speaks and writes frequently on the abortion issue in his community and teaches a debate course dealing with the controversy. He has been associated with the right-to-life movement for many years.

Donald Granberg, Ph.D., is a Professor of Sociology and Research Associate at the Center for Research in Social Behavior at the University of Missouri, Columbia. He received his doctorate from Pennsylvania State University. In 1976, while on leave at Oregon State University, he began doing research on abortion and has published over fifteen articles on the topic. His research is based mainly on national surveys of the public, of activists, and with voting patterns within the U.S. Senate.

Nat Hentoff is a staff writer for *The Village Voice*. He is also a columnist for *The Washington Post* and a staff writer for *The New Yorker*. He did graduate work at Harvard University, was a Fulbright Fellow at the Sorbonne, and received a Guggenheim Fellowship in education. In 1980, the American Bar Association awarded him the Silver Gavel Award for his coverage of law and criminal justice. He has also authored a number of books, including his memoir *Boston Boy*.

William C. Hunt has a doctorate in theology and a master's degree in business administration. He taught biomedical ethics at the graduate level for ten years and has been active in the pro-life movement since 1967. He is a founding member of Minnesota Citizens Concerned for Life and American Citizens Concerned for Life and was an early organizer of the National Right to Life Committee. He has written and spoken extensively on the major bioethical issues of the day.

Mary R. Joyce of St. Cloud, Minnesota is the author of numerous books and articles on issues of human life and sexuality. Her book, *Women and Choice*, exposes the puritan and playboy mentalities controlling women's minds as they defend the abortion choice. A founding member of Minnesota Citizens Concerned for Life, she co-authored with her husband, Robert Joyce, *Let Us Be Born: The Inhumanity of Abortion*. Her latest book, *Friends for Teens*, is a psychology of chastity for young people.

David Mall is a Midwest-based writer/scholar who specializes in the rhetoric of social movements, particularly those that involve the cultural transmission of biomedical ethics. He has been a participant observer of the American pro-life movement for many years and has helped found several of its organizations, including Minnesota Citizens Concerned for Life and the National Youth Pro-Life Coalition. He wrote and co-edited a number of books, including *New Perspectives on Human Abortion* and *In Good Conscience: Abortion and Moral Necessity*.

B.F. McClerren, Ph.D., earned his doctorate in rhetoric, philosophy, and history at Southern Illinois University in Carbondale, Illinois. He has taught speech communication at the State University of New York at New Paltz and has been a graduate professor in rhetoric and philosophy at Eastern Illinois University. McClerren is widely published and speaks extensively throughout the United States. For many years he has been interested in the relationship between biomedical ethics and rhetorical theory.

Monica Migliorino Miller, Ph.D., earned her doctorate in theology from Marquette University where she teaches part-time. She is known for her activism and has been associated with the right-to-life movement for many years. She is a member of Feminists for Life of America and is a director of Wisconsin Citizens for Life. She writes from a feminist perspective.

John J. Potts, J.D., is a Professor of Law at Valparaiso University School of Law in Valparaiso, Indiana. He was educated at the University of New Mexico, Boston College, and Northeastern University. Before teaching, he practiced law in New Mexico and became Chairman of the Board of Directors, Section of Taxation, New Mexico State Bar Association. Since beginning his teaching career, he has been involved in a large variety of pro-life activities and organizations.

Milton C. Sernett, Ph.D., is a Professor in the Department of African American Studies and Adjunct Professor of Religion at Syracuse University, Syracuse, New York. He is a historian of American intellectual, social, and religious history, with special interest in African American history and religion. His most recent publication is *Bound for the Promised Land: African American Religion and the Great Migration*, forthcoming from the University of North Carolina Press.

John C. Willke, M.D., is a physician, author, lecturer, and expert in human sexuality. He served for ten years as president of the National Right to Life Committee and is the president of the Life Issues Institute. Dr. Willke practiced medicine in Cincinnati, Ohio, for forty years, where he was on the senior attending staff at the Providence and the Good Samaritan hospitals. With his wife Barbara he wrote the classic *Handbook on Abortion*, considered by many to be the most widely read book in the world presenting the scientific case for the unborn.

Index

TO SET THE DAWN FREE

Designed by Carol Tornatore
Composed at DMI
by Ingrid Mauer in Garamond Book
Printed by BookCrafters
on Glatfelter Booktext Natural
with felt endpapers by Ecological Fibers
Bound by BookCrafters
in Holliston Roxite linen and
stamped in gold

Library of Congress Cataloging-in-Publication Data

When life and choice collide : essays on rhetoric and abortion /
    edited by David Mall ; with an introduction by Nat Hentoff.
        p.   cm. -- (Words in conflict series)
    Includes bibliographical references and index.
    Contents: v. 1. To set the dawn free.
    ISBN 0--9608410-3-2 (alk. paper) : $30.00. -- ISBN 0-9608410-2-4
(pbk. : alk. paper) : $15.00
        1. Abortion--United States--Moral and ethical aspects.
    2. Abortion--Social aspects--United States.   I. Mall, David.
    II. Series.
    HQ767.5.U5W49   1993
    363.4'6'0973--dc20   93-20573
                                                                  CIP